THE
EVIL EYE

THE
EVIL EYE

An Account of this Ancient
and Widespread Superstition

Frederick Thomas Elworthy

BELL PUBLISHING COMPANY
NEW YORK

Copyright © 1989 by OBC, Inc.

This 1989 edition is published by Bell Publishing Company,
distributed by Crown Publishers, Inc., 225 Park Avenue South, New York, New York 10003

Printed and Bound in the United States of America

Library of Congress Cataloging-in-Publication Data

Elworthy, Frederick Thomas, 1830–1907.
The evil eye.

Reprint.
Includes index.
1. Evil eye. 2. Charms. 3. Magic. 4. Superstition.
I. Title.
BF1553.E6 1989   133.4′25   89-21
ISBN 0-517-67944-2

h g f e d c b a

CONTENTS

CHAPTER VII

CHAPTER VIII

CHAPTER IX

CHAPTER X

CHAPTER XI

CHAPTER XII

LIST OF ILLUSTRATIONS

FOREWORD

"Ah whither roam'st thou? Much-enduring man!
O blind to fate! What led thy steps to rove
The horrid mazes of this magic grove!
Each friend you seek in yon enclosure lies,
All lost their form, and habitants of sties.
Think'st thou by wit to model their escape?
Sooner shalt thou, a stranger to thy shape,
Fall prone their equal; first thy danger know,
Then take the antidote the Gods bestow.
The plant I give, through all the direful bower
Shall guard thee, and avert the evil hour."

—from the *Odyssey* of Homer,
translated by Alexander Pope,
Book X, lines 281-292

Magic is composed of spells and counterspells cast to bring about an action or displace an anticipated result. Magic is no flat, monolithic science proceeding smoothly along the linear path of time. Fueled by the forces of belief and superstition, like the multi-dimensional web of Fate, magic runs in every place and direction throughout our history and our lives. Much like Odysseus in the above quotation, who annulled Circe's enchantments

with a counterspell provided by a friendly god, and so
avoided being turned into a pig for the rest of his life,
we are often made aware of the pitfalls waiting for us
around the corner. If we can perceive these dangers, we
may sometimes avert them with our more modern
counterspells.

Perhaps this was too primitive a philosophy for
Frederick Thomas Elworthy, the author of *The Evil
Eye*. Elworthy was not a magician, but a dispassionate
academic polymath whose comprehensive work on
superstition has become one of the classic references in
this field. Elworthy gathered his information on this
darkest and most fascinating superstition from an active
interest in and research into folklore originating from his
work as a linguist. He wrote and worked in an age when
the Western world was deeply involved in a so-called
second age of exploration. Man was busy digging up the
ruins of Western civilization to expose the foundations
of Neo-Classicism, or analyzing the history and origins of
the human race through the practices of contemporary
"Stone Age" tribes. It was a unique time when cultural
synthesis and a knowledge explosion made possible great
technical and theoretical progress—yet the remnants of
primitive culture and superstition were still firmly in
place and available for study in the field.

With *The Evil Eye*, Elworthy brings his measured
and orderly mind to bear on an unusually rich subject.
His obvious fascination with the multiple meanings of
the evil eye do not distract him from detailed, and poly-
lingual, discussions of the minutiae of formula, image,
and antidote. His source material stems not only from his
own extensive researches into country dialects, but also
from the great anthropologists and folklorists of his time.

He quotes Sir James George Frazer's *The Golden Bough* on the customs of primitive fire and harvest festivals; he cites Carl Lumholtz's *Among the Cannibals* for the example of the tribe that ate congealed human blood "to acquire the courage and strength of their enemies." Many of his sources are culled from the treasures of Greek and Roman literature, such as Pliny's theories on the medicinal and antidotal uses of the rue plant. Other sources, Greek, Etruscan, and Egyptian, describe the placement of eyes on both sides of the prow of a boat to perceive and ward off the evil demons of the sea, a practice still in use among primitive peoples even today. Elworthy by no means neglects another of the great primary sources for information about superstition—the Scriptures and early Christian works of art, stating, among other examples, that the figure of St. Mark in a sixth-century Italian mosaic (illustrated in the book) holds his right hand raised high, palm open and thumb extended, perhaps making a gesture against the evil eye.

Although the evil eye is but one small element of superstition as we know it, with *The Evil Eye*—and perhaps contradictory to his intentions—Elworthy leads us directly into the more arcane fields of magic, exploring spells with intent to harm, charms to ward off evil, and methods of curing. Drawing on sources from ancient Egypt through the dawn of the twentieth century, he discusses symbols, gestures, and sympathetic, active, and passive magical practices. He grounds his arguments with ample quotations from primary sources, and illustrates this work—so much more comprehensive with visual amplification—with drawings and photographs from his extensive personal collection. For folklorists and anyone interested in the way superstitious magic has affected our lives throughout history, *The Evil Eye* will be an erudite source of information and a stimulus to further thought on the relationship of magic to superstition.

LOIS HILL

New York
1989

PREFACE

THE following pages are intended as a simple record of facts, gathered under varying circumstances from many sources during many years. They are put forward merely as typical, and by no means as exhaustive of the subject.

Long ago while noting the peculiarities of my native dialect I became fully aware that the belief in a personal evil influence was not only prevalent but almost universal. Familiarity with the modes of thought of country-folk convinced me that every obscure ailment and every unaccountable misfortune was habitually considered to be a " wisht thing." At the same time I have known, ever since I can remember, one or more persons whose business it was to discover the witch, or, in other words, the possessor of the evil eye.

For very many years jottings on this subject have been made side by side with others on dialect : one result is that my note-books have attained such a plethoric condition as to be by no means the least curious fact I have had to deal with.

Frequent and protracted visits to Italy and Southern Europe have enabled me to collect many charms and amulets, some of which are depicted in these pages.

Having no pet theories to propound, I have been under no temptation either to suppress or to exaggerate; consequently I have not been careful to hide inconsistencies.

I have only further to express my obligation to several kind friends, especially to the Rev. F. W. Weaver for having read the proofs—a work for which I must confess to having myself an evil eye; to Mr. Neville Rolfe and Dr. Meredith for several valuable hints and investigations; and to others for the loan of rare books.

I have also to thank Miss Twining and Mr. John Romilly Allen for kind permission to copy illustrations from their respective works. Messrs. G. Bell and Sons, Mr. David Nutt, and Mr. John Murray have also permitted me to do the like from books of which they hold the copyright, and I desire to recognise the obligation.

I believe that I have given my authority for every statement, except those put forward on my own responsibility. If in any case I have failed to do so, I now desire to thank my unknown informant, and to assure him that the omission of his name, or of his book, has been unintentional.

F. T. E.

THE
EVIL EYE

THE EVIL EYE

CHAPTER I

INTRODUCTION

" THERE be none of the affections which have been noted to fascinate or to bewitch, but love and envy; they both have vehement wishes, they frame themselves readily into imaginations and suggestions, and they come easily into the eye, especially upon the presence of the objects which are the points that conduce to fascination, if any such there be. We see likewise the Scripture calleth envy an evil eye." [1]

So wrote one of our greatest philosophers, and on the same subject he says: "Of all other affections, it is the most importunate and continual; . . . therefore it is well said: 'Invidia festos dies non agit,' for it is ever working upon some or other. It is also the vilest affection and the most depraved; for which cause it is the proper attribute of the Devil, who is called 'The envious man that soweth tares amongst the wheat by night.'"

As to the word *fascination*, even in Bacon's time it had acquired its modern sense, implying the influence or effect we now associate with

---

[1] Bacon, Essay IX. "Of Envy."

animal magnetism. Notwithstanding this, the word was used by various writers down to the end of the seventeenth century in its original, technical meaning, as an alternative for "evil eye." Nowadays it has practically lost its older sinister sense, and except among scholars has retained only the pleasant one in which Bacon used it.

A fascinating person now, is one who charms delightfully, who excites feelings of pleasure, who is in every way attractive. Similarly in our everyday talk the alternate word *bewitch* has retained only in polite society its pleasant side. A bewitching woman is one who excites the passion of love alone, and the simple use of either synonym conveys now no implication of malevolence to the conventionally educated.

The quotation from Bacon with which we started well marks the progress always going on in the development of word-meanings. In the Elizabethan age, to fascinate or bewitch had in literature even then arrived at a double position, applicable to either love or hate ; whereas in earlier days these words were wholly confined to maleficence in signification. This of course only applies to literary language and polite society ; among the peasantry the Latin form, *fascination*, is unknown, while everything relating to *witch* or *witching* still bears an evil sense only.

In proof of all this we have only to compare the modern colloquial significance of the terms fascinating or bewitching, as used in speaking of a person by the educated, with witch, witching, or the west country dialectal "wisht," as used by the peasantry.

The belief that there is a power of evil working, which is ejaculated (as Bacon says) upon any object it beholds, has existed in all times and in all countries. It was adopted and sanctioned alike by the Fathers of the Church, by mediæval physicians, and all writers on occult science; while in our own day it still exists among all savage nations, and even here in England in our very midst. Heliodorus [2] makes Charicles say of his host: " I fancy an envious eye has looked upon this man also; he seems to be affected much in the same manner as Chariclea. Indeed I think so too, I replied; and it is probable enough, for he went directly after her in the procession." [3]

The origin of the belief is lost in the obscurity of prehistoric ages. The enlightened call it superstition; but it holds its sway over the people of many countries, savage as well as civilised, and must be set down as one of the hereditary and instinctive convictions of mankind.

The stories that might be adduced of the constancy of the belief in a blighting power of influencing other persons, and of controlling events injuriously to others, even in these days of board-school enlightenment are almost infinite. Here, in Somerset, the pig is taken ill and dies—"he was overlooked." A murrain afflicts a farmer's cattle; he goes off secretly to the "white witch," that is the old witch-finder, to ascertain who has "overlooked his things" and to learn the best

[2] *Theagenes and Chariclea* (Trans. 1789), vol. i. p. 145. Heliodorus, Bishop of Tricca in Thessaly, about A.D. 380, was a very firm believer in the evil eye, and frequently refers to it in his works, no doubt faithfully reflecting the opinions of his day.

[3] See an article on the " Evil Eye" in Chambers's *Encyclopædia*. For numerous quotations on the subject see *New Eng. Dict*. s. v. "Evil Eye."

antidote, "'cause they there farriers can't do no good."

A child is ill and pining away; the mother loses all heart; she is sure the child is overlooked and "is safe to die." Often she gives up not only hope but all effort to save the child; the consequent neglect of course hastens the expected result, and then it is: "Oh! I know'd very well he would'n never get no better." "'Tidn no good vor to strive vor to go agin it." This is no fancy, or isolated case, but here in the last decade of the nineteenth century one of the commonest of everyday facts.

The author of the pious graffito (still *in situ*) :—

> Things seen is Intempural,
> Things not seen is Inturnel,

referred to in the *West Somerset Word-Book*, p. ix, is a man far above the average in intelligence. He lodged where the daughter of the family had some obscure malady. She became a patient at the County Hospital, but only grew worse. In this case the mother does not at first seem to have believed in occult influence, but went about and spread a report that "they'd a-starved her maid, into thick there hospital"! At the same time the writer ascertained that the girl had been all the while receiving extra nourishment. She was removed, and of course grew worse. On speaking to the lodger about the starvation theory, he said: "Oh! I knows 'twaddn that." "What do you think it was?" "Oh! I knows." After many times declaring "I knows," he at last said: "Her was overlooked—her was; and I knows very well who don'd it." After much persuasion he mentioned the name of a poor ignorant old woman, who certainly did not bear the best of characters. The whole family devoutly believed that the girl's death, which happened very soon, was brought about by this old woman. No doubt a century or two ago she would have been burnt as a witch.[4]

Several cases of precisely the same kind are well known to the writer and his family—especially relating to children. Visits have been often paid to the sick children of persons whose names might be given, where "'tis very wisht vor to zee the poor chiel a-pinin away like that there." Not much is said to strangers, but those who know are perfectly aware of what the mother means.

> Beshrew your eyes,
> They have o'erlook'd me and divided me;
> One half of me is yours, the other half yours.
>
> *Merchant of Venice*, Act iii. Sc. 2.

The imputation by St. Paul, that the foolish Galatians[5] had been spellbound, meant that some evil eye had "overlooked" them and worked in them a blighting influence. It was an apt allusion to the then, and still, universally prevalent belief in that power of "dread fascination" which the writer of the Epistle[6] so well knew they would comprehend, and he therefore used it as a striking metaphor.

[4] A long account of a prosecution of a white witch, who pretended that a woman was ill of a "bad wish" in a case much like the foregoing, is given in Pulman's *Weekly News*, June 14, 1892. Similar reports are frequently appearing in the local press. At this moment (October 1894) two persons are dying in Wellington parish (one of phthisis !) who firmly believe, and are believed, to be suffering solely from having been "overlooked."

[5] See Lightfoot, *Epistle to the Galatians*, iii. 1, p. 133.

[6] The expression of St. Paul, though translated "bewitched" in our A.V., is in the Vulgate *fascinavit*, precisely the same as that used by Virgil (*post*, p. 10). In the Septuagint also the sense of the passage is identical, referring to the influence, so well understood, of the evil eye. On this see Frommannd, *Tract. de Fasc.* p. 11.

Abundant testimony exists in the oldest monuments in the world that among the ancient Egyptians belief in and dread of the evil eye were ever present; their efforts to avert or to baffle it, both as regarded the living and the dead, who they knew would live again, were perhaps the most constant and elaborate of any, of which we can now decipher the traces.

We see evidence of this in the very beginning of Egyptian mythology. Ptah, the Opener,[7] is said to be the father of the gods and of men. He brought forth all the other gods from his eye, and men from his mouth—a piece of implied evidence of the ancient belief that of all emanations those from the eye were the most potent.

How strong the feeling was among contemporary Orientals, the many passages in Scripture[7a] referring to it distinctly prove. Indeed it is found in the literature of every people, in every land since history began to be written. No science, no religion, no laws have been able to root out this fixed belief; and no power has ever been able to eradicate it from the human mind; so that even amongst the cultivated and the enlightened it still exists as an unacknowledged, mysterious half-belief, half-superstition, which nevertheless exercises, though secretly, a powerful influence on the actions of mankind.

We in these latter days of science, when scoffing at superstition is both a fashion and a passion, nevertheless show by actions and words that in our inner-

---

[7] E. Wallis Budge, *The Nile-Notes for Travellers in Egypt*, 1890, p. 77.
[7a] *e.g.* Deut. xxviii. 54, 56; Job vii. 8; Psa. xxxv. 21; Prov. vi. 13; Isa. xiii. 18; Lam. ii. 4; Ezek. ix. 5. Especially also Prov. xxiii. 6, xxviii. 22; Matt. vi. 22, 23, xx. 15; Luke xi. 34; Mark vii. 22; Psa. liv. 7, lix. 10, xcii. 11, with many others.

most soul there lurks a something, a feeling, a superstition if you will, which all our culture, all our
boasted superiority to vulgar beliefs, cannot stifle,
and which may well be held to be a kind of
hereditary instinct.[8]

Not only do the pages of Brand's *Popular
Antiquities*, Brewster's *Magic*, and Hone's *Everyday Book*, as well as the local press, provide endless
stories and examples, which we need not here repeat,
but the more modern publications of the Psychical
Research Society also record plenty of them ; at the
same time the latter throw over them a glamour of
quasi-scientific investigation.

Among the Greeks, who got their art and many
of their customs from Egypt, the belief was so
universal that they had a special word to express this
mysterious power, βασκανία,[9] whence, all authorities
say,[10] comes the Latin word *fascinatio*.

This latter word Cicero himself discusses, and
explains as *invidere*, to look too closely at : hence
invidia, envy, or evil eye, the instigator of most
deadly sins—the vice which is even now most
frequently named in connection with its sequences,
"hatred, and malice, and all uncharitableness."

Delrio[11] and Frommannd trace the Greek word
to Chaldean, and discourse upon the etymology as

---

[8] " In spite of the schoolmaster we are still as firm believers in witchcraft
and the evil eye as were the shepherd swains of Theocritus and Virgil, and
many who, if directly questioned on the subject, would indignantly deny the
impeachment, are none the less devout believers in such occult powers."—W.
F. Rose, *Somerset and Dorset Notes and Queries*, vol. iv. June 1894, p. 76.

[9] In Modern Greek this is κακὸ μάτι.

[10] *Tractatus de Fascinatione*, Christian Frommannd, Nuremberg, 1674,
p. 4 ; Nicolo Valletta, *Cicalata sul Fascino*, Napoli, 1787, p. 12 ; Potter,
Archæologia Græca, 1824, i. 414; Lightfoot, *Ep. to Gal.* 1890, p. 133,
who all give long lists of authors and quotations in support of this etymology.

[11] *Disquisitionum Magicarum libri sex*, Auctore Martino Delrio, Societatis
Jesu presbytero.   Moguntiæ, apud Johannem Albinum, 1603.

well as the meanings of *fascinatio* at great length, in language and allusions unfit for reproduction, which are, moreover, beside our present purpose. It may, however, be remarked that Frommannd throws much light upon the ancient ideas connected with the evil eye, and with the means taken to baffle it, backed up by an array of authorities such as no other writer on the subject has brought together, but of such a nature that we can only here direct the student to the book itself.[12] Many objects to be seen in Egypt, Greece, and Italy, especially at Pompeii, are by this extraordinary treatise made to assume an entirely different shape and signification from those given them by the guidebooks or the *ciceroni*.

It was firmly believed by all ancients, that some malignant influence darted from the eyes of envious or angry persons, and so infected the air as to penetrate and corrupt the bodies of both living creatures and inanimate objects. "When any one looks at what is excellent with an envious eye he fills the surrounding atmosphere with a pernicious quality, and transmits his own envenomed exhalations into whatever is nearest to him."[13]

It has also been fully believed, both in ancient and modern times, that many persons by the glance of their eye have caused injurious effects, without their consent and even against their will, so that

---

[12] Potter's *Archæologia Græca* will be found a mine of information ; indeed it would be easy to load our pages with references to authors classical and mediæval, but sufficient indication is here given for the student to find all that has been written on the subject.

[13] Heliodorus, *Thea. and Char.* i. 140. There can be no doubt that Saul was believed to have the evil eye when we read : " And Saul eyed David from that day and forward " (1 Sam. xviii. 9). In the context we see all the circumstances we have been describing—envy and its consequences.

in some cases mothers [14] would not venture to expose their infants to the look of their own fathers.

A story is related of an unhappy Slav,[15] who with the most loving heart was afflicted with the evil eye, and at last blinded himself in order that he might not be the means of injury to his children.

Frommannd (p. 10) draws attention to the very remarkable passage in Deut. xxviii. 54, in confirmation of the possession of this terrible power acting against the will of the possessor.

Jahn [16] remarks upon this, that as smell, speech, bodily presence and breath work their influence upon those with whom they come in contact, so in a yet higher degree does the glance from the eye, which, as all know, affects so much in love.[17]

Domestic animals, such as horses, camels, cows, have always been thought in special danger. In the Scotch Highlands if a stranger looks admiringly on a cow the people still believe she will waste away from the evil eye, and they offer him some of her milk to drink, in the belief that by so doing the spell will be broken and the consequences averted.[18] The Turk and the Arab think the same of their horses and camels. Above all the Neapolitan cabman of to-day believes in the great danger to his horse from the eye of the *jettatore*

---

[14] Jahn, "Ueber den Aberglauben des bösen Blicks bei den Alten": *Berichte der Gesellschaft der Wissenschaften zu Leipzig*, 1855, p. 35.

[15] Woyciki, *Polish Folk Lore* (Trs. by Lewestein), p. 25.

[16] *Ut supra*, p. 33.

[17] In Ireland the belief has always existed, and in old legends we are told of King Miada of the silver hand, who possessed a magic sword, but who nevertheless fell before "Balor of the Evil Eye" (Elton, *Origins of Eng. Hist.* 2nd ed. p. 279).

[18] *Notes and Queries*, 1st ser. vi. p. 409.

Camden says the Irish believe some men's eyes have the power of bewitching horses.[19]

Young animals of all kinds were, and are, thought to be peculiarly susceptible. Virgil (*Ec.* iii. 103) puts into the mouth of a shepherd, what everybody quotes : " Nescio quis teneros oculus mihi fascinat agnos." Plutarch [20] also says that certain men's eyes are destructive to infants and young animals because of the weak and tender constitution of their bodies, but have not so much power over men of strong frames. . . . He says, however, the Thebans had this inimical faculty, so that they could destroy not infants only but strong men.

The Cretans and the people of Cyprus had in ancient times the reputation of being specially endowed with the faculty, and the same belief continues down to this day as recounted by General de Cesnola.

The special dread of fascination for domestic animals is implied by the author of the Book of Judges (viii. 21), for the word translated *ornaments* in the A.V. is given in the margin as "ornaments like the moon" that were on their camels' necks.[20a]

Who can doubt that those ornaments were the exact prototypes of the identical half-moons we now put upon our harness? We shall see later that these have ever been among the most potent amulets against the evil eye. The belief still prevails everywhere, that horses are specially subject to its influence : it is found in India, China, Turkey, Egypt, Greece, England, Scotland, Ireland, and in all countries where horses abound, but above all in Italy.

[19] *Ancient and Modern Manners of the Irish*, quoted by Brand, iii. 304.
[20] *Sympos.* lib. v. quæs. 7.
[20a] The R.V. has " the crescents that were on their camels' necks."

In Scotland [21] and in England all kinds of cattle are thought liable to its malignity. To this day any ailment or misfortune to a domestic animal is at once set down to its being "overlooked." [22] In Ireland in Elizabeth's time they used to execute eye-biting witches for causing diseases among cattle. Cows are particularly subject to fascination in Scotland, and the various preventive remedies are enumerated by Pennant in his *Voyage to the Hebrides*. [23] In England, of all animals the pig is oftenest "overlooked." This may be because he has more owners of the peasantry class, or perhaps because of the difficulty of administering physic; and hence his frequent maladies have become mysterious. It is the common saying that "there idn no drenchin' a pig when he's a-tookt bad; there idn no cure vor'n but cold steel." [24]

Pliny also says that the Thibii in Pontus, and many other persons as well, have a double pupil in one eye, and in the other the figure of a horse, and

[21] See Brand, vol. iii. p. 46 (Bohn).

[22] *Spectator*, "Somerset Superstitions," March 24, 1894. Last week (October 1894) a man much wanted to buy a heifer from an unwilling seller. "Nif he do want'n, I tell ee, you'd better let'n have'n," said a neighbour. There was no question of price, but the reason was obvious.

[23] Dodwell, *Classical Tour*, vol. ii. p. 37. I cannot find what Pennant says, if anything; indeed Dodwell's references are very untrustworthy.

[24] Pliny says (*Nat. Hist.* vii. 2; vol. ii. pp. 126, 127, Bohn) that in Africa there are families of enchanters who can cause cattle to perish, trees to wither, and infants to die. That among the Triballi and Illyrii are some who have the power of fascination with the eyes, and can even kill those on whom they fix their gaze, more especially if their look denotes anger. A still more remarkable circumstance is that these persons have two pupils in each eye. Apollonides says that there are certain females of this description in Scythia who are known as Bythiæ. Quoting Cicero he declares "feminas omnes ubique visu nocere, quæ duplices pupillas habent." Cf. also Horace, *Epist.* i. 14. 37 :—

> "Non istic obliquo oculo mea commoda quisquam
> Limat, non odio obscuro morsuque venenat."

See also Bacon, Essay IX. p. 78, and Frommannd, *Tractatus*, p. 11.

that these people will not sink in water even if weighed down with clothes.[25]

It is thus easy to see from Pliny, whence the idea came which led people in the Middle Ages, and even later, to put reputed witches to the water ordeal. If they sank they were innocent, but of course then they were drowned, and spite was appeased; while if they floated they were, as in Pliny's time, accounted guilty and then burnt.[26]

Those who were under the influence of anger or of envy were most dangerous in this terrible faculty, while those who were in the enjoyment of special happiness or good fortune were the most liable to injury, because exciting the greater *invidia* of the *fascinator*.

Those who had been highly praised, by others or even by themselves, were liable to be blasted.

Narcissus was thought to have *fascinated* himself, and hence his untimely fate, for it has always been held that too much praise or admiration of any person or object by whomsoever given, even by himself, would bring upon him the curse of fascination.

How surely this belief still exists even here in England is proved by the following :—A few weeks ago a respectable farmer had a very nice-looking

---

[25] Ovid says (*Amores* i. Eleg. 8. 15) :—

> "Oculis quoque pupula duplex
> Fulminat et geminum lumen ab orbe venit."

And again (*Metamorph.* vii. 364) that the people of Rhodes as well as the Telchinas injured everything by looking at it. See also Frommannd, p. 12.

[26] On this swimming of witches, see Brand, vol. iii. p. 21 (Bohn). "Nature has thought fit to produce poisons as well in every part of his body, and in the eyes even of some persons, taking care that there should be no evil in existence, which was not to be found in the human body" (Pliny, *Nat. Hist.* vii. 2; Bohn, vol. ii. p. 128). This chapter of Pliny is well worth careful reading; also Dr. Bostock's notes.

horse in his cart, which the writer, his landlord, admired, and said would bring him a long price for a certain purpose. The owner began to expatiate on the good qualities of the animal, but suddenly stopped and said: "But there, I don't want to zell'n, and mustn' zay too much for fear o' bad luck" (Nov. 15, 1893).

Even the most enlightened of us has constantly heard and perhaps said: "I never like to boast of my things; if I do I am sure to lose them." "Only yesterday, I was saying I had not broken anything for years, and now I have let fall this old glass that belonged to my grandmother!"

A story upon this question is told by Plutarch [28] which he puts into the mouth of his friend Soclarus at a supper in the house of a certain Metrius Florus. There had been a discussion on the evil eye, and some one having asserted that fascination was all nonsense, the host insisted that the power was undoubted, and called on his friends to testify that "we ourelves have known men who could inflict potent injury upon our children by merely looking at them." Plutarch then explains that the voice, the odour, the breath, are emanations which may easily injure those susceptible of them, and particularly is this true of the eyes, which dart out fiery rays, producing a wonderful effect, especially as may be seen in the influence of love through the eyes. Another of the friends agrees: he says that envy exerts an evil influence through the eye; and Plutarch affirms these to produce most direful results, from the envious looks which pierce like poisoned arrows. He goes on to say it is wise to employ charms and antidotes to turn aside these

[28] *Sympos.* v. prob. 7.

evil glances. Soclarus then mentions the fact that fathers and relatives sometimes bewitch their own children unintentionally, and that some even fascinate themselves by their own gaze.

He reminds them of the story of Eutelidas, who like Narcissus fell a victim to the admiration he felt for his own likeness.

> Fair was Eutelidas once, with his beautiful hair,
> But admiring his face in the stream, on himself he inflicted
> A dread fascination, and wasted away with disease.

Theocritus also tells a story of a certain Damætas who had been boasting of the impression his own beauty had made upon him when he had seen his image reflected in the water. He, however, seemed well aware of what might be the consequence, for he adopted a well-known remedy against fascination, by spitting three times on his breast. This will be referred to later on.[29]

Further, among the Greeks and Romans, statues of Nemesis were erected, which were adored and invoked to save their worshippers from fascination.

Few of the old classic writers[30] fail to give an account of the dread power which some individuals exercised over others. Women and children seem to have been accounted by all as the most liable to injury, while also some women were held to be the most powerful fascinators. Not only was the effect supposed to be produced by the eye—ὀφθαλμὸς βάσκανος, the fascinating eye of the Greeks—but it was asserted that some could blast trees, kill children, and destroy animals merely by their voice. In Gozola, a town in Africa, a fascinator called Elzanan

---

[29] Theocritus, *Idyll.* vi. 39.
[30] A long list of these with quotations is given in Dodwell, vol. ii. p. 35. Delrio and Frommannd also give endless references.

killed by his evil art no less than eighty persons in two years.[31]

In Rome the faculty of fascination was so well recognised that, according to Pliny, special laws were enacted against injury to crops by incantation, excantation, or fascination. The belief in those days was so universal that when a person was ill without apparent cause the people cried : " Mantis te vidit " —"some fascinator (lit. *grillo*, grasshopper) has looked on thee"; just as would now be said, "Thou art overlooked." [32]

It was believed anciently that even the gods also looked enviously upon man's good fortune, and often with malicious joy destroyed it for him. The injurious effect of this envy which seemed to men of old so mysterious (because beyond their comprehension), with the gods was thought to be but the natural outcome of their superhuman power. The belief was also held that the gods were envious of each other, and cast evil glances upon the less powerful of their own fraternity—hence the *caduceus* always carried by Mercury as a protector.

Although we no longer believe in divine enmity, any close observer can yet discover for himself, that a belief in the same malignant power of envy, though less outspoken, is still prevalent as ever. Here in the west we have a common expression of the peasantry, which keeps alive and tersely expresses this firm belief. Any untoward event which has brought misfortune, is described as "a very wisht thing." The death of a parent

[31] Story, *Castle of S. Angelo*, p. 149, quotes Andreas Thuetas.

[32] " Mantis, locustæ genus, quæ in stipulis enascitur, si quod inspexerit animal protinus illi quippiam producit mali. Hinc Proverbium : Mantis te vidit."—Frommannd, *Tract.* p. 19.

leaving young children, a child sick without any
apparent disease, a fatal accident, or any unexpected
calamity is thus spoken of.   A person forlorn, sickly,
or otherwise pitiable, is always "a wisht poor blid."
The phrase extended would be "illwished," *i.e.*
blasted or injured by the envious malignity of some
person by whom the sufferer has been "overlooked,"
by whom the maleficent glance has been cast.   The
word is so common, and of such regular use, that it
would be uttered by many, who would repudiate
any such superstitious belief as that of the evil eye.[34]

In connection with envy, it was customary amongst
the Romans when praising any person or thing to
add, *præfiscini dixerim,*[35] which may be freely

---

[34] See *West Somerset Word-Book*, pp. 365, 548, 835.   Blackmore, *Perly-cross*, p. 191, and elsewhere, wrongly writes "weist."

[35] The full sentence, of which the foregoing was only the colloquial form, is given by Plautus :—

> "Præfiscini hoc nunc dixerim ; nemo me etiam accusavit
> Merito meo ; neque me Athenis est alter hodie quisquam,
> Cui credi recte æque putent."—*Asinaria*, Act ii. Sc. 4. 84.

This subject is discussed at much length by Frommannd, *Tract. de Fasc.* pp. 60-63.   He gives very numerous instances and quotations from classics and scholiasts ; amongst others he says Vossius notes an instance of a girl named Paula being immoderately praised (*immodicè*), when another person interrupting in fear of fascination says : "Paula mea, amabo, pol tu ad laudem addito præfiscini, ne puella fascinetur."   (This passage is also quoted by Jahn, *Aberglauben*, p. 62.   Frommannd also gives an account of the *Fescennine* songs (*Fescennini versus*) which were most unchaste and lascivious, and were sung at weddings in the belief that they would avert the evil eye. It was usual to interpolate the most disgraceful and obscene expressions, thinking that the more abominable these were, the more certain in effect. Nemesis, Cunina, and Priapus were all invoked in these licentious songs.

Besides the authors referred to by Frommannd, both Catullus and Horace speak of these nuptial songs.   The latter says :—

> "Fescennina per hunc inventa licentia morem
> Versibus alternis opprobria rustica fudit."—*Epist.* i. 2. 145.

St. Augustine speaks of them as celebrated in his day, *cum tanta licentia turpitudinis* and *exsultante nequitia,* for a whole month in honour of the god Liber.   He gives details unfit for repetition (*De Civitate Dei,* vii. 21).

Pliny, *Nat. Hist.* xv. 24 (Bohn, vol. iii. p. 315), says that the walnut was used along with the fescennine songs at nuptials, because it was a "symbol consecrated to marriage," and a protector of offspring in manifold ways.

Valletta, referring to these songs, says: "Anzi dal fascino molti dicono esser

translated : " Fain evil ! I should say." The same
custom still holds in certain parts of Italy, where in
like circumstances it is said : "Si mal occhio non ci
fosse." The object of these conventional sayings
was, and still is, to prove that the speaker was
sincere and had no evil designs in his praise. We
in the West have similar little speeches, though
perhaps no set formula. " Mus'n zay too much."
" That ever I should zay zo." " I don't wish 'ee no
harm, so I on't zay no more," etc. etc., are very
common sayings after praise.

It would be easy to multiply ancient quotations
all bearing reference to the evil eye, not only
from the Scriptures, but from hosts of early writers,
which prove not only the prevalence, but the universality, of the belief.

All those who were supposed to possess the evil
eye were specially avoided by the ancients. " Eat
thou not the bread of him that hath an evil eye "
(Prov. xxiii. 6) is just as much a maxim to-day as it
was in the time of Solomon. At the appearance of
a person having the reputation, a cry, *jettatore !* is
passed, and even in a crowded street of Naples it
causes an instantaneous vanishing of everybody,
a rush up entries, into shops, or elsewhere ; the
charms and antidotes, of which we have to speak
later on, notwithstanding.

An amusing incident occurred to the writer. I
had been searching the book-shops of Italy from

appellati versi *fescennini,* quelli, che nelle nozzie alle soverchie lodi si aggiun-
gevano per allontare la jettatura." In a note he says further : "Questi versi
contenevano molta licenza nelle parole " (Nicolo Valletta, *Cicalata sul Fascino
volgarmente detto Jettatura,* p. 22. Napoli, 1787).

Story, *Castle of S. Angelo,* p. 200, speaks of this rare book, and of a
portrait in it, as printed in 1819 ; the writer possesses an earlier edition, dated
1787, but there is no portrait in this latter.

one end to the other for *Cicalata*, by Nicolo Valletta. At Venice I entered a large second-hand establishment, and was met by the padrone all smiles and obsequiousness, until he heard the last words of the title of the book wanted, *sul Fascino*. Instantly there was a regular stampede; the man actually turned and bolted into his inner room, leaving his customer in full possession of his entire stock. Nor did he even venture to look out from his den, so long as I waited to see what would happen. He evidently thought even the dread word a fatal omen, or at least that a foreigner using it must be a *jettatore*. Generally there is no hesitation among the people, at least the tradespeople, to talk about the *jettatura* as an abstract fact, but to get at their own personal feelings about it, or to get instances of its effects related, is much more difficult.

The fascinator of infants, *jettatore di bambini*, as he is called in Italy, is everywhere the most dreaded. A gentleman on three occasions acted as sponsor at Naples, and singularly all three of the children died; upon which he ever after got the reputation of having the *malocchio*, so that mothers who knew him took all sorts of precautions to keep their children out of his sight; and no one would, for the world, venture to ask him again to be godfather to a child.

The writer's friend, Mr. Neville-Rolfe, tells many similar stories (*Naples in 1888*. Trübner), and they might be multiplied to any extent. One such ought to be reported respecting a kind of fascination he terms "suspensive," the peculiarity of which is to disarrange whatever is being done. "If you meet him (the fascinator) when going to the train you will

assuredly miss it.   If you are going to see a friend
by appointment you will find him out; if a friend is
coming to see you he will be disappointed."

" How is your case getting on ? " we once said to
a Neapolitan friend, who was engaged in a trouble-
some litigation; "it was heard yesterday, was it
not ?"   "No," replied he, very crestfallen; "on my
way to the Court I met Mr. C——, and he has a
jettatura sospensiva, so I knew what would happen;
my case was adjourned *sine die*."

It may be mentioned *en passant*, that in Tuscany
the influence is called *affascinamento*, or *mal d'occhio;*
while in Southern Italy *jettatura* is the common
term.   In Corsica,[36] however, where the belief is
universal, it is called *Innocchiatura*.   In other parts
of Northern Italy it is known by several names,
which seem to include all the varied influences
of fascination, as well as those of the evil eye
especially.[37]

Valletta records[38] that a servant of the Duke of
Briganzio caused a falcon to drop down dead, *con
occhi jettatori*.   Also that it is registered in the Acts
of the Academy of Paris that a dirty old hag
(*vecchiaccia*) in 1739 went near and paused before a
highly polished mirror, which, from her glance,
absorbed so much greasy matter (*grassume*), that
collected together it was proved to be a very powerful poison.   Finally, he says, there was one who by

---

[36] Valletta, *Cicalata sul Fascino*, p. 9.

[37] In a note to the preface of an edition in the writer's possession of
Capricci sulla Jettatura, de Gian Leonardo Marugi, Napoli, 1815, is the
following :—" Se questa Operetta capitasse nelle mani di un Italiano più set-
tentrionale, piacemi d'avvertirlo che Jettatura suona lo stesso, che *stregoneria,
sortilegio, fattucchieria*," etc.   " Questo vocabolo Napoletano è de buonissima
lega, e l'etimologia n'è chiara.   Viene dalla frase latina *jacere sortes*, gettar
le sorti, incantare, ammaliare, e quindi i maliardi, o *Jettatori*."

[38] *Cicalata*, c. 12, pp. 55, 59

looking on a block of marble dashed it in pieces (*lo spezzo*). Also there was in Rome, Titinnia, who by her evil eye caused the orator Curio to remain speechless when making a peroration against the Senate.

He relates moreover many other misfortunes which befell sundry people known to him, especially how he had himself prepared a memorial to the king, setting forth his labours and claims, and making requests which had always been granted to his predecessors. But, alas! as he was getting into the carriage which was to convey him to Caserta, a friend whom he had long known as a terrible *jettatore* presented himself, and said: "*It is difficult*"; consequently there was as much misfortune as could possibly happen on the journey: pouring rain, a drunken coachman, horse taken ill or lame, and at last when approaching the royal presence to present his memorial, he could not find it in his pocket, where he had carefully placed it! The worst of all was that *quel maledetto jettatore* laughingly reminded him every day of the occurrence and of his blighted hopes.

The professor concludes: [39] "Every people, every race, believes, and hopes to avoid sinister events and *la jettatura*, by benedictions, by happy auguries, by those precautions and remedies which experience shows to be most valuable and opportune." He afterwards goes on to philosophise on the *invido sguardo*, and speaks of the antipathy between the Lion and the Cock. He says (p. 105) the eyes of cocks cause melancholy (*mestizia*) and fear to the poor lion; that there are seeds in the body of the

[39] *Cicalata*, p. 61.

cock inimical to the lion.   Curiously too he quotes
Bacon's ninth essay, on Envy.   Speaking of the
various antidotes, he says (p. 144): " For preservation
against incantations and evil enchantments (*malefici*)
I have found the following to be recommended :
invocation of the Goddess Nemesis ; the good
prayers of those who do not gaze with admiration
on or bepraise others ; the blessings of those who
wish to inspire courage are valuable to keep off the
evil eye (*togliere il fascino*) ; the carrying on the
person (*adosso*) certain natural articles, such as rue,
certain roots, a wolf's tail, the skin of a hyena's forehead (*fronte della iene*), the onion, which they say
the devil respects because the ancients adored it
equally with himself ; and that herb with strong-
smelling root called *Baccharis*, *Baccari*,[40] vulgarly
called *Guanto di nostra signora* (Our Lady's glove),
because it constipates the passages, and restrains the
overflow of the spirits which excessive praise produces ; whence it closes the door to fascination."

Valletta was evidently himself a profound believer

[40] Valletta, *Cicalata*, p. 145.

> " La Damaccia, ch' à la schiena
> Corta corta, e piena piena,
> Se a jettar staravv 'intanto,
> Voi prendetevi del *guanto*,*
> Ed in petto lo ponete,
> O la fronte vi cingete."—Marugi, *Capricci*, p. 111.

* " This is a flower called *Guanto di nostra signora*, known to the ancients
under the name of *Baccar*, which they bound to the foreheads of the sick " (note
by Marugi, p. 111).   He quotes Loyer as to its being *valevolissimo* against
evil tongues, and Virgil as to its virtues against *jettatori*.

Gerard (p. 791) says : " About this plant *Baccharis* there hath been great
contention amongst the new writers."   He in the end identifies it with *Plowman's Spikenard*, a name which Britten says was probably invented by Gerard.
Britten says the plant is *Inula coniza ;* Dr. Prior (*Popular Names of British
Plants*, p. 187) says it is *Conyza Squarrosa*.

Gerard says : " *Baccharis* or Plowman's Spikenard is of a temperature very
astringent or binding," and generally he describes its " vertues " much the
same as Professor Valletta.   There does not appear to be any plant-name
known in England at all like " Our Lady's glove."

in fascination of every kind, whether of eye, bodily presence, or actual touch, and finishes up his essay by offering a reward of from ten to twenty scudi for answers to thirteen questions, according as the *notizia* may excite in him more or less interest. They are as follows, translated literally :—

1. If a man or woman is the more powerful (*jetta più*)? 2. If more, he who has a wig ? 3. If more, he who has eye-glasses ? 4. If more, the woman *enceinte ?* 5. If monks more (than others), and of what order ? 6. If he is able *jettare* (to fascinate) more, who approaches us after the evil which we have suffered ? *i.e.* Is the second time worse than the first, or do we become increasingly subject to the influence ? 7. At what distance does the *jettatura* extend ? 8. If it is able to come from things inanimate? 9. If it operates more on side, front or back (*di lato, di prospetto, o di dietro*) ? 10. What gait (*gesto*), what voice, what eye, and what character of will have *jettatori*, and (how) do they make themselves known ? 11. What devotions (*orazioncine*) one ought to recite to preserve oneself from the *jettatura* of monks (*Frati*) ? 12. What words in general ought one to repeat to escape the evil eye (*si debban dire per evitare la jettatura*) ? 13. What power therefore have the horn, or other things ? [41]

It was anciently believed that women have more power of fascination than men. Varro accounts for their increased evil influence as the result of their unbridled passions,[42] and he fully describes how to discern between those who have greater or less dan-

---

[41] A comparison of these queries with those quoted by Story, *Castle of S. Angelo*, p. 200, will show that the later edition of Valletta's book used by him had been considerably altered.

[42] " Quia irascendi et concupiscendi animi vim adeo effrenatam habent."

gerous power. In modern times, however, it has generally come to be believed that the evil eye is possessed more by men than women.[43]

Ever since the establishment of the religious orders, monks have had the special reputation of possessing the fatal influence.

In 842, Erchempert, a monk of Monte Cassino, the most famous convent in Italy, wrote that Landulf, Bishop of Capua, used to say that whenever he met a monk, something unlucky always happened to him during the day.[44] To this day there are many persons who, if they meet a monk or priest, on first going out in the morning, will not proceed upon their errand or business until they have returned to their houses and waited a while, so as to be able to make a fresh start.

In Rome are many noted *jettatori*:[45] one of them is a most pleasant and handsome man, attached to the Church, and yet, by odd coincidence, wherever he goes he carries ill-luck. If he goes to a party, the ices do not arrive, the music is late, the lamps go out, a storm comes on, the waiter smashes his tray of refreshments, something or other is sure to happen. Some one said the other day : " Yesterday I was looking out of my window, when I saw —— (a well-known *jettatore*) coming along. 'Phew !' said I, making the sign of the cross and pointing both fingers, 'what ill-luck will happen now to some poor devil that does not see him ?' I watched him all down the street however, and nothing occurred ; but this morning I hear that after turning the corner

<hr>

43 " The fear of the evil eye of a woman is very prevalent in Spain, but the panacea is to drink horn shavings."—Murray's *Handbook to Spain*, by Richard Ford, 3rd ed. 1855, p. 632.

44 Valletta, p. 54.   45 Story, p. 197.

he spoke to a poor little boy, who was up in a tree gathering some fruit, and no sooner was he out of sight than, smash! down fell the boy and broke his arm."

A story was told the writer in Naples of an event which had just happened : a certain Marchese, having this evil repute, was invited to a ball, and people who knew he was coming were sure something would happen. He did not arrive till late, but he had no sooner set his foot in the ball-room than down fell the great glass chandelier in the centre of the room. Fortunately no one was immediately beneath it at the moment, but the chandelier was smashed to atoms, and of course he was the cause. Endless stories of this kind are to be heard in Naples, the home *par excellence* of the *jettatura*.

Truth (Nov. 4, 1893), of a party to a *cause célèbre*, says: "In Italy, however, it would be believed that he is a *jettatore*—that is to say, a person who, from no fault of his own, has the singular attribute of bringing some misfortune on others wherever he goes. The only way for any one brought in contact with such a person to avoid ill consequence is to point two fingers at him. Pope Pio Nono was supposed to be a *jettatore*, and the most devout Catholics, whilst asking his blessing, used to point two fingers at him. I remember once in Nice there was a gentleman who had this reputation. The *Préfet*, being a Frenchman, invited him to a ball. He soon, however, discovered that if the *jettatore* came many others would not, and he had to convey to him delicately the request not to accept the invitation."

Ask a Roman about the late Pope's evil eye

reputation, and he will answer: "They said so, and it seems really to be true. If he had not the *jettatura*, it is very odd that everything he blessed made *fiasco*. We all did very well in the campaign against the Austrians in '48. We were winning battle after battle, and all was gaiety and hope, when suddenly he blessed the cause, and everything went to the bad at once. Nothing succeeds with anybody or anything when he wishes well to them. When he went to S. Agnese to hold a great festival, down went the floor, and the people were all smashed together. Then he visited the column to the Madonna in the Piazza di Spagna, and blessed it and the workmen ; of course one fell from the scaffold the same day and killed himself. He arranged to meet the King of Naples at Porto d'Anzio, when up came a violent gale, and a storm that lasted a week ; another arrangement was made, and then came the fracas about the ex-queen of Spain.

"Again, Lord C—— came in from Albano, being rather unwell ; the Pope sent him his blessing, when, pop ! he died right off in a twinkling. There was nothing so fatal as his blessing. I do not wonder the workmen at the column in the Piazza di Spagna refused to work in raising it unless the Pope stayed away ! "

Mr. Story tells another tale—of Rachel and a rosary blessed by the Pope, which she wore on her arm as a bracelet. She had been visiting a sister who was ill in the Pyrenees, but one day she was so much better, that Rachel left her to visit another sister. While laughing and chatting merrily, a message arrived that she must return instantly as a fit had come on. Rising like a wounded tigress, she seemed to seek some cause for this sudden blow. Her eye fell on the rosary, and in rage and disappointment she tore it from her wrist, and dashed it to the ground, exclaiming: "O fatal gift! 'tis thou hast entailed this curse upon me!" and immediately sprang out of the room. Her sister died the day after.

Another acquaintance of Mr. Story, the Marchese B——, had the reputation of being a *jettatore*, and he called on a company of friends who were paying a visit at a villa in the country. All were gay and in good spirits, just on the point of setting off in carriages, on donkeys and mules, for a picnic. At once there was confusion and dismay. Some wished to put off altogether, others thought it would have a very ugly look in his eyes, and that they had better go, after taking all possible precautions to avert the *jettatura ;* and so it was decided. The gaiety, however, was at an end; every one expected ill-luck, and so it happened! They had hardly gone a mile when the horses in one of the carriages bolted, upset the carriage, and so frightened and hurt those who were in it, that they refused to go farther, and the picnic was given up. "Ah, you laugh!" said my friend; "you laugh; but it is no less a fact that wherever the Marchese goes he carries ill-luck. *Dio mio!* what a *jettatore* he is! The other day we were going into the country to spend the day when we had the ill-luck to meet him. '*Buon viaggio !*' he cried as we passed. '*Si divertino.*' We knew at once it was all up with us, and debated whether we should postpone our journey till another day. But that was a disappointment, and then we had made all our preparations, so on we went; but within half

a mile, off came the front wheel ; and, *bon gré mal
gré*, we were obliged to go back."

At a concert at the Sala Dante, in Rome, on
December 20, 1876, one of the main gas-pipes burst,
but fortunately, though the room was crowded, no
one was injured. *La Libertà* next day concluded
an account of the occurrence thus : "A friend coming
out of the Sala Dante explained the unfortunate
scene which had just taken place, attributing it to
the presence in the hall of certain individuals well
known as *jettatori*. Who knows that our friend is
not right ? "

Dumas in *Le Corricolo*, which is mostly about
Naples, has a short chapter on *La Jettatura*. He
says that it is an incurable malady,[46] one is born a
jettatore and so dies ; one is compelled to become
such, and when once begun there is no power to
throw it off. Generally they are unaware of their
fatal influence ; hence it is the worst possible compliment to tell a man that he has it. Constantly
you see in Naples two men chatting in the street,
one of them keeps his hand clasped (*pliée*) behind
his back. Mark carefully the one with whom he is
talking ; he is a *jettatore*, or at least one who has
the misfortune to pass for one. A stranger arriving
in Naples begins by laughing at the evil eye ; but
little by little he thinks over it, and at the end of three
months you will see him covered with horns from
head to foot, and his right hand eternally *crispée*.
Nothing guards against it except the means indicated.
No rank, no fortune, no social position, can place
one above its reach. All men are equal *devant elle*.

Dumas finishes his chapter with a citation of

[46] Vol. i. p. 183.

the same questions put by Valletta (see p. 22), but they are taken from a different edition of the *Cicalata* from either that used by Mr. Story, or that in possession of the writer.

In a previous chapter (vol. i. p. 177) Dumas speaks of King Ferdinand, that though he had lived seventy-six years and had reigned sixty-five, yet the Neapolitans sought to discover something supernatural in his death at last.

This is what they discovered. The king, who was a firm believer in the power of the evil eye, especially in priests, had been tormented for fifteen years by a certain Canon Ojori, who sought an audience to present some book of which he was the author. Ferdinand had all along persistently refused, but at length, on January 2, 1825, overcome by the persuasions of those about him, he fixed the morrow for this long-sought interview. In the morning the king wanted to set out for Caserta for a day's shooting, an excuse he always deemed sufficient; but he was dissuaded. He remained in Naples, received Dom Ojori, who passed two hours with him, and departed leaving his book behind. The day after, King Ferdinand was dead! The doctors unanimously declared that it was an attack of acute apoplexy, but the people would not believe a word of it. The true cause was that this audience had given an evil chance to Canon Ojori, who was known as one of the most terrible *jettatori* in Naples.

In Abyssinia potters and ironworkers called *Budas* [46a] were believed to have been specially endowed with the maleficent faculty, hence, in that so-

[46a] I have read somewhere, quite recently, that there are Budas still in Abyssinia.

called Christian land, these people were excluded
from the more sacred rites, notwithstanding that as a
class they professed to be most religious, and were sur-
passed by none in strictness of observance.   Certain
ailments are still set down to their influence, and
they are believed to have had the old-world power of
the *loup garou*, or were-wolf—that of changing themselves into hyenas or other ravenous beasts, the
counterparts of the wolves of the north.

Nathaniel Pearce, an old African traveller, declares
that a friend of his had seen one of these transformations with his own eyes, and that the peculiar earrings
worn by the descendants of the *Budas* had frequently
been seen by him (Pearce) in the ears of hyenas that
have been trapped.   This story is as old as Herodotus, who recounts that the *Budas* were reputed then
to be evil-minded enchanters who for one day in
every year changed themselves into wolves; but he
himself did not believe it.

The belief in the power of transformation [47] seems
in all countries to have been closely allied with
witches and with those possessed of the evil eye.
The idea is very common in the stories of ancient
mythology, and from the Middle Ages down to the
present time it has possessed the popular mind.
The hare, the wolf, the cat, and the sow seem nowadays to be the favourite animals whose shape is
assumed, though many others are believed in. [48]

[47] Story, p. 153, tells a very remarkable story from India by Major-
General Sleeman in 1849-50, of a boy who always seemed more than half
wolf, and never could be tamed.

[48] Old Higden tells us by Trevisa, his translator, that in Ireland and in
Wales "olde wyfes and wymmen were i-woned, and beeþ ȝit (as me pleyneþ) ofte
forto schape hem self in likness of hares . . . and ofte grehoundes renneth
after hem and purseweþ hem, and weneþ þat þey be hares.   Also some by crafts
of nygromancie makeþ fat swyne . . . and selleþ hem in chepinge and in feires;
but anon þese swyne passeþ ony water þey torneþ aȝen in to her owne kynde. . . .

Giraldus, so often quoted by Higden, says that Ossory men were periodically turned into wolves in his day; and Spenser says "some of the Irish doe use to make the wolf their gossip." These traditions naturally lead to such stories as that of *Little Red Riding Hood* of our nursery days. In India it is very firmly believed that certain people can change themselves into tigers, and again resume their natural shape at pleasure.

The ancient name *versipelles* sufficiently expresses the idea of those who could assume strange forms, or turn their skins. We ourselves bear witness to the old belief in the common saying : "Ready to jump out of their skins for joy."

It is easy to see how the belief in their power of transformation by witches has begotten that ever-present dread of ill omens, when one of the animals, supposed to be one of those whose form is usually

But þese swyne mowe not be i-kept by no manere craft for to dure in liknesse of swyn over þre dayes" (Higden, *Polychron.* Rolls Series, i. 360).

There must surely be some allusion to this ancient belief in Jer. xiii. 23, "Can the Ethiopian change his skin, or the leopard his spots? *then* may ye also do good, that are accustomed to do evil."

For a long disquisition on the whole subject of Lycanthropy, see Frommannd, lib. iii. p. 560, who assigns the entire power to the devil, by whose means magicians not only took the form of a wolf, but his voice or cry, his odour, touch, taste and appetite in devouring flesh (p. 564). He gives, moreover, many wonderful stories and quotations respecting transformations.

See also St. Augustine, *De Civ. Dei*, xviii. 18. Pliny, *Nat. Hist.* viii. 34 (Bohn, vol. ii. p. 284), gives the origin of the word *versipellis*, and although he says he does not believe them, records several wonderful stories.

The following shows that the belief still exists here in our very midst. In 1875 there had been some proceedings regarding the death of a "varth o' paigs," and one of the reputed authors of the mischief had fallen into the fire and been burnt to death, etc. "On the morning of this sad event, the harriers on the adjacent hill lost their hare among some stone walls, where it was next day picked up dead. The man who found it took it to his master's house, but on bringing it into the kitchen, the maids immediately rushed out in terror and 'wouldn't bide' in the house, declaring it was old Mrs. —— (the old woman burnt to death). It is a common belief that witches have the power of transforming themselves into hares. . . . I suppose there was a vague idea that the witch and her double had passed away at the same moment" (Rev. W. F. Rose, *Somerset and Dorset Notes and Queries*, June 1894, p. 77).

assumed, crosses the path. The writer knows people who would scorn the notion of being uneducated or superstitious, but who are terrified if a hare or a sow cross their path, and fully expect some misfortune presently to happen.

> Nor did we meet, with nimble feet,
>   One little fearful *lepus*,
> That certain sign, as some divine,
> Of fortune bad to keep us.

Even so serious a writer as Burton[49] mentions the fear of accident or of prodigies which trouble us "as if a hare cross the way at our going forth."[50]

In Scotland it is most unlucky to see a hare or a pig cross the path, and the fisher folk turn their backs if they see either. In Somerset, a hare crossing the path in front of the spectator is a sign of death ; but since the Ground Game Act this belief is likely to be soon forgotten.

Fishermen everywhere avoid mentioning at sea the name of a hare, pig, salmon, trout, or dog, but go out of their way to find some other word when it is needful to indicate either of these.

The fear of mentioning the name of any sacred or dreaded animal is common in India.

The weasel, or as Trevisa called it, and we still call it, the "veyre," crossing the path, is also a bad omen, doubtless from the same notion, though there does not seem to be any record of witches assuming its shape. "I have known people who have been put into such terrible apprehensions of death by the squeaking of a weasel, as have been very near bringing on them the fate they dreaded."[51]

[49] *Anatomy of Melancholy*, 1621, 4th ed. p. 214.
[50] Much on this subject is to be found in Brand, vol. iii. p. 201 *et seq*.
[51] *Secret Memoirs of Duncan Campbell*, 1732, p. 60. See Brand, iii. 203.

On the other hand a frog was considered a good omen. Many other objects are still considered, when met, to be the forerunners of misfortune, such as a deformed person,[52] a black cat, a shaggy dog, a barefooted woman; but above all to meet a person who squints, is here in England thought to be as unlucky as in Italy it is to meet a *jettatore sospensivo*. In fact there are still living people by no means unintelligent to whom omens of bad or good fortune are matters of very considerable importance, and who, without perhaps confessing it, are yet guided in their actions to an unsuspected degree by feelings engendered by such notions as are here hinted at.

The same custom of deprecating over-praise, before referred to, is common among the Turks, among modern Italians, and among ourselves, who each and all have a similar formula. A well-mannered Turk will not pay a compliment without "*Mash-allah!*" an Italian will not receive one without "Grazia a Dio"; an Irishman without "Glory be to God"; or an English peasant without "Lord be wi' us." The idea is the same with all peoples: by acknowledging a higher power as the protector, the danger of fascination is averted; this, and not gratitude, must be confessed to be the motive in all cases, and that there is little of what is called Christianity in any.

There were two kinds of fascination among the ancients, the moral and the natural, and this belief is still held. The moral power was that exercised

---

[52] In Italy, and generally in Southern Europe, a hunchback is a good omen. At Monte Carlo, gamesters believe that if they can but touch a *gobbo* when going to play, good luck is certain. We have more to say on the *Gobbo* later.

by the will. It was against the users of this, that
the special laws of the Romans were directed.
These included all those who practised incantation
and malignant arts. More terrible were, and still
are, those in whom the faculty of the evil eye was
natural, whose baneful look was unconscious, whose
eye threw out *radios perniciosos*, which by a sort
of mesmeric power acted upon the nervous system
of the victim. It has always been recognised
as a rule of good manners never to praise immoderately lest the speaker should *fascinate* against his
will. Hence the conventional exclamation before
referred to, *præfiscini dixerim*, which put the hearer
on his guard to use some antidotal formula for
himself.

Heliodorus narrates [53] that a Greek girl, daughter
of Calasaris, fell ill, and that in reply to the question
what was the matter, it was said that it was no
wonder, seeing that she had been seen by so great
a crowd of people—and of course among so many
she had drawn upon her the evil eye of some one;
and the speaker goes on to explain that the air,
infected by the malign influence, penetrates the eyes,
nose, and breath of the victim, and carries with it the
bitterness of the envy with which it is surcharged.
He argues forcibly that love is of the same origin
as disease, which through the sight strikes passion
into the soul.

Consider besides, O Charicles, how many have been infected
with inflammations of the eyes, and with other contagious dis-
tempers, without ever touching, either at bed or board, those who
laboured under them, but solely by breathing the same air with

---

[53] *Theagenes and Chariclea* (Trans. 1789), vol. i. p. 141. See also Jahn,
Aberglauben, etc., p. 33.

them. The birth of love affords another proof of what I am explaining, which, by the eyes alone, finds a passage to the soul; and it is not difficult to assign the reason; for as, of all inlets to our senses, the sight is the most lively, and most various in its motions, this animated quality most easily receives the influences which surround it, and attracts to itself the emanations of love.

He ends with saying, if some give the stroke of the evil eye unconsciously to those they love, how much more must the effect be when malignant will is added to the force of nature.

It was currently believed in England at the time of the Black Death, that even a glance from the sick man's distorted eyes was sufficient to give the infection to those on whom it fell.[54] No doubt it was to this belief that Shakespeare refers in

> Write "Lord have mercy on us" on those three;
> They are infected; in their hearts it lies;
> They have the plague, and caught it of your eyes.[55]

The same speaker, Biron, had just before in the same scene called attention very significantly to

> Their eyes, villain, their eyes!

The eye was, and is, certainly considered the chief medium of communicating evil, but there were also those of touch, of bodily presence, and of the voice; further again there was the whole class of actions spoken of as enchantments or incantations, practised quite as much with the object of working evil, as of frustrating or counteracting it.

Those students who are curious upon the strange and manifold ramifications of the belief in fascination are once more referred to the exhaustive treatise of Christian Frommannd.

---

[54] W. J. Loftie, *London*, vol. i. p. 353.
[55] *Love's Labour's Lost*, Act v. Sc. 2.

Another remarkable book is[56] that of Martin Delrio, a Jesuit of Louvain, who published in 1603 six books folio, in which he also quotes a great number of authorities both ancient and modern. He says he will not argue whether *maleficium* exists, he takes it for granted, and that the calamities of mortals are the work of evil spirits. He declares that "Fascination is a power derived from a pact with the devil, who, when the so-called fascinator looks

[56] The full title of the author's copy is *Disquisitionum Magicarum libri sex in tres tomos partiti*, Auctore Martino Delrio, etc. Moguntiæ, apud Johannem Albinum, 1603.

Of these, Book I. treats *De Magia in genere, et de naturali et artificiali*. In it he discusses at great length the questions whether the power of characters, rings, seals or images is such as the Magi contend ; whether in words or incantations there is power to raise the dead or to perform miracles. He sums up one of his discussions with " Respondeo stultorum esse numerum infinitum," p. 32. He also treats at length of alchemy as a magic art. Book II. is *De Magia Dæmoniaca*. He asserts that such is proved to exist, and that by means of power derived from the devil. He inquires by what compact with the devil the fascinator can inflict his deadly influence ; and by what other pact can the Magi perform miracles. As to *incubi* and *succubæ*, he says (p. 141) : " Dicimus ergo ex concubitu incubi cum muliere aliquando prolem nasci posse," etc. Again (p. 145) that there are pygmies, and that they are the offspring of demons, etc. Whether demons can restore youth to old age ? he believes they can. He declares (p. 193) that the souls of the dead are able sometimes to appear to the living ; and (p. 231) discusses apparitions of demons or spectres. There were certain demon wrestlers, who forced men to wrestle with them ; for this he quotes (p. 243) Pausanias and Strabo. He discourses also of fauns and satyrs, and gives a long list of Scripture *emendata et explicata* from both Old and New Testaments. Book III. is *De Maleficio et De Vana observatione*. P. 26 is a chapter *De Fascinatione*, in which he repeats many well-worn stories, including that of Eutelidas and self-fascination, with others of Plato, Plutarch, and Heliodorus. Speaking of depraved love, he declares that " not by form only are they who love, captivated ; but to each, that which he loves appears to be beautiful ; hence, ' Quisquis amat ranam, ranam putat esse Dianam.' "

P. 35 contains the old discussions on the etymology of fascination, and makes reference to the evil eye of the tender and delicate woman mentioned so plainly in Deuteronomy xxviii. 56, 57. In his final chapter (p. 94) he treats at inordinate length of the many means "malis depellendis et morbis sanandis," such as the offering of money obtained in charity,* which is thought specially efficacious ; crosses made or bought by alms ; wax or other matters offered to saints ; mixing hair of men and sick animals ; plunging images in water ; certain ligatures against depriving cows of milk ; " qui per annulum desponsationis meiunt, " and many more, all for the purpose *ut liberentur maleficio*.

* In Berkshire it is thought that a ring made from a piece of silver collected at the Communion is a cure for convulsions and fits (Brand, vol. iii. p. 300).

at another with an evil intent, or praises, by means
known to himself, infects with evil the person at
whom he looks." He distinctly says that fascination
may be received by touch, or by inhalation, but
of these, the latter is not only most fatal but most
contagious.

As we go on we cannot but see that fascination,
in many of its aspects, is nothing more nor less than
what we now call Mesmerism or Hypnotism, by
which, as we all know, certain people have an extraordinary influence over others. In a recent magazine
article was a very remarkable story from a Physician's
Note-Book which precisely shows what we mean.
A girl, well educated, gentle, refined and perfectly
sane, was found to be detained in a lunatic asylum,
during the Queen's pleasure, for murder. She had
shot a man whom she did not know, and against
whom personally she could have had no enmity. The

In paragraph *decimaoctava* (p. 103) he directs us to join parallel rods, with
the force of certain words, in the centre, and to bind them in the form of a
cross ; and to suspend from the neck ; or to apply a piece of round wood to
the throat, with a certain muttering, *ut Turcæ faciunt.* He shows how
women were taught to use certain nails called *hoefnageln*, as love charms, etc.

He recounts endless particulars, and continues : "Recently I have discovered
here in Brabant, in order to learn if a sick man is about to die, they commonly place salt in his hand unawares (*ignaro*) and watch whether or not the
salt dissolves." In fact the whole book is a perfect mine of folk lore, though
not entirely bearing on our special subject.

Book IV. treats *De Divinatione* and discusses the *Urim and Thummim.*
He settles the vexed question thus : "Sic ergo statuo, *Urim et Thummim
fuisse has ipsas gemmas* XII. ut volunt Josephus, Lyran., Tostat., Oleaster et
Ribera."

In this book he also writes *De Chiromantia* both physical and astrological,
and refers to a people practising it who lived between Hungary and the empire of the Turks, Zigenos *appellamus.* (Gypsies, German *Zigeuner.*)

Book V. deals at equal length and in similar detail *De officio judicum
contra maleficos*, and Book VI. *De officio confessarii.*

Each book is furnished with a complete and separate index, as well as a
full summary of contents. On the whole the book is curious and valuable to
students of Mediæval Magic, but upon the subject of fascination it is vastly
inferior to the later work of Frommannd, 1674, which goes into the details of
the evil eye as exhaustively, though not quite at such length, as Delrio does
into magic.

story is told with much circumstantial detail, and, extraordinary as it is, seems probable enough. The upshot is that she had become subject to the influence of a physician, who had taken to practise hypnotism, and whose power over her had become unbounded. The man's own confession unfolds the tale : he had some reason of his own to hate the murdered man, and in his heart wished him dead. He himself does not appear to have been specially bad, but he certainly harboured and encouraged in his own mind the evil feeling. One day the girl met the man whom her doctor secretly hated, and at once felt a violent antipathy ; this grew and grew, until at last the girl felt herself absolutely impelled, constrained, to murder him. She, a delicate girl who otherwise would have feared even to touch such a weapon, took a pistol of her father's, called upon the victim, and as soon as she got into his presence, shot him dead.

We have heard many instances of a similar kind, where certain people have had mysterious and very extraordinary influence over others. Some years ago a lady hypnotist acquired a marvellous power over some of the undergraduates at Oxford—a power real and overmastering, which science can in no way explain ; and however much chicanery there may be mixed with its practice, it is certainly a fact, that the effect produced first by the eye of the mesmerist is greatly strengthened by the actual touch.

In all ages and in all countries the power of touch has been fully recognised.

Many of our Lord's miracles were performed by the aid of touch, usually as an actual means, but on one notable occasion the healing was effected by the woman's touching Him. When Naaman went to be cured of his leprosy, he expected that the prophet would touch him "as well as call upon his God." Here in our west country "the doctor" is the well-understood name for a seventh son, though really according to popular faith he should be also the son of a seventh son. The familiar name comes from the firm belief that his touch alone has healing power. The touch of the king for the cure of scrofula, even within the last two centuries, has given to that particular kind the name of the King's Evil.[57]

Our dialectal word to *bless* signifies to touch by making the sign of the cross on the part affected. Here in the west, goitre is a rather common ailment, for which the best cure is believed to be the touching of the swelling by the hand of a corpse—the sex being different from that of the person afflicted. I have known many cases of its application, but cannot testify to the effect.

Whatever opinion we ourselves may hold as to the existence of a power or influence such as we are discussing, however much we may be inclined to ridicule the belief so far as concerns human beings, no one can deny that a very powerful influence does exist among animals both as regards the effect of certain species upon others, and as to the power of man upon the eye of savage beasts. Without admit-

---

[57] See W. Beckett, *Impartial Enquiry into the Antiquity and Efficacy of touching for the King's Evil*, 1722. T. Badger, *Collection of Remarkable Cures of the King's Evil by the Royal Touch*, 1748.

It is evident that this practice was common within the time named, as we find recorded by Hone (*Everyday Book*, 1830, p. 682) a notice respecting Charles II. in 1664 that "his sacred Majesty having declared it to be his royal will and purpose to continue the healing of his people for the evil during the month of May, and then give over till Michaelmas next, I am commanded to give notice thereof, that the people may not come up to the town in the interim and lose their labour."

ting the truth of what Virgil and Pliny refer to as to
the fact that he whom the wolf sees before he is
himself seen loses his voice,[58] yet we believe, and it is
generally maintained, that no animal can retain his
fierceness under, nor endure, the steady gaze of man.
Moreover the experience recorded by Dr. Livingstone when being actually torn by a lion, goes to
prove that the senses become deadened, that the
terror of his position had disappeared, and that the
previous nervous dread was the only suffering he
experienced : that in fact he felt no pain, nor any
acute desire to escape from his terrible assailant.

It is but reasonable, at least, to hope that some
such feeling is mercifully provided for animals in
general, and that the daily slaughter which is going
on everlastingly in nature, may not be attended with
all the nervous and physical pain with which, judging by our human feelings, we usually associate it.[59]

It is certain that some animals can and do exercise
a great and mysterious influence over others, fables
notwithstanding.[60]   Snakes especially seem to have

---

[58]   "Vox quoque Mœrim
         Jam fugit ipsa ; lupi Mœrim videre priores."
                                   VIRGIL, *Eclogue* ix.
   Pliny, *Nat. Hist.* viii. 34 (Bohn, vol. ii. p. 283), says : "It is supposed
that it will instantly take away the voice of a man if it (the wolf) is the first
to see him."   A note says : " Hence the proverbial expression applied to a
person who is suddenly silent upon the entrance of another, ' Lupus est tibi
visus.' "
   [59] Pliny says that near the sources of the Nile is found a wild beast called
the catoblepas ; "an animal of moderate size . . . sluggish in the movement
of its limbs, and its head is remarkably heavy. Were it not for this circumstance,
it would prove the destruction of the human race ; for all who behold its eyes,
fall dead upon the spot."—*Nat. Hist.* viii. 32 (vol. ii. p. 281, Bohn).
   [60] "The camel has a natural antipathy to the horse " (Pliny, *Nat. Hist.*
viii. 26 ; vol. ii. p. 276, Bohn : mentioned by Aristotle, *Hist. Anim.* vi.
17, also by Ælian).   This feeling is on all hands believed to be mutual.
George Eliot in one of her novels refers to the well-known fact that a horse
trembles with fear when first he sees a camel.   This is not fright like that
caused by a railway engine, but an actual nervous dread or involuntary
excitement, which shows itself by shaking and unwillingness to come near.

the power of exciting fear and aversion in nearly all other creatures, while with some, especially birds, they have at the same time a power of attraction, which can only be described as fascination.

This feeling is strikingly illustrated by the action of the frog when chased by a snake; for he utters a piteous cry while trying to escape from the creature of which he has an instinctive terror. "When fairly seized, however, it gives itself up to its fate, and seldom attempts to struggle."[61]

One species, *Bucephalus Capensis*, is generally found upon trees, to which it resorts for the purpose of catching birds. The presence of one is soon discovered by the birds of the neighbourhood, which collect around it, flying to and fro, uttering the most piercing cries, until some one of them, more terror-struck than the rest, scans its lips, and almost without resistance becomes a meal for its enemy. During the proceeding the snake is generally seen with its head raised ten or twelve inches above the branch round which the body is entwined, with its mouth open and neck inflated, as if anxiously endeavouring to increase the terror it was aware would sooner or later bring within its grasp some one of the feathered group.

Notwithstanding all that may be said in ridicule of fascination, it is nevertheless true that birds, and even quadrupeds, are under certain circumstances unable to retire from the presence of certain of their enemies, and, what is even more extraordinary, unable to resist the propensity to advance from a

---

The elephant is commonly said to have an antipathy to the pig, and especially to its squeal. The following shows how old is this notion : " Elephantes porcina vox terret " (Seneca, *De Ira*, ii. 12).

[61] *Museum of Animated Nature*, vol. ii. p. 107.

situation of actual safety into one of the most im-
minent danger. "This I have often seen exemplified
in the case of birds and snakes, and I have heard of
instances equally curious, in which antelopes and
other quadrupeds have been so bewildered by the
sudden appearance of crocodiles, and by the grimaces
and contortions they practised, as to be unable to
fly or even to move from the spot, towards which
they were approaching to seize them." [62]

A remarkable snake story is recorded in *Household Words* (vol. xvii. p. 139) of a cobra and an old
soldier in India, who became quite good friends,
and who used to remain in company together two
or three hours at a time while the soldier kept
singing. One day a hawk chasing its prey came
near the cobra, which raised its head and hissed.
"The hawk gave a shriek, fluttered, flapped his
wings, and tried very hard to get away; but it
would not do. Strong as the eye of the hawk was,
the eye of the snake was stronger. The hawk, for
a time, seemed suspended in the air; but at last he
was obliged to come down and sit opposite the snake,
who commenced with his forked tongue, keeping
his eyes on him all the while, to slime his victim all
over. This occupied him for at least forty minutes,
and by the time the process was over the hawk was
perfectly motionless. I don't think he was dead,
but he was very soon, for the snake put him into a
coil or two and crackled up every bone in the hawk's
body." He then gave him another sliming, made a
big mouth, and soon made a meal of him.

In our childhood we used to be told that the fox
was in the habit of sitting under a tree whereon a

[62] Smith, *Reptilia*, quoted by Story.

bird was perched, that he fastened his eyes and kept them steadily looking up at it, until at last the bird became quite overcome with the fascination and fell from its perch to become an easy victim to sly Reynard.

The ancients again, according to Ælian and Athenæus, believed that other animals besides serpents had the same power, and moreover that the animals themselves were so far conscious of it, that some birds kept certain stones and plants in their nests in order to protect themselves from it. Doves were said to spit in the mouths of their young for their safe keeping. It was from the belief of the Greeks that the cricket or grillo had this power of the eye, both protective and injurious, over all other animals, that Pisistratus set one up on the Acropolis as an amulet, to protect the citizens against the evil eye.

Again, we all know from experience the powerful attraction, the positive fascination, which a strong light has for some creatures, and the negative or deterrent effect it has upon others.

The experience of our lighthouse-keepers proves to us how migratory birds are attracted to their destruction by their powerful light; while our own senses have told us of the fatal attraction of a light for insects of most kinds, except the common house fly, whose familiarity with the domestic candle has bred a salutary contempt. The *raison d'être* of our common country sport, *bird-batting*, depends upon the fascination of birds by a strong light; on being disturbed at night they fly straight to the light and are caught in the net which is held up in front of it. Toads, too, are said to be so attracted by light that

they actually rush into the fire, and that the burning so far from checking them seems to stimulate
them to crawl towards the hottest parts, even though
being roasted to death ; just as the poor moth or bee
whose wings have been already singed, tries again
and again to reach the flame, until at last over-
powered and burnt to death.   Fish also are lured to
their destruction by a light.

On the other hand, light and fire are terrifying
and abhorrent to many animals.   Among insects,
scorpions are driven away by light, and beetles,
cockroaches, bugs, with their congeners, scuttle away
into hiding as soon as a light appears.   Moreover, we all know that a fire is the well-recognised
protector against night-prowling wild beasts, which
will not come near a strong light.   The well-known
difficulty of getting a horse out of a stable on fire,
where he but too often defies all efforts to save him,
and remains to be burnt to death, may possibly be
due to either of the influences referred to—either
fear to move and face the fire he dreads, or that he is
fascinated by it like the moths, and will not escape
his fate.   Perhaps the latter is the true explanation,
for it is said that a horse will press against a knife
held against his chest until he is stabbed to the
heart.   The writer cannot vouch for this as a fact,
but he has often heard it asserted.

CHAPTER II

SYMPATHETIC MAGIC

In further pursuing this subject, it must be borne in mind that besides the direct influences of fascination, including those of simple bodily presence, breathing, or touching, there is a whole class of operations directly connected with it, comprehended in the terms Magic, Enchantment, Witchcraft.

A great authority,[63] who has dealt exhaustively with the subject of the Occult Sciences, including Omens, Augury, and Astrology, does not even allude to the belief in the evil eye, which we take to be the basis and origin of the Magical Arts. About these the earliest known writings and the most ancient monuments give abundant evidence. Dr. Tylor calls the belief in magic "one of the most pernicious delusions that ever vexed mankind"; and considering magic merely as the handmaid, or the tool, of envy, this description accords well with that of Bacon, as the vilest and most depraved of all "affections."

The practice of magic as defined by Littré, "Art prétendu de produire des effets contre l'ordre de la nature," began with the lowest known stages of civilisation; and although amongst most

---

[63] Tylor, *Primitive Culture*, vol. i. p. 101.

savage races it is still the chief part of religion,[64] yet it is not to be taken in all cases as the measure of the civilisation of the people practising it. The reason we assign is, that outward circumstances, such as local natural features, or climate, tend to make the mental condition of certain people specially susceptible of feelings, upon which magical arts can exert an influence altogether out of proportion to the culture of the persons affected. In fact, the more imaginative races, those who have been led to adopt the widest pantheon, have been mostly those upon whom magic has made the most impression ; and what was once, and among certain races still is, a savage art, lived on, grew vigorously, and adopted new developments, among people in their day at the head of civilisation. Thus it has stood its ground in spite of all the scoffs of the learned, and the experimental tests of so-called scientific research, until we may with confidence assert that many practices classed as occult, and many beliefs which the educated call superstitious, are still performed and held firmly by many amongst ourselves, whom we must not brand as ignorant or uncultured. No doubt the grosser forms of enchantment and sorcery have passed away ; no doubt there is much chicanery in the doings of modern adepts ; yet, call it superstition or what we may, there are acts performed every day by Spiritualists, Hypnotists, Dowsers and others, which may well fall within the term Magic ; yet the most sceptical is constrained to admit, that in some cases an effect is produced which obliges us to omit the word *prétendu* from our definition.

[64] R. Stuart Poole in Smith's *Dict. of Bible*, s.v. " Magic."

We cannot explain how, but undoubtedly there is
in certain individuals a faculty, very occult, by which
the divining rod does twist in the grasp of persons
whose honour and good faith are beyond suspicion.
The writer has seen the hazel twig twist in the
hands of his own daughter, when held in such a
position that no voluntary action on her part could
possibly affect it. Moreover, a professional Dowser
makes no mystery or hocus-pocus about it; he
plainly declares he does not know how, or why, the
twig or watch-spring moves when he passes over
water; nor can he even teach his own sons to carry
on his business. Of all arts we may say of his,
nascitur, non fit.

Again, there are certain phenomena in thought-
reading, which are well-established facts, clear to our
senses. Above all, there are the strange powers
possessed by Hypnotists over their patients, which
we can no more explain than we can that minutely
recorded act of the Witch of Endor[65] who "brought
up" Samuel, and instantly discovered thereby that
Saul himself was with her. Without believing either
in magic or the evil eye, the writer fully agrees that
"much may be learnt"[66] from a study of the belief,
and of the many practices to which it has given rise.
It is needful, however, to approach the subject with
an open, judicial mind, and not to reject all, like the
"Pharisees of Science,"[67] that our superior understanding is unable to explain. Our senses, our
experience, alike tell us that there exist many facts
and appearances, which appealed strongly to the
despised judgment of our forefathers, rude and

---

[65] 1 Samuel xxviii. 7 *et seq.*
[66] Tylor, *Primitive Culture*, vol. i. p. 101.
[67] *Spectator*, July 14, 1894, p. 45.

cultured alike, which never have been either disproved or explained, and some of these facts have
been held as firm articles of belief in all ages.

Mr. De Vere[68] expresses precisely what we mean
when he says of the imaginative, rather than the
critical mind of our chivalrous ancestors of the
Middle Ages, that "they delightedly believed much
that many modern men unreasonably disbelieve to
show their cleverness."[69]

It is easy, and the failure of modern science has
made it safe, to call everything we cannot understand
contemptible superstition. It is however satisfactory
and even consolatory, in pursuing our subject, to
know that the same word superstition has been
applied by "superior persons," indifferently and im-
partially, to the most sacred doctrines of Christianity,
to the belief in our Lord's miracles, to most solemn
mysteries, and creeds other than those of our infallible selves, to the magic omens and portents
which many believe in, and to the incantations or
enchantments of charlatans, wizards, and sorcerers.[70]

The more, however, we study with unbiassed
mind the subjects which are called occult, the more
evident will it become, even to the least advanced or
enlightened amongst us, that there is a whole world

[68] "Mediæval Records," *Spectator*, January 6, 1894, p. 14.

[69] These remarks are suggested by a "scientific gentleman," who was a
witness with the writer of the twisting of the rod above mentioned, and who
had the taste to assert that the young lady was in league with the Dowser.

[70] Since this was written we have been favoured with Mr. Huxley's *ex
cathedra* deliverance in the *Times* of July 9, 1894, on Mr. Lang's book,
Cock Lane and Common Sense, which may be shortly summed up: "I do
not understand these things, therefore they are not."

No doubt superior people would nowadays accept the consequence, which
John Wesley put so plainly when he said "to give up belief in witchcraft was
to give up the Bible" (Farrar. Smith's *Dict. of Bible*, s.v. "Divination,"
vol. i. p. 445). We, however, venture to believe that there is a middle
course, that of determining what we mean by witchcraft. As vulgarly understood and practised we are of course uncompromising unbelievers.

of facts, operations, and conditions, with which our human senses and powers of comprehension are quite incapable of dealing. This has certainly been the experience of all people in all ages ; we see in his magic but the feeble efforts of feeble man to approach and to step over the boundary his senses can appreciate, into what is intended to be, and must always remain, beyond his ken—essentially the supernatural.

Man, having come to associate in thought those things which he found by experience to be connected in fact, proceeded erroneously to invert this action, and to conclude that association in thought must involve similar connection in reality.[71]

Here no doubt we have the true reason for that association of ideas with facts which a recent author[72] calls Sympathetic Magic. He says : " One of the principles of this is that any effect may be produced by imitating it." So concise a definition may well be borne in mind, for we are told that it lies at the very foundation of human reason, and of unreason also. We Christians, however, certainly cannot agree to call this association of ideas with facts a superstition in the conventional sense ; for we must see that the principle, perhaps to suit our humanity and our limited reason, has been appointed and adopted for our most sacred rites. Surely in the act of baptism we hope for the spiritual effect we imitate or typify by the actual use of water. So in that highest of our sacraments we spiritually eat and drink, by the actual consumption of the elements.

Leaving sacred things, which are merely mentioned here, with all reverence, by way of illustration, and to show how association of ideas with facts

[71] Tylor, *Primitive Culture*, vol. i. p. 104.
[72] Frazer, *Golden Bough*, vol. i. p. 9.

is not necessarily superstitious, but a fundamental principle of human ethics, we find that in practice it has nevertheless been more often perverted to the accomplishment, actual or fancied, of the basest designs of malignant spite, than to the higher purposes of religion.

To illustrate his meaning of the term Sympathetic Magic, the author [73] says: "If it is wished to kill a person, an image of him is made and then destroyed, and it is believed that through a certain physical sympathy between the person and his image, the man feels the injuries done to the image as if they were done to his own body, and that when it is destroyed he must simultaneously perish." The idea herein expressed is as old as the hills, and is practised to-day.[74] The ancient Egyptians believed that the *ushebtiu* or little figures of stone, wood, or pottery (Figs. 1, 2, and 3) which they placed, often in such numbers, in the tombs of their dead, would provide the deceased with servants and attendants to work for him in the nether world, and to fight for him against the many enemies he would there have to combat. Their name signifies *respondents*,[75] as if to answer to the call for help. The same curious belief is shown in the imitations or re-

---

[73] Frazer, *Golden Bough*, vol. i. p. 9.

[74] In the Pitt Rivers Museum at Oxford, is the original clay figure actually made to represent a man, whose death it was intended thereby to compass. This happened no longer ago than 1889 in Glen Urquhart, where the image was placed before the house of an inhabitant. That this is not an uncommon act is proved by their having in Gaelic a distinct name for the clay figure—Corp Creidh, the clay body, well understood to mean the object and purpose above described. The great antiquity of this mode of working evil is shown by the discovery at Thebes of a small clay figure of a man tied to a papyrus scroll, evidently to compass the destruction of the person represented and denounced in the scrip. This figure and papyrus are now in the Ashmolean Museum. We refer again to this subject in Chapter XI.

[75] Wilkinson, *Anc. Egypt.* vol. iii. p. 492.

presentations of food, such as terra-cotta bread,[76] and other articles placed with the dead for his use and sustenance.

Maspero in his lectures on the "Egyptian Hell" (see a long notice in the *Times* of August 22, 1887)

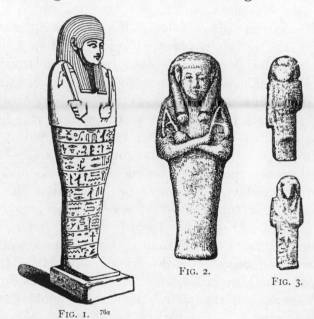

FIG. 2.

FIG. 3.

FIG. I.   [76a]

dwells upon the reasons which induced the ancients to provide their dead with arms, food, amulets, and slaves, for it was thought the dead would be liable to the *corvée* as well as the living. Besides all these things the dead were furnished with a funereal

[76] Maspero, *Archæol. Egyp.* p. 245. Of the ancient Greeks, we are told that in some "places they placed their infants in a thing bearing some resemblance to whatever sort of life they designed them for. Nothing was more common than to put them in vans, or conveniences to winnow corn, which were designed as omens of their future riches and affluence" (Potter, *Archæol. Græc.* vol. ii. p. 321). We are further told these "things" were not real but imitations.

[76a] Fig. I is from Wilkinson, *Anc. Egyp.* Figs. 2 and 3 from author's collection.

papyrus, now known as the "Book of the Dead," which Maspero describes as a "Complete Handbook to Hell," giving not only an itinerary of the route but all the spells, incantations, and prayers for each stage of the journey.

The very curious part of these provisions is that idealism seems to have run riot, as though the dead himself, in whose actual existence there was devout belief, would be satisfied with a mere make-believe, or even the picture of the article he needed. They seem to have thought that in the future state the person deceased would be so readily deceived, as to consider himself provided for by the most innocently transparent counterfeits.[77]

This remarkable belief in the easy gullibility of the departed was by no means confined to the ancient Egyptians, for among the Chinese is found a custom at present, which, seeing that in China habits change not, we may conclude to be of ancient date.

Archdeacon MacCullagh, long resident in China, says that Chinamen still believe that paper money passes current in the next world as it used to do with them in this. They also believe that as the person is dead, so must his money be with which he is to be furnished in the place to which he has gone. They therefore kill the money for him by burning it, in order that he may have dead or killed money.

[77] "C'étaient des simulacres de pains, d'offrandes destinés à nourrir le mort éternellement. Beaucoup de vases qu'on déposait dans la tombe sont peints en imitation d'albâtre, de granit, de basalte, de bronze ou même d'or, et sont la contrefaçon à bon marché des vases en matières précieuses, que les riches donnaient aux momies."—Maspero, *Archæol. Egyp.* p. 245. Upon this subject see also Maspero, *Histoire Ancienne des peuples de l'Orient,* p. 53 sq. ; Ib. *Trans. Bibl. Archæol. Soc.* vol. vii. p. 6 sq. ; Mariette, *Sur les Tombes de l'Ancien Empire,* p. 17 sq. ; Brugsch, *Die Ægyptische Gräberwelt,* p. 16 sq.

Paper currency has been for many centuries abolished in China, but the people will not believe it to be so in the world of spirits.   They therefore prepare spurious paper money in imitation of the old extinct currency, which they burn at the funeral, and also annually at the grave of their departed relative. The Egyptians did almost the same thing : they broke the arms placed with the dead.   This killed them, and set their ghosts free to follow their dead master.[78]

Such deception, which they think suitable for the spiritual world, evidently will not do for the present : at the death of a Chinaman, his friends present coins, of small value indeed, but real, to all comers, in order to make friends for the departed who may possibly meet him in the place where he is gone. The terra-cotta cakes at the Ashmolean Museum, so like modern Neapolitan loaves, must be such as would be placed with the dead man, by way of satisfying his appetite on his journey to the happy hunting grounds.

Nor can we say that this notion of being able to deceive the dwellers in the unseen world is confined to ancient or specially superstitious people, when we see altars in churches, dedicated to departed saints, bedecked in their honour with flowers of painted tin or coloured calico, stuck in sham vases of tinselled wood.

Again, nearer home, when we see the wreaths of beads strung on wires, of tin leaves and tinted flowers placed under glass shades upon the graves in our cemeteries, we wonder if the " Ka," or the

[78] Maspero, *Études Égyptiennes*, vol. i. p. 192.   See also Mariette, *Sur les Tombes*, p. 8.   Closely allied to this is the breaking of votive offerings to SS. Cosmo and Damian, referred to later.

shade of the departed, when it visits the cast-off
mortal coil, will be deceived by these cheap counterfeits. We fear we must conclude that such things
can only be classed, even in this nineteenth century,
as mere examples of the performances of sympathetic
magic, to be summed up in the famous words of
Erasmus to Sir Thomas More : "Crede ut habes
et habes."

In our Somerset County Museum at Taunton
is to be seen more than one heart, said to be those
of pigs, stuck full of pins
and thorns, which have
been found not long ago
in old houses near the
writer's home. The illustrations are careful drawings from the originals
and represent actual size.[79]
These hearts are also said
to be malignant in design
as well as protective: that
the persons who stuck
those pins into the hearts,
had special ill - will, and

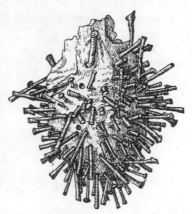

FIG. 4.

desired to work injury against the person in whose
house they were found. They entertained the old,

[79] Fig. 4 was found October 1882 in a recess of a chimney in an old house
occupied by Mrs. Cottrell in the village of Ashbrittle. It was wrapped in a
flannel bag, black and rotten, which crumbled to pieces. Some of the old
people declared it to have been a custom when a pig died from the "overlooking" of a witch to have its heart stuck full of pins and white thorns, and to
put it up the chimney, in the belief that as the heart dried and withered so
would that of the malignant person who had "ill wisht" the pig. As long
as that lasted no witch could have power over the pigs belonging to that house.
Fig. 5 was found nailed up inside the "clavel" in the chimney of an old house
at Staplegrove in 1890. One side of this heart is stuck thickly with pins,
the other side, here shown, has only the letters M. D. which are considered
to be the initials of the supposed witch.

old belief that the heart is the seat of life, and therefore a fit representative or symbol of a living person.
They believed that the heart of the hated person
would suffer from the pricking inflicted upon the pig's
heart, and that as the latter dried up and withered, so
would the heart and the life of the victim against
whom the act was designed.

The Bakongo people "believe the spirit is situated in the middle
of the heart, and
it is regarded as
the mainspring of
action, so that to
bewitch the spirit
in a man's heart
is to cause him
to waste away
and die."[80]   The
charm doctor is
the great spiritual
power : his busi-
ness is to find out
the witch who has
eaten the heart of a newly deceased person.

Fig. 5.

A few years ago, also in this same neighbourhood,

[80] Herbert Ward, *Five Years with the Congo Cannibals*, 1890.

Only ten years ago an old woman died here in the Workhouse, who was
always a noted witch.   She was the terror of her native village (in the Wellington Union), as it was fully believed she could " work harm " to her neigh-
bours.   Her daughter also, and others of her family, enjoyed the like reputation.
Virago-like she knew and practised on the fears of the other inmates of " the
House."   On one occasion she muttered a threat to the matron, that she would
" put a pin in for her."   The other women heard it, and cautioned the matron
not to cross her, as she had vowed to put in a pin for her, and she would do it.
When the woman died there was found fastened to her stays a heart-shaped
pad stuck with pins ; and also fastened to her stays were four little bags in
which were dried toads' feet.   All these things rested on her chest over her
heart, when the stays were worn.

A farm boy left his employment in a neighbouring parish against his

an onion was found hidden in a chimney, with a paper stuck round it by numberless pins; on this was written the name of a well-known and highly-respected gentleman, a large employer of labour.

The other day I [81] was at the Court House, East Quantoxhead, and was shown in the chimney of a now disused kitchen—suspended—a sheep's heart stuck full of pins. I think Captain L—— told me that this was done by persons who thought themselves "overlooked" or "ill-wished"; also to prevent the descent of witches down the chimney. . . . The heart is in good preservation.

In 1875 the village of Worle, near Weston-super-Mare, was in a commotion about the death of a "varth o' paigs," and the owner sent for a "wise man" from Taan'tn, who laid it to the charge of four

master's wish, "to better himself," and took service near. Soon after, he was seized with a "terrible" pain in his foot, so that he could neither stand nor drive home the cows. An acquaintance coming by took him home in his cart, and advised him to consult "Conjurer ——." The latter told him at once, "Somebody's workin' harm 'pon thee." In the end the boy was advised to go back to his old place, and to keep a sharp watch if Mr. or Mrs. —— took anything down out of the "chimbly." "'Nif they do, and tear'n abroad, they can't never hurt thee no more." After many questions he was taken back into the house again, and in a short time he saw Mrs. —— take an image down from the chimney. "'Twas a mommet thing, and he knowd 'twas a-made vor he." He saw that the feet of the little figure were stuck full of pins and thorns! As soon as he found out that the thing was destroyed, he went off again to farmer ——'s, because his feet got well directly, and he knew they could not work harm a second time.

Fifteen years ago, at a town in Devonshire, lived for many years an unmarried woman, the mother of several children. The woman left, and a neighbour searching about the house found, in the chimney as usual, onions stuck thickly with pins, and also a figure made unmistakably to represent *das mannliche Glied*, into which also were stuck a large number of pins. The people who crowded to see these things had no doubt whatever as to their being intended for a certain man who kept a little shop near, and had been known as a visitor of this woman, who thus vented her spite upon him.

The names of the parties to all these stories are known to me, and the "Conjurer" up to his death a few years ago occupied a cottage belonging to my father.

The pins in an onion are believed to cause internal pains, and those in the feet or other members are to injure the parts represented, while pins in the heart are intended to work fatally; thus a distinct gradation of enmity can be gratified.

[81] Letter from Mr. J. L. W. Page (author of *Explorations of Dartmoor, Exmoor*, etc.), October 20, 1890.

village wives, all of whom he declared he would bring to the house of the aggrieved party to beg for mercy and forgiveness.

The heart of one of the defunct pigs was stuck full of pins and then thrown on the fire—the owner and his wife sitting by and "waiting for poor old Mrs. —— to come and ask why they were hurting her." The remarkable coincidence followed these proceedings, that the old woman, who bore a bad reputation for "overlooking," should have met her death by falling into the fire on her own hearth. We are not told how soon this event followed the burning of the heart.[82]

Another recent instance in Somerset. An old woman living in the Mendip district had her pig "took bad," and of course at once concluded that it was "overlooked." As usual in such cases, a white witch was applied to.[83] The following is what took place in obedience to his orders.

A sheep's heart was stuck full of pins and roasted before the fire. While this was being done, the assembled people chanted the following incantation :—

> It is not this heart I mean to burn,
> But the person's heart I wish to turn,
> Wishing them neither rest nor peace
> Till they are dead and gone.

At intervals, in response to a request of "Put a little more salt on the fire, George," the son of the old woman bewitched, sprinkled the fire, thus adding a ghastly yellow light to the general effect. After this had gone on far into the night, the inevitable "black cat" jumped out from somewhere, and was pronounced to be the fiend which had been exorcised.[84]

---

[82] W. F. Rose, *Somerset and Dorset Notes and Queries*, vol. iv. part xxvi. p. 77 (1894).

[83] Those whose profession is to counter-charm and to discover witchcraft are white witches or "wise men," or more commonly "conjurers." They are usually, but not always, men.

[84] H. S. in the *Spectator*, Feb. 17, 1894, p. 232.

Closely allied to these practices is that of the maidens in Shropshire, who drop needles and pins into the wells at Wenlock, to arrest and fix the affections of their lovers.[85] Nor is this particular form of sympathetic enchantment, which here in Somerset is a very common one, by any means confined to this country.

A year or two ago a friend showed me in Naples an almost identical object, within a few days of its discovery: the following is his own account of it :—

In 1892 Mr. William Smith, English grocer at Naples, in course of cleaning his house, took down his curtains, and on the top of the valence-board found the object. Mrs. Smith presented it to Mr. Neville Rolfe, knowing that he took an interest in such things. He showed it to his cook, an old man, who was as ignorant and superstitious as ever a Neapolitan could be ; and he was so horror-stricken (thinking it had been sent to the house by some evil-disposed person) that he declined to remain in the house unless the object were at once sent out of it ! Mr. Rolfe, accordingly, lent it to the Museum at Oxford. It consists of an ordinary Neapolitan green lemon, into which twenty-four clout-headed nails and half a dozen wire nails are stuck, the nails being secured by a string twisted round their heads. The cook asserted that after the thing was made by the witches, they put it above a brazier, and danced round it naked, thus making it of deadly power. Many stories are current in Naples of the efficacy of the incantations practised by the witches, and especially of one who resided in Mergellina, a part of Naples still mainly inhabited by fishermen.

It appears that in Southern Italy the article is so common as to have a regular name, *Fattura della*

In all the foregoing instances, it will be noted that the hearts or onions were to be scorched either by being actually thrown on the fire or by being placed in the chimney, where they would be exposed to much heat. The inside of the clavel beam would be a particularly hot place. A specimen of the same kind of heart as Fig. 5, at Oxford (Pitt Rivers Museum), has also a large nail through it, to fasten it to the wooden clavel.

[85] Mrs. Gaskell in *Nineteenth Century*, Feb. 1894, p. 264.

This, however, is somewhat wide of our subject, and belongs rather to the widely-extended belief in holy wells and sacred springs. (For full information on this subject, see Mackinlay, *Folk Lore of Scottish Lochs and Springs*, 1894.)

morte (deathmaker), and that it is constantly employed in the same manner, and for the same purpose, as the pig's heart or onion is with us. Fig. 6 is from a drawing of this remarkable object now in the Pitt Rivers Museum.[86] The string or yarn twisted

FIG. 6.

about the nails, though now blackened by dirt and age, seems to have been originally coloured.

Who can deny that along with the onion as an eatable tuber, which almost certainly came to us from Italy, we may also have received the practice of the *fattura della morte* ?

The winding of the thread or yarn amongst the nails has doubtless its especial meaning, and is certainly a relic of ancient days, for Petronius, writing of certain incantations performed for the purpose of freeing a certain Encolpius from a spell, says : " She then took from her bosom a web of twisted threads of various colours, and bound it on my neck."[87]

[86] In the same case are to be seen one or two other hearts of the same character as Figs. 4 and 5, though less perfect as specimens.

[87] Petronius, *Sat.* 131. Story, *Castle of S. Angelo,* p. 211. Jahn, *Aberglauben,* etc., p. 42, says : " Bunte Fäden spielten bei allen Zauberwesen eine grosse Rolle," and gives numerous references to classics and scholiasts.

The same custom of tying threads of many colours
on the necks of infants as part of a charm against
fascination is mentioned by Persius.[88]

The foregoing examples are intended to show
sympathetic magic in its destructive or evil-working
side, but we may easily find instances of its use for
beneficent or at least harmless purposes. The idea
prevails in various parts of South Wales, where at
certain holy wells, each having a separate reputation
of its own for specific diseases, the faithful hang a
piece of rag, after having rubbed it over the part dis-
eased, upon some special tree or bush near the well,
in the belief that the rag absorbs the ailment, and that
the sufferer will be cured. One or more of these
trees are covered with pieces of rag placed on it by
the believers. There is, in some instances, an accompaniment of dropping pins into the well, but it does
not appear whether this act has any particular connection with the rag ; though it is suggested that the
pin or button dropped into the well is a make-believe
votive offering to the presiding spirit. There are
besides many famous wishing wells, where by the
practice of certain acts, such as dropping pins,
maidens learn who is to be their lover ; also on the
other hand ill-wishing is practised ; for corks stuck
with pins are set afloat in them, and the hearts of
enemies are wounded thereby.[89]

One of our commonest cures for warts is : "Take
a dew-snail and rub it on the wart, then stick the

[88] Persius, *Sat.* ii. 31. There is also a very common practice both in
England and elsewhere of tying a bunch of many-coloured ribbons to horses'
heads. "During the panic caused in Tunis by the cholera some extraordinary remedies were eagerly run after by the populace." Among others one
woman "sold bits of coloured ribbon to be pinned on the clothes of those
who were anxious to escape the epidemic" (*Hygiene*, Nov. 17, 1893, p. 938).

[89] On this subject see *Sacred Wells in Wales*, by Professor Rhys, read
before the Cwmrodorian Society, January 11, 1893.

snail upon a white thorn, and as the snail dries up
and 'goes away' so will the wart."[90] Another is :
" Steal a piece of fresh raw beef and rub that upon
the wart, then bury it where nobody sees, and as
the meat perishes, so will the wart."   In both these
cases secrecy is of the essence of the act—if any one
is told or knows what is done, except the person
performing, the result will be nothing.   Sympathetic
medicine is no less an active force than the evil-
working magic of which examples have been given.
The following recipe, called " The Cure of Wounds
by the Powder of Sympathy," is a serious one, and
throws light upon the art and science of surgery
just two hundred years ago.

Take good English Vitriol which you may buy for 2d. a
pound, dissolve it in warm water, using no more than will dissolve it, leaving some of the impurest part at the bottom undis-
solved, then pour it off and filtre it, which you may do by a
coffin of pure gray paper put into a Funnel, or by laying a sheet
of gray paper in a sieve, and pouring your water or Dissolution
of Vitriol into it by degrees, setting the sieve upon a large Pan
to receive the filtred Liquor : when all your Liquor is filtred boyl
it in an Earthen vessel glazed, till you see a thin scum upon it ;
then set in a cellar to cool covering it loosly, so that nothing may
fall in : after two or three days standing, pour off the Liquor, and
you will find at the bottom and on the sides large and fair green
Chrystals like Emerauds : drain off all the water clean from them,
and dry them, then spread them abroad in a large flat earthen
dish, and expose them to the hot sun on the Dog-days, taking
them in at Night and setting them out in the Morning, securing
them from the rain ; and when the Sun hath calcin'd them to
whiteness, beat them to powder and set this powder again in the
Sun, stirring it sometimes, and when you see it perfectly white,
powder it, and sift it finely, and set it again in the Sun for a day,
and you will have a pure white powder, which is the Powder of
Sympathy, which put in a glass and stop it close.   The next year
when the Dog-days come if you have any of this powder left

---

[90] Compare this with the many examples of sending away various diseases
by hanging articles on trees, given by Dr. Tylor, *Primitive Culture*, vol. ii. p. 137.

you may expose it in the Sun, spreading it abroad to renew its
vertue by the Influence of the Sunbeams.

The way of curing wounds with it, is to take some of the blood
upon a Rag, and put some of the Powder upon the blood, then
keep only the wound clean, with a clean Linnen about it, and in
a moderate temper betwixt hot and cold, and wrap the Rag with
the blood, and keep it either in your Pocket, or in a Box, and the
Wound will be healed without any Oyntment or Plaister, and
without any pain.   But if the wound be somewhat Old and Hot
and Inflamed, you must put some of this Powder into a Porringer
or Bason full of cold water, and then put anything into it that
hath been upon the wound, and hath some of the blood or
matter upon it, and it will presently take away all Pain and
Inflamation as you see in Sir Kenelm's *Relation of Mr. Howard.*

To staunch the Blood either of a Wound or bleeding at the
Nose, take only some of the Blood upon a Rag, and put some
Powder upon it ; or take a Bason with fresh water and put some
Powder into it ; and bath the Nostrils with it.[91]

"A few years ago in India, during a cholera scare,"
a witness tells the writer, "a woman dressed in
fantastic style was led by two men up to an infected
house, with the usual following of tom-toms and
musicians.   A fire with much smoke was made outside, and the woman, who represented the cholera
spirit, was completely fumigated amidst much ceremony, prayers, and great din.   Nothing whatever
was done to house or patient; in two days, however, the cholera had ceased."

We also include here all the many harvest customs,
the Maypoles, the Jacks in the Green, with all their
dancing and merrymaking, as being more or less
dramatic representations of the ends all these acts
and ceremonies were originally intended to produce.
Surely the Lord and Lady of the May, the King and
Queen of the May, the actual marriage of trees, are
something more than mere types or emblems of

[91] *The True Preserver and Restorer of Health,* by G. Hartman, Chymist,
1695, servant of Sir Kenelm Digby.

animal and vegetable fertility, which, primarily, all these things were believed and intended to procure or to stimulate.

There is abundant evidence that those now practised are survivals of very ancient rituals : that the marriage of Dionysus and Ariadne, said to have been acted every year in Crete, is the fore-runner of the little drama acted by the French peasants of the Alps, where a king and queen are chosen on the first of May and are set on a throne for all to see.

Persons dressed up in leaves represent the spirit of vegetation ; our Jack in the Green is his personi-fication. In several parts of France and Germany the children dress up a little leaf man, and go about with him in spring, singing and dancing from house to house.

Throughout Europe, the Maypole is supposed to impart a fertilising influence over both women and cattle as well as vegetation.

Sometimes these May trees, and probably our west country [92] Neck, like the ancient Greek *Eiresione*, were burnt at the end of the year, or when supposed to be dead ; and surely it is no unfair inference to assume that such burning was a piece of ritualistic worship of the life-giving Sun, whose bright rays are so needful to the progress of vegetation. Again all the little by-play with the water which occurs in our business of " Crying the Neck," and the throwing water over the priest of the sacred grove in Bengal, with many other examples in several parts of Europe of the sousing with water over the tree, the effigy, or the real person representing the rain spirit, are

[92] See " Crying the Neck," *Transactions Devon Association*, 1891.

but acted imitations of the end desired.   The object
of preserving the Harvest May, Neck or *Eiresione*,
from one year to another, is that the life-giving
presence of the spirit dwelling in it may promote the
growth of the crops throughout the season, and when
at the end of the year its virtue is supposed to be
exhausted, it is replaced by a new one.   How widely
spread these ideas are found, and among what
essentially different races, can be proved by the
fact that precisely analogous customs are found
in Sweden and Borneo, in India, Africa, North
America, and Peru.[93]

Referring to sun-worship, mentioned above, there
are still remaining amongst us many vestiges, besides
those relating to the Beltan fires,[94] in Scotland,
Ireland, and Northern England.

An Irish peasant crawls three times round the
healing spring, in a circuit that imitates the course
of the sun.[95]   It is everywhere thought most unlucky
to progress in a direction opposite to the course of
the sun ; indeed so well is this understood that we

[93] At the Pitt Rivers Museum, Oxford, are many specimens of this Harvest
figure from several parts of the world.   Particularly several " Kirn babies "
from Scotland, made from the last of the corn cut, and thus supposed to contain the corn spirit.   Though not precisely alike in form, they are exactly
analogous in motive to the " Neck " of Devon and West Somerset.   Upon
" Kirn babies," Brand fell into the error that *Kirn* meant *corn*, from
similarity of sound.   The word really means *churn*, and is precisely analogous
to *kirk* and *church.*   At harvest time in Scotland there has always been a
great churning of butter for the festival, and hence the *Kirn* has developed
into the name for the festival itself.   Baby is but the old English name for a
doll or " image," as Brand recognised.   Therefore the *Kirn baby* has nothing
to do with the word *corn*, but means a " Harvest-festival doll."   Theories
built up upon its meaning *corn-maiden* are without any foundation except that
of connection with the end of harvest.   No doubt these figures are made from
the last of the corn, and do represent the spirit of vegetation, but their
signification is by no means implied in their Scotch name.   Mr. Frazer
(*Golden Bough*, vol. i. p. 344) has therefore been misled by Brand.   See
N. E. Dict. s.v. " Corn-Baby."

[94] See Brand, vol. i. p. 226 *et seq.*

[95] Elton, *Origins of English History*, 2nd ed. p. 282.

have a special word, *widdershins*, to express the contrary direction. It is a well-known rule of Freemasons not to go against the sun in moving within the Lodge, and there are other plain survivals of sun-worship in other points of masonic ritual. In the Hebrides the people used to march three times from east to west round their crops and their cattle. If a boat put out to sea, it first made three turns in this direction, before starting on its course; if a welcome stranger visited the islands, the people passed three times round their guest.[96] A flaming torch was carried three times round a child daily until it was christened.[97]

The old Welsh names for the cardinal points of the sky, the north being the left hand and the south the right, are signs of an ancient practice of turning to the rising sun.[98]

In the Highlands of Scotland [99] and in Ireland it was usual to drive cattle through the needfire as a preservative against disease.[100] In these last examples we see customs almost analogous to making the children pass through the fire to Moloch.

We know that our British forefathers were Sun-

---

[96] Martin, *Description of Western Islands*, quoted by Elton, *Orig.* p. 282.

[97] In ancient Greece, " on the fifth day after the birth, the midwives, having first purified themselves by washing their hands, ran round the fire hearth with the infant in their arms, thereby, as it were, entering it into the family " (Potter, *Archæol. Græc.* vol. ii. p. 322).

[98] Rhys, *Welsh Philology*, p. 10.

[99] Kemble, *Saxons in England*, vol. i. p. 360, has a long note on this act in Perthshire during the present century, and also in Devonshire.

[100] We refer to these fires later on, but they were undoubtedly relics of sun-worship.

" In Munster and Connaught a bone (probably the representative of the former sacrifice) must be burnt in them (Baal fires). In many places sterile beasts and human beings are passed through the fire. As a boy I with others jumped through the fire 'for luck,' none of us knowing the original reason."—Kinahan, *Folk-Lore Record*, vol. iv. 1881, quoted *Notes and Queries*, 8th ser. v. 433.

worshippers, though the Sun does not appear to have been the chief of their divinities. Lug was the personification of the sun ; he was the son of Dagda [101] "the good god," who was "grayer than the gray mist," and he had another son named "Ogma the sun-faced," the patron of writing and prophecy.

It may well be maintained that all our modern notions included in the general term Orientation are but survivals of the once universal sun-worship.

A great authority [102] says that the ceremony of Orientation "unknown in primitive Christianity . . . was developed within its first four centuries."

This statement (and here he differs from his usual practice) is unsupported by any authority ; with all deference we would submit that there is much evidence to the contrary. Sun-worship was undoubtedly an abomination to the Jews, but the very facts recorded in connection with Ezekiel's horror (ch. viii. 16) at the idolatry of the twenty-five men who worshipped the sun in the temple of the Lord, show first a careful Orientation of the temple itself, in accordance with the plan the Israelites had learnt in Egypt ; and next that general importance attached to the directions of east and west. Thus, although actual sun-worship was considered as idolatry, the Sun was both actually and typically regarded as the almighty life-giving power of nature—giving his own name to the great emanation, the only begotten Son of the Father, the Light of the World, the Sun of Righteousness. Surely these very names speak eloquently of the idea, if not of the practice implied in the term Orientation. Primitive Christianity

---

[101] Elton, *Origins of English History*, p. 276.
[102] Tylor, *Primitive Culture*, vol. ii. p. 387.

will doubtless be admitted to have been developed from the older Judaism, and even if no distinct intimation of any actual ceremony which might be called Orientation can be found among Jewish rites, yet the fact that Daniel (ch. vi. 10) prayed with his windows opened "towards Jerusalem" shows that he attached importance to position, even though Jerusalem, where he believed his God to reside, was situated to the west of Babylon.

It was an ancient custom among the heathen to worship with their faces towards the east.[103] This is confirmed by Clement of Alexandria, who says that the altars and statues of pagan temples were placed at the east end, so that those who came to worship might have their faces towards them.[104] This account scarcely accords with the construction of Egyptian temples, yet we read immediately : "Nevertheless the way of building temples towards the east, so that the doors being opened should receive the rays of the rising sun, was very ancient, and in later ages almost universal." Moreover we know that Orientation in building was an important factor in pagan worship long antecedent to Christianity ; while the traditional burial of Christ Himself, looking eastwards, shows that the ceremony of Orientation was at least practised in the earliest days of the Church, though it can be no more called an act of idolatrous sunworship, than is our still-observed custom of burying our dead with their feet eastwards, so that the body may rise to face the Lord at His second coming in

[103] Selden says : " 'Tis in the main allowed that the heathens did in general look towards the east when they prayed, even from the earliest ages of the world."

[104] Potter, vol. i. pp. 223, 224. Upon the subject of " Bowing towards the Altar" much is said in Brand, vol. ii. pp. 317-324 (Bohn, 1882).

the east.   Here again we see Christianity and
heathendom hand in hand, for among the aboriginal
Australians, who are still cannibals, the graves have
a direction from east to west, and the foot of the
grave is toward the rising sun.   " If the deceased was
a prominent man, a hut is sometimes built over his
grave.   The entrance, which faces east, has an
opening through which a grown person may creep.
Near Rockhampton I saw several graves not more
than a foot deep, in which the feet were directed
towards the rising sun."[105]

The care observed by the ancient Egyptians in
building their temples properly east and west is remarkable, and while perhaps involving something
more, still plainly points to the idea that the sun was
the almighty power.   Nowhere is this seen more
distinctly than in the two rock-hewn temples at
Abou Simbel.   These are carefully constructed to
meet the rising sun upon two anniversaries.   The
great temple was hewn out to commemorate the
victory of Rameses the Great over the Cheta, and
was specially dedicated to Ra, the God of Light.[106]
The writer was fortunate enough to see the rays at
sunrise penetrate to the extreme end, and light up
the statues at the innermost part of the sanctuary,
on the very anniversary of the famous battle—
February 24.[107]   The smaller temple also commemorates a victory of Rameses, but evidently at a later

[105] Lumholtz, *Among Cannibals*, 1889, p. 276.
[106] Brugsch, *Egypt under the Pharaohs*, vol. ii. p. 412, 2nd ed.
1881.
[107] The facts given here are those observed, and those related on the spot
traditionally.   It is however clear that although this temple may have been
truly orientated by Rameses for the day of his great battle, yet that date could
not then have corresponded with the present season of February 24, owing to
the precession of the equinox.   Upon this subject see Norman Lockyer in
The Dawn of Astronomy, reviewed in the *Times*, February 2, 1894.

period of the year, as its axis points north of that of
its greater companion. All the Egyptian temples
are carefully orientated with the sanctuary at the
west, so that the sun's rays enter at the east end
and light up the sacred statues only on certain dedi-
cation days. The same system was adopted by the
Greeks, and later by the Romans in their temples.
The Roman basilicas were also constructed in like
manner, and have thus left their mark on the
churches now called Basilicas, where the main
entrance—as at St. John Lateran, St. Peter's, S.
Paolo fuori le mura, Sta. Maria Maggiore, and
others—is at the east, and the sanctuary at the west.
These facts all tend to show a general adaptation of
what had been good, or unobjectionable, in pagan
customs to the requirements of the Christian faith;
just as the pagan and Jewish lustrations, ancient and
almost universal, were perpetuated in the Christian
rite of baptism, both by the example and precept of
the Church's divine Master; proving that practical
customs, harmless in themselves, were not forbidden,
but were consecrated by adoption as sacred ceremonies into the then reformed Jewish worship which
we call Christianity. We find, too, that baptism itself was in the early Church closely allied to Orientation, in the position in which the catechumen was
placed.[108]

It is not generally known that in pagan temples
there was a vessel of stone or brass, called
περιρραντήριον, filled with holy water, with which all
those admitted to the sacrifices were sprinkled, and

---

[108] As we proceed we shall see other striking examples of this eclecticism
of modern Christianity, and a lesson of tolerance may well be learnt from the
spectacle.

beyond this it was not lawful for the profane to pass,[109] until purified by water. By some accounts this vessel was placed at the door of the temple; thus the holy-water stoups, outside the doors of so many of our old churches, are not of Christian origin at all, but merely an adaptation of the lustration used in rites we now call heathen.

Although it was usually considered that a small sprinkling was sufficient, yet sometimes, before participation in the sacred rites, the feet were washed as well as the hands.[110] So also the water was required to be clear and free from all impurities. The Jews used the same rite as the pagans, and were careful to have clean water for their washing of purification, hence St. Paul's expression (Heb. x. 22), "Our hearts sprinkled from an evil conscience, and our bodies washed with pure water." In Ezekiel (xxxvi. 25) we read: "I will sprinkle clean water upon you, and ye shall be clean."

Whether or not Orientation be in idea and in practice a quasi sun-worship, we, who would repel the suggestion of idolatry, have customs, keeping their place amongst us, notwithstanding all our enlightenment and culture, to which no such exception can be applied, for they surely partake of both sun-worship and sympathetic magic.

The very common custom, still maintained, of passing a child afflicted with congenital hernia through a split ash-tree is precisely such a case. The rite has to be performed on a Sunday morning at, or just before, sunrise—the opening must be made in the direction of east and west, for the child

---

[109] Potter, vol. i. pp. 224, 261.
[110] *Ibid.* vol. i. pp. 262, 263.

must be passed through it towards the rising sun.[111]

Another custom almost similar is reported from Gweek, in the parish of Wendron, Cornwall,[112] where the Tolvan or holed stone was in repute as a means of curing weak or rickety infants, who were brought, often from a distance, to be passed through the hole.

In ancient Greece, such as had been thought to be dead, and on whom funeral rites had been celebrated, but who afterwards recovered, such also as had been long absent in foreign countries, where it was believed they had died, if they should return home, were not permitted to enter into the temple of the Eumenides until after purification. This was done at Athens, by their " being let through the lap of a woman's gown, that so they might seem to be new born."

So in Rome, such as had been thought dead in battle, and afterwards returned home unexpectedly, were not allowed to enter at the door of their own houses, but were received at a passage opened in the roof,[113] and thus, as it were, in full view of the sun.

These rites can be considered as nothing short of dramatic representations of that which it is desired to accomplish, *i.e.* remedy of congenital or ceremonial imperfection by a new birth.

The homœopathic notion that like produces or

[111] Mead, *Proceed. Som. Arch. and Nat. Hist. Soc.* vol. xxxviii. p. 362, 1892. Also F. T. Elworthy in *Spectator*, February 5, 1887. The tree itself about which this notice in the *Spectator* was written is now in the Somerset Archæological Society's Museum at Taunton.

[112] First Report of Committee on *Ethnographical Survey of the United Kingdom* (Sec. H, British Association), 1893, p. 15.

[113] Potter, vol. i. p. 265.

cures like, is by no means new. One of the oldest remedies for a bite, here in England, was a hair of the dog that bit you; or the best way to staunch blood from a wound was to place in it the knife or sword which caused it. A friend of the writer, the Rev. R. P. Murray of Shapwick Vicarage, Dorset, relates that in May 1890, while at Arucas, in Grand Canary, he saw a dog fiercely attack a native boy, and that although he rushed to the boy's assistance, the latter was badly bitten in the hand, and his clothes much torn. The howling of the lad and the shouts of Mr. Murray caused a hue and cry, so that the dog was quickly caught amid much gesticulation and brandishing of knives, which my informant thought were to polish off the beast in no time. Instead of this, however, a handful of his shaggy hair was cut off, and the boy, well knowing what was to be done, held out his bleeding hand: the hair was placed on the wound, a lighted match was applied, and a little fizzled-up heap of animal charcoal remained upon it. No doubt the cautery was a good remedy, but all the virtue was believed by the natives to be in the hair of the dog that caused the wound.

Another curious form of the association of ideas with facts, or rather perhaps of persons with their belongings, is shown in the care which many people take to prevent anything they have owned or used getting into the possession of an enemy.

A South Sea Island chief persisted that he was extremely ill, because his enemies the Happahs had stolen a lock of his hair, and buried it in a plantain leaf for the purpose of killing him. He had offered the Happahs the greater part of his property if they would but bring back his hair and the leaf, for that otherwise he would be sure to die.[114]

It is for this reason that nothing whatever is to be seen but ashes on the spot where gypsies have encamped, unless it be the little peeled stick, left sometimes standing upright in the ground, most likely as a secret signal to friends who may be passing that way. One of these was noted very recently by the writer (Dec. 1893). Everything else is carefully burnt or otherwise made away with.

The aboriginal Australians believe that an enemy getting possession of anything that has belonged to them, can employ it as a charm to produce illness or other injury to the person to whom the article belonged. They are therefore careful to burn up all useless rubbish before leaving a camping ground. Should anything belonging to an unfriendly tribe be found, it is given to the chief, who preserves it as a means of injuring the enemy. This *Wuulon*, as it is called, is lent to any one who desires to vent his spite against a member of the unfriendly tribe. When thus used as a charm, the *Wuulon* is rubbed over with emu fat mixed with red clay and tied to the point of a spear-thrower, which is stuck upright in the ground before the camp fire.

The company sit round watching it, but at such a distance that their shadows cannot fall on it. They keep chanting imprecations on the enemy till the spear-thrower, as they say, turns round, and falls in the direction of the tribe the *Wuulon* belongs to. Hot ashes are then thrown in the same direction with

[114] D. Porter, *Journal of a Cruise in the Pacific*, vol. ii. p. 188. Dawson, *Australian Aborigines*, tells other stories of this nature.

Frazer, *Golden Bough*, vol. i. p. 198, gives many references to authors who have recounted instances of this common belief.

hissing and curses, and wishes that disease and misfortune may overtake their enemy.[115]

One cannot but wonder if the little stick stuck up by our gypsies is in any way connected with this custom. These latter are said to have come from India, and their habit of burning up all refuse after them, like the far-away Australians, seems to point to a common origin.[116]

A recent traveller in Australia says that "in order to be able to practise his arts against any black man, the wizard must be in possession of some article that has belonged to him—say, some of his hair or of the food left in his camp, or some similar thing.[117] On Herbert River the natives need only know the name of the person in question, and for this reason they rarely use their proper names in addressing or speaking of each other, but simply their clan names."

Another apt illustration comes from the West Indies. In Demerara it is to-day firmly and widely believed by the negroes and others, that injuries inflicted even upon the defecations of persons will be felt by the individual by whom they were left; and consequently it is often sought thus to punish the author of a nuisance. In 1864 the town of Georgetown was nearly destroyed by fire, and upon close investigation into its origin, it was proved to have been in consequence of some boys who, having

---

[115] Dawson, *Australian Aborigines*, p. 54.

[116] Here we have another link in that remarkable chain of beliefs so ably demonstrated by Dr. Tylor, at the British Association meeting, 1894, in his lecture on the "Distribution of Mythical Beliefs as evidence in the History of Culture," which seems also to prove the common parentage of widely-separated races. The ultimate relationship of the Nagas of Assam, with the Australian aborigines, through migration by way of Formosa, Sumatra, and the Indian Archipelago, is traced by Mr. Peal in "Fading Histories," *Journ. Asiatic Soc. of Bengal*, lxiii. part iii. No. 1, 1894.

[117] Lumholtz, *Among Cannibals*, 1889, p. 280.

found the excrement of another in a newly-constructed house, said : " Ki! let us burn it ; now we make him belly ache " ; and accordingly they got some shavings and made a fire over what they had found—the consequence was a vast destruction of property. The foregoing fact can be distinctly substantiated by the writer's informant, who was then a medical officer on the spot. Moreover, the like belief is still held even here in Somerset. About the year 1880 the child of a well-to-do farmer's wife was ill, and in the course of her explanations to the doctor, the mother expressed great displeasure with the nurse, especially at having discovered that she had thrown the child's excrement on the fire, and continuing, said : " You know this is very bad for the baby and ought not to be done, as it causes injury." She could not be drawn out to say what injury or malady was to be expected, but she said enough to show that the belief was commonly and strongly held. This woman is still living, and she and all her family are well known to the writer.

Further inquiry in other quarters completely clears up the question as to the injury to be expected from this proceeding, and very remarkably confirms the story from Demerara. An old midwife, questioned (May 14, 1894) upon this piece of nurse lore, at once said : " 'Tis a very bad thing to throw a child's stooling on the fire, 'cause it do give the child such constipation and do hurt it so in his inside." She said she had proved it ; she knew it was a bad thing, and had always heard, ever since she was a girl, that it was bad for the child. On the same day Mrs. S——, aged 85, said that when she was a girl at Taunton, she well remembers people saying that it was a bad thing, as it gives the children constipation and hurts them ; but she did not believe in it. She had not heard anything about it for years now. The day following, Mary W——, 80, and Anne P——, 70, two old women in the Workhouse, one a native of Devon, on being asked about it, said : " Lor! did'n you never hear o' that ? " Both believed it, and had always heard that it was hurtful to a child. Several other old women—indeed all there were—knew all about it. These inquiries led to the further discovery that the piece of the *funis umbilicus* should be taken off at the proper time and burnt ; that if this is not done, and if it is allowed to drop off naturally, especially if it should fall on the floor, the child will grow into a —— which, politely expressed, means afflicted with nocturnal enuresis, an uncleanly habit. Squabbles among the women " in the House " are not uncommon, from this cause. Much more might be said as to other reasons given for the careful attention to this operation, especially as to the different treatment of a boy from a girl, but they are wide of our subject, and scarcely desirable for discussion here.

Very strange belief in sympathy, even in the present day, appears in the following :—

A friend of mine, not long ago, told me that the wife of his coachman had been confined some time before the event was expected. He thereupon went to his own cook to tell her to send food to the woman and to render what help she could.

The cook said : " I knew how it would be, sir ; it's all along of them lionesses." She repeated the expression, and my friend, not understanding what she meant, inquired what the lionesses had to do with the matter.

" Why, don't you know, sir, that when the lionesses have their cubs very early, women have always a tendency to be brought to bed prematurely ? "

She appeared surprised that he had never heard of this "fact"; and on inquiry of a medical friend— or friends—he told me that the superstition seems to be a very prevalent one among the old "Mother Gamps."

One would have supposed this belief must be peculiar to London, the *locale* of this story, where alone the presence of lionesses can be effective ; still the facts are of much interest as a proof of a continued survival. On close inquiry, however, even here in Somerset, there are traces of the like notion. The old women in the Wellington Workhouse say : " If a lioness dies in whelping, the year in which that happens is a bad one for women to be confined in." This belief is quite common ; Mrs. M—— the matron has often heard it. All this suggests the idea that the British Lion may be not merely a fanciful object of heraldic blazonry, of which the people know nothing, but that he must be the Totem of our Celtic forefathers.

It is strange that the notion should be so stoutly maintained as to the injury done to a person by burning one thing, while on the other hand it is equally held that a child's milk-teeth, his nails, and hair should be burnt, lest injury come to him through neglect of that precaution. Stranger still is it to find how very widely these old and deep-seated beliefs are entertained by people of races so different as Somerset peasantry and West Indian negroes.

Such facts as we have given above cannot fail to

suggest that the burning of the effigy of a hated person means, at the bottom, a good deal more than a mere demonstration, and at least in times past was thought to injure by actual bodily suffering the person represented.

The student of man tells us that the reason for the reluctance to disclose one's name, was of the same nature as that which makes savages, and nations far above the savage state, feel anxious that an enemy should not get possession of anything identified with one's person as a whole, especially if such enemy is suspected of possessing any skill in handling the terrors of magic. In other words, the anthropologist would say that the name was regarded as part of the person, and having said this, he is usually satisfied that he has definitely disposed of the matter. . . . The whole Aryan family believed at one time, not only that his name was a part of a man, but that it was the part of him which is termed the soul, the breath of life, or whatever you may choose to define it as being.[118]

May we not add to this, that what relates to persons may by the same reasoning be applied to things ? Hence, of course, comes the belief of the modern Neapolitan, that in the absence of the amulet or charm the mere utterance of its name is equally effective as a protection, and that force is added thereto by the repetition of the name.[119]

Professor Rhys says that the Irish "probably treated the name as a substance, but without placing it on one's person, or regarding it as being of one's person, so much as of something put on the person at the will of the name-giving Druid, some time before the person to be named had grown to man's estate." Something of the same kind is found among Australian aborigines. They "have this peculiarity in common with the savages of other countries, that

[118] Prof. Rhys, " Welsh Fairies," art. in *Nineteenth Century*, Oct. 1891, p. 566. *Cf.* also remark on Herbert River natives, p. 73.
[119] Jorio, *Mimica degli Antichi*, p. 92.

they never utter the names of the dead, lest their spirits should hear the voices of the living and thus discover their whereabouts."[120]   Did not the Witch of Endor "call up" Samuel, that is by uttering his name?

The connection of a man's shadow with his body, as evidenced in the proceedings of Australian savages, is also a very widespread belief at the present time throughout the East amongst the races from which the Australians originally sprang.   An injury to a man's shadow, such as stabbing, treading on or striking it, is thought to injure his person in the same degree; and if it is detached from him entirely, as it is believed it may be, he will die.

In the Island of Wetar in the Eastern Archipelago, near Celebes, the magicians profess to make a man ill by stabbing his shadow with a spear, or hacking it with a sword.   Sankara, to prove his supernatural powers to the Grand Lama, soared into the air, but as he mounted up, the Grand Lama, perceiving his shadow swaying and wavering on the ground, struck his knife into it, upon which down fell Sankara and broke his neck.[121]   The ancient Greeks, too, believed in the intimate association of a man or beast with his shadow.   It was thought in Arabia that if a hyena trod on a person's shadow it deprived him of the power of speech; also that if a dog were standing on a roof, and if his shadow falling upon the ground were trodden upon by a hyena, the dog would fall down as if dragged by a rope.   Again it was thought, on the other hand, that a dog treading upon the shadow of a hyena rendered the latter dumb.[122]

[120] Lumholtz, *Among Cannibals*, p. 279.
[121] Bastian, *Die Völker des östlichen Asien*, v. 455.
[122] Torreblanca, *De Magia*, ii. 49.

Whoever entered the sanctuary of Zeus on Mount Lycæus was believed to lose his shadow and to die within the year. Here in the west country there is an old belief that many have sold their souls to the devil, and that those who do so, lose their shadow— from this it would seem to be thought, that the shadow contains the soul, *i.e.* the "Ka" of ancient Egypt.

In olden times it was believed in many widely separated countries [123] that a human victim was a necessity for the stability of any important building; indeed the idea was by no means confined to paganism, for we are told that St. Columba [124] found it necessary to bury St. Oran alive beneath the foundation of his monastery, in order to propitiate the spirits of the soil, who demolished at night what had been built during the day.

Here in England, throughout the Middle Ages, the common saying, "There's a skeleton in every house," or, "Every man has a skeleton in his closet," was hardly a figure of speech. The stories of finding the skeletons of faithless monks and nuns walled up alive,[124a] seem to have sprung from a much earlier notion ; and it is now well established that these are by no means myths, but very facts. At Holsworthy, in North Devon, the parish church was restored in

[123] Tylor, *Primitive Culture*, vol. i. p. 94 *et seq.* gives a number of very remarkable instances of foundation sacrifices from all parts of the world ; as for instance, quite in modern times even in our own possessions in the Punjaub—the only son of a widow was thus sacrificed. But perhaps the strangest account of all is that of several willing victims, making the story of Quintus Curtius seem quite commonplace.

[124] Baring-Gould, art. "On Foundations," in *Murray's Magazine*, March 1887, pp. 365, 367. Tylor tells the same story, *op. cit.* i. 94.

[124a] These stories are sifted and disproved in *The Immuring of Nuns*, by the Rev. H. Thurston, S.J., Catholic Truth Society, 1st ser. p. 125 ; but he by no means controverts facts relating to long antecedent beliefs.

1845. On taking down the south-west angle wall a skeleton was found imbedded in the stone and mortar. There was every appearance of the body having been buried alive, and hurriedly. A mass of mortar was over the mouth, and the stones were heaped and huddled about the corpse; the rest of the wall had been built properly.

Many similar accounts are given of finds of a like nature in various parts of Germany, and the superstition that walls would not stand without a human victim, existed among Celts, Slavs, Teutons and Northmen. Even so late as 1813 when a Government official went to repair a broken dam on the Elbe, an old peasant sneered at his efforts, and said: "You will never get the dyke to hold unless you first sink an innocent child under its foundations." Several stories are told of parents who sold their children for this purpose, and of others where the victim, often a woman, was kidnapped and built into the foundations.

At the building of the castle of Henneberg a mason had sold his child to be built into the wall. The child had been given a cake, and the father stood on a ladder superintending the work. When the last stone had been put in, the child screamed in the wall, and the man, overwhelmed with self-reproach, fell from the ladder and broke his neck.

At the castle of Liebenstein, a mother sold her child for this purpose. As the wall rose about the little one it cried out: "Mother, I still see you!" then later, "Mother, I can hardly see you!" and lastly, "Mother, I see you no more!"[124b] Several other castles have similarly ghastly stories connected

[124b] For authorities see Note 124, p. 79.

with them.   The latest authentic instance of the
actual immuring of a human victim alive, occurred at
Algiers, when Geronimo of Oran was walled up in
the gate Bab-el-Oved in 1569.

Most so-called Devil's Bridges have some story
associated with them, keeping alive the old idea of
sacrifice, though sometimes substituting an animal
for a human victim.   The most usual account is
that the devil had promised his aid on condition
of having the first life that passed over the bridge,
and then follow the dodges by which he was cheated,
showing that his wits were not estimated much higher
than those of the Giant in *Jack the Giant-Killer*.

In all ages it has been customary in sacrifice to
substitute a victim of less value for one of more importance.   The same idea, as that involved in the
substitution of the sham for the real in the offerings
made to the dead, is found running through sacrifice.
This latter is defined as "primarily a meal offered to
the deity,"[125] and the offering up of a human victim
has been in all ages considered the highest and most
important.

The Romans substituted puppets for the human
sacrifices to the goddess Mania.   They threw rush
dolls into the Tiber at the yearly atoning sacrifice
on the Sublician Bridge.   How curiously this corresponds with a find here in Devon !   A few years
ago the north wall of Chumleigh Church was pulled
down, and there, in it, was found a carved crucifix,
of a date much earlier than the Perpendicular
wall of the fifteenth century, when this figure was
built into it as a substitute.   Not far off, at Holsworthy, at about the same time, as we have just

[125] Robertson Smith, art. " Sacrifice," in *Ency. Brit.*

noted, the church wall was built upon a veritably living victim. Was Chumleigh more advanced in civilisation in the fifteenth century, or less devout in its belief in the efficacy of real sacrifice? or were the Holsworthy people less chary of human life, and, equally believing in the value of the rite, determined to fulfil it to the ideal, so as to ensure a good result?

Substitution in sacrifice, however, was of much earlier date than either Chumleigh or Roman offerings. The Egyptians who put off their dead with counterfeits, offered an animal to their gods instead of a man, but they symbolised their intended act by marking the creature to be slain with a seal bearing the image of a man bound and kneeling, with a sword at his throat.[125a]

When once the notion of substitution has got in, whether in offerings to gods or men, the decadence becomes rapid, and in these latter days takes the form of buttons and base counters in our offertory bags.

In modern Greece at the present day it is still customary to consecrate the foundation of a new building with the sacrifice of some bird or animal ; but sometimes, perhaps on a great occasion, upon which in old times a human victim would have been offered, the builder who cannot do this, typifies it by building on a man's shadow. He entices a man on to the site, secretly measures his body or his shadow, and buries the measure under the foundation stone. It is believed, too, in this case that the man whose shadow is thus buried will die within the year.[126]

The Roumanians have a similar custom, and they,

[125a] Robertson Smith, art. "Sacrifice," in *Ency. Brit.*

[126] Schmidt, *Das Volksleben der Neugriechen*, p. 196 *et seq.* Frazer, *Golden Bough*, vol. i. p. 145, also quotes as above, and gives many other authorities. See also Baring-Gould, *Murray's Magazine*, March 1887, p. 373.

too, believe that he of the buried shadow will die within the year ; it is therefore common to cry out to persons passing a newly begun building : "Beware lest they take thy shadow!" Not long since all this was thought necessary for securing stability to the walls, and there were actually people whose trade it was to supply architects with shadows.

Our own very commonly uttered sentiment, "May your shadow never grow less!" is at least a co-incidence.

From the shadow the step is but very short to the reflection, consequently we find many savage people who regard their likeness in a mirror as their soul. The Andaman and Fiji Islanders, with others, hold this belief, and of course its corollary, that injury to the reflection is equivalent to injury to the shadow, and so to the person reflected.

Far away from these islanders, it was believed that the reflection may be stabbed as much as the shadow. One method among the Aztecs of keeping away sorcerers was to leave a bowl of water with a knife in it behind the door. A sorcerer entering would be so alarmed at seeing his likeness transfixed by a knife, that he would instantly turn and flee.

Surely here we have in this very ancient and widespread belief, the basis of that very common one amongst our own enlightened selves, of the terrible calamity which awaits the person who destroys his own image by breaking a looking-glass. Some hold that "he will shortly lose his best friend," which may of course mean that he will die himself, others that it portends speedy mortality in the family, usually the master.[127]

[127] Dyer, *English Folk Lore*, p. 277.

In Germany, England,[128] Scotland, and other places even as far off as India and Madagascar, it is still believed that, if after death a person see his image reflected in a mirror in the same room as the dead, he will shortly die himself; hence in many places it is customary to cover up looking-glasses in a death-chamber. Bombay Sunis not only cover the looking-glasses in the room of a dying person, but do so habitually in their bedrooms before retiring to rest.[129]

The Zulus and Basutos of South Africa have almost precisely similar notions. We have no need however to go so far afield for instances of a belief of a similar kind.

The following story is given by a correspondent of the *Spectator*, of February 17, 1894, as told to him "last month" by an old woman, in a Somerset village about ten miles from Bristol.

"Old John, that do live out to Knowle Hill, have a-told I, his vaether George had a sister, an' when her wer' young, a man what lived next door come a-courten of she. But she wouldn't have none on him. But she were took bad, an' had a ravennen appetite, an' did use to eat a whole loaf at once. Zoo her brother thought she wer' overlooked; an' he went down to Somerton, where a man did bide who wer' a real witch, and zo zoon as George got to un, he did zay: 'I do knaw what thee bist a-cwome var; thy zister be overlooked by the neighbour as do live next door. I'll tell 'ee what to do, an' 'twont cost thee no mwore than a penny.' Zoo her told un to goo whoam an' goo to the blacksmith an' get a new nail, an' not to let thick nail out of her hand till her'd a-zeed un make a track, then her were to take an' nail down the track. Zoo George did as her wer' twold, an' when her zeed the man make a track, her took the nail in one hand an' the hammer in t'other, an' a-nailed down the track. And the man did goo limping vrom

[128] Dyer, *English Folk Lore*, p. 109. *Folk-Lore Journal*, vol. iii. p. 281.
[129] *Punjaub Notes and Queries*, vol. ii. p. 906, quoted by Frazer.

that time, and George's sister she got well. Zome time arter that, the man wer' took very bad, an' George's wife did work vor a leädy, an' she twold her missus he wer' ill. Zoo her missus gied her a rhabbut to teäke to the man, but when she got to his house some men outzide the door twold her he wer' dead. Then she did offer to goo an' help lay un out, and wash un, because she wanted to look wether or no there wer' anything wi' his voot. Zo she went and helped lay un out, an' zhure enough there wer' a place right under his voot, as if so be a nail had been hammered into un. An' this, John her son twold I as it were certain true." [129a]

The strange notion, that the soul goes out of the body with the shadow or the reflection, is carried still further by many savage people, and obstinately remains with some civilised ones, who think it unlucky to be photographed or to have their portraits painted. They have a fancy that it will shorten their days, just as many have about insuring their lives. This idea is the secret of the savage's unwillingness to be photographed, or to have his likeness sketched, which may be said to be almost universal.

A recent traveller [130] gives a graphic account of his experience among the Ainus after having apparently in another place (Volcano Bay) been permitted to paint the people unmolested, except by inquisitiveness. He says that a young lad came over to see what he was doing, and that being told the author was painting a group of his people, " the news seemed to give him a shock. . . . He rejoined the others, excitedly muttered some words, and apparently told them that I had painted the whole group, fish and all. Had any one among them been struck by lightning, they certainly could not have

[129a] The recorder of this story doubtless gives the facts correctly ; but his rendering of the dialect is quite literary.
[130] A. H. S. Landor, *Alone with the Hairy Ainu*, p. 13.

looked more dismayed. . . . The fish was thrown aside, but not the knives, armed with which they all rushed at my back." He describes how his paint-box and apparatus were smashed, the painting destroyed, and he himself knocked down and "a big knife was kept well over my head."

The dread of being pictured is found all over the world. The writer has often heard Somerset people object to having their likenesses taken on the ground that it is unlucky, and that so and so was "a-tookt," but soon afterwards she was "took bad and died." Of course these persons would indignantly repudiate any suggestion of superstition; indeed they would do the same about any other belief, such as the death-watch, or an owl's hooting, nevertheless they confess to the feeling and are strongly influenced by it. Quite recently the wife of a gardener near the writer's home objected to have her photograph taken upon the ground that she had "a-yeard 'twas terrible onlucky"; and that "volks never didn live long arter they be a-tookt off," i.e. photographed.

Whence then do these notions come, if they are not the heritage of untold ages?

CHAPTER III

TOTEMS, PORTENTS, TREE-WORSHIP

A BELIEF so strong, so universal, so founded on fear, as that connected with fascination, would naturally in the earliest days of humanity have led to the study and search for means to baffle or to counteract its dreaded effects. The causes of most kinds of evil, indeed of all that could not be easily accounted for by the senses, were set down to the supernatural action of invisible but malignant spirits which in one form or other were worshipped as divinities. Without going far into the field of primitive religion or of pagan mythology, it becomes abundantly evident that more thought was bestowed upon propitiating the angry or the destructive deities, than in the worship of those whose attributes were beneficent; we find that fear and dread have in all human history been more potent factors in man's conduct than hope and gratitude or love. Even the earliest records of worship in our ancient Scriptures point in the same direction. The sacrifices of Abel and of Cain were, we imagine, more propitiatory of an offended power, than as thank-offerings in grateful remembrance of blessings received. It is true we hear later of acts of devotion by way of acknowledgment and in gratitude for mercies bestowed, but they were the result of an express command, recognising man's innate weakness of fear, rather than the outcome of spontaneous thanksgiving. Our very words, to atone for sins, atoning sacrifice, imply acts to appease, to submit, to propitiate anger, to avoid the punishment due to offences.

As men degenerated from the monotheistic sun-worship, every power and attribute of nature became personified ; even Time became Chronos the de-stroyer, the avenger, the Saturn of the Romans with his scythe, who ate up his own children ; and in our day is the personification of Death the terrible. Zeus or Jupiter, the king of heaven, the giver of all his blessings and miseries to man, was generally represented as the holder of the thunderbolts, whose wrath had to be appeased. The stories of the various metamorphoses of Jove into a swan, a bull, a satyr or goat, do but carry back the later, even the present superstitions, as to the power of uncanny persons to assume animal shapes. Juno, too, the Queen of the Gods, though often a protectress and benefactress, was on the whole more dreaded than beloved, and was the very type of jealousy and spite. A sow and a ewe lamb were the offerings she most accepted, and these animals were consequently sacred to her, as representing or symbolising her attributes. Surely we may conclude that in the witch lore of to-day the misfortune of a sow crossing the path implies the envious anger likely to be felt and displayed by somebody towards the person to whom Juno exhibits herself in this guise. Certain objects and certain animals seem by primæval habit to have been sacri-ficed as propitiatory offerings to the various deities who were supposed to watch over, for good or for evil, the doings of mankind. Moreover certain other objects or animals were supposed to partake of their special natures, and hence were held to be especially under their protection, and to be their particular favourites. Consequently these became sacred, and like the modern totems[131] of many savages, or the sacred animals of India, must on no account be killed or molested.[132]

In early days no doubt the swan was the totem of some tribe, and being also the most famous metamorphosis of Jupiter, it would naturally follow that this bird should be held specially sacred. The Irish saga shows the strength of the belief :—

> Then was it Erin's sons, listening that cry,
> Decreed : "The man who slays a swan shall die."[133]

"Lir" was an ocean-god of both Ireland and Britain. According to Irish romance, the children of Lir were turned into swans by enchantment ; and the men of Erin were so grieved at their departure, that they made a law and proclaimed it throughout the land, that no one should kill a swan in Erin from

[131] The word "totem" is North-American Indian, almost unchanged. Among the Algonquins *dodaim* is their name for their tribe-animal or *totem*, and hence the term has been adopted by ethnologists everywhere to express the idea (Tylor, *Prim. Cult.* ii. 213). Ogilvie spells it *Totam.*

[132] "The term *totem* signifies the device of a gens or tribal division ; it may be an animal or a vegetable, or any natural object or phenomenon, or even a mere quality. The nature of *totemism* as a system is shown by the fact that among the Australians the totem is the symbol of a group of kinsmen. It is thus equivalent to a family name, and it is properly defined as a 'badge of fraternity,' answering to the 'device of a gens.' . . . The gens is founded on two chief conceptions, the bond of kin and non-intermarriage of persons belonging to the same gens. This obligation applies not only to human beings, but also to the totem group of objects which are regarded as sacred by the members of the gens, although they may be killed and eaten by persons not belonging to it. . . . The fundamental basis of *totemism* is to be found in the phase of human thought which supposes spirits to inhabit trees and groves, and to move in the winds and stars, and which personifies almost every phase of nature."—C. Stanisland Wake, "Definition of Totemism," *British Association Report*, 1887, p. 906.

[133] *Foray of Queen Meave*, p. 96, quoted in *N. and Q.* 8th ser. iv. p. 431.

that time forth. In Welsh histories he appears as " Lear." [134]

Totemism cannot after all be so very savage a cult, for we are told by Mr. G. L. Gomme [135] that various animals are still held sacred in Britain. Among these he places the seal, wolf, fowl, cat, hare, magpie, butterfly, sparrow, swan, raven, and otter. To these we should add many others which sentimentally are held to be sacred by various individuals, such as the wren, robin, swallow, lady-bird, bat, cuckoo, dog, fox, horse, swine, salmon, goose, cow, toad, deer. [135a] " The robin (in Irish, the *spiddóge*) is, as is well known, a blessed bird, and no one, no matter how wild or cruel, would kill or hurt one, partly from love, partly from fear. They believe if they killed a robin a large lump would grow on the palm of their right hand, preventing them from working and from hurling. It is fear alone, however, that saves a swallow from injury, for it is equally well known that every swallow has in him three drops of the devil's blood." [136] In Somerset much the same notion still exists. [137]

[134] Elton, *Origins of English History*, 2nd edition, p. 279.
[135] " Lecture on Totemism," *Standard*, April 17, 1889.
[135a] " There is a small black spider that often gets on clothes or hats ; this is called a ' money spider,' and if you kill it you will be sure to suffer from the lack of the needful."—*Choice Notes from N. and Q.* (" Folk Lore") p. 164.
[136] Le Fanu, *Seventy Years of Irish Life*, 1894, p. 41.
[137] " Hold a robin in veneration : to kill one is most unlucky. This bird is said to tap three times at the window before the death of any member of the family. Always take off your hat to a magpie, or at any rate bow respectfully to him, or evil will surely follow."—" Somerset Superstitions," in *Somerset County Herald*, Nov. 8, 1892. The magpie seems to be held everywhere as a portentous bird.

> Augurs and understood relations have
> By magot-pies and choughs and rooks brought forth
> The secret'st man of blood.—*Macbeth*, Act iii. Sc. 4.

Nearly every district has its own special version of the omens to be interpreted by the numbers seen at any one time. Our Somerset one is—

The root idea of totemism seems to be that whatever connection there may be, either in character or temper, between a person and his totem, is of benefit to both sides. Hence the totem becomes the man's protector, and the man will not kill or injure his totem. The totem is not a fetish to be worshipped like an idol: it includes a whole class of objects like the whole family of wolves or bears; it is not often inanimate, and very rarely artificial. It may belong to an entire class, or to one sex in the tribe, but not to the other: again it may belong to an individual without passing to his descendants. Members of the same totem may not intermarry.

How strong all these so-called savage beliefs still are may be seen almost on the surface of things. Who can doubt that the prohibition of certain marriages between persons having no blood kinship, however canonical, is after all the outcome of this belief in some indescribable, impalpable relationship described politely as affinity, but among the un-civilised as totemism; such, for instance, as that between god-parents, or between a man and his wife's kin? Surely it is pure totemism which in Shropshire makes it unlucky to kill a bat, and else-where, as here in Somerset, to kill a swallow, wren, or robin.

The belief in the owl's hooting being a death por-

> One, sign o' anger; two, sign o' muth;
> Dree, sign o' wedding-day; vower, sign o' death;
> Vive, sign o' zorrow; zix, sign o' joy;
> Zebm, sign o' maid; an' eight, sign o' boy.

The belief that the magpie is the devil's own bird is no doubt the reason of the well-known custom alluded to above. Our vernacular "Always take off your hat to the devil," conveys the same notion, which may be considered as a free paraphrase of "A soft answer turneth away wrath," that is, disarms malignity, and so neutralises the baneful glance of an enemy's eye.

In Ireland (Le Fanu, *op. cit.* p. 104) it is lucky to see two pies, but un-lucky to see one. This seems the universal belief.

tent is very widely extended, and it is said to be unlucky to shoot an owl.[137a]   Even among the Australian natives the kokok or great owl is a bird of ill omen : " It smells death in the camp, and visits the neighbourhood of a dying person, calling Kokok! Kokok!"[138]   The "bad spirit" also is said to employ owls to watch for him; hence owls are birds of ill omen, and hated accordingly.   When one is heard hooting, the children immediately crawl under their grass mats.[139]

In Tonquin every village chooses its guardian spirit (or totem), often in the form of an animal, as a dog, tiger, cat, or serpent.   Sometimes a living person is selected as the patron divinity.   Thus a beggar persuaded the people of a village that he was their guardian spirit, so they loaded him with honours and entertained him with their best.[140]   The names of many Irish kings are said to be taken from their totems, and instances are given of the wearing of dresses to imitate curious animals on particular festival days.[141]

Almost all savage beliefs are nowadays traced back by the savants to totemism.   Why then should not the origin of similar ones held by refined and educated people be stretched back a little, so as to cover the time of their evolution from outward or undisguised savagery ?

[137a] I have shot many owls, and have often "had bad luck."   I scarcely attribute the bad luck to the owls.

[138] Dawson, *Australian Aborigines*, 1881, p. 52.   [139] *Ibid.* p. 50.

[140] Frazer, *Golden Bough*, vol. i. p. 40.   Bastian, *Die Völker des östlichen Asien*, vol. iv. p. 383.

[141] For a full and comprehensive review of totemism, see Frazer, *Golden Bough*, vol. ii. p. 337 *et seq.*   For particulars of various *gentes*, with their customs, stories, legends, but especially for lists of birds, animals, and objects adopted as totems with their native names, see "Anthropological Report," *British Association Report*, 1889, p. 819 *et seq.*

Where is the family in which some member does not believe in luck, or fatalism, in the dire calamity to follow the spilling of salt, in "thirteen at dinner" foreboding death? Whose heart has not beat at the sound of the death-watch? Where is the house which is not considered lucky to have a swallow's nest under the eaves, but especially against a window? Does not every household contain some one who dreads to hear an owl hoot, or a raven croak? Since this was written we have read in the papers of the heroic doings of the "Thirteen Club," who bravely defy the terrors which their very buffoonery shows they acknowledge. Their splendid temerity is well matched by their singular ignorance, to which the *Spectator* and other journals did sufficient justice at the time. Did we not note the names of more than one acknowledged savant, among the famous "thirteen" group?

In all lands there is something more than mere dread of deadly animals. They are looked upon by human beings with that same sort of physical shrinking, that negative attraction, with which all wild creatures, familiar with his appearance, regard a man— they fly from him. The stoutest of us, even here in England, will admit an involuntary shock, at least a momentary flutter, when he suddenly perceives he was about to step on a viper. The same instinct unrestrained, is that which causes some silly women to shriek at the sight of a mouse in the room, as though a lion were in the path. We superior people flout the idea of superstition, or of anything akin to the belief that there is anything uncanny in venomous beasts, yet very often the writer has remarked that a sportsman will call the keeper to kill an adder, when a stroke from himself would have done it. Neither is it entire tenderness of heart which causes "my lady" to ring for Perks or the butler to kill the mouse. Mankind is the same everywhere at bottom, whether in Belgravia or in Uganda.

Hindoos especially hold the tiger in superstitious awe: many would not kill him if they could, nor are they always willing to show where he may be found, even when he has been killing their comrades or their cattle, from the fear that he may haunt them, or do them mischief, after he is dead. . . . In certain districts they will not pronounce his name.[142]

They do the same as regards the wolf; but as a general rule they are glad that others should destroy both wolf and tiger, and make great rejoicing when either is killed. "All sorts of powers are ascribed to portions of the tiger after death: the fangs, the claws, the whiskers are potent charms, medicines, love philtres, or protectors against the *evil eye*, magic, disease, or death. . . . It is difficult to preserve the skin of a tiger with claws and whiskers intact; the natives steal them if possible." Not only does this apply to tigers, but to lions, leopards, hyenas, cheetahs, wolves, jackals, wild dogs, and bears. "It is believed that these bears *(Ursus labiatus)* sometimes carry off women, hence perhaps one of their names, Adam-Zad."[143]

Everywhere it is thought that the raven[144] is a bird of ill omen, and in Scotland this is well expressed in

---

[142] Sir Joseph Fayrer, "Deadly Wild Beasts of India," in *Nineteenth Century*, August 1889, p. 223.   [143] *Ibid.* p. 236.

[144] The owl shriek'd at thy birth,—an evil sign;
The night-crow cried, aboding luckless time;
Dogs howl'd, and hideous tempest shook down trees;
The raven rook'd her on the chimney's top,
And chattering pies in dismal discords sung.
                    3 *Henry VI*. Act v. Sc. 6.

the gilly's proverb : " Nae gude ever cam' o' killin' black craws."

The belief that bees have an affinity with the family of their owners is strongly held even now in Somerset. If a death occurs in the house to which the bees belong, they must be formally told of it before the corpse is carried away, or they will all die before the year is out.[145] It is considered a death portent in the family if the bees in swarming should settle on a dead tree.

In Northampton[146] if at a funeral the hearse has to be turned after the coffin is placed in it, it is a sure sign of another death in the family quickly to follow. Besides these portents, are the firm beliefs that certain objects used in a special way are not merely bad omens, but actual producers of death. For instance, here in Somerset it is steadfastly believed far and wide that " May "— the flower of the hawthorn—if brought into the house will cause death in it shortly. To put that common household implement the bellows on the table is equally fatal. The writer has known this to produce fright little short of convulsions in the " gudewife."

In some places the crowing of a hen, or rather the attempt, for it is at best only a poor and laughable imitation of her lord and master, is looked upon as foreboding ill-luck to the owner, and death is quickly dealt out to her in consequence ; the idea being that taking her life will avert the impending trouble. On entering a farm-house in Somersetshire recently, I saw on the table a beautiful plump fowl, all picked and trussed ready for cooking, the farmer's wife explaining to me that her husband, seeing the hen in the yard in the act of crowing that morning, caught her at once, and then and there despatched her without

---

[145] *West Somerset Word-Book*, p. 55 ; also Brand, vol. ii. p. 300 ; also " Superstitions," in *Somerset County Herald*, Nov. 8, 1892.
[146] *Notes and Queries*, Oct. 21, 1893, p. 328 (8th ser. iv.).

delay, his prompt action in the matter proving how strong and firmly rooted was his belief in the superstition.[147]

Mr. Gomme says that certain trees are English totems, that they are particularly identified with the life of certain animals; that in many places in Ireland, and also in Scotland, misfortunes which have happened to families are said to have been occasioned by the cutting down of trees.

The curious antipathy of many people, particularly the Scotch, to the cutting down of trees, not on account of their beauty, but from the feeling that it is unlucky, or that it will lead to misfortune to do so, may surely be traced to the ancient worship of trees. We find in Scripture abundant evidence of this. The very earliest mention of them lends a sort of inspiration to the tree of knowledge and the tree of life, planted in the garden of our first parents. Then before they became objects of idolatry we read how Abraham planted a tree (grove, in the A.V.) in Beersheba, which was evidently of special sanctity, for there he called on the name of the Lord (Gen. xxi. 33). Later on when the Israelites had come under Egyptian influence, trees became objects of direct idolatry; the planting of a grove of trees near the altar of the Lord was strictly forbidden, "Neither shalt thou set thee up any image, which the Lord thy God hateth" (Deut. xvi. 22).[148]

---

[147] *Wellington Weekly News*, June 13, 1889.

[148] It should be borne in mind that the word "grove" in the A.V. must not be always, nor indeed generally, taken in its present sense. Authorities agree that Jezebel's groves were idols of a special kind called *Asherah* in Hebrew. They were symbolic trees, of which several representations are preserved in Babylonish sculptures. The worship was particularly licentious and obscene. Full information may be found in Smith's *Dict. of the Bible*, s.v. "Asherah-Grove," and in Daremberg et Saglio, *Dict. des Antiquités*. Those who require more detailed particulars must consult books like Forlong's *Rivers of Life*, Inman's *Ancient Faiths*, Higgins's *Anacalypsis*, etc. The latter is a learned and very interesting book.

Among the ancient Egyptians [149] many trees and plants were held to be specially sacred. The peach was sacred to Athor, and to Harpocrates; while the sycamore was sacred to Nut. The tamarisk, so common in Egypt, was a holy tree, from having been chosen to overshadow the sepulchre of Osiris; the chest containing his body was found by Isis lodged in its branches, when driven ashore by the waves. The legend is quite in accord with our own experience, for the tamarisk is almost the only tree which will grow by the sea, where salt spray can reach.

Garlic and onions were treated as gods by the Egyptians when taking an oath, says Pliny,[150] while Juvenal satirises [151] them for their veneration of these garden-born deities. The palm branch represented a year in ideographic writing. The ivy was called Chenosiris, or the plant of Osiris.[152] Evergreens seem to have been special favourites in ancient times; among the Romans, the myrtle was sacred to Venus,[153] and it was on this account that the myrtle had always to be excluded from the components of a maiden's wreath. The laurel and bay were sacred to Apollo, and the olive to Minerva. The pine has been held in reverence by many races. In ancient Greece it was sacred to Poseidon, Dionysos, and Zeus. It was especially the tree beloved of virgins. The *Pinea Corona* was the emblem of virginity which Daphne took from Chloe and placed upon her own head. Among the Romans the chaste Diana was crowned with a chaplet of pine.[154]

---

[149] Wilkinson, *Ancient Egyptians*, iii. 349; see also *Ib.* pp. 110, 131, 132.
[150] *Nat. Hist.* xix. 32. The inhabitants of Pelusium were devoted to the worship of the onion and garlic.
[151] Juvenal, *Sat.* xv.   [152] Plutarch, *De Iside*, s. 37.
[153] Pliny, *Nat. Hist.* xv. 35 (Bohn, vol. iii. p. 328).
[154] In Silesia (*Cultus Arborum*, privately printed 1890, p. 76) " Frau

Clement of Alexandria mentions thirty-six plants dedicated to the genii who presided over the signs of the zodiac.

In classic days tree and plant worship was prevalent both in Greece and Italy. Pliny tells us that in the Forum at Rome there was a sacred fig-tree named *ruminalis*, which was worshipped from the time of Romulus down to his day,[155] and dire consternation would have arisen if any evil had befallen it. Tacitus also speaks of this tree, while the writer can testify that it is still to be seen on the Forum, sculptured on one of the two remarkable monuments, said to have been erected by Trajan, each of which has the Sustaurovilia or Suovetaurilia on one of its sides. The tree appears in the bas-relief which commemorates the foundation of an orphanage. Another sacred tree in Rome grew on the Palatine, and whenever in a dry season this tree seemed to be drooping, Plutarch says a shout was raised, and people ran from all sides with pails of water as if to put out a fire. The story of Daphne being changed into a laurel-tree is all in keeping with this ancient faith.[156]

Fichte," the pine, is credited with great healing powers, and is believed to preserve animals from harm. Boughs of it are hung up on stable doors to keep off the evil spirits. In Bohemia, too, the pine kernel from the topmost cone is thought to make the eater invulnerable against shot. In other parts of Germany to tie a knot in the highest shoot of a pine-tree is a sovereign remedy for gout ! (Doubtless !).

[155] Pliny, *Nat. Hist.* xv. 20 (Bohn, vol. iii. p. 310).

[156] Among the sacred trees and plants we cannot omit the large number which in a way are, even amongst ourselves, dedicated to or named after Our Lady. First are those into which the name enters, as in Marigold, Marsh Marigold, Rose Mary, Mary Buds (*Calendula officinalis*).

> Winking Mary-buds begin
> To ope their golden eyes. —*Cymbeline*, Act ii. Sc. 3.

St. Mary's Seed (*Sonchus Oleraceus*, Sow thistle), Mary's Tears, or Sage of Bethlehem (*Pulmonaria officinalis*).

Then we have Lady Glove (*Digitalis purpurea*). This is very different from the Italian *Guanto di nostra Signora.*

Uncivilised man all the world over, from the extreme east in Kamtschatka to the extreme west in the Rocky Mountains, has always believed that trees held not only living spirits, but that they were animate themselves.

Trees are regarded by some people as the body itself of a living being, and by others as the abode of a spirit, but in either case as capable of feeling, and hence they must not be cut down or injured. In Livonia there is a sacred grove, where it is believed that if any man cuts down a tree, or even breaks a branch, he will die within the year. The tree spirit had always to be appeased before the wood could be cut. In ancient Rome, before thinning out trees, a pig had to be sacrificed to the deity of the grove.

One remarkable and widespread belief regarding trees was that certain kinds had the power of granting easy delivery to women. In Sweden there was a sacred tree near every farm, which no one was allowed to touch, not even to pluck a single leaf. The women used to clasp this tree

---

Our Lady's Cowslip, Our Lady's Cushion, Lady's Keys (*Primula veris*), called also in German *Frauenschlüssel*.

Our Lady's Mantle (*Alchemilla vulgaris*).

Lady's Meat, Lady's Milk, Lady's Milkwort, Our Lady's Seal (*Tamus communis*), "Sigillum Sanctæ Mariæ."

Our Lady's Thistle (*Carduus Marianus*).

Virgin Mary's Candle (*Verbascum Thapsus*).

Virgin Mary's Cowslip and Virgin Mary's Milk-drops (*Pulmonaria officinalis*).

Virgin Mary's Pinch (*Polygonum Persicaria*).

Virgin's Bower (*Clematis vitalba*).

With very many more. We do not of course include amongst these any plants which are not manifestly intended by their names to indicate the B.V.M. There are very many of these—such as Lady's Slipper, Lady's Garters, My Lady's Looking-glass—to be found in the old herbals, but more readily in Britten's *Eng. Plant-Names* (E. Dial. Soc.), or in Prior's *Popular Names of British Plants*.

with their arms during pregnancy to ensure easy delivery.[157]

The same thing is done in Congo, and the women also make themselves garments from the bark of their sacred tree, because they believe that it will deliver them from the peril of childbirth.

How old this belief is, may be seen from the Greek story of Leto, that when about to give birth to Apollo and Artemis, she clasped a palm and an olive, or, according to some, two laurels, that she might obtain painless delivery.

It is still believed that certain trees have the power of producing fertility; moreover the exact converse has been believed in all ages regarding other plants. Among the ancient Greeks and Romans it was firmly held that certain plants had the property of rendering women pregnant. In Turkestan, the Kirjiz women, if barren, roll themselves on the ground under a solitary apple-tree in order to obtain offspring. This ancient faith in the fertilising power of the tree spirit is shown still in the common custom in many parts of Europe of placing a green branch on May Day before the house of a sweetheart. A similar custom is placed to the account of the Irish : "they fancy a green bough of a tree fastened on May Day against the house will produce plenty of milk." In Germany also peasants set up May-trees, one for each horse or cow, before the stable doors, in order that the cows may give more milk.

Moreover, May Day customs have always been accompanied by much dancing, which has been held to have a mystic meaning in connection with fertility,

---

[157] Mannhardt, *Der Baumkultur der Germanen und ihrer Nachbarstämme*, p. 51. For much information on this subject see Frazer, *G. B.* i. 74.

but somewhat outside our subject, as treated for the general reader.

Most of our May Day festivities if traced to their ultimate origin will be found to be branches of tree-worship, and to lead to the old faith, typified by the death of the spirit of vegetation, and its resuscitation in the spring. The harvest wail in our "Crying the Neck" to-day, the Μανέρως or Λίνος of the ancient Greeks, the "Dirge of Isis" of the still dimmer antiquity, alike point to the central belief of humanity that the deity should be slain and die that he might rise again to give life to man. The joyous shout following the wail in all these cases typifies the gladness of the world at the revival of the dead god, just as the May Day rejoicings all over the temperate part of the northern hemisphere commemorate the spring, or the uprising of dead vegetation.

This must be the true meaning of all those curious customs of which Brand, Hone, and others give so many particulars. If such were doubtful, it is proved by the fact that in more northern latitudes, where vegetation is much later in the season, all these rites are postponed. In Sweden they set up their *Maj Stänger* on St. John's Eve (June 23), with elaborate decorations of leaves and flowers, round which they dance. They have also large bonfires like the Beltan fires, to be danced around and jumped over. In some parts of Bohemia also the pole is set up on Midsummer Eve, and like bonfire customs are observed there, together with much climbing of the pole by the men, after the garlands and ribbons fixed to it by the maidens. All these things are said to have typical relation to subjects nearly akin to the revival of vegetation, and to many grosser rites, that can be no more than hinted at in these pages.[158]

The Congo natives place calabashes of water under certain trees, that the tree spirit may drink when thirsty. In parts of India a marriage ceremony is performed between trees, as between human beings ; while in the Moluccas,[159] clove-trees in blossom are treated like pregnant women. No loud noise must be made nor anything done to frighten the tree, lest she should drop her fruit like the untimely deliverance of a woman. This same idea of pregnancy is held with regard to rice in bloom, by the Javanese, and in Orissa. Red Indians of North America and old Austrian peasants are equally averse to cutting down green trees, from the belief that they are animate, and feel wounds as acutely as a man himself. The Mundaris[160] in Assam have a sacred grove near every village, and the grove deities are held responsible for the crops ; at all great agricultural festivals they are especially honoured.

Philippine Islanders believe the souls of their fathers to dwell in certain trees, and cut them only on compulsion.

Among the Bechuanas the blackthorn is held sacred, and it is a very serious offence to cut a bough from it and carry it into the village during the rainy season ; but when the corn is ripe they go and cut a branch, which each man brings back.[161] The juniper is much venerated, according to De Gubernatis, in Italy and in Northern Germany,

---

[158] Upon this subject see Forlong, *Rivers of Life ;* Hargrave Jennings, *Phallicism ;* Phallic Series ; Payne Knight's *Worship of Priapus*, etc. etc.

[159] Frazer, *Golden Bough*, vol. i. p. 60 *et seq.* Much information is given and very many authorities are quoted.

[160] Dalton, *Ethnology of Bengal*, p. 188.

[161] J. Mackenzie, *Ten Years North of the Orange River*, p. 385.

as a protector against evil spirits. " Frau Wach-
holder," the juniper spirit, is invoked to discover
thieves by bending down certain of the branches.
There are many Italian stories and legends about
the juniper in connection with Our Lady, who was
hidden by one in her flight, and who blessed it in
consequence. In Italy branches of juniper are
hung up at Christmas just as the holly is in
England, France, and Switzerland. "In the sacred
cemetery at Meccah, the aloe, here as in Egypt, is
hung like the dried crocodile over houses as a talisman against evil spirits." [162]

Of all trees, the oak seems to be the sacred one
par excellence of the Aryan people in those latitudes
where it grows. It certainly ranked first among the
holy trees of the Germans, and was indeed their
chief god; distinct traces of its worship have survived almost to the present day. To the ancient
inhabitants of Italy the oak was sacred above all
other trees. The image of Jupiter Capitolinus at
Rome was nothing but a natural oak-tree, according
to Livy. The Greeks worshipped Zeus as residing
in the sacred oak at Dodona, and the rustling of its
leaves was his voice. The civic crown of the Romans
was of oak ; and a chaplet of oak was the reward of
eminent services rendered to the State. Acorns
having been the staple food of man till Demeter
introduced corn, boughs of oak were carried in
her mysteries at Eleusis. The Druids all consent-
ing pitched on the most beautiful oak-tree, cut off
its side branches, and then joined two of them to
the highest part of the trunk, so that they extended

[162] Sir R. F. Burton, *Pilgrimage to Meccah and Medinah*, ed. 1893,
ii. 248.

themselves on either side like the arms of a man ;
this was the Thau or God.[163]

Frazer[164] says the presumption is that in the
primitive fire festivals, the essential feature was
the burning of a man who represented the tree
spirit, and that the tree so represented was the
oak. These sacred fires were of oak kindled by
the "needfire," which was always produced by the
friction of two pieces of wood, and these pieces,
among Celts, Germans, and Slavs, were always of
oak.[165] In Scotland until quite modern times the
Beltein,[166] or Baal's fire as it is (wrongly) called, was
kept up in Ayr on St. Peter's Day, and in Perth on
May Day ; in Northumberland and Cumberland at
Midsummer, and in Ireland, known as La Bealtine,
on May Day. The first of May is called in Irish
La Beal-tine, "that is, the day of Beal's fire." Beal
and Phœnician Baal are said to be one and the
same deity—the sun.[167] Another writer[168] says :
"On St. John's Eve, the 23rd of June, still may be
seen a few bonfires on the mountains ; in the old
days they blazed on every hill and in every farm.
No field was fruitful into which a burning brand
had not been thrown, no horse or cow which had
not been touched by fire on that night." The date

[163] Borlase, *Hist. of Cornwall*, p. 108.

[164] *Golden Bough*, vol. ii. p. 291 *et seq.*

[165] In the Pitt Rivers Museum is a complete collection of apparatus such as
was used for the "needfire," and is still employed by some savage races.

[166] Brand, *Pop. Ant.* vol. i. pp. 226, 228, 318, 337. Elton, *Orig. Eng.
Hist.* p. 261. See also Kemble, *Saxons in England*, vol. i. p. 361.

[167] See *New Eng. Dict.* s.v. "Beltane." "The rubbish about *Baal,
Bel, Belus*, imported into the word from the O.T. and classical antiquity, is
outside the scope of scientific etymology." The word is pure Celtic ; in
Gaelic *bealltainn* is the name of the 1st of May. The word has nothing to
do with Baal, and is but one more instance of popular etymology. The very
fact that the name was applied to fires lighted at different seasons completely
destroys the Baal theory.

[168] Le Fanu, *Seventy Years of Irish Life*, 1894, p. 101.

here does not accord with other accounts, though the custom is abundantly recorded.

Here in Britain we all believe in the sacred groves of our Druid forefathers, whose worship is said to have always been under an oak. The Saxons held their meetings under an oak, and there are endless stories connected with that tree, all of which may be said to be kept alive by our still commemorating the 29th of May as "Oak Apple Day," with boughs of oak—a notable example of popular inaccuracy. The date of the Restoration being perpetuated by the memory of King Charles's escape on quite a different occasion. We are too apt to forget that besides King Charles's oak, all this tree-worship is in our very midst, and is kept up to this day. What is the old Christmas custom of wassailing the apple-trees, which the writer himself has often heard going on, but a worship, a pouring out of a libation to the tree spirit? [169]

In the typical representation of "plenty" known to all Freemasons, we have in the "ear of corn near a fall of water," not only a reminder of the ancient worship of the spirit of vegetation, symbolised by the corn, but also another example of association of ideas with facts—the dramatic representation of the desired result. The corn irrigated by the water from this point of view is a singularly appropriate symbol of abundance.

Our Scandinavian forefathers were less acquainted

---

[169] See *W. Somerset Word-Bk.* p. 820. Brand, *Pop. Ant.* vol. i. pp. 9-29. An account of the recent performance of this curious ceremony appeared in the *Devon and Somerset Weekly News*, Feb. 20, 1890, although Brand says the custom is discontinued. Raymond in *Sam and Sabina* (Pseudonym Library) gives a good account of wassailing apple-trees, and also of burning the ashen faggot.

with the oak.   With them the ash, Igdrasil, the tree
of life, was especially sacred.   We find the survival
of this amongst ourselves in the passing of a child
afflicted with congenital hernia through a growing
ash,[170] always an ash, with certain formulæ connected
with sunrise and Sunday, by which a new-born life
is typified.[171]   Several instances of this cure are
recorded in the *Gentleman's Magazine* for 1804, p.
909.   The writer of these says the rupture returns
whenever the tree is cut down.   Other beliefs are
still entertained respecting the ash in various parts of
England.   The following evidently relates to War-
wickshire: "Tom was in a state of as blank un-
imaginativeness concerning the cause and tendency
of his sufferings, as if he had been an innocent shrew-
mouse imprisoned in the split trunk of an ash-tree
in order to cure lameness in cattle."[172]

The old west country custom of burning an
ashen faggot on Christmas Eve points to the
sacredness of the ash.   From it, an old Norse
tradition says that man was first formed.   It is
believed that idols were made from it: "He planteth
an ash, and the rain doth nourish it. . . . And the
residue thereof he maketh a god, even his graven
image" (Isaiah xliv. 14-17).   Hence probably was
developed our Christmas custom, which is no less

---

[170] This tree was evidently highly prized by the ancients who had the oak
as well ; for Pliny (*Nat. Hist.* xvi. 24 ; Bohn, iii. 365) says that the leaves
of the ash yield an extract which is a specific for the bites of serpents ; that
no serpent will ever lie in the shadow of an ash, either morning or evening,
and that they keep the greatest possible distance from it.   He states positively
that if a serpent and a lighted fire are placed within a circle formed of the
leaves, it will rather throw itself into the fire than encounter the ash leaves.

[171] Referred to *ante*, p. 69.   Newspapers and magazines in plenty testify
to the prevalence of this well-known custom.   See *Gentleman's Mag.* June
1804 ; also *Cultus Arborum*, Phallic Series, privately printed 1890, p. 67.

[172] George Eliot, *Mill on the Floss*, p. 126.   See also Brand, iii. 290.

than the burning of Igdrasil, the tree of life, emblem-
atical of the death of vegetation at the winter sol-
stice.   It is supposed that misfortune will certainly
fall on the house where the burning is not kept up,
while, on the other hand, its due performance is believed to lead to many benefits.   The faggot must
be bound with three or more "binds" or withes,
and one or other of these is chosen by the young
people.   The bind which first bursts in the fire shows
that whoever chose it will be first to be married.
Hence at the breaking of each bind the cider cup
goes round to pledge the healths first of the lucky
ones and afterwards of "our noble selves," etc.[173]

The old idea of a spirit residing in trees is ex-
panded into one embracing all vegetation.   Hence
the corn spirit, which the Romans worshipped as the
goddess Ceres, was a cult which still exists unconsciously at our very doors.   The little plaited ears
of corn hung up in a farmhouse kitchen, which the
writer has seen within the past few days (December
1893), speak of the slaying of a divinity, such as the
Egyptian Osiris, and of the subsequent resurrection
of the life-giving corn.[174]

The remarkable similarity in customs all over
Europe points to the conclusion that tree-worship
was once an important element in the early religion
of mankind, especially of the Aryan stock, and that
the singular uniformity of the rites and ceremonies
which can easily be shown to exist in widely
separated countries, fully warrants us in believing
that they have not much changed from very remote

---

[173] Many curious beliefs as to the power of the ash-tree will be found in
Brand, vol. iii. p. 290 sq.
[174] "Crying the Neck," by F. T. Elworthy, *Trans. Devon Assoc.* 1891.

ages, and that the practices continued down to a very
recent period by peasantry, some even among ourselves, were substantially identical with the same
rites and ceremonies observed by Egyptians,
Etruscans, Greeks and Romans. [175]

In further reference to trees and plants it should
be noted, that there is a strange and very remarkable antipathy as well as sympathy amongst certain of
them, just as there is between certain animals.   The
laurel is said to be fatal to rosemary and the vine :
the cabbage will not grow under either vine or olive.
We all know that the fir will not grow with the elm ;
that hardly anything will grow under the beech.   On
the other hand, the vine and the poplar have a special
affinity ; so has the mushroom for the chestnut, and
rue for the fig.   Between the oak and the olive
there exists a hatred so inveterate, that trans-
planted, either of them, to a site previously occupied
by the other, they will die. [176]

The same attraction or repulsion is very evident
between certain animals and reptiles, and still more
is this the case as between some men and some
animals.   Man and beast alike have an inborn
repugnance to snakes; "dog-and-cat life" is a
common description of habitual domestic squabbling.
Some persons cannot endure cats, and the very
presence of a cat, even if not seen, throws them into
convulsions.   Bats, too, have the like effect upon
certain people.   An Italian physician, Antonio

[175] " Tree-worship may be traced from the interior of Africa not only into
Egypt and Arabia, but also onward uninterruptedly into Palestine and Syria,
Assyria, Persia, India, Thibet, Siam, the Philippine Islands, China, Japan
and Siberia, also westward into Asia Minor, Greece, Italy, and other
countries."—*Gen. of Earth and Man*, p. 139, in Smith's *Dict. of the Bible*.
[176] Pliny, *Nat. Hist.* xxiv. i. (Bohn).   The whole chapter is upon the
antipathies and sympathies which exist among trees and plants.

Vallisneri, relates a curious instance of this kind. He shut up a bat in a box which he placed in the room of his patient, who on entering, though utterly ignorant of the presence of the bat, was immediately seized with convulsions, which continued until the bat was removed. Those of us who have visited tombs and ruins where many bats live, can more readily accept this story, from the peculiar and pungent odour they emit.

Antipathy and sympathy among men and women have existed from the beginning, and create a feeling we cannot call mere prejudice, viewed from either side of the attraction we now call fascination.

> Non amo te, Sabidi, nec possum dicere quare;
> Hoc tantum possum dicere—non amo te ! [177]

is but the old-world form of our modern

> I do not love you, Dr. Fell !
> The reason why, I cannot tell ;
> But this alone I know full well,
> I do not love you, Dr. Fell.

Many authors from Plato and Aristotle down to Descartes and William Hazlitt have written upon this subject, which may be said to fall within the scope of fascination, although here we have only space to hint at it.

On reflecting upon all the strange cults and practices in connection with the annual death and resurrection of the spirit of vegetation we are struck by the apparent repetition of the same old idea of the slaying and the resurrection of a god, figured in the ancient Egyptian myth of Osiris preserved on the wall at Philæ; in the very remarkable cult of Diana Nemorensis, wherein her priest was slain

[177] Martial, *Epigr.* i. 33.

by his successor after he had plucked the golden
bough ; and in our own familiar custom of "crying
the neck," already referred to.

Mr. Frazer has worked out at considerable length
and with striking force, the belief which seems to lie
deep down in the heart of man, inherited from his
very earliest ancestors, that not only was a human
victim a fitting, but a necessary object for sacrifice,
whether to atone for past offences or to propitiate
for future favours.　The faith of Abraham was tested
in a way evidently familiar, and not apparently
shocking or unreasonable according to the customs
of his day.　The killing of a substitute for a god,[178]
may be observed in many of the human sacrificial
rites performed by savage or semi-savage people.
The view that the victim is also an embodiment of
the spirit of the deity to be slain, is shown by the
great pains taken "to secure a physical correspondence between him and the natural object," whose
spirit or embodiment he is made to represent.
Thus the Mexicans killed young victims for the
young corn, and old ones for the ripe.　The full
identification of the victim with the corn spirit or
deity is shown by the African custom of putting
him to death with spades and hoes, and by the
Mexican, of grinding him like corn between two
stones.

Stranger still, the same author shows plainly and
at great length the custom of sacramental eating the
representative body of the slain god to be prevalent
as the survival of a cult long anterior to Christianity.

Not only did the Pawnee chief devour the heart
of the Sioux girl, slain as a sacrificial offering, but

[178] Frazer, *Golden Bough*, vol. i. p. 391 ; vol. ii. p. 67 *et seq.*

other savages ate the victim's flesh not as cannibals,
but as a sacred rite. Even in pious Sweden the
flour from the grain of the last sheaf, supposed
to contain the corn spirit, is baked into a loaf
in the shape of a girl, which is divided amongst
the whole household and eaten by them. In Scotland, too, the last sheaf is made up into a female
form and is called "the Maiden," but we are told
nothing as to its being eaten in any special way—
it is rather kept; but everywhere the eating of a
loaf made from the last sheaf is certainly thought to
be eating the god of the corn. At La Palisse, in
France, moreover, the dough man, made of the last
of the corn, cut at the end of harvest, is actually
broken in pieces by the mayor and given to the
people to eat.

The custom of eating bread sacramentally as the
body of a god was practised by the Aztecs before the
discovery and conquest of Mexico by the Spaniards.
A long account of the ceremonies used is given by
Acosta (Hakluyt Society); and another writer (Ban-
croft) gives further details of this rite, especially how
a priest took a flint-tipped dart, and hurled it into
the breast of the dough image, piercing it through
and through. This was called "killing the god
Huitzilopochtli, so that his body might be eaten."
The image was divided into minute pieces, one of
which every male, even down to the babe in the
cradle, received to eat, but no woman might taste a
morsel. The ceremony was called *torqualo*, that is
"God is eaten." Mr. Frazer also produces evidence
of sacramental eating of bread as practised by ancient
Romans at Aricia, near Albano, and traces the
custom of eating animals and men by various races,

in the belief that the eater acquires the physical, moral, and intellectual qualities of the animal or man so eaten.

There can be no doubt of the totem origin of the ritual of sacrificial offerings, especially that of eating the slain god. "The victim is not only slain, but the worshippers partake of the body and blood of the victim, so that his life passes into their life, and knits them to the deity in living communion." [179]

The same belief comes to us from Australia, where the cannibal aborigines consider that "the most delicate morsel of all is the fat about the kidneys. By eating this they believe that they acquire part of the slain person's strength, and so far as I could understand, this was even more true of the kidneys themselves. For according to a widespread Australian belief, the kidneys are the centre of life." [180] The natives on Herbert River are particularly fond of the fat of a dead foe, which is not only eaten as a delicacy and as strengthening food, but is also carried as an amulet.

In the north-east of Burmah are mountain tribes who eat the congealed blood of their enemies. "The blood is poured into bamboo reeds, corked up, and in course of time hardens. When the chief wants to treat his friends to this kind of food, the reed is broken and the contents devoured with the greatest relish." The natives believe that they "will thereby acquire the courage and strength of their enemies." [181]

In further support of this idea, an authentic story comes from India,[181a] where it is very firmly believed

---

[179] Prof. W. Robertson Smith, *Ency. Brit.* s.v. "Sacrifice," p. 138.
[180] Carl Lumholtz, *Among Cannibals*, 1889, p. 272.   [181] *Ibid.* p. 274.
[181a] Letter from Mr. Samuel Peal, resident in Assam.

that the flesh eaten imparts to the eater the fierceness
or other qualities of the animal so consumed.

Mr. Evans, a Wesleyan missionary, who has been
living in the Kassia hills, but who has evidently no
knowledge of native religions, relates that the people
there are primitive and old-world in their beliefs,
although it appears that he has a considerable flock
who have adopted Christianity. Not long since, a
certain Captain Crawley, who was on a visit, heard
that a goat had been killed by a tiger close to the
village. After the usual preparations he shot the
tiger, whereupon the natives asked to have the
flesh given to them; this was agreed to on condition
that he should have the skin and head. The people
(we presume the men) then took the carcase and
made a hearty meal off it. On the following day,
being Sunday, they attended Mr. Evans's chapel,
and he was at once aware of the overpowering
odour from the people's breath—so much so that
he was obliged to adjourn to the open air, but even
there he had to conduct his service with much dis-
comfort.

Among Mr. Evans's congregation was a milkman,
to whom of course the cows were quite accustomed.
On that Sunday morning however, on going to milk
his cows, they became instantly frantic, and the usually
docile creatures burst from their fastenings and rushed
away. They would not permit their own attendant
to come near them, and had to be milked by another
man who did not smell of tiger. It does not appear
that these people liked tiger meat, but it seems
to have been eaten under the impression that it
would make them strong and fierce, by the absorp-
tion into their bodies of the tiger qualities through

eating his flesh ; and looking at the fact that Hindoos hold the tiger in awe as the embodiment of a deity, they were performing a sort of sacramental rite, which their adoption of Christianity by no means tended to modify or to influence.

There is nothing uncommon in the notion that the flesh of oxen gives strength and courage, while that of sheep does not.   This is said to be the reason why our soldiers and sailors are fed on beef and seldom taste mutton.

We are thus brought to see that some of the most sacred and mysterious rites of our religious faith have had their beginning in the beliefs and customs of those we now call pagans, and that these crude though firm ideas, planted in the heart of primæval man, have but been purified, purged from their gross accretions, and adapted to our still imperfect intelligence, as suitable to the limited vision of our humanity.   So far from investigations of this nature tending to injure or to lower our convictions of the truth, or the reality of Revelation, the veil seems to be somewhat lifted, to enable us to see how consistent and prearranged is the divine plan to meet the usages and forms of thought implanted in the human breast.   The various types, allegories, and parables, whereby we are instructed in Holy Scripture, are but adaptations of that innate association of ideas with facts, which seems to have been one of the very earliest creations of man's reasoning faculties.

CHAPTER IV

SYMBOLS AND AMULETS

IF so many strange beliefs still exist in these days of science and enlightenment, it is easy to see how in olden times a fanciful people, full of imagination, who personified not only every aspect of nature, but every virtue and every vice, got to look upon the trees or animals they thought sacred, as symbols of the deity to whom they were sacred. Perhaps of all nations we English are the most materialistic and matter of fact, yet in what endless ways do we even now make use of symbols, to denote not only objects, but events and abstract ideas! Every letter that we write or print is said to be the survival of some primitive picture, and thus to be the symbol of a separate idea. In Christian art symbolism occupies as large a place, as in the pagan mythology of old. A figure holding a key with sometimes a cock in the background is at once known as St. Peter; a man in a boat typifies Noah; a figure with a loaf and a basket signifies the feeding of the multitude; the fish is a symbol of our Lord, said to be a Greek acrostic as well as a sign; the dove represents the Holy Spirit; the cross is a symbol not only of a great event, but of a great doctrinal fact; while the hand, or *Dextera Dei*, of which we have much to say, represents power, and thereby the person of the Almighty Father.

Even latter-day Puritans, "who are eager to banish the cross and the crucifix, with everything that has to them even a faint association with the terrible word idolatry,[182] accept that most symbolic of romances, *The Pilgrim's Progress*, as a true exemplar of their special views," and thus provide the best possible evidence that no religious feeling worthy of the name will consent to live without some imaginative expression for those urgent and intimately varied spiritual yearnings, for which there is no definite and rigidly accurate language.

This love of symbol and the eagerness for its artistic use are said to be rapidly reviving[183]—a fact which does but prove how history repeats itself, and that the primitive notions of mankind are constantly reasserting themselves; that we are but now re-adopting the methods which have prevailed intermittently throughout all human time.

In this way we get a clue to the primitive use of emblems and symbols by way of protection, against evils that people believed might be averted, through the intervention of the powers or divinities to whom they specially appealed; hence the reverence for, the half-worship of, the symbols representing those powers to their own minds. Moreover the uncultured mind does not readily discriminate between the symbol itself and the person, object, or fact which it is intended to represent.

In view of the looseness with which words of

[182] *La Migration des Symboles*, Comte Goblet d'Alviella, Hibbert Lectures, 1890-91 : Husenbeth, "Emblems of the Saints in Art," *Spectator*, June 29, 1889.
[183] Chapman, *Sermons on Symbols*, 1888.

different significance are often used to represent the
same ideas, and, on the other hand, the same word
used to imply different meanings, it is well here
to define what we mean by emblem and symbol.
Curiously both words were originally derived from
concrete objects, very far removed from the ideas
they ultimately came to signify. *Symbol* properly
means the separate contribution of each person towards the cost of a Greek drinking party. To
ensure due payment it was customary for each
person to pledge his signet ring to the caterer, to be
redeemed on his paying his share of the bill. This
custom was also adopted by the Romans, and by
the time of Plautus the ring itself had got to be
called *symbolum*. The signet ring having thus
become the most easily available, as well as trust-
worthy of credentials, *symbolum* developed quickly
into signifying the credential itself. From this, by
a further development, in ecclesiastical language, as
in the *Symbolum Apostolicum*, it expressed a definite
creed, and at last has become a term for the conveyance of any idea, but more particularly of such as
appertains to religious belief. We may now define a
symbol as a means of conveying ideas and facts to
the mind, through representations more or less
pictorial. By constant repetition these pictures become in a way so conventionalised and stereotyped,
that the mere portrayal, or even the mere mention,
of a certain object conveys a distinct and well-defined
train of thought to the mind.

An *emblem* was an inlaid or raised ornament on
a vessel, but inasmuch as the subjects of the designs
were always figures of persons, generally mytho-
logical, so the word *emblem* came to imply repre-

sentation, more or less allegorical, of some person
or attribute personified ; and in the end, by the
same process of repetition, the emblem became conventionalised like the symbol, so that certain representations always conveyed to the beholder the idea
of a certain fact or event, or of some being, or
personification ; with this difference, that the *emblem*
expressed more fully and distinctly, while the *symbol*
only hinted at the idea conveyed.[184]   To make what
we mean more clear, the crucifix is an emblem, a
dramatic representation of a great event, carrying
with it all its history and consequences, while the
simple cross is a symbol no less expressive, but yet
conveying by a mere hint all the history, all the
doctrine, all the significance, of the more elaborate
representation.

Justice, again, as an *emblem* is represented as a
blindfolded female figure, holding the sword of
punishment in one hand, with the balance of judgment in the other.   As a *symbol* of justice, either the
sword, or the *balance* alone, conveys the idea, though
in a more abstract form.   Victory, too, has for her
emblem a winged female figure holding a wreath or
a palm branch, while the *symbol* of victory is the
wreath or the palm alone.

It will be readily understood how a *symbol* may
be easily developed from an actual pictorial *emblem*,
into a mere description, either spoken or by gesture
acted, so as to convey the same idea.   Thus when
the hand is raised in the act of benediction, the three

---

[184] "*Emblema* licet cum isto ænigmatum génere in ratione symboli conveniat,
differt tamen, quod rem sublatis ænigmatum velis purius liquidiusque pro-
ponat.   Est enim proprie symbolum aliquod ingeniosum, suave, et moratum,
ex pictura et lemmate constans, quo aliqua gravior sententia indicari solet."—
De symbolica Ægyptorum sapientia.   Nicolaus Caussinus.   Coloniæ, 1623,
p. 17.

extended fingers are the well-known symbol of the
Holy Trinity; so when we speak of bearing the
cross, wearing the wreath or the palm, we symbolise and convey our meaning just as clearly as
though those symbols were actually painted or
carved.

Precisely as a miniature in a locket brings back
to the wearer the individuality of the person portrayed, so does the symbolic representation of the
deity, whose aid is sought, bring back to the mind of
the beholder the whole conception of the attributes
and power of the being so represented. An ancient
Roman believed that Juno would protect him against
certain dangers; forthwith he paints or carves a peacock, her own bird, and is thus reminded of her.
In theory he prays to her as often as he looks upon
her symbol, while he honours or worships her by
wearing it.[185]

The practice, if not the belief, still survives
amongst us.

Some eight or ten years ago a gentleman well known to me
went to call on an intimate friend of his. Unfortunately for him,
he had the eye of a peacock's feather in his hat. When the
lady of the house saw it, she snatched it from him and threw it
out of the hall-door, rating him as if he had been guilty of some
great moral offence.

Some years ago, in North Yorkshire, an old servant came to
the house where I was, and found some peacocks' feathers above
the mantelpiece in one of the bedrooms. She expressed her
horror to the young ladies of the house, and said that they
need never expect to be married if they kept such things for
ornaments.[186]

---

[185] " On the main gateway of the Old City (Citta Vecchia) at Malta is a statue
of Juno, ancient protectress of Malta, bearing her cognisance of a peacock."—
Col. R. L. Playfair, *Murray's Handbook to the Mediterranean*, 1882,
p. 199.
[186] *Notes and Queries*, 8th ser. iv. p. 531 (December 30, 1893).

In Shropshire also it is believed to be very unlucky to bring peacocks' feathers into the house.[187]

No doubt the belief that to keep peacocks' feathers is unlucky, comes from the ancient cult of Juno—her anger being in some way excited by the plucking of the feathers of her favourite bird ; while the idea that so long as they are kept in the house no suitors will come for the daughters, points to the old attribute of spite and jealousy in love or matrimonial matters, with which that goddess was always accredited.[188]

From keeping and using such objects or signs, as reminders of the worship due to the beings symbolised, the history of the word *symbol* shows that it is but a very short step to the belief in the efficacy of the symbol itself, and hence we are led to the universal use of what have been of old called amulets.

These are described [189] as "anything worn about the person as a charm or preventive against evil, mischief, disease, witchcraft," etc. In Smith's *Dictionary of Antiquities* we find it said that the word signified something suspended, and that it was used for objects such as a stone, plant, artificial production, or piece of writing, which was suspended from the neck, or tied to any part of the body—seemingly ignoring the many other uses of amulets both ancient and modern. Even in Pliny's time amulets were not merely worn, but were used as ornaments or objects having special purposes, fixed or otherwise, as they are to this day, about the houses, carriages, and fields of widely diverse races. The word *amulet* is nowadays very

---

[187] Mrs. Gaskell in *Nineteenth Century*, February 1894, p. 264.
[188] See *Notes and Queries*, November 25, 1893, p. 426.
[189] *New English Dictionary*, s.v. "Amulet."

commonly used as synonymous with talisman,
whereas in meaning it is entirely distinct. The
latter means a "sigil engraved in stone or metal,"[190]
and it served a double purpose, namely, "to procure
love, and to avert mischief from its possessor," while
an *amuletum*, derived from *amolior* to do away with,
or to baffle,[190a] had for its sole end the protection of the
owner. Pliny, writing on the cyclamen (*tuberterræ*)[191]
says, it "ought to be grown in every house, if it be
true that wherever it grows noxious spells can have
no effect. This plant is also what is called an *amulet*."
Boccaccio speaks of "the skull of an ass set up on a
pole in a cornfield as a potent amulet against blight."
As a modern parallel to this we are told that at
Mourzak, in Central Africa, the people set up the
head of an ass in their gardens to avert the evil eye
from their crops.[192]

FIG. 7.—King's *Handbook of Gems.*

Pisistratus too is re-
corded by Hesychius
to have set up, in the
Acropolis at Athens,
the figure of a grass-
hopper (cricket) or
grillo, as a charm or
amulet to avert the
evil eye from the citi-
zens.[193] This insect is
constantly found engraved on gems (Fig. 7) with a

---

[190] See *The Gnostics*, by C. W. King, 1874, p. 115. Also Frommannd,
Tract. de Fasc. p. 278, who makes a long disquisition on this subject, giving
the etymology and origin of *talisman* as Arabic.
[190a] King, *op. cit.* p. 115. According to *N. E. Dictionary*, "a word of
unknown origin." [191] *Natural History*, xxv. 67 (Bohn, v. p. 125).
[192] *Notes and Queries*, 1st ser. vii. p. 496.
[193] On this see Lobeck, *Aglaophamus*, p. 973. He quotes Pliny, xxix. (6)
39, but I cannot find this in Pliny. Lobeck says Hesychius calls this amulet
κερτομια προσβασκάνια.

similar intention.[194]   The grillo or locust is said [195] to
have been adopted as an amulet from its likeness to
a skeleton, which is still the emblem of Chronos or
Saturn, and a powerful charm against the evil eye.

The Maltese, who are full of beliefs about the
evil eye, have set an amulet upon
the base of a statue in front of the
Church of Crendi near Valetta,
which the writer sketched on the
spot (Fig. 8)—a crescent with a
serpent coiled about it.   When we
come to speak of the Cimaruta and
the specific charms used in Italy,
we shall see clearly that this relief can only
be intended as an amulet.   Abundant evidence will
be produced later on to show that amulets were used
also as household ornaments, much as we now use
vases and other nicknacks upon our chimney-pieces
and tables.   It is very probable that the teraphim,
translated *images* in our Authorised Version,[196] which
Rachel stole from Laban, were really amulets of the
kind not to be worn, but used as protecting objects;
these, like the Lares and Penates of subsequent times,
were looked upon almost as objects of worship,
though not as actual gods.   Indeed we can have no
reason to believe Laban idolatrous, or that Rachel
carried them off with the intention of worshipping
them.   Still it is evident they were highly prized.[197]

FIG. 8.

[194] King, *Gnostics*, p. 116.   [195] *Ibid.* p. 212.
[196] Genesis xxxi. 19.   See Frommannd, *Tract. de Fasc.* p. 715, who says
Luther called these *Silberne Götzen*.   These are called *teraphim* in the R.V.
[197] Professor Huxley says (*Science and Hebrew Tradition*, 1893, p. 309):
"The teraphim were certainly images of family gods, and as such in all prob-
ability represented deceased ancestors," and further that Jacob was not "scan-
dalised by the idolatrous practices of his favourite wife . . . for the teraphim
seem to have remained in his camp."   Other authorities say (Reginald
Stuart Poole in Smith's *Dict.* s.v. "Teraphim, Magic."   Also W. Aldis

We are told [198] that "the ear-rings" mentioned
in Gen. xxxv. 4 and Hosea ii. 13 were really
amulets, and were connected with idolatrous worship. Amulets, however, were mostly worn round
the neck, or rather suspended from a necklace and
forming its centrepiece. We find this custom
coming down to us here in England, through the
classic and Middle Ages to our own times, though
just now out of fashion, in the various lockets containing hair, etc., with other articles of a like kind
forming the central ornament of necklaces. In some

Wright, s.v. "Nehushtan") "there is no evidence that they were ever worshipped." There seems to be a consensus of opinion that the teraphim, whatever they were, had much to do with magic. It is here suggested that many
of the numberless little bronze statuettes, to be seen in various museums, probably represent the Teraphim of the Hebrews and the Lares of Rome, and
are not mere ornaments. Fig. 105 is surely one of these, and its original
cannot be later than the time of Jacob. The terra-cotta figures too, beginning
with the crude forms found at Mycenæ, and developing into the beautiful
artistic statuettes of later Greece, must have been of the same character ; for
we cannot suppose that as mere ornaments they would have been so carefully
deposited along with the dead. · Nor does there appear to be any evidence
that the Greeks or Romans ever imbibed the Egyptian notion of placing
figures of this kind with the dead, as *ushebtiu*, to attend on the departed in
the next world.

It seems rather an assumption than a certainty that teraphim were images
only of persons. It is suggested that among such may be included several
other objects, looked upon as prophylactic, or otherwise sacred. The bronze
hands, dealt with in the chapter on the Mano Pantea, would distinctly come
into this category. Further we find proof of this in the point noticed by
Huxley (p. 310), that it was not until the time of Hezekiah that the brazen
serpent of Moses was destroyed. During the thousand years of its existence
it had been preserved, and at length from a protective teraphim had become
Nehushtan. All this seems to show that the brazen serpent, and all such
objects as we now call amulets, like the grillo of Athens, the crocodiles of
Seville and Venice, were not originally worshipped idolatrously, but were looked
upon as magically endowed with the power of countervailing the effect of the
malignant eye—the fertile source, as it was thought, of every evil to mankind.

It has been well suggested (Farrar in Kitto's *Cyclopædia of Biblical Literature*, s.v. "Teraphim") that the teraphim, and to them we would add protective
symbols in general, were looked upon much in the same way that pictures and
images are now looked upon by Roman Catholics, who indignantly repudiate
the notion of idolatry. No doubt the denunciations of the prophets point to
the same line of teaching as that of modern Protestants, who can perceive no
difference between the reverence paid to the image itself, and that which all
would admit to be due to the person depicted.

[198] Smith's *Dictionary of the Bible*, s.v. "Amulets."

countries these things are still worn, not as mere
ornaments, but avowedly as protective amulets
against dread fascination. By no means were all
hung round the neck, for the phylacteries which
were worn as the "frontlets between thine eyes"
(Exodus xiii. 16) were true amulets. One kind of
phylactery was bound upon the bend of the left arm,
and the other on the forehead. They were little
leather boxes containing strips of parchment on
which were written the four following passages of
Scripture, called the Tetragrammaton, namely, Exod.
xiii. 2-10 and 11-16; Deut. vi. 4-9 and xi. 13-21.
They were certainly worn by all Jews over thirteen
years of age in the time of our Lord.[199]

Slips from the Koran, the Scriptures, or other
writings, are now worn on the person, or upon horses
and camels, by Arabs, Turks, Abyssinians,[200] Greeks,
Italians, and even English. They are all avowedly
worn for the purpose of averting the evil eye;
and seeing that the dread of it was perhaps even
greater in old days than now, it seems but reasonable to assume that the direct object of the biblical
phylactery was then, as it is to-day, to baffle the
malignant glance.

It is curious that Turks, and, indeed, all Mahomedans, once used animals and figures of men,
representing various deities, as amulets against
fascination, but since their conversion from
heathenism they have discarded most of these,
and now wear sentences from the Koran, avowedly
to guard them against the evil eye. Little silver
cases to contain them, such as are shown on Fig. 112,

---

[199] Upon this, see Farrar in Smith's *Bib. Dict.* s.v. "Frontlets."
[200] See the remarkable Ethiopic charm in Chap. XI.

p. 259, are regular articles of sale in all Eastern bazaars. At Constantinople they may be bought by the dozen.

It was said by Plutarch[201] that when Isis brought into the world Harpocrates, the posthumous son of Osiris, she wore an amulet round her neck, in the shape of a *vase*, the "emblem of Ma," the goddess of truth. The vase was also a symbol of Osiris.[201a] This vase represented water; hence the vivifying power of nature, *i.e.* Osiris the personification of the Nile,[202] which was thus typified by a vase.

Among the ancient Egyptians not only were protecting amulets worn by the living, but in that land where the belief in a future life seemed to absorb so much of the care and interest of the present, they placed them in profusion on their dead, in order that they might be protected from evil spirits and the blighting eye, during the dark passage from this world to the next.

Maspero[203] says these amulets (speaking of scarabs)

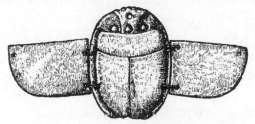

FIG. 9.—From Author's Collection.

were "symboles de durée présente ou future," placed, *ailes déployées*, upon the breast of the dead along with a written prayer (Fig. 9), that the heart (of the

[201] Wilkinson, *Ancient Egyptians*, iii. 130.   [201a] *Ib.* iii. 80.
[202] Plutarch, *De Iside*, s. 32; Wilkinson, iii. 74.
[203] *Archéologie Egyptienne*, p. 236. See also Wilkinson, vol. iii. p. 486.

person) whose form the beetle was made to represent, would never bear witness against the dead
in the day of judgment. The commonest of all
Egyptian amulets, except the scarab, was that
known to English people as the Eye of Osiris :
" L'œil mystique (Fig. 10), l'ouza lié au poignet ou
au bras par une cordelette, pro-
tégeait contre le mauvais œil,
contre les paroles d'envie ou de
colère, contre la morsure des serpents." These scarabs and mystic
eyes were worn equally by the living
and the dead "as amulets against
evil magic." [204] Moreover the mystic eye appears
everywhere painted on walls. One such, of especial
size and prominence, is to be found over the door of
one of the upper chambers in the temple of Denderah, and it is seen constantly as one of the hieroglyphics translated *ut'a*. [205]

FIG. 10.

We find the eye also used for two other signs in
Egyptian writing. It was said to be that of Shu or
Horus as the god of stability, and was carried in
funeral processions along with the sacred boat. [206]
Wilkinson says it " was placed over the incision in
the side of the body when embalmed, was the
emblem of Egypt, and was frequently used as a sort
of amulet and deposited in the tombs." [207]

[204] Brugsch, *Egypt under the Pharaohs*, vol. i. p. 468. Wilkinson, vol. ii.
p. 334, gives a number of necklaces, in nearly all of which the mystic eye
appears, while in some it is the only element, and in others is alternated
with other charms.

[205] *The Nile*, E. Wallis Budge, p. 61.

[206] One of these processions showing the eye is given as Plate lxvi. in
Wilkinson, vol. iii. p. 444.

[207] In the British Museum is a case full of these mystic eyes of all sizes.
There are also necklaces composed entirely of them. Three of these in blue
enamel are shown on Fig. 81, p. 203.

It was natural from the association of idea with fact, or "sympathetic magic," that representations of the eye itself should among all people have been considered potent amulets against its malign influence. The Phœnicians certainly used it as an amulet. In the Museum at Carthage, among the objects found in the ancient tombs, there are numerous examples of the head of an animal in blue pottery, having a very large eye at the side of the head (Fig. 11). These were all provided with eyelets for suspension.

FIG. 11.

Precisely the same thing was, in 1889, to be seen in the Ashmolean Museum, from Beirut, showing it to have been a common object among the Phœnicians. Similar amulets are to be seen in the museums of the Louvre and at Athens. The Etruscans also had an amulet of this kind. The head itself is said[208] to be that of a panther, and from the number of specimens of this identical amulet which the writer has seen in various museums, brought from widely separated countries, yet all in the track of the Phœnicians, we may take it as established, that this form of the eye amulet was most in use among that ancient people.

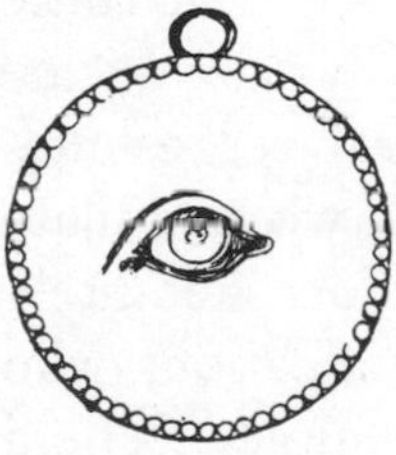

In the Louvre among the gems is a medal-shaped amulet (Fig. 12), with an eye alone in the centre; and Jahn gives several other examples of the single eye used as an amulet, especially in two necklaces drawn on Taf. V. of his article. In one, the eye is

FIG. 12.

[208] See Dennis, *Cities of Etruria*, vol. i. p. 471.

the pendant to a necklace formed of *conchæ veneris;*
this latter (Fig. 13) a potent charm in itself against

FIG. 13.

fascination among the Greeks of
old, and among the Turks, Arabs,
and Nubians of to-day. Jahn
considers the head of which
this eye is the most obvious
feature to be that of a fowl (or
cock).[209]

As we proceed with the consideration of the various charms
and amulets used by ancients and
moderns alike, we shall find that not only were
single objects, such as the eye, the hand, and many
others to which we shall refer later, used as such,
but that there was a combination, a sort of piling up
of emblems and symbols, so that we constantly find
objects of a highly composite character differing very
essentially in their several component parts, but yet
on the whole presenting a sort of similarity; while
it is perfectly obvious that the design or purpose of
these compound amulets was in all cases the same.

We shall endeavour to discover as we go on
what was the special import of each item of these
many compounds, and as far as possible to decide
what deity was typified by the several representations made use of—for at the outset we postulate
that every one of the symbols used, does definitely
represent some deity or other personification, who
was believed by the possessor of the amulet to be a
protector against maleficent influence. The com-

---

[209] It is suggested that the head here produced may be that of the Gnostic
god Abraxas, who is very frequently represented with the head of a cock.
See the many engraved gems showing this in *Abraxas seu Apistopistus*
Johannis Macarii. Antwerpiæ, 1657. Also in King's *Gnostics.*

bination of symbols we find to be as various both in number and description, whether we take ancient or modern dates, as is now the cult of the various saints in the calendar ; so that when we find an amulet of unusually complex character, bearing a great number of symbolic figures, we may take it to be the prototype and the equivalent of the latter-day summing up of " All Saints" or "all the company of heaven." A singular comment upon this accumulation of protectors is seen in an inscription of the first year of our Christian era, A.U.C. 754, found quite recently in the Tiber near the Church of Sta. Lucia della Tinta.

Under the consulship of Caius Cæsar and Lucius Paulus, a freedman named Lucius Lucretius Zethus was warned in a vision by Jupiter, to raise an altar in honour of Augustus, under the invocation of "Mercurius Deus Æternus." Following these directions, Lucretius Zethus had the altar made, and unwilling apparently to hurt the feelings of the gods in general, dedicated it not only to Mercury Augustus, but at the same time to Jupiter, Juno, Minerva, the sun, the moon, Apollo, Diana, Fortune, Ops, Isis, Piety and the Fates. From an epigraphic point of view, this monument ranks among the very best discovered in the works of the Tiber.[210]

A great number of ancient compound amulets in the shape of marble reliefs, medals and engraved gems, have been found, in which an eye is the central object, while grouped around it are various animals or other emblems of protecting divinities.

Jahn in his well-known paper gives no less than six different medals and gems, which have for each the eye as a centre, surrounded by a greater or less numerous grouping of symbolic figures, and all are undoubted amulets of ancient date against the evil eye.

No. 2 in Jahn is taken from Caylus rec. vi. 38,

---

[210] Rodolfo Lanciani, *Athenæum*, No. 3313, April 25, 1891, p. 543.

3 (Fig. 14), and is a struck medal having in the
centre the eye, surrounded by a crocodile, swan,
serpent, cock, dog, lion, winged phallus, scorpion,
and thunderbolt.

No. 3 (Fig. 15) is from Arneth, *Gold- und
Silbermon*, S. iv. 96 G.—a medal with eyelet for

FIG. 14.   FIG. 15.   FIG. 16.

suspension.   It has the eye in centre, with crocodile
or lizard, thunderbolt, elephant, scorpion, phallus (as
seen at Pompeii), lion, dog, swan, around it.

No. 4 is from Caylus rec. v. 57, 1, 2 (Fig. 16),
also a medal with eye in centre, surrounded by
thunderbolt, lizard, phallus, scorpion, star, elephant,
swan, fish, serpent.   The medals are
all of silver.

No. 5 (Fig. 17) is an engraved
gem, from the Florence Museum.
It has the central eye, with lizard,
scorpion, frog, bee, serpent, crab,
bee again, and tortoise, surrounding.

No. 6 (Fig. 17) also a gem from
Antike Paste in Berlin, described by

FIG. 17.

Winkelmann, p. 554.   It has the eye in the centre
with tortoise, lizard, scorpion, frog, bee, serpent,
crab, and another bee, surrounding.[211]

---

[211] Nos. 5 and 6 have precisely the same objects upon them, though differing
in size.   Therefore one illustration here applies to both.

No. 7 (Fig. 18) is an engraved onyx[212] from Gerhard's collection, with central eye, but with Jupiter's or Serapis's head, eagle, thunderbolt, and dolphin, surrounding. On this last, Jahn remarks that it is evidently a symbol of the highest protecting divinity.[213]

FIG. 18.

Still more remarkable than any of the foregoing amulets given by Jahn is that of an engraved sard from the Praun gems, of which an illustration is given by King, *Gnostics*, p. 115, and also *Handbook*

FIG. 19.—From King's *Gnostics*.

of Engraved Gems, p. 81, where the central eye is surrounded by an owl, serpent, stag, scorpion, dog, lion and thunderbolt (Fig. 19).

212. This gem is a *cameo*, upon which it may be remarked, that this word is said to be Persian. "*Camahem* is a loadstone or fibrous hæmatite, the usual material for Babylonish cylinders, and in use there down to the time of the Cufic signets. The Arabs knowing no other motive for engraving of stones than their conversion into talismans (amulets), gave the name of the one most frequently used to the whole class; and the Crusaders introduced it into all European languages in this sense. Matthew Paris has *lapides quos cameos vulgariter appellamus*, which marks its foreign origin " (King, *Gnostics*, p. 112). Mr. King does not give his authority. Dr. Murray (*N.E.D.*) says, "Of the derivation nothing is yet known." I do not find the above among the "guesses" alluded to by Dr. Murray.

213 The value of medals whether to be worn as amulets, or used as talismans to procure objects desired, or to cure diseases, is by no means a notion con-

On this blood-red gem King remarks (*Gnostics*, p. 238) that it shows "the evil eye surrounded by antidotes against its influence for every day in the week, in the attribute of the deity presiding over each, namely, the lion for *dies Solis*, the stag for *dies Lunæ* (*Diana venatrix*), the scorpion for *dies Martis*, the dog for *dies Mercurii*, etc." To these we must add the thunderbolt for *dies Jovis*. The owl, however, was sacred to Athene or Minerva, and must have been substituted as the symbol of *dies Veneris*, for Venus does not seem to have been regarded as a protectress against fascination, unless we look upon her as identical with Isis, Ishtar, and Diana ; whereas Minerva, the bearer of the Gorgon's head, was always one of the most potent protecting deities. The serpent, too, was the symbol of Hecate,[214] one of the attributes, as we shall see later, of Diana Triformis, and was considered one of the most powerful of all the antidotes. Scarcely any compound amulet occurs without the serpent, and hence we must suppose in the case we are considering that it was adopted as the symbol applicable to *dies Saturni*.[214a]

In considering this gem, we must not forget its Gnostic character, and that its origin was Græco-Egyptian, though the work of a European hand.

fined to the ancients. In Ireland "some five-and-forty years ago a temperance medal was found to be a specific for every ailment ; not all medals, however, but only those which had been blessed and given by Father Mathew. Rubbing with one of these at once relieved rheumatic pains. I have seen ophthalmia treated by hanging two of these medals over a girl's eyes " (Le Fanu, *Seventy Years of Irish Life*, 1894, p. 114).

[214] Jahn, *Aberglauben*, etc., p. 98, says that " the dog as the beast of Hecate has to do with all magic " (*Zauberwesen*). In later times it was thought that by dogs' blood all evil witchery could be kept off.

[214a] Since this was written the Python at the Zoo has (Oct. 1894) swallowed his mate (or his child ?), thus proving the serpent to be a singularly practical symbol of Saturn.

Hence every symbol must be interpreted as Egyptian from a Greek point of view. Now as we know, and as Pliny[215] long ago related that there are no stags in Africa, it is clear that the designer of this amulet must have denoted by the stag a deity of the Græco-Roman mythology ; and we must therefore look for one whose prototype is to be found in Egypt, and whose attributes were the same as the Ephesian Diana whom undoubtedly the stag represented in his idea. This could be no other than Hathor, whom we must look upon like Diana, as distinctly a moon goddess.[216] So the thunderbolt, in like manner, would represent Serapis, the great Sun-god.

Thus considered, every one of the symbols on this week-day amulet ultimately resolves itself into one or other of the great Gnostic gods, the Sun and Moon.

The use of the eye as the central object in amulets involving sympathetic magic, may be taken to be universal. "Arab amulets at the present day bear the figure of the thing against which they exert their virtue, and all oriental practices in this line come down from immemorial antiquity."[217]

The Maltese, partly Arab and partly Italian, holding the beliefs and customs of both parent stocks,

---

[215] Pliny, *Nat. Hist,* viii. 51 (vol. ii. p. 302, Bohn). Diana is often represented as accompanied by a dog, the most sagacious and watchful of animals. The dog was a symbol of Diana, Thoth, Hermes, Mercury, Anubis (Payne Knight, *Symb. Lang.* p. 113). "The dog as a symbol of destruction was sacred to Mars as well as to Mercury" (Phurnutus, *Nature of the Gods,* xxi) ; hence "the dogs of war."

[216] See the story of Osiris and Isis-Athor in Wilkinson, iii. 75 *et seq.* ; also of Isis and her connection with the Dog-star, *Ib.* p. 106.

[217] Cesnola, *Cyprus,* 1877. Appendix by C. W. King (author of *Gnostics,* etc.), p. 385. Fig. 20 is from Pignorius (*Vetustissimæ Tabulæ,* Venice, 1605), p. 16 *in dorso,* and is by him called a phallic engraved amulet.

FIG. 20.

are specially in dread of the evil eye, and being a
maritime people too, we should look for marks of this
in connection with their principal calling, for perils
by the sea are everywhere believed to be constant
sources of danger subject to maleficent influence.
Consequently we find the native boats, as a regular
part of their decoration, have a large eye painted on
each side of the bows, giving them a very weird and
uncanny appearance, much enhanced by the high
prolongation of the stem. The same kind of stem
is seen in the Neapolitan boats, though without the
eyes.

The writer has seen boats having eyes on either
side of the prow in some other places, at Smyrna, or
one of the Greek ports, but having missed his note
cannot recall at which port it was. This custom is
evidently of great antiquity. The eye was placed
on boats by the ancient Egyptians,[218] and also by the
Etruscans.[219] Dennis remarks : [220] " The presence of
eyes on the bows of ancient vessels, perhaps originating in the fancied analogy with fish, or to intimate
the vigilance necessary to the pilot, is well known
—'they were charms against the evil eye.' " [221]

Besides the conventional *ouza* or *œil mystique*
already referred to, the Egyptians wore eyes as
amulets of a more realistic character. They were
in pairs, looking fully to the front, and were pierced

---

[218] Wilkinson, vol. iii, p. 353.

[219] In the Grotta de Cacciatore, near Corneto, "is depicted a boat with a
high, sharp stern and a low bow, on which is painted an enormous eye—a
fashion that has descended from Etruscan times to the fishermen of modern
Italy " (Dennis, *Cities of Etruria*, vol. i. p. 312).

[220] *Ibid.* vol. i. p. 471.

[221] On a vase in the British Museum representing Ulysses (tied to the mast)
and the Sirens, the vessel has a large eye upon the prow—suggesting that
another was upon the other side not seen. A plate of this is given in Smith's
Classical Dict. p. 784, ed. 1877.

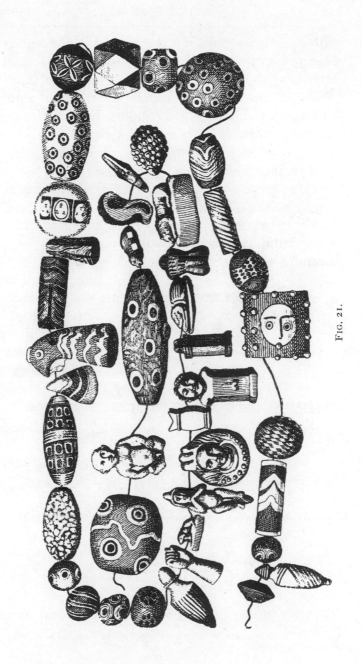

FIG. 21.

with the usual hole for the string. A number of examples of this kind may be seen in the Ashmolean Museum at Oxford.

In the remarkable necklace or string of amulets found in a tomb at Kertch, taken by Jahn from the Russian work of Achik,[222] a great many of the separate objects have markings on them which can only be intended for eyes (Fig. 21).

Jahn, page 41, says that necklaces with separate pendants as amulets are extremely common in Etruscan art-work. Among other people, girdles of various kinds, arm-bands with amulets thereon, are common, and specially in Italian art-work.

FIG. 22.

Among the Etruscans a prominent eye was often placed on objects which can hardly be called amulets, but on which the eye may well be considered to take the place it does at present on

FIG. 23.

Maltese boats. It was in itself a powerful amulet,

222 Achik, *Antiq. du Bosphore Cimmérien*, vol. iii. p. 210. See also Daremberg et Saglio, p. 257.

and was therefore used as a conspicuous object of decoration.

FIG. 24.—From Woburn Marbles.

Fig. 22 is from Vulci.[223]   Fig. 23 is an Etruscan winged deity.[224]

[223] Dennis, *Etruria*, vol. i. p. cxxi and p. 462.
[224] *Ib.* vol. ii. p. 160. All the illustrations from Dennis are reproduced by the kind permission of Mr. John Murray.

Perhaps the most noteworthy of all the amulets in which the eye forms the central object in combination with several other emblems, is the very remarkable relief illustrated in Millingen's paper in vol. xix. of *Archæologia*, p. 74, and referred to by Jahn.[225] It is one of the Woburn marbles (Fig. 24) in the collection of the Duke of Bedford, and measures 1'6" × 1'5", but this last dimension is not perfect, being broken on the left side. There was a framing, and it is usually thought to have been built into a wall, as a house-decoration, but still more as a protection. The centre is a large human eye, and, as Jahn says, " the left, which may be considered a special feature of its sinister intention, and moreover the pupil is strongly marked." [226] Over it is a very prominent eyelid and an arched brow. Above this is seated a beardless man in a Phrygian cap, with his back towards the spectator, and his head turned backwards. He is squatted down with both hands on his knees, has his shirt pulled up, and strikingly exemplifies the description of Pomponius :—

" Hoc sciunt omnes quantum est qui cossim cacant." [227]

Moreover it is evident that he is in that position which even now conveys in its full reality (in England no less than in Germany) the common

[225] The illustration here given is from Millingen's original plate, and differs in many respects from the copy of it attached to Jahn's article.

[226] In consequence of the stress laid by Jahn upon the eye represented being the left, I have carefully examined all the eyes upon amulets which have come under my notice, and among a great number of examples I have found no marked preponderance either way, but on the whole should say there are more right eyes than left. The very common phrase " sinister expression," come to us from classic days, may have suggested to Jahn the idea that the left eye is especially malignant, but I can see no evidence in support of it, and believe the phrase has no connection with the evil eye, but that it springs from another and quite different set of beliefs.

[227] Nonius, see *cossim*, p. 40, verb *incoxare*, p. 39. Jahn, p. 30.

typical expression of the utmost contempt.[228]   In fact, the figure is sitting on the eye in a most indecorous position, and as we explain later, any object or gesture which gave rise to an indecent or obscene idea was looked upon as specially effective in the way of a protection against fascination.   One cannot help once more remarking here, how strikingly this mockery of the evil eye, this challenging of its malignity in the old Roman days of Septimius Severus, to which period this marble is ascribed, are reproduced in this enlightened nineteenth century by the heroic performances of the " Thirteen Club." Surely the dinner with its brave defiance of the Fates is a very eloquent and convincing piece of evidence that so-called civilisation, enlightenment, culture and all the rest of it, have not even yet eradicated the feeling, which has existed in man's breast from the remotest antiquity—that there is a power, an influence, a something passing from certain persons to others, which though unseen, unfelt, unmeasured and incapable of explanation, at least is dreaded by many, and perhaps most by some of those who scoff loudest, and outwardly defy it most ostentatiously.

It is well known that at the present day Neapolitan and other Italian sailors use this same identical attitude, turning themselves thus towards a contrary wind, in the belief that by such contemptuous defiance of the adverse spirit of the wind, its direction may be changed.[229]

[228] Striking examples of this act have not long since come under the notice of the writer, in one of which a man used this means of grossly insulting a woman—about his equal in refinement—with whom he had had a quarrel.

[229] This gesture was evidently of widespread use in ancient times.   We are told that in the ceremony of going down the Nile to the festive worship of Bast at Bubastis the crowded boats, as they passed near a town, came close to

On the right of the spectator in our illustration is another figure with his face turned towards the Phrygian, the former appears to be a gladiator wearing the distinctive girdle called the *subligaculum*. In his right hand is the trident, with which he seems to stab the eye, and in his left a short sword[230] (*fuscina*). The yoke-like object on his left shoulder, and the armlet he wears, recognised as the *galerus*,[231] prove that he was a *Retiarius*, one of those who fought with a net, which he tried to throw over his opponent the *Mirmillo*, so as to entangle him and his shield ; and then he attacked him with the trident. The *Retiarius*, moreover, used to fight bare-headed like the figure here. There was most likely (Jahn says, *ohne Zweifel*) a figure on the opposite side of the bas-relief, which is now broken off, and it is here suggested that the latter may have represented the opposing *Mirmillo*, though Jahn says nothing upon that subject.

On the lower part of the marble are five animals seemingly attacking the eye with great fury. These are a lion, a serpent, a scorpion, a crane, and a raven or crow — each one a distinct amulet in itself.

Millingen remarks that no doubt can be entertained but that the evil eye or *fascinum* is here represented, and in this opinion he is fully supported

the bank. " Some of the women continue to sing and strike cymbals ; others cry out as long as they can, and utter reproaches against the people of the town, who begin to dance, while the former pull up their clothes before them in a scoffing manner" (Herodotus, ii. 60, quoted by Budge, *Nile*, p. 111).

The writer can testify to having witnessed a similar performance by a woman on London Bridge at ten o'clock in the morning !

[230] The trident and sword are separate amulets, as shown later.

[231] This is taken from Jahn, p. 30, but according to Smith, *Dict. of Gr. and Rom. Antiq.*, the *galerus* was a helmet or head-dress.

by Jahn ; while to any candid observer the relief
itself is by far the best evidence.[232]

It was usual to ornament the coffins or mummy
cases of the ancient Egyptians with two large open
eyes, with two monumental doors on the left, while
on the right they placed three doors.   These eyes
could only have been intended to answer the same
purpose on the outside as the *œil mystique* within.

The remarkable scene here given (Fig. 25)
from an amphora found at Vulci, now in the British

FIG. 25.

Museum, is but a sample of the eyes found on
painted vases like this, not only of Etruscan, but also
of undoubted Greek origin, which are fully recognised,
says Dennis, as charms against the evil eye.[233]

The curious representation of the great eyes
(evidently the feature of the whole) upon the conventionalised wings of two Sirens, and upon those of a
Fury in the collection of Sig. Bargagli at Sarleano,
described by Dennis,[234] forms another connecting
link in the chain which we hope to forge, by which
we shall connect the sirens of modern Naples with

[232] On the other hand, in the same volume (xix. of *Archæologia*, at p. 99),
the Rev. Stephen Weston contests this view, and tries to prove that the whole
piece of sculpture is a representation of the sacred rites of Mythra ; but his
views in support of his Mythraic theory are speculative and fanciful in face of
the materialistic story of the marble itself.   Upon this point Jahn, p. 31,
says : "Es kann kein Zweifel sein und ist von allen erkannt, dass es
bestimmt war Schutz gegen den Zauber des bösen Blicks zu gewähren."
[233] Dennis, *Etruria*, vol. i. p. 471.   [234] *Ib.* vol. ii. p. 364.

the ancient mythology of Egypt, Greece, and Rome. The Etruscans ornamented their vases and furniture with eyes very conspicuously depicted, as may be seen in the *Museo Gregoriano* in Rome and else- where. On these Dennis[235] remarks, that they "have evidently an analogy to those so often painted on the Hellenic vases, and have probably the same symbolic meaning."

The ancient Egyptians, too, were accustomed to adorn their pottery with the eye as a special feature of the design. The strange combination of three fishes with three lotus flowers here given (Fig. 26) is from Maspero, *Arch. Egypt.* p. 255.[236]

FIG. 26.

Except upon Maltese and some other boats, or in masonic sym- bolism, the eye seems to have passed out of modern use, and as an amulet almost exclusively to be a thing of the past; even among the ancients it was by no means the commonest emblem used against its own influence. Eyes, however, made of wax or silver are extremely common to-day as *ex votos*—hung up in churches, before *Notre Dame de bon secours*, and some other favourite saints, such as SS. Cosmo e Damiano. We must ever bear in mind that it was, and continues to be, believed that the first glance of the evil eye was the

---

235 Dennis, *Etruria*, vol. ii. pp. 77, 331.
236 It is the rounded bottom of a blue bowl. The fish here compounded with *l'œil mystique*, and the no less mystical lotus, is undoubtedly the sacred Lepidotus, fully described by Wilkinson (vol. iii. pp. 340 *et seq.*). It surely is not unreasonable to consider that a form of decoration common to Egyptians, Etruscans, and Greeks was not a mere coincidence, but had a well-understood common significance. The original bowl is in the Berlin Museum. The same illustration is in Wilkinson, vol. ii. p. 42.

most fatal, and therefore it was of the utmost importance that any object intended to protect against its
influence should be such as should attract the first
or fatal stroke ; for it was just as firmly held, that
whatever diverted it for the moment from the person
or animal liable to injury, absorbed and so destroyed
its effect.   Anything, therefore, calculated to excite
the curiosity, the mirth, or in any way to attract the
attention of the beholder was considered to be the
most effectual.   There were three methods generally
accepted for averting fascination, whether it were
of look, voice, touch, or bodily presence of the
fascinator.[237]   These were, by exciting laughter or
curiosity ; by demonstration of good fortune so as to
excite envy in the beholder and so to draw his evil
glance upon the object displayed ; and by doing
something painfully disagreeable to cause him an
unpleasant feeling of dread lest he, the fascinator,
should be compelled to do likewise.[238]

Plutarch in a remarkable passage [239] declares that
the objects that are fixed up to ward off witchcraft
or fascination, derive their efficacy from the fact that
they act through the strangeness and ridiculousness
of their forms, which fix the mischief-working eye
upon themselves.[240]

It was this firm belief which led to the design of
those extremely grotesque figures amongst the
Romans of which they were so fond, and of

---

[237] " Fascinatio est actio, qua corpori noxa visu, verbis, contactu aut effluviis
malis occulto modo agentibus per vim seu naturalem seu supernaturalem inferri
putatur."—Frommannd, p. 7.

[238] These are thus summed up by Vincentius Alsarius (" De Invidia et
Fascinatione," *Thesaur. Antiq. Rom.* vol. vii. p. 890) : " Quodam ridiculo
spectatoribus objecto : . . . fortunæ secundæ dissimulatione ; . . . casu aliquo
adversa sponte suscepto et contractu," quoted by Frommannd.

[239] *Symposia,* v. 7.

[240] See remarks on Gurgoyles, Appendix II.

which we have such numberless examples in every museum of ancient gems. These amulets, all intended for the same purpose, are now called

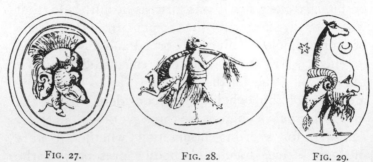

FIG. 27.   FIG. 28.   FIG. 29.

Grylli, from modern Italian *grillo*, signifying both a cricket or grasshopper, and also a caprice or fancy.[241]

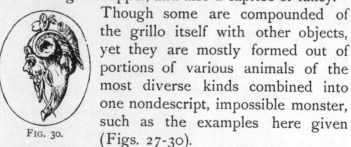

FIG. 30.

Though some are compounded of the grillo itself with other objects, yet they are mostly formed out of portions of various animals of the most diverse kinds combined into one nondescript, impossible monster, such as the examples here given (Figs. 27-30).

These grotesques formed of the creatures, sometimes called *Chimeræ*, have been by some considered as Gnostic remains; but it is urged on the other side,[242] that besides never exhibiting the symbols which are characteristic of Gnosticism, the style of work proclaims them to the least experienced eye to belong to a much earlier date—that of the best period of

[241] The alternative meaning of *grillo* in modern Italian is said to be a classic survival : " Antiphilus jocosis nomine *Gryllum* deridiculi habitus pinxit, unde id genus picturæ *grylli* vocantur " (Pliny, *Sympos.* xxv. 37).

[242] King, *Handbook of Engraved Gems*, p. 81. The four grylli here reproduced are from Mr. King's books. I am indebted to Mr. David Nutt and Messrs. George Bell and Sons for permission to copy them.

Roman art.[243]   In any case the strange combination of various animal forms in one is certainly a practice handed down from ages long antecedent to either

FIG. 31.   FIG. 32.   FIG. 33.

Gnosticism or Roman history.   Early Etruscan bronze amulets were very commonly formed by the union of two animals in one body, as well as by very rude re-presentations of a single one.   This may be seen in the cuts herewith (Figs. 31, 32, 33), from the Etruscan Museums of Bol-ogna and Cortona, and Figs. 34, 35, 36, 37, 38, from the Ashmolean at Oxford.   More-over we have the famous vision of

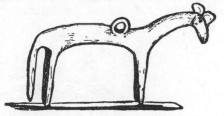

FIG. 34.

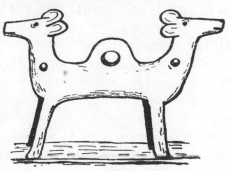

FIG. 35.

Ezekiel in which the faces of a man, lion, ox, and eagle were conjoined, and these components have

[243] It is certain that as works of art a vast number of the objects used as amulets were of a very debased kind indeed ; but it should always be remem-bered that the virtue of an amulet or talisman lay in the type it embodied, and in its own material substance—the manner of execution of the potent sigil was altogether unconsidered.   This will become abundantly plain when we come

in Christian art been separated and become the symbols of the four Evangelists.

In treating of amulets it behoves us to give an early place in our consideration to that which of all others may be taken as the first, the original germ,

FIG. 36.   FIG. 37.

FIG. 38.

at least so far as noticeable in Greek art—the head of the Medusa, or as it is commonly called, the Gorgoneion.

The story of Perseus and of his killing the Medusa, whom he only ventured to look at in a mirror, need not here be detailed, but in it we have at least a very early incident in the primæval belief in the evil eye. So far as Greek art goes, we have in the hideous representation of her dog-toothed, split-tongued visage, the earliest example which we can positively assert to be a prophylactic charm against the fatal glance which she was believed to have possessed ; for though there are plenty of Egyptian

to consider the very rough and crude objects made in these latter days for con-stant use in Naples—where the thing represented is of the rudest, coarsest work, while all the time it is of the most imperative necessity that each article should be of sterling silver, which must be attested by the hall-mark.

amulets of earlier date, it cannot be certainly declared
what was their precise intention.   This very remarkable object is of so much importance that we must
make it a subject to be treated apart ; [244] suffice it here
to say that from being the earliest of amulets known
to European art, so the illustration on p. 160, Fig. 49,
shows it to be one of the latest, if not the latest, used in
Christian times to baffle the evil eye.   We also see by
the same illustration that it is one of the most debased
among the many examples of declining art.   It is of
course out of our province, and beyond our ability,
to decide whence the Greeks obtained the story, and
we must leave that question to experts who are con-
tent to contract more narrowly their investigations.
The obvious development of the early idea of the
Gorgon's head, from its first conception of the
intensest ugly frightfulness, until it became at last
by the gradual refinement of taste, as shown in
classic art, the ideal of female beauty, culminating
in the well-known Strozzi Medusa,[245] demands careful
attention.

The step from the famous death-dealing visage, as
a protection against the very evil it was believed to
produce, is but short to that of hideous faces in
general; and hence we find that strange and contorted
faces or masks were certainly used as objects to
attract the evil eye, and so to absorb its influence, and
to protect the person wearing or displaying the mask.
The very origin of the name *mask* is said to be but

[244] Jorio, *Mimica degli Antichi*, p. 235, says : "The common people (of
Naples) are absolutely ignorant of everything concerning the Medusa's head ;
but they are fully persuaded that the eyes of the Basilisk (of which also they
know nothing) have the same power as that attributed to the fabulous head."
[245] Another beautiful Medusa is that upon the Onyx cup in the Naples
Museum, called the Tasse Farnese.   A print of this is in Daremberg et
Saglio, *Dict. des Antiq.* p. 103.

a corruption of the older Greek βασκα, whence
βασκανία, *fascina* or amulets.   " From this custom of
regarding hideous masks as amulets can be explained
a circumstance otherwise a problem to every archæo-
logist—the vast number of such subjects we meet
with in antique gems." [246]   Not only so, but their
importance is still more impressed upon us by the
fact that the highest skill known to Roman art was
lavished upon the engraving of masks.

Nothing, as is well known of all ages, so much
attracts or excites curiosity as obscenity and inde-

FIG. 39.   FIG. 40.

cency ; [247] and hence of all amulets, those partaking
of this character were the most potent, and therefore
the most used.   Anything strange, odd, or uncommon, as likely to attract the eye, was considered
most effectual, and consequently the objects viewed
as protective against it were almost infinite in number.   For the reasons given we find in compounded
amulets that the commonest of all objects was the
phallus, or some other, suggesting the ideas conveyed by it.

[246] King, *Handbook of Gems*, p. 85.   Figs. 39, 40, come from a number
of these masks in Mr. King's books, namely, the above and *The Gnostics*.

[247] " Everything that was ridiculous and indecent was also supposed to be
inimical to the malignant influence of fascination by the oddness of the sight."—
Dodwell, *Class. Tour through Greece*, 1819, vol. ii. p. 34.

Amulets then which protect against the power of fascination would naturally be of three classes. First, those whose intention was to attract upon themselves the malignant glance. These were necessarily either worn on the outside of the dress, or openly exposed to view like the grillo of Pisistratus at Athens, the brazen serpent set up by Moses, or the various household objects displayed for the same purpose. Secondly, there were all those charms, worn or carried secretly, or hidden beneath the dress; and thirdly, the written words of Scripture, Koran, and other sacred writings, or the cabalistic figures and formulæ considered so powerful.

The former class were the most numerous, and of them we have the greatest number of examples, both ancient and modern. For the reason above stated, amulets consisting alone of *das männliche Glied*, or compounded with it as the attractive feature, were so common that they obtained a technical name from the purpose they were intended to serve. The usual term among old writers was *fascinum*.[248]

Other writers, especially Varro, call one particular form which was commonly suspended from the necks

---

[248] "Quid? quod libelli Stoici inter Sericos
        Jacere pulvillos amant?
      Illiterati num minus nervi rigent,
        Minusve languet fascinum?
      Quod ut superbo provoces ab inguine
        Ore allaborandum est tibi."—Horace, *Epodon* viii. 15.

(This epode is omitted in the expurgated editions.) See also Frommannd, *Tract. de Fasc.* p. 5, who says: "Per fascinum virile membrum, quod fascia tegi solet sive campestribus, hic intelligi Commentator et Cruquius dicunt. Fascinum autem vocarunt partem illam, quoniam fascinandis rebus hæc membri deformitas apponi fuit solita."

He goes on to connect the reason of the name with the licentious cult of Liberus. He also writes much on the subject which is unfit to be reproduced here, referring frequently to the worship of Priapus, and to the sayings of Enothea, priest of Priapus.

of children *turpicula res, scæva* or *scævola*, and he discusses at some length the development of the word.[249]

Dodwell (vol. ii. p. 34) says : " They are frequently found in Italy of bronze, and the other extremity of the symbol is terminated by a hand which is closed ; the thumb protruding between the fore and middle fingers.[250]

This is but a very partial description of a most remarkable object much easier portrayed than described. It is of so obscene a character that it cannot here be reproduced.

A full-sized illustration of one in bronze from the Dresden collection is given (p. 81) in Jahn's *Ueber den Aberglauben*, etc. It is evidently a pendant-amulet, having three extra eyelets, from which probably little bells were hung, such as will be seen later on in our illustrations of the Sirens and Sea-horses. One branch of the pendant consists of a phallus such as Frommannd describes (p. 5), *tam rigidum reddere quam cornu;* while to balance it, is an arm ending in a fist with the thumb protruding as stated by Dodwell. The central part or body is composed of another membrum, of the kind constantly found as a separate amulet. Any number of these may be seen both as amulets and as *ex votos* in the private Museum at Naples, and also in the Museum of the Collegio

---

[249] " Potest vel ab eo quod pueris turpicula res in collo quædam suspenditur, ne quid obsit bonæ scævæ causa : unde scævola appellata. Ea dicta ab scæva, id est sinistra, quod quæ sinistra sunt bona auspicia existimantur : a quo dicitur comitia aliudve quid ; sic dicta avis, sinistra quæ nunc est. Id a Græco est, quod hi sinistram vocant σκαιαν : quare quod dixit Obscœnum Omen, est omen turpe, quod unde (id) dicitur, Osmen ex quo S extritum."—Varro, *De Lingua Latina*, viii. 97. Ed. Sprengel, Berlin, 1885.

[250] " Inserto pollice inter medium et indicem, ita ut pollex ipse insertus emineret, et apparet, reliquis digitis in pugnum contractis."—*De Pollice*, p. 42, Lipsiæ, 1677.

Romano.   A very beautiful specimen of a *turpicula res* is in one of the cases of antique jewellery in the Louvre Museum.   It is of gold, and measures about an inch and a half wide, and itself forms the pendant to a complete necklace, having above it as part of the pendant a fine amethyst cut as a scarab.   There may be others in other museums, but the above is by far the most elaborate known to me, and is a most interesting study.   In the same case are several other amulets against the evil eye, among which is the medal (Fig. 12).

In the Naples Museum are many bronze examples of various sizes, but all similar in pattern ; in all cases the thumb is between the first and second fingers.   There are also many phalli with eyelet holes to enable them to be worn as charms.

The vast antiquity of the phallic necklace can be easily demonstrated : it was very ancient even in the days of Horace and Varro ; and it may be that the Romans got their *fascinum* from Egypt.   In a recently discovered tomb at Thebes, near that of Rekhamara, the account of which has not yet found its way into the guide-books, the writer was struck by a singularly fresh and distinct painting of a necklace—the colour as bright as the day it was painted, more than three thousand years ago.   It is formed of a chain fastened by a serpent's head, such as may be seen in our own shops to-day.   The ornaments are three pendants—the phallus,[251] the most conspicuous, in the centre, the symbol of stability, and the *ankh*, or symbol of life, on either side.

[251] Upon the importance of the phallus, and its consecration to Osiris, with the reasons for the place it took in the Egyptian system, see Wilkinson, vol. iii. p. 77, and various notices in vols. i. ii. concerning the God Khem.

The necklace so carefully painted is being presented by one female figure to another, but there are no special attributes by which to decide whom they are meant to represent. The attitude of the figures, and the prominence given to the three pendants of the offering, show that it was intended to be received and worn as a protective amulet.

Although of course the *turpicula res* is no longer to be found in actual use, yet the fist with protruding thumb is to-day one of the commonest of objects worn as a charm for the watch-chain. The complete survival of the ancient amulet is no longer permitted by the papal censors, but the hand - part of it is still the ordinary baby's sucker or plaything hung upon a child's neck in Rome, where of old the grosser object held its place. In fact this hand in silver is to the Roman child of to-day what our "coral and silver bells" was to us in our childhood—the regulation christening gift. Fig. 41 is from the writer's collection ; actual size. It is of silver, and was bought in a shop close to the Campo dei Fiori, where it was one of a large bunch of at least twenty exposed for sale, showing that it is an article in large and regular demand. The same thing may be seen in almost any silversmith's shop out of the beat of the ordinary tourist. This special article seems to be confined to Rome and its neighbourhood, for, as we shall see later, something

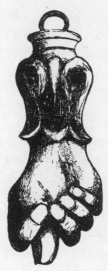

FIG. 41.

very different is worn by the babies in Naples and Southern Italy.

In making purchases of this and of the many other charms in the writer's possession, it has always been his practice to inquire of the seller what was the object of the article. In every case the answer has been the same—"*Contra malocchia*" in Rome ; "*Contra la jettatura*" in Naples.

The antiquity of the phallus as an amulet is shown by the number found among Egyptian sculptures. No visitor to Egyptian antiquities needs to be told this. Indeed, it was held to have been consecrated by Isis herself.[252] The phallus was the most sacred amulet worn by the vestal virgins of ancient Rome.[253] Moreover, we find that Sesostris of the early twelfth dynasty, who conquered Asia, set up memorials of a phallic nature among the people who had acted bravely, but among the degenerate, female emblems engraved on *stelæ* were set up.[254] Who shall say these objects may not have been the origin of those still to be found so universally throughout India ? In the ruins of Zimbabwe, in Central Africa, are to be seen phalli carved upon stone, similar to those found in Sardinia, which are said to be Phœnician.[255] The like have been seen by the writer on the so-called Phœnician ruins of Hajar Khem in Malta. Again, numbers of phallic amulets in bronze are found in the earliest Etruscan tombs as well as in the museums of the Collegio Romano, of Cortona and of Bologna, marked

---

[252] Wilkinson, iii. p. 77.
[253] Smith's *Dict. of the Bible*, s.v. "Fascinum."
[254] Wilkinson, *op. cit.* i. p. 20.
[255] Bent, *Ruined Cities of Mashonaland.* Perrot and Chipiez, *History of Art in Sardinia*, p. 57. *Spectator*, November 26, 1892.

as belonging to the *prima età di ferro*—a time which,
like Egyptian monuments, makes the objects of
Classic Rome things of yesterday. The objects on
Fig. 42 are in the Museum at Bologna. In the
Naples Museum are a number of vases of different
shapes, ornamented with vine leaves and tendrils

FIG. 42.

alternating with a phallus, forming a belt of decoration round the belly of the vase.

The object described as *satirica signa* by Pliny,
and so constantly referred to, appears not only upon
the amulets of which the eye is the centre, but is
that to be seen over so many of the doorways in
Pompeii. It by no means signified that which the
ciceroni now tell the tourist ; [255a] but was placed there
as a protective amulet against fascination. We
read [256] that it was the common sign over a blacksmith's forge, and no doubt inasmuch as the horses
who came to him to be shod were specially liable to
the malign influence, so the smith would naturally
provide the best possible protector for the animals
by whom he got his living.

"That such representations were placed by the
ancients on the walls of their cities, there is no lack
of proof.[257]   They are found on several of the early

[255a] That houses so marked were Lupanari.

[256] Dennis, *Cities of Etruria*, vol. ii. p. 119. It was of course not confined to this purpose at Pompeii.

[257] Dennis, as above. He refers to Pliny, but cannot find the passage.
Dennis believes in their being thus placed to defy the enemy. I recommend
the student to read this chapter.

cities of Italy and Greece, on masonry polygonal as well as regular." At Alatri it is tripled, sculptured in relief on the lintel of a postern or passage in the polygonal walls of the citadel. It is also tripled on the Pelasgic walls at Grottatore. Another is found on the ancient wall of Terra di Cesi, near Terni, and again on the ancient fortifications of Todi on the upper waters of the Tiber, where it is in high relief, and is well known as *il pezzo di marmo*. There is one on a block in the wall of Oea, in the island of Thera in the Ægean Sea, with an inscription accompanying it, which distinctly proves it to have been intended to avert the evil eye. The same thing has been found on the doors of ancient tombs at Palazzuolo in Sicily, at Castel d'Asso in Etruria, and in the Catacombs of Naples. Of all places, however, the greatest number now to be seen are amongst the tombs and temples of Egypt.

Jahn gives plates of a very remarkable kind, of objects sculptured on the amphitheatre at Nismes, to be seen at the Dresden and other museums; he pursues this subject at greater length than can be here followed. To have omitted all notice of it would have been to leave out really the part on which ancient and mediæval writers have dwelt longest; still it is unsavoury, and we are glad to have done with it, the more so as we have so many facts and objects to be found in the life of to-day which seem to have been singularly overlooked by those who have written on the evil eye.

Repeated mention is made in these pages of the many amulets to be found in the Etruscan Museum at Bologna. Of the accompanying illustrations, Fig. 43 is taken from Burton's *Etruscan Bologna*,

p. 68, who gives it as a *pelekys* or axe, which he
says is an amulet against fascination.   Fig. 44 is
from a sketch by the writer from the same museum.

FIG. 43.   FIG. 44.

It also suggests an axe in shape, about one and a
half times the size of illustration, and from its being
evidently for suspension, it is here suggested that it
may be an amulet.   Being of bronze, and very thin,
it is possible that its use may be the same as the

FIG. 45.   FIG. 46.

very numerous handled half-moons of about the
same size, found there and in other museums, which
are well known to be ancient razors.   In the object
here shown, there is but one possible cutting edge,
that at the bottom.   Figs. 45, 46 represent an
Etruscan coin [258] of the town of Luna.   The devices
engraved upon it almost certainly prove that they

[258] From Dennis's *Etruria*, vol. ii. p. 63.

were intended as amulets. The axe and sword were
each considered to be such, while as to the two
crescents, we may accept one as being a rebus of
Luna, and the other to be the consort of the central
solar disc. The head on the reverse may be the
personification of the city or of Diana.

CHAPTER V

THE GORGONEION

WHETHER looked at as the emblem of a hideous fable or simply as a mask, the Gorgoneion has in all ages been "reputed one of the most efficacious of amulets." [259] If further proof were required to sustain this assertion, beyond the frequency of its use, it would be found in the inscription upon a gem in the collection of the late Rev. C. W. King, of which he gives a drawing (Fig. 47). On this, beneath the head is: ΑΡΗΓΩ ΡΩΡΩΜΑΝ-ΔΑΡΗ—"I protect Roromandare."

FIG. 47.

It may have been the universality of the belief in the Medusa's power that led to masks becoming such favourites as protectors. Probably the root idea of the efficacy of any amulet lying in its strangeness, whether provocative of fear or laughter, may have led to the grotesque and impossible faces which are so frequently to be seen. Actors in classic days adopted a mask to hide their features, most likely from the general dread of the evil eye, lest among the crowd, gazing upon the performer, some may

---

[259] King, *Gnostics*, pp. 67, 223. Lucian says: "It was an amulet against the evil eye : what could be more potent than the face of the Queen of Hell?"

have possessed that fatal influence which Heliodorus
records respecting the daughter of Calasiris.   The
masks, whether worn by actors or painted on walls
by way of decoration, were commonly of hideous
grotesqueness.   In Rome, certain of these by long
usage developed into conventional faces, just like
that of our modern
Punch, two of which
typified, respectively,
Tragedy and Comedy.
These latter are now
only used for decor-
ative purposes, on
theatres and such like
buildings, while the
Medusa, the prototype
of masks, has con-
tinued to be used as
a common ornament
down to the present
day.   The very ugly
specimen depicted on
Fig. 67, p. 183 (Chap.
VI.) is one of the early
Greek type, from a

FIG. 48.

terra cotta in the Museum of Syracuse.[260]   Others, also
showing the mocking split-tongue, are of probably
the same age.   Fig. 48 is called by Dennis (vol. ii. p.
318) "the Anubis vase."   It is Etruscan black ware
from Chiusi in the Museo Casuccini.   It is 20 inches
high and has many grinning masks, some of which
are unmistakable Medusas.   The rest of our illustra-

[260] There are several similar ones, quite flat at the back, and, like this,
perforated with holes for suspension, in the Museums of Palermo and Girgenti.
They were evidently intended to be hung up against a wall or other flat surface.

tions speak for themselves, showing how the idea
had developed from the ugliness of the early Greek
ideal, to beauty in the Augustan age of Rome, and
how it had again declined both in art and in comeli-
ness during the period of Byzantine Christianity, as
exhibited in the annexed (Fig. 49), known as the

FIG. 49.

"Gnostic Gorgon." The inscription upon this undoubted amulet (actual size) from King's *Gnostics* [261]
(p. 67) being translated, reads : " Holy, holy, Lord of
Sabaoth, hosanna in the highest, the Blessed." [262]

A Medusa's head very similar to the one last mentioned is given in *Gnostics* (p. 119) as the seal of S. Ser-
vatius, Maestricht Cathedral, which of course brings it

[261] For permission to copy illustrations from the works of the late Rev. C.
W. King, I am indebted to the kindness of Mr. David Nutt, and Messrs. G.
Bell and Sons.

[262] Αγιος αγιος κοας φαωθ ωσανας τοις υψιστοις ευλογιμενος.   This legend, full
of corruptions, is intended for : "Αγιος, "Αγιος, Κύριος Σαβαώθ, ὡσαννὰ τοῖς ὑψίστοις
εὐλογημένος (King, *Handbook of Engraved Gems*, p. 377).

down as an amulet to much later times.   We know
that both on seals and on coins objects prophylactic
against fascination were common even in the late
Middle Ages, and were used down to a period long
since the Reformation.   Our own Anglo-Saxon kings
adopted such devices on their coins.[263]   Not only were
the Greek and Etruscan Gorgons common in Europe,
representing a widely-received myth, but in the East,
Bhavani, the Destructive Female Principle, is still
represented with a head exactly agreeing with the
most ancient type of the Medusa : with huge tusks,
tongue thrust out, and with snakes twining about the
throat, just as may still be seen in the Etruscan tomb
of the Volumni at Perugia, and such as was described
by Hesiod of old.   " In the centre of that tomb [264] is an
enormous Gorgon's head, hewn from the dark rock,
with eyes upturned in horror, gleaming from the
gloom, teeth bristling whitely in the open mouth,
wings on the temples, and snakes knotted over the
brow.   You confess the terror of the image, and
almost expect to hear

> " Some whisper from that horrid mouth
>   Of strange unearthly tone ;
>   A wild infernal laugh to thrill
>   One's marrow to the bone.
>   But, no ! it grins like horrid Death,
>   And silent as a stone."

A lamp of earthenware was suspended over the
doorway of this same chamber, having another
Medusa's head on the bottom.   A similar lamp
was suspended from the ceiling of the central
chamber.

[263] A large number of these may be seen in *Archæologia*, vol. xix. ; and in
the *Proceedings of the Somerset Arch. and Nat. Hist. Society*, vol. i. 1849.
[264] Dennis, *Cities of Etruria*, vol. ii. p. 441.

The illustration here given is from the under side of a very beautifully wrought bronze lamp in the Museum at Cortona, intended for suspension, and it would seem from these several instances, that this mode of depicting the Gorgon's head was, as we are told,[265] a very common Etruscan sepulchral decoration.

FIG. 50.

Fig. 50 is from a poor print sold at the Museum, but it gives a better idea of the Medusa and her surroundings than either of the plates in Dennis's book. About this lamp he says (vol. ii. p. 402): "But the wonder of ancient wonders, in the Museum of Cortona, is a bronze lamp of such surpassing beauty and elaboration of work-manship as to throw into shade every toreutic work of this class yet discovered in the soil of Etruria." It is circular, about 23 inches in diameter, hollow like a bowl, but from the centre rises a sort of conical chimney or tube, to which must have been attached a chain for its suspension. Round the rim are sixteen lamps of classic form, fed by oil from the great bowl, and adorned with foliage in relief. Alternating with them are heads of the horned and bearded Bacchus. At the bottom of each lamp is a figure in relief—alternately a draped siren with

[265] Dennis, *op. cit.* vol. i. p. 199.

wings outspread, and a naked satyr playing the
double pipes, having a dolphin beneath his feet.
" In a band encircling it are lions, leopards, wolves,
griffons in pairs, devouring a bull, a horse, a boar,
and a stag."   The bottom is hollowed in the centre
and contains a huge Gorgon's face.   " It is a libel on
the face of fair Dian, to say that this hideous visage
symbolises the moon. . . . There is every reason
to believe it was suspended in a tomb, perhaps in a
temple as a sacrificial lamp. . . . It is undoubtedly of
ante-Roman times, and I think it may safely be
referred to the fifth century of Rome, or to the close
of Etruscan independence."[266]

Gorgon's heads are found also on the cinerary
urns, "winged and snaked, sometimes set in
acanthus leaves."   Some of these, coloured to the
life, are now to be seen
in the Museum at Per-
ugia.

Fig. 51 is from a vase
at Chiusi, which Dennis
says (vol. ii. p. 221) is
typical of the early Etruscan style ; but whether the
Greeks or the Etruscans
first discarded hideousness
is uncertain.   It is how

FIG. 51.

ever clear that the latter people had done so before
Roman times, for in the same tomb of the Volumni,
where the frightful face is on the ceiling, is to be
found an " ash chest " with a *patera* at each angle,
having a Gorgon's head, " no longer the hideous

[266] The writer knew the lamp well, and possessed the print here copied,
many years before reading Mr. Dennis's description.

mask of the original idea, but the beautiful Medusa of later art,[267] with a pair of serpents knotted on her head and tied beneath her chin, and wings also springing from her brows."[268]

Not only did the pictorial idea change and develop, but as extremes meet, so it came in time to be believed, that it was her marvellous beauty and not her hideousness, that had turned beholders into stone.[269]

One of the most beautiful Medusas of late Greek

FIG. 52.—From Naples Museum.

art is to be seen in Rome. It is a highly sculptured relief in the Villa Ludovisi, where also is the Aurora of Guercino, now unfortunately closed to the public. She is there represented as a woman of severe though grand beauty, in her dying moments. There are no snakes about her head, but her hair lies in suggestive snake-like tresses about her neck and shoulders. Her eyes are closed, but yet she does not appear dead. This beautiful sculpture is ascribed

[267] Dennis, *op. cit.* vol. ii. p. 439.

[268] None of the early Medusas are given by Montfaucon, whose "Antiquity" does not seem to include anything but quite late objects.

[269] The accompanying heads, Fig. 52, from the Naples Museum, are simply door-knockers from Pompeii, but they admirably represent the transition period from the earlier grim and ferocious face, to the smiling and beautiful. It will be noted that the protruded tongue is retained in two, while in one there is an indication of the old splitting.

to the Macedonian period of Greek art. A much later type still is shown in the triskelion arms of Sicily, in the chapter on Crosses (p. 290).

The legend of the Gorgoneion although apparently unknown to the Egyptians is traceable in the far East, whence indeed the story of Perseus is said to have been brought. It is known in Cambodia and Borneo, in Tahiti and in far-off Peru. The accompanying illustrations amply support this statement. Fig. 53 was taken from the exhibits at the Paris Exhibition of 1889. Those from Peru are from Wiener's *Pérou et Bolivie*, Paris, 1880. The dog-tooth Medusa seems to have been quite a common object in ancient Peru, judging from the variety of examples given by Wiener. This

FIG. 53.
From Tahiti.

looks like another link in the chain of evidence whence both the South Seas and South America were originally peopled. There were almost identical heads from Cambodia. In the Museum at Taunton are several Dyak shields from Borneo. Every one has for its centre a hideous face with the conventional tusks, just like those here shown from Peru (Figs. 54, 55). These representations are doubtless the survival of primæval habit and spring from the central idea embodied in the Medusa.

By some it was held long ago that the Gorgon's head was a symbol of the lunar disc, hence the allusion by Dennis to "fair Dian." Another theory has been broached in modern times, that "the Gorgon of antiquity was nothing but an ape or ourang-outang, seen on the African coast by some early Greek or Phœnician mariner; and that its ferocious air, its

horrible tusks, its features and form caricaturing
humanity, seized on his imagination, which reproduced the monster in the series of myths."[270]

The story of the Medusa is but an incident in the
early belief in the evil eye, and should be carefully

FIG. 54.   From Peru.   Fig. 55.

studied by any who are interested in the subject.
After using it effectually in the turning of his enemy
Polydectes into stone, Perseus presented the terrible
head to Pallas, the Athenian goddess, who placed it
on her ægis, and in nearly all her statues, and those
of her Roman counterpart Minerva, she bears this
notable mask as an amulet.[271]

Originally the ægis was a goat's hide worn as a
protective garment, but later it became a breastplate,
and afterwards a shield. When Minerva is represented with a shield as the war goddess, she has
the gorgon's head emblazoned upon it. Thus was

[270] Dennis, *op. cit.* vol. ii. p. 221.

[271] At Athens new-born infants "were commonly wrapped in a cloth, wherein was represented the Gorgon's head, because that was described in the shield
of Minerva, the protectress of that city, whereby, it may be, infants were
committed to the goddess's care" (Potter, *Archæol. Græc.* ii. p. 320).

first set the fashion of bearing some prophylactic device by men in battle, which should first attract the angry glance of their enemies and then baffle their malignity. A custom once begun, and by so powerful a deity as the Goddess Athena, would not long want imitators; consequently representations of fighting men, especially on Greek vases, the oldest-known European pictures, show some object or other depicted upon breastplate or shield, but always one that was considered effective as a protector.[272] As the number of protectors came to be more numerous, so the variety of device upon the shield became greater: each warrior-chief naturally adopting that in which he placed the greatest faith. According to Plutarch, Ulysses adopted the dolphin as his special charm; both on his signet and on his shield. It is said that he chose this fish to commemorate the saving of Telemachus from drowning by its means.

Since then the dolphin has become a favourite device, and was in Roman times one of the special charms against the evil eye.[273] On an ancient vase at Arezzo[274] is a representation of Hercules and Telamon fighting the Amazons, who are all armed with round shields. The shield of one of the Amazons bears the Gorgoneion; another who is wounded bears a Cantharus or two-handled cup on her shield, and on her

[272] The same objects appear over and over again in later times, avowedly as charms against the evil eye.

[273] See gem, Fig. 18; also Water Bottle, Fig. 179, from the British Museum.

The dolphin is the badge of the well-known Somerset family of Fitz-James, two of whom, Richard, Bishop of London, and his nephew, Sir John Fitz-James, Lord Chief Justice, were the two principal founders of Bruton School, A.D. 1519. The original foundation deed, a most interesting document, is given at length by the Rev. F. W. Weaver in *Som. and Dor. Notes and Queries*, iii. xxii. 241.

[274] Plates in Dennis's *Etruria*, vol. ii. p. 387.

cuirass a lion. The hero Telamon bears a round shield just like the Amazons with a large lion passant upon it. Each of the figures represented may be taken as a leader, and so of course each of that leader's following would bear the same device. When under the Roman Empire the usages of war had become regulated by minute laws, the distinguishing badges of the various legions were prescribed with great exactness. The devices of several are referred to by Tacitus and also by Ammianus. They were borne by each man on his shield, and fortunately we are still able to see what many of those designs were.

A few of these devices here given (Figs. 56-66) are from *Notitia Dignitatum*,[275] by Guido Pancirolo, Lugduni, 1608.[276] Of the various subjects adopted by authority as the "cognisances" of the Roman legions, we have made a typical selection. One main idea seems to have influenced the choice of design. In all the scores of representations preserved in this remarkable book nearly all had a symbol of the sun in some form or other as its centre. There are twenty-one different insignia of the Thracian legions, of which sixteen are here given ; all but one of the twenty-one had a circle in

---

[275] Coloured copies of these insignia will be found in Logan's *History of the Scottish Gael*.

[276] " This valuable record," Mr. Hodgkin says (*Italy and her Invaders* A.D. 376 to 476. Oxford, 1880, vol. i. p. 200) "was compiled in the fifth century. It is a complete Official Directory and Army List of the whole Roman Empire, and it is of incalculable value for the decision of all sorts of questions, antiquarian and historical." The work of Pancirolo consists of the original text, compiled as above, together with his lengthy and important Commentarium.

In the Bodleian Library is a very beautiful MS. copy (Canon. Misc. 378) of the text of the *Notitia*, and containing the whole of the insignia ; moreover, all are highly coloured, so that the curious may learn precisely what these various badges were like. This is the more important because, even in those days, as the work fully explains, colour in itself entered largely as an element into the several designs.

its centre.[277]   Many had the crescent as well as the sun ; and one, the Thaanni, had six stars (probably the Pleiades) enclosed within the crescent.

FIG. 56.—Auxilia Palatina XVIII. p. 21.

Many of the shields bore various animals as "supporters." These may have been intended to represent the sun, or as symbols of it.[278]

[277] It may be accepted as a fact that recognition of the sun was quite characteristic of the army of the East, while there are many more exceptions to the rule, in that of the West.

[278] Surely it is no straining of Scripture to suggest that the Psalmist must

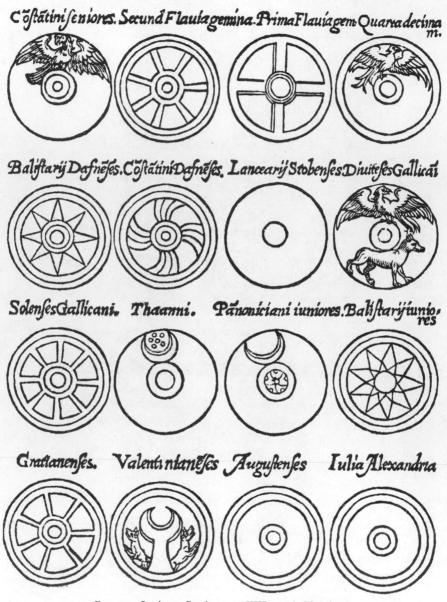

FIG. 57.—Legiones Comitatenses XXI. p. 36 (Thracians).

In the descriptions given, it is quite clear that the colours, as well as the devices, had each their symbolic meaning.[279]   The Ascarii Seniores had their shield half white and the rest *ferruginea*. There were two purple hemicycles united in the

Neruij.   *Fortenſes.*   *Hercul ani iuniores.*

Braccanſiлmiores   *Bataui ſeniores.*   *Martiarÿ iuniores*

FIG. 58.—Legiones Palatinæ XV. p. 20.

centre with two half-circles.   Pancirolo calls the whole a skilful design of symbol (*arguta symboli inventio*), for purple is the imperial colour.

The description of the insignia of the Ascarii in which the above occurs, if it had been in modern heraldic language, might well apply to mediæval coats.[280]

have been well used to the device as the central ornament, and familiar with its object, when he says : " For the Lord God is a sun and shield " (Psalm lxxxiv. 11).

[279] " Ascarii Juniores, in luteo clypeo, quem latus limbus rubeus circum-scribit, orbem aureum ferunt : unde octo luteæ cuspides acutæ exeunt.   In Madruciano, globus nigris lineis in septem partes dividitur, quæ forte septem terræ habitatæ climata referunt, eaque Imperio Rom. subesse."—*Notitia*, p. 39.

[280] Many similar allusions to the colours of the various badges might be given, but in the Oxford MS. these all tell their own tale.   It will be noticed that there was another legion—Ascarii Juniores—but these belonged to the Western Army and had a different shield.

We are told that the Honoriani Seniores (cavalry) bore a white shield, in which a golden centre (*aureus umbilicus*) was surrounded by a yellow circle.

Secŭda Flavia

I. *Flavia Theodosiana.*　II. *Felix Valen. Thebeorŭ.*　*Cŏstant Thebeorŭ.*

FIG. 59.—Legiones Comitatenses IX. p. 33.

The Martiarii Seniores had two jackals rampant supporting an orb with a Greek cross, surmounted by a crescent.　The Cornuti had two griffins' heads joined on a pedestal, with the inevitable sun circle in the centre, thus providing a "difference" to distinguish them from the Celtæ, who belonged to the Western Army.[281] Long ages before the Roman period to which these insignia belong, Grecian heroes carried on their shields what we may fairly term "armorial bearings."　The earliest known pictures, such as the vase paintings before referred to, show that the device

Petulantes iuniores.

FIG. 60.
Auxilia Palatina VI.

[281] The popular notion regarding coats of arms is no doubt accurately reflected by the leader-writer who penned the following: "Armorial bearings, we may presume, were originally adopted to distinguish a military leader in the throng of fighting men from a host of others similarly accoutred, and all with their vizors down.　They served, in short, as a sort of hieroglyphics, invented in an unlettered age, before the capability of reading a more conventional form of writing had become general" (*Standard*, June 9, 1894). He will therefore perhaps be surprised to see how much like mediæval shields were those of the Roman legions.

could not have been intended to distinguish
any leader from his following. They give
plenty of examples of both helmets and shields.
None of the helmets had visors, which appeared
at a much later period, while the shields had

Felices Theodosiani.   *Tervingi.*   *Traces.*   *Falconarii.*

FIG. 61.—Auxilia Palatina XVIII. p. 30.
(All the foregoing belong to the Army of the East.)

a common device for each clan or troop — of
these by far the most frequently seen was the
Gorgoneion. The various ancient representations

Herculiani.   *Iouian.*   *Celtæ.*   *Ascarijiun.*

FIG. 62.—Army of the West, p. 124 (Selection).

of objects depicted on shields seem to show that
these were adopted at the special or separate
pleasure of the individual chieftains, and the device
may be said to depict his clan totem. They were,
like the cognizances of our mediæval knights in
their day, not specially distinctive of family, but
more like the Roman insignia, the badges of particular corps. Thus, according to Æschylus, in a

story dating from the dawn of history, the heroes at the siege of Thebes bore distinctive devices on their shields, which the poet describes, and we may at least accept his statements as of historic value.

FIG. 63.—Army of the West, p. 125.

One, Parthenopæus, had on his shield a sphinx devouring a prostrate Theban; another, Typhon (our devil) belching forth flames and smoke. The mention of a sphinx as a device naturally leads one to Egypt, but there is a remarkable absence of anything which could be called a *cognizance* upon the arms of ancient Egypt, so that we of course conclude

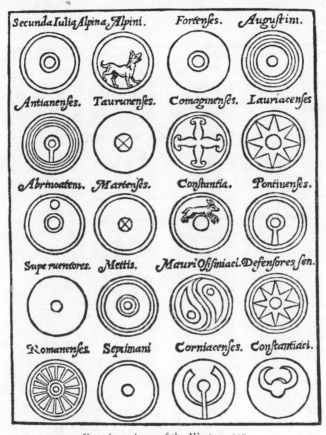

FIG. 64.—Army of the West, p. 127.

that in this particular the Greeks obtained their notions elsewhere.[282]

[282] The combination of protective symbols upon the same shield is by no means a feature peculiar to *mediæval* blazonry or modern heraldry. The ancient Etruscans were adepts at it, for on a *coupe* found at Vulci, now in the Berlin Museum (given in Daremberg et Saglio, p. 187), is a combat between Poseidon and Ephialtes. On the shield of the former are depicted a dolphin, scorpion, stag, serpent, lizard and crab, while on that of the latter there is only a horse rampant (the modern arms of Kent) with the legend KALON.

The variety of devices upon Chinese shields, and
the known unchangeable antiquity of everything in
China, make it a fair assumption that the early
Greeks and Etruscans obtained the custom of paint-

FIG. 65.—Army of the West, p. 125.

ing their shields from oriental people, and not from
Egypt. Among the Japanese, enormous fans are
used as ensigns in war, with various devices painted
upon them; moreover the armorial bearings, the
totems of families, are painted on fans. The fan is

considered as a symbol of life—the rivet end is the
starting point, and as the rays expand, so the road
of life widens out.[283] The suggestion that the
original custom of emblazoning strange devices upon

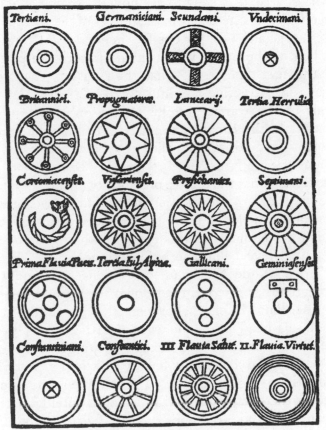

FIG. 66.—Army of the West, p. 127.

warriors' shields, to catch the eye of the enemy, is an
Oriental one, lends additional weight to the contention that in the Medusa's head we have the germ of
armorial device, because, as before mentioned, Bhavani

[283] "Fans of Japan," M. Salwey in *Spectator*, Mar. 17, 1894.

corresponds to and is most likely the prototype of the Greek Gorgon, whereas there is no evidence of anything analogous in ancient Egyptian mythology.

Having then, as we believe, run the original idea to its source, it is easy to see how it became adopted practically. The belief in the power of the malignant eye, especially of a furious foe, needed something to be held up before it, which should absorb the poison of the first glance. What then so effective as a strangely attractive pictorial device, to be carried in front of the warrior on his shield, on which might first alight the dreaded eye? It was thought that a protection against the dire invisible blow was a much greater safeguard than the best shield or buckler against the stroke of sword or spear. Hence the habit of presenting a strange sight to the enemy grew and developed until it crystallised into a custom which has endured to this day, but whose origin and meaning have been utterly forgotten.

To continue the chain of evidence, we find the Roman insignia continued down to Norman times. In the long interval between the placing of the Medusa's head upon the ægis of Athena, and even the Greek, or still later Roman age, a great variety of device had been adopted by fighting men, to be painted on their shields. The stranger and more bizarre the design, so much the more potent.

In the Bayeux tapestry, the figures upon the shields of the Norman knights were generally simple and single, carrying on for the most part the style of the Roman shields. This is the more easily accounted for when we remember that the Franks and Gauls had, from Constantine's time onwards, been the chief material of the Roman

armies, and that after the destruction of the
Empire, they would be likely to maintain, or at
least not to forget, the institutions and traditions
of the school in which they had been trained. We
therefore expect to find that down to a moderately
late period, the arms and discipline of the Franks
would perpetuate, in the main, those of their Roman
teachers. In another branch of our subject we see
how various emblems and simple amulets came to
be used not only singly, but compounded and combined, from the most simple to the most various and
complicated types, in all intervening stages ; so also
we find that the devices called armorial bearings
became compounded and complicated during the
age known as that of Chivalry, until at last a
systematic form of such combination developed
itself into a quasi - science, which we now call
Heraldry. Of course in the meantime the old
notion of specially favourite amulets (shall we call
them totems ?) had become fixed, and thus certain
devices had been adopted by heads of families or
tribes which their dependants adopted as their own
special *cognizance*, and naturally when families became
united by marriage, each party contributed his or her
own special family device, and hence arose what is
known as " quartering of arms." This having grown
into a well-recognised system with its official experts
and exponents, the combination of totems, amulets,
or special devices, has at length arrived at the position
of a pictorial family history, read with greater pride,
and, in these enlightened days, more highly valued,
than any other records however compiled. It preserves the mark of lineage to the highest and the
noblest born, through means which, though retained

and still believed in by humbler people, are treated with scoffing and contempt by those most interested. Superstition and ignorance are the mildest words to express the opinions of the adepts in heraldry, for those who still cherish the root notions on which heraldry is founded. Who are the totemists, who are the really ignorant, but those who boast loudest of their refinement, their cultivation, their enlightenment, as proved by their long pedigree, recorded by amulets?

CHAPTER VI

CRESCENTS, HORNS, HORSESHOES

EVERYBODY is familiar with the lunar appearance popularly known as "the old moon in the arms of the new," in which a dark disc is seen within the crescent. Precisely this phase was adopted as one of the most frequent crests to be seen upon the head of more than one of the Egyptian gods and goddesses. Thoth or Tehuti,[284] the scribe who weighed the souls when brought to judgment ("in one aspect he is the god of the moon"), and Chonsu, the hawk-headed, are both represented with the crescent and disc. Isis, and Hathor who was closely connected and sometimes actually confounded with her,[285] bear the disc with the horns of the crescent much prolonged, so as to assume the appearance of the horns of a cow. Hathor is often represented with the head of a cow on a human body, and also frequently as a cow, having the disc and horns on its head. At Philæ, Denderah, and elsewhere, she is represented as beautiful, while at the same time she has a sort of half-human, half-bovine face. Hathor became in late Greek and Roman times completely identified with Isis. "Isis is the female and receptive principle of generation."[286]

---

[284] Budge, p. 93 sq.   [285] Wilkinson, iii. p. 110.   Herodotus, ii. 4.
[286] Plutarch, *De Iside et Osir.* 53.

It is with the crescent and disc head-dress that we now have to do. Of course the deities thus distinguished by the crescent were moon-gods; but in the case of the gods Thoth and Chonsu the disc represented the sun also, from their intimate connection with Ra, the Sun-God of Egypt. Among the Greeks, who got much of their mythology from Egypt, the counterparts of Isis and Hathor were Artemis and Iö, the latter of whom became at length identical with Hera; all of these were symbolised by the Crescent.[287]

The Greek Iö was frequently represented by a cow,[288] as at Amyclæ. She is said to have been changed into a cow by Hera, and she was considered in the heroic age to be the cow-goddess Hera herself. The latter is called, from her cow-face, βοῶπις by Homer. In the battle of the gods, Hera took the form of a white cow, *Nivea Saturnia vacca*.[289] Cows' heads were on the coins of Samos, where was the most ancient temple of Hera. In Corinth[290] she had the epithet βουναία, and white cows were sacrificed in her honour.[291] The priestesses of Hera rode in a car drawn by white bulls to her temple at Argos.[292] It is said that the Egyptian Isis was born at Argos,[293] and that she was identified with the cow-shaped Iö, who, as before stated, was the same as Hera, and both were represented in Egypt as well as in Greece with cows' horns.[294] In the religious mysteries of Argos, Iö continued to be the old name

[287] "The emblem of Isis is that of a beautiful woman with cow's horns, just as the Greeks make Iö."—Payne Knight, *Symbolical Language of Ancient Art and Mythology*, p. 37.

[288] Pausanias, iii. 18. 13.   [289] Ovid, *Metamorphoses*, v. 330.
[290] Pausanias, ii. 4, 7.   [291] *Ib.* ix. 3, 4.   [292] Herodotus, i. 31.
[293] Diodorus Sic. i. 24, 25.   Apollodorus, ii. 1, 3.   [294] Herod. ii. 41.

for the moon.[295]   We are further told distinctly and repeatedly, that the cow horns of Iö-Hera, who was also often represented with a cow's face, like that of Isis-Hathor, were derived from the symbolic horns of the crescent moon.[296]

Hera, under her old moon-name Iö, had a celebrated temple on the site of Byzantium, said to have been founded by her daughter Keroëssa, "the horned."[297] The crescent, which was in all antiquity and throughout the Middle Ages the symbol of Byzantium, and which is now the symbol of the Turkish Empire, is a direct inheritance from Byzantium's mythical foundress Keroëssa, the daughter of the moon-goddess Iö-Hera; for it is certain the Turks did not bring it with them from Asia, but found it already the "cognizance" of Byzantium. The name Bosphorus is said to be "the passage of the cow": Iö, according to the legend, having there crossed into Europe in that form.[298]

The intimate connection of Hera and all her relatives with the crescent, is shown by the remarkable figures in coarse terra cotta, of which so many were discovered by Schliemann at Mycenæ, and now to be seen in the Athens Museum. The illustrations herewith (Fig. 68) are from the writer's own sketches from the original painted pottery at Athens, but a coloured plate of one of them appears in Schliemann's book on Tiryns and Mycenæ. He calls them Hera images, and the strange association of the female form with the crescent rather confirms the opinion that these were the household gods (like

---

[295] Eustath. *ap.* Dionys. Perieg. 92, 94. Also Jablonsky, *Pantheon,* ii. p. 4.
[296] Diod. Sic. i. 11.   Plutarch, *De Is. et Os.* 52.   Macrobius, *Sat.* i. 19.
[297] O. Müller, *Dorier,* i. 121.   Steph. Byz. *s.v.* Βυζάντιον.
[298] Bostock, note to Pliny's *Nat. Hist.* vol. i. p. 326 (Bohn).

Penates or Teraphim) of those ancient Greeks, who
relied upon their protection against the evil eye.[299]
They certainly belong to that class of objects, of
which we have other striking examples. They are
in any case very remarkable evidences of the em-
blematic treatment of a divinity at a very early date ;
for it must be admitted that the use of the crescent
as the body of the figure in each of the many
examples at Athens is of itself remarkable, and it
is certainly reasonable to maintain that all relate
to one and the same personality.

When the several attributes of the various deities
came to be represented by concrete shapes, as,
for example, the "lowing one" by horns, the
early figurative significations were forgotten, and
they became so mixed up, confused, and conventionalised, that a cow - face, a crescent, or a cow's
horns stood alike for Isis, Hathor, Iö, Hera, or
Demeter ; while an owl represented Athena as the
type of wisdom and as one of the goddesses of the
dawn. In fact the cow, the crescent, the horns,
and the owl became their recognised attributes or
symbols—precisely as in Christian art the man's

[299] Freeman (*Studies of Travel, Greece*, p. 141) says of the objects found at
Mycenæ, that they are " of an age which, though beyond the reach of
chronology, we can hardly call unrecorded . . . they are work of the period
which Homer sung" : consequently, they were historically ancient even in
his day.

"Hera, Iö, and Isis (Hathor) must at all events be identical also with
Demeter Mycalessia, who derived her epithet, 'the lowing,' from her cow-
shape, and had her temple at Mycalessus in Bœotia. She had as doorkeeper
Hercules, whose office it was to shut her sanctuary in the evening and open
it again in the morning. This service is identical with that of Argus, who in
the morning unfastened the cow-shaped Iö, and fastened her again in the
evening to the olive-tree which was in the sacred grove of Mycenæ.

"Iö-Hera, as deity of the moon, would receive her epithet βοωπίς from
the symbolic horns of the crescent moon, and its dark spots, resembling a face
with large eyes ; whilst Athena, as goddess of the dawn, doubtless received
the epithet γλαυκωπίς, the owl-faced, to indicate the light of the opening
day."—Schliemann, *Mycenæ*, p. 21.

face, the winged lion, the bull, and the eagle have become the recognised symbols or attributes of the four Evangelists.

Having then shown that the same symbols represented beings which originally were held to be distinct and separate, it is not difficult to see how their separate identities became lost, and from the same symbol each and all would at last come to be regarded as one and the same person. Not only a number of goddesses did actually become mixed and confused into one, but several of the gods likewise.

" Jove, Pluto, Phœbus, Bacchus, all are one," was sung by Orpheus,[300] thus adopting the grand principle of Hindooism—that all the various deities are but names for the different attributes of the Almighty one. In further confirmation of this idea, we find that Virgil treated Bacchus the Wine God, the god of orgies and debauch, as only another form, we may call it an effect, of the life-giving, wine-producing sun. He makes Bacchus and Ceres stand for Osiris and Isis, the sun and moon, typified in the disc and crescent. Hence Bacchus is often represented with horns.[301] " In Hebrew a 'radiated' and a 'horned' head is signified by the same word. Hence, when Moses came down from the Mount, *cornuta fuit facies ejus*, according to the Vulgate ; and in virtue of this mistranslation hath the Lawgiver ever been graced with those appendages." [302]

---

[300] King, *Gnostics*, p. 83. The above takes for granted the identity of Roman and Greek divinities, in thus translating Ζεύς, Ἀΐδης, Ἥλιος, Διόνυσος.

[301] Among the Gnostic gems in the British Museum is a figure of the mummied Osiris with very distinct horns on his head.

[302] King, *Gnostics*, p. 84. In Pignorius, *Expositio Mensæ Isiacæ*, p. 15 *in dorso*, is a head of a man, with horns growing out of his forehead, from an ancient relief.

Without entering into the nice controversy here foreshadowed, it is quite enough for the present purpose to point to the fact that the authors of the Vulgate translation believed, from their own training and habit, that the Hebrew meaning was that the great, almost divine Moses, came down with actual horns upon his head. Moreover, this view has been actually maintained by more than one commentator.[303]

As with gods, so with regard to goddesses, we find the same pervading idea ; and as we proceed, this will have constant illustration in the manifold combination of attributes certainly relating to one and the same being, but in their inception belonging to many distinct personifications.

"Apuleius quoque Isin—Deum Matrem, Minervam, Junonem, Dianam, Cererem, Venerem, Proserpinam, Hecatem unam, eandemque esse prædicat."[304] If then all these various goddesses, like

[303] Smith's *Dictionary of the Bible*, s.v. "Horn."

Michael Angelo's famous statue in San Pietro in Vincoli, of which a copy exists at South Kensington, whereon the horns are very concrete in substance, serves to show the continuance of the old classic notions referred to above. That horns are typified by the shape of a bishop's mitre is well known, and the belief that Moses had actual solid horns must have been firmly held in the Middle Ages. Bishop Reginald of Bath, 1174-1191, is represented on his seal as having actual horns projecting from his head while in the act of benediction, besides the conventional ones of his mitre. Moreover, it is evident that horns were typified by the points of the mitre and were believed to have the power of keeping off evil and of appearing terrible to evil persons. The words now used in the consecration of a bishop in the Roman Church fully keep alive this belief. In placing the mitre on the head of the newly-consecrated prelate, the consecrator says : "We set on the head of this prelate, Thy champion, the helmet of defence and of salvation, that with comely face, and with his head armed with the horns of either Testament, he may appear terrible to the gainsayers of the truth," etc.— "Order of Consecration of a Bishop-elect." Translated from *The Roman Pontifical* (Burns and Oates, 1893), p. 14.

[304] *Symbolica Dianæ Ephesiæ*, p. 10. The author continues, "nevertheless celebrated by diverse names, and worshipped by various races in many different ways" (*multiplici specie*), "Isis, Hathor, Aphrodite, and Venus are all one and the same personage" (Payne Knight, *Symb. Lang. of Anc. Art*, p. 35).

the gods sung by Orpheus, are "one and the same"
—mere names representing various attributes of one
great divinity—our oft-recurring difficulty in explaining the strange combination of charms in one complex amulet, vanishes, and that which was obscure
becomes quite clear.[305]

The remarkable inscription found by Lanciani
(see p. 129) does but confirm what we are trying to
make plain, that one and the same deity appears
over and over again under different names, representing diverse attributes.

To return to Isis : she "sometimes signifies the
Moon when she is represented by a crescent ; sometimes the Earth, as fecundated by the waters of the
Nile.   Hence water, as the issue of Osiris, is carried
in a vase in her processions.   Osiris is signified by
an eye, also by an eye and a sceptre combined :
his name being compounded of *Os*, many ; and *Iris*,
eye." [306]   We have seen how completely Isis, Artemis,
and Diana were identical, and hence all three are
habitually represented with the horned crescent, as
their particular accompaniment or symbol : and
further by the cow's head or cow's horns so often
seen.   When we speak of Diana the chaste huntress,
it is manifestly under a very different aspect from
that of the Ephesian Diana, whose typical statues
are to be seen at Naples and elsewhere.   Fig. 69 is
from Menetrius,[307] and represents one of the Roman
ideas of the Ephesian goddess.   In these statues
the great feature is the numerous mammæ which

---

[305] On this subject see *La Migration des Symboles*, par le Comte Goblet
d'Alviella, Paris, 1892.

[306] King, *Gnostics*, p. 42.

[307] *Symbolica Dianæ Ephesiæ Statua*, a Claudio Menetrio.   Romæ.   Typis
Mascardi, MDCLVII.   The loan of this rare book, with permission to copy,
has cleared up the Siren question in Chap. X.

mark her as the type of human fertility. This latter conception is of purely Asiatic origin, though the

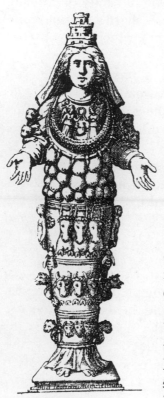

FIG. 69.

same fertility was ascribed to Isis; moreover, the Diana of Ephesus whose "image fell down from Jupiter," is, like Isis, allowed to be in that aspect the same person as the Indian Parvati. The multiplicity of mammæ was the symbol of abundance of nutriment. The same symbols are used in representations of the Babylonian Ishtar and the Indian Devaki.[308] The wide difference between the fertile matron of Ephesus and the chaste maiden of the Romans has to be carefully borne in mind. The illustrations we give in Chap. X. of statues of the former, show how the Romans ignored the most prominent of her Asiatic attributes, and portrayed her, by way of compromise, as a portly female of uncertain status, rather suggestive of her patronage, as Diana Lucina, of the monthly nurse.

Looking at Isis as the mother of Horus,[309] in the

---

[308] "St. Jerome says Diana of Ephesus was called *Multimammia*." Several paps were ascribed to Isis also. Isis had sometimes a flower on her head; Diana always a tower (Montfaucon, vol. i. p. 96).

[309] Pignorius, *Expositio Mensæ Isiacæ* (*Vetustissimæ Tabulæ*), p. 16, alludes to Mercury having placed horns made out of the head of a cow upon the head

act of nursing him (Fig. 70, from Wilkinson, iii.
112), one of the commonest forms in which she is
represented, and remembering, too, that in the use
of the same symbols, those of the crescent and horns,

FIG. 70.   FIG. 71.[310a]

she was succeeded by Artemis and Diana, one cannot
but be struck with the wonderful similarity between
her and the present-day Madonna and Child.

In one of the rock chambers at Silsilis on the
Nile, is a relief of Isis suckling Horus, said[310] to be
"one of the most perfect specimens of Egyptian
sculpture at its best period." It is treated in such a
manner, and without the usual head ornaments, that
one would be ready to believe the old Italian
painters Lippi and Botticelli must have gone there,

of Isis. He also later refers to the horns upon the head of Moses: "qui a
congressu Domini Dei Exercituum faciem cornutam referebat."
[310] Murray's *Handbook for Egypt*, 1888, p. 517.
[310a] Fig. 71 is from an ancient bronze in possession of the author.
Similar ones are common in most Egyptian museums.

and have made true copies of what they saw, to be
reproduced at home as the "Holy Family." In
India, the infant Chrishna, the incarnate deity, in the
arms of Devaki, is another very striking example [311]
(Fig. 72) of precisely the same subject. Moreover,
in this the child is black with woolly hair—a thing

FIG. 72.

strange in India. Those who have seen the black
figure at the top of the Scala Santa at Rome will
not fail to be struck with the remarkable resemblance
not only of the mother and child, but of the ray of
light or nimbus round both heads. It is of a piece
with the black Virgins to be seen elsewhere. [312]

[311] From Moor's *Hindoo Pantheon*, Plate lix.
[312] The idea is, however, distinctly foreign to the uneducated Italian mind.
Having taken an old Italian servant who had lived with us in Florence to
Rome, she of course made her pilgrimage to the Scala Santa and devoutly
ascended on her knees. The thing which struck and astonished her most on

In the statues of Diana of Ephesus (supposed to
represent the original "image which fell down") at
Naples and elsewhere, the face, hands, and feet, are
of black marble, showing that it was intended to represent a black goddess; and it is maintained by some writers that the primæval belief of mankind was that the
Mother of the Gods was black.[313]

Ishtar was adored in ancient Baby-

beholding the famous painting was that he was black.
"Ma! non ho capito mai che fu Moro!" was her first
remark.

Upon the remarkable halo surrounding the heads of both
the Indian mother and child one might almost say that it
belonged to a Christian work and not a heathen. The
nimbus is, however, far older than the nineteen centuries of
Christendom. Rays were said to have proceeded from the
head of Isis; and they have been called the proper attributes of Juno, of Isis, or the "Mother of the Gods"
(Pignorius, *Vetustissimæ Tabulæ*, p. 16).

FIG. 73.

[313] Inman, *Ancient Faiths embodied in Ancient Names*, vol. i. p. 105.

A learned writer remarks that not only was Diana black, but that so was
Christna of the Hindoos. Isis, Horus, Cneph, Osiris, Buddha, Mercury,
and the Roman Terminus, were typified by black stones. There was a black
Venus at Corinth. "Venus, Isis, Hecate, Diana, Juno, Metis, Ceres, and
Cybele, were black, and the Multimammia in the Campidoglio in Rome is
also black." To this list are added Jupiter, Apollo, Bacchus, Hercules,
Asteroth, Adonis, Apis, Ammon. The same author states that the Roman
and Greek emperors who claimed to be gods, had their statues in black
marble with coloured draperies (Higgins, *Anacalypsis*, vol. i. p. 286).

The famous Virgin of Einsiedeln in Switzerland, to whom 150,000 pilgrims
annually resort, is a black image. Black is appropriated to the female creator
for reasons given, but not here producible, by all Oriental nations (Inman,
Ancient Faiths, p. 266).

Higgins in his very remarkable book (*Anacalypsis*) gives much learning
and many references : indeed, we strongly urge those who are interested in
this particular subject to study the book. He says, in speaking of the negro
Chrishna, that he presumes man to have been originally negro, and that he
improved and developed as he travelled westward (vol. i. p. 284). He also
refers to Venus and the other divinities as all black ; and remarks (p. 286)
that "all wood and stone deities were black." This is not quite the fact in
these modern days. In the Pitt Rivers Museum is a Siva, having a trinity of
heads ; while besides the principal pair of arms, are three other subsidiary
pairs, all rising one over the other. The three faces all show tusks like the
Cambodian and Peruvian Gorgons, without a protruded tongue ; but the
whole figure is black. On the other hand, Thagya, the Buddhist Angel of
Life, a wooden figure, is represented as of a light colour.

Another author (Lieut. Wilford, "On Egypt and the Nile, from the
Ancient Books of the Hindus," *Asiatic Researches*, vol. iii. pp. 389, 406) says :

lon much in the same manner as the Virgin is now ; and amongst her other titles was "The Mother of the Gods."[314]   Fig. 73 is Ishtar, from Rawlinson's *Ancient Monarchies*, vol. i. p. 176.   The same figure is reproduced in Layard, *Nineveh and Babylon*, p. 477 ; and in Inman, *Ancient Faiths*, vol. ii. p. 254.   (See Appendix I.)

Again, the analogy of Diana Lucina and Diana Pronuba, the goddess of childbirth and of marriage,

FIG. 74.[314a]

represented by the crescent, is well preserved in her successor the Madonna del parto, who in the well-known attribute of "Madonna Immaculata,"[315] is always depicted as standing on the crescent.   It is easy to trace the chain of ideas.   We must not forget that in one of her aspects Diana was a tree spirit or sylvan deity. Like the tree spirits before referred to, she helped women in travail.[316]

Somewhat allied to the foregoing is the belief

"It cannot reasonably be doubted that a race of negroes had formerly preeminence in India."   Professor Huxley says Australians believe white men to be the reincarnated spirits of black men (*Science and Hebrew Tradition*, 1893, p. 317).   [314] Inman, *op. cit.* vol. ii. p. 254.

[314a] Fig. 74 is the Hindu Indranee and Child (from *Journ. Asiat. Res.* vi. 393), and is one more example of the all-pervading belief in the same motherhood.

[315] In the Museo del Prado at Madrid are the masterpieces of Murillo's *vaporosa* style, representing this subject.   All these, as well as the more famous but less beautiful replica in the Louvre, represent the central figure as standing on the crescent.

[316] Roscher, *Lexikon d. Griech. u. Röm. Mythologie*, 1007.

in what is understood by immaculate conception—
another of those remarkable instincts which seem to
have existed throughout the ages, and long antecedent
to the Jewish prophecies.   In the far East the
Persian Mazda worshippers looked for the birth of a
Saviour from a virgin mother.   In the sacred books
of Zoroaster we read : "We worship the guardian
spirit of the holy maid Esetât-Jedhri, who is called
the all-conquering, for she will bring him forth who
will destroy the malice of the demons and of men." [317]
It was this firm belief which brought the Magi,
many long centuries after the above was written,
from the land of Zoroaster to worship Him whom
they had heard of, as born of a virgin to be the
King of the Jews.   Ages upon ages earlier still, the
belief was current in Egypt, for, according to some,
Aroeris or the Elder Horus (the Greek Apollo) was
born of Isis from a conception previous to her own
birth; [318] and we constantly see the unmistakable
foreshadowing by Isis and Horus of the latter day
Madonna e Bambino.

We know, too, that both Greeks and Romans
fully believed in the facts implied, and they further
believed that certain plants had the property of
rendering women pregnant.

Diana was called the "Mother of the World," [319]
strangely like the title given to the Babylonian
Ishtar.   The Egyptian priests styled the moon,
whose personification was Isis, "The Mother of
the Universe." [320]

[317] Dr. L. H. Mills, "Zoroaster and the Bible," in *Nineteenth Century*, Jan.
1894, p. 51.   [318] Wilkinson, *Anc. Egyp.* iii. 61.
[319] Payne Knight, *Symb. Lang.* p. 99.
[320] Plutarch, *De Isid. et Osir.* p. 48.
Diana was frequently represented by a sea-crab (Payne Knight, *op. cit.*
p. 100), a symbol often placed upon her statues, and to be seen upon the

Domestic cattle were supposed to be under the special protection of Diana, hence we may well trace the extreme prevalence of amulets, symbolic of her attributes, upon horses. Diana was also identified through Artemis with the Greek Ilithya, the servant of Hera, and goddess of birth. She also was originally a moon-goddess, and the moon was always believed to exercise great influence on growth in general, but especially of children ; so the attributes of Ilithya were passed on along with her moon-symbol, and consequently all those deities, ancient or modern, whose principal sign is the crescent, are looked upon as the special protectors of women and children against malign influence. The wearing of the crescent is a visible worship of the powerful being whose symbol it is, whether known as Isis, Parvati, Devaki, Kali,[321] Bhavani, Artemis, Athena, Minerva, Diana or Madonna, who are all, as shown before, *unam eandemque.*

Seeing how every phase or attribute of nature had its special divinity, we are not surprised to learn that, in Imperial times, according to Varro, there were in Rome three temples on the Esquiline dedicated to the goddess of fever, and one to Mephitis. Readers of Tacitus will remember that a temple of

---

breast of the Ephesian Artemis (Fig. 69). She was the sovereign of humidity, her nymphs or subordinate personifications came to her from the ocean. She was the protectress of women, the patroness and regulator of nutrition, and of passive generation both in man and beast. As among the ancients " the moon's orbit was held to be the boundary between the celestial and terrestrial world, so Diana was held to be the mediatrix between the two."

[321] " Kali, one character of Bhavani, appears in sculpture as a terminal figure, the exact counterpart of the Ephesian Diana. Even the stags, those singular adjuncts to the shoulders of the latter, are seen in a similar position springing from Kali's hands. The numerous breasts of the Ephesian statue were also peculiar to Isis, who is allowed to be the Indian goddess in her form Parvati."—King, *Gnostics*, p. 171.

Mephitis was the only building left standing after the sack of Cremona.   There was also an altar dedicated to the evil eye (*Mala Fortuna*).   " Near the Prætorian Camp, there was an altar to Verminus, god of microbes, and in the very centre of the Forum an altar to Cloacina, the goddess of typhoid." Those who know the spot can join the writer in testifying that she still reigns there with unabated power.   The example of ancient Rome does but illustrate how ignorant people fly to the supernatural and miraculous, whenever attacked by evils of which they cannot understand the cause.   Hence the increase of divinities in pagan times, when not only aspects of nature, but every disease, and almost every idea, had its personification.   In mediæval days there was no advance in real belief, but simply a transfer of these old-world ideas : having set up separate deities, they merely transposed them into attributes of the great Christian goddess, successor of Diana, whose cult then became all-supreme.   It is a curious fact that when Rome, after the fall of the Empire, relapsed into its insanitary condition, the old worship re-appeared in another shape, and a chapel arose near the Vatican to the " Madonna della Febre," [322] the most popular in Rome, in times of sickness or epidemic.

As a parallel to this, here in Britain, " the goddess of love was turned into St. Brychan's daughter ; and as late as the fourteenth century lovers are said to have come from all parts to pray at her shrine in Anglesea."   Another similar example " is found in the confusion of St. Bridget and an Irish goddess whose gifts were poetry, fire, and medicine.   The

[322] Lanciani, *Ancient Rome*, pp. 44, 52 *et seq.*

saint became the Queen of Heaven, and was adored as 'Mary of the Gael'; but almost all the incidents in her legend can be referred to the pagan ritual." [323]

Having sketched briefly the cult which may be called Isis-Diana worship, whose principal attributes were symbolised by the horned moon, we arrive at the conclusion that, to-day, horns, in one form or another, are of all objects the most common as amulets against the evil eye, whether affecting man or beast; so much so that it has at last come to be fully believed by Neapolitans that, in default of a horn of some shape in the concrete, the mere utterance of the word *corno* or *corna* is an effectual protection. [323a] Further than this, the common name by which every charm or amulet against the evil eye is known, even the most elaborate, such as the *Cimaruta*, or *Mano Pantea*, is simply "*un corno.*"

In one of her aspects Hecate was identical with the Gorgon, and hence we find very numerous instances, widely separated in locality, of the Medusa being furnished with horns. In Fig. 53, from the Paris Exhibition of 1889, though the moustaches seem to imply a male face, yet it is one of several hideous masks, all of which are ornamented with horns, while the eyebrows and moustaches are alike formed of the black horns of smaller animals. Some, from Cambodia, may, with every reason, be considered to represent the oriental Bhavani, the original of the Greek Gorgoneion. From Senegal were exhibited many roughly-carved wooden figures— images or gods, but mostly with horns projecting

[323] Elton, *Origins of Eng. Hist.* 2nd ed. p. 269.
[323a] Jorio, *Mimica degli Antichi*, p. 92.

high above the head. There were two head-dresses ornamented with cowries, charms in themselves; but above each head-dress there were two antelope horns standing up conspicuously. The central object of the exhibits at Paris from Senegal was a typical house, ornamented at the four corners of the roof with large cow's horns turned upwards. From

FIG. 75.

Tahiti was exhibited an idol, with two large horns on its head carved in wood; moreover, this figure had the right hand raised with palm exposed.[324]

Fig. 75 is from Peru,[325] and the horns on this mask are of much the same character as those found in Tahiti (Fig. 53).

[324] In the British Museum there are two masks from Ceylon. That for a man has a large boar's tusk by way of horn projecting from each side. That for a horse has one long upright horn, like that of a unicorn.

[325] *Pérou et Bolivie*, Ch. Wiener, Paris, 1880, p. 649.

On p. 44 Wiener gives a plate showing the interior of a tomb. Above the group of figures and utensils it contains, is fixed, near the apex of the roof, a large mask with immense horns. This is evidently an amulet to protect the dead.

Fig. 76 is a horned Medusa from the bust of one of the Emperors, in the Doria Gallery in Rome, showing that, in the time of the Empire, horns had

FIG. 76.

been applied to the Medusa, in addition to the retention of her hideousness. These examples are sufficient to show that in all parts of the world not only is the Bhavani-Gorgoneion used as an amulet, but to add to its power, horns have been given to it; whether or not these are to replace the snakes does not appear.[326] Later we shall show how the horns of the crescent are represented by a snake, thus combining the efficacy of two separate symbols into one powerful charm. Not only is the horn found upon the head of the dead Medusa, but in many places upon the head of the living man. In the many passages of Scripture, where it is mentioned, the horn seems to have become the emblem of dignity and honour, though it may originally have been adopted as an amulet.[326a] There is some reason for this suggestion from the analogy

[326] Later developments of the Medusa show it with wings, while the snakes are conventionalised into curls. Such is the face in the well-known triskelion of Sicily, of which Fig. 133 is a good representation. We cannot help noticing the strange coincidence of the winged face of the Medusa with those winged faces called "cherubs" so very commonly seen on funereal monuments of the last century, and as attending in crowds the Madonna Immaculata, when standing on her crescent, especially in Murillo's pictures called *vaporosas*.

[326a] In Ilton Church, Somerset, is the figure of a "horned" lady, of whom a print will be found in *Som. and Dor. Notes and Queries*, December 1894.

of the phylactery, an undoubted amulet, worn as a "frontlet" for a protection against the evil eye.

We know how in our Lord's time the wearing of these had become a fashion ; how they got to be enlarged and exaggerated, until they were looked upon as a badge of sanctity, a mark of worldly honour. So much had they become, in this way, the instruments of hypocrisy, that they brought upon the Pharisees the Master's denunciation. Why should not the use of both phylactery and horn have had the same origin? The defiling of his horn in the dust by Job (xvi. 15) and the exalting of his horn by the Psalmist (lxxxix. 17, 24 ; xcii. 10) seem both to point in the same direction, and to show that it was worn as a mark of distinction—something to attract attention and to bespeak respect. In the present day, the curious spiral ornaments worn on each side of the head by Dutch women, must surely be something more than a mere coincidence, in their resemblance to the ram's horns so often seen upon the heads of Jupiter and Bacchus. The women of the Druses of Lebanon wear silver horns upon their heads, larger or smaller, to distinguish the married from the single. The writer can bear witness that the Jewesses of Tunis also wear, as part of their regular costume, a sort of pointed cap, much higher on the matron than the maid. It is quite well understood there that this head-dress is the survival of the Scriptural horn. In South Africa [327] the women of some tribes ornament their heads with buffalo horns. Horns are worn as amulets by Africans of both sexes ; [328] and we see that

[327] Livingstone, *Missionary Travels*, pp. 430-431. See also Smith, *Bib. Dict.* s.v. "Horn." [328] Livingstone, *Zambesi*, c. xxv. p. 523.

Fig. 77.—From Catlin, i. 146.

elsewhere they are not now restricted to female wear, any more than in the time of David. Catlin[329] gives portraits of many North American Indians who wear the skins of bisons on their heads with the horns attached. We reproduce one (Fig. 77), that of *Mah-to-wo-pa*, as it contains another important amulet, besides the very conspicuous horns upon his head. Also it should be noted that on his spear are two horns, with a feather close by in a conspicuous place, to draw attention to them, like the pheasant's tail on the Neapolitan harness. Not only, however, were these worn on the head of the savage, but on the *helmet* of the warrior, as a crest which his enemy might not fail to see, in case the shield, bearing some other amulet, should not attract the first fatal glance. In the Naples Museum and in that of the Louvre are several ancient Greek bronze helmets (Figs. 78, 79). Each one bears a pair of branching horns of flat plate much of the same

FIG. 78.   FIG. 79.

From Naples Museum.

shape as the conventional horns of Isis. In the Louvre is a full-sized Greek helmet of gold,[330] having the high branching horns.[331] The helmet of the ancient Belgian

---

[329] Catlin, *North American Indians.* 2 vols. 1844.

[330] A drawing of this helmet is given in Daremberg et Saglio, p. 1534.

[331] The ancient Etruscans wore a helmet with horns precisely like one of those here shown (Fig. 78). Like it there was a small square fork upon the apex, apparently for fixing some crest or plume to add to the attractiveness of the whole. An Etruscan helmet of this shape is given by Gen. Forlong, *Rivers of Life,* vol. ii. p. 254, Pl. xii. In the *Bullettino Archeologico Napoletano* (An. II. Tav. XI.) is a man on horseback, apparently an ancient Roman or Greek soldier. From the back of his helmet rise two large horns, forming a complete crescent, while at the same time preserving their distinct horn shape; even the rings at the root of a cow's horn are well indicated. In the British Museum is an Anglo-Saxon helmet with two large horns. There is also an ancient Mexican helmet

"was ornamented with horns and a high plume."[332] We may reasonably conclude that the high plume was not only ornamental, but, like the pheasants' tails now stuck on horses' heads, was intended to attract the eye of the malevolent and to direct it upon the protecting horns.   Who will undertake to assert that the horns on the Greek, Etruscan, Belgic, or Saxon warrior, were worn for a purpose different from those on the head of Catlin's Mandan chief?

Besides those borne on the helmet by Greeks and others, horns were worn as amulets by man and beast ;

FIG. 80.

so they are to this day.   The ancient Egyptian one (Fig. 80) is from the Ashmolean Museum, Oxford.   It is carved out of cornelian or some hard stone.   Horns of this kind are often thus made at Constantinople, of two tusks united, or like this, carved out of fine stone so as to form a crescent.

Among the Louvre ancient gems are horns of agate set in gold with eyelets for suspension, especially Nos. 726, 727, while No. 729 has three horns so set.   Compare this with the modern Italian charm, the hand holding three coral horns suspended, see centre of Fig. 81.[333]

Necklaces and bracelets formed of suspended crescents and horned heads of oxen are common in every collection of ancient jewellery.[334]

with large horns.   The attachment of horns to the helmet by way of special protection must have been quite familiar to the writers of Isaiah (lix. 17) and Ep. to Ephesians (vi. 17).   The horns made it the helmet of salvation or of safety.   This idea is rather confirmed by 1 Thess. v. 8, where it is called the " hope of salvation," implying the belief in its efficient protection.

[332] Elton, *Origins of Eng. History*, 2nd ed. p. 113.

[333] Plutarch says (Daremberg et Saglio, p. 168) that horns of stags were offered to Diana ; horns of all kinds, we know, are symbolical of her.

[334] At the Louvre are many—Nos. 196, 198 especially should be noted.

There is abundant evidence, moreover, that our own British forefathers wore these things, for in the

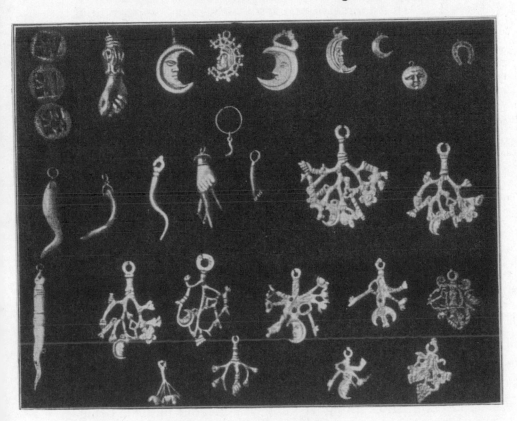

FIG. 81.—From the Author's Collection.

tumuli which have been opened in various places in England, have been found "crescents made of wolves'

No. 198 is a necklace with eight horned heads as pendants, precisely like those ornamenting the front of the statue of the Ephesian Diana, Fig. 69. No. 196 has the head of Jupiter Serapis, of a larger size than the *capo di bove*, as the single pendant, with two horns. This is a very fine specimen, and the head may well be compared to that of Moses. "The most ancient altars were adorned with horns" (upon this see Potter, *Arch. Græc.* i. 229), while the expression "horns of the altar" in Psalm cxviii. 27 is familiar to all.

teeth and boars' tusks, which were perforated and worn as charms." [335]

In a Dorsetshire barrow was found a perforated boar's tusk.[336] Crescents made of boars' tusks are favourite ornaments on horses' breasts in Constantinople, where dread of the evil eye for his horse makes the Turk forget his antipathy to the pig.

In Naples, horns both in the form of crescents and like those of animals are as common as blackberries, upon the trappings of horses. Examples of each are to be seen in Figs. 83, 84; but the single pendent horn, whether of brass or white metal, of silver, coral, pearl, or bone, may be said to be almost invariable upon man and beast in Italy. A horn of one or other of these materials is to be seen hanging to the watch-chain of nearly every Italian one meets, who wears any such things; while many wear them as hidden charms on the breast, next the skin.[337]

Of the common Neapolitan cart harness, shown on Fig. 82, the ornaments are literally made up of charms and prophylactics. Photogravure cannot adequately represent this, for it fails to show that the whole thing is kept very bright; and all being of polished brass, it has a flashing and most attractive appearance, which cannot be overlooked, in any sense of the word. On his head the horse carries a

---

[335] Elton, *Orig. of Eng. Hist.* 2nd ed. p. 145.

[336] *Archæologia*, xliii. 540, quoted by Elton, *op. cit.* p. 145.

[337] " Mascagni, like so many other Italian artists, is also said to carry in his pockets an extraordinary collection of amulets against the superstition of the 'evil eye,' the list including corals, horns of mother-of-pearl, ivory, and ebony, some of them bearing the effigy of his patron saint, St. George, besides a goodly number of lucky chestnuts."—*Daily News*, June 23, 1893. Much more is said about horns as a Neapolitan hand-gesture in Chap. VII.

FIG. 82.—From the Author's Collection.

bell, with four jingling clappers, surmounted by a crescent; another crescent, having horns pointing downwards, shows beneath the bell. On the off cheek is a piece of the inevitable wolf skin, a warning to every *versipelle* whose wicked eye may light upon the horse. Outside the wolf skin is a bunch of bright, many-coloured ribbons, and upon them is hung the single pendent horn. The colours, which do not come out in the photograph, as before explained, are a part of the business, for coloured threads and ribbons enter largely into all matters relating to witchcraft. Besides all these things, the bridle or head-stall is bedecked with a pheasant's tail, another attractive object to be seen on nearly every Neapolitan or Roman horse's head - gear. The bright brass-plating, engraved with saints or angels, completes this powerful battery of resisting charms, so that an evil glance must be fully absorbed, baffled, or exhausted before it can fix itself upon the animal.

It may be well here to point out other peculiarities of horse gear which, though so very common in Naples, are not generally known, and perhaps have passed unnoticed by many, who are familiar with the general appearance. There is no bit in the horse's mouth, but a metal plate with two projecting arms rests on the nasal bone above the nostrils; to these the reins are attached, and a subsidiary strap, on each side passing through a ring, is fastened to a jointed plate with rough edges resting on the under jaw opposite the nose plate. Any pull on this latter causes the nose and jaw to be held in a powerful grip, far more effective than a common bit. Nearly all the cab horses are driven with a contrivance of this kind.

Neapolitan horses being small, and the carts having very high wheels, the shafts have to be kept at a considerable distance above the animal's back, and the loads are so adjusted as to bear very little on him. The very high pommel and brightly-plated saddle are peculiar to Southern Italy and Sicily. In Naples the two brazen flags, swinging about, above the horse's back, are almost invariable. They are said to be typical of the "flaming sword which turned every way" (Gen. iii. 24), and they are no doubt intended as part of the guard, protecting the life of the horse bearing them ; for they are an unfailing attraction to the eye whether evil or not.[338] The high pommel ends in another patch of wolf skin and more red worsted round the spindle of the vanes.[339] The figure standing upon the little round barrel at the back of the pommel is San Gennaro. This ornament varies according to the fancy of the

---

[338] "The flaming sword finds its analogue in the weapon of the Babylonian god Merodach, a revolving circular disc surrounded with flaming points. This weapon is called among other names *littu*, which is letter for letter the same as the Hebrew word translated flaming."—Lenormant, *Les Origines de l'Histoire d'après la Bible et les Traditions des Peuples Orientaux*. *Athenæum*, July 31, 1880, p. 137.

[339] I have often seen here in Somersetshire (even so late as 1894) cart horses, each with a bunch of many-coloured ribbons on his cheek, and others with a half-moon on the forehead. One of our commonest of crest ornaments is a small disc pivoted, in a kind of horned or crescent-shaped frame, which swings backwards and forwards glinting in the sun, as the horse moves his head. Surely this is the Babylonian disc of Merodach, analogous to the Neapolitan vanes, and moreover it must represent also the disc and horns on the head of Isis. If not, the coincidence is strange indeed. Further, Pluto was represented with a disc on his head like Venus and Isis (Payne Knight, *Symb. Lang.* p. 104). From Pluto to Vulcan the step is short, and they may well be confounded. If then our disc is the symbol of Vulcan, it is a most suitable horse amulet. A disc framed like this, but having also a face upon it, is on the Barone lamp in Chap. X. Not long ago I saw what I remember as very common—the " vore 'oss " of a team had a board about 18 inches long mounted on two irons, which held it well above the collar into which they fitted. This board had hung beneath it a row of about six large jangling bells which, when the horse moves, can be heard for half a mile. To complete this pixy-driving apparatus is a fringe concealing all the bells, but made of the inevitable, bright, many coloured worsted threads.

owner, but the little round barrel is invariable, so is the row of studs on the front of the pommel ; but I have never been able to learn the meaning of

FIG. 83.—From the Author's Collection.

either. These pommels are, however, like the prows of Venetian gondolas, all alike.

In Figs. 83 and 84 are examples of amulets, one or more of which are to be found upon every cab horse in Naples. The small branching horns at the left

corner of Fig. 84 are carried on his head between
his ears, and very few horses are to be seen without
this particular article, though of course varied in form ;

FIG. 84. — From the Author's Collection.

some are of brass and some of white metal. The
pendent horn next the pair of horns, is that which
is worn on the off cheek with the ribbons, wolf skin,
and pheasant's tail. The pendent crescents are
often worn fastened upon the loin strap on each side,
as well as on the forehead—a favourite place for a

half-moon, just as it is here in Somerset. All the other amulets shown on both figures are screwed into the pommel of the little pad on the horse's back, and in some cases form a stud for the bearing rein. In one, the screw by which it is fixed is shown. All these are avowedly carried *contra la jettatura*, and each owner chooses the one he thinks most effectual or ornamental. This is anything but an exhaustive collection, yet it very well represents the horse furniture of to-day. It is the result of many and long-separated visits to the shops, well known to the writer, where these things are made. Each may be taken as typical of the class of amulet to which it belongs, but there are many varieties of each kind, and of many more among the thousands of Neapolitan *carosselle*, which could not be procured unless specially ordered.

Of all the different objects upon the horses' backs, and no back is without one, by far the most numerous are the hands, in various positions or gestures. On a long rank of fourteen *carosselle*, we once saw three horses only which did not carry a hand. Of course this was rather exceptional, but it would be no exaggeration to say that up to a year or two ago, nearly every other cab horse in Naples carried a hand on his back. We shall speak of each of these horse amulets separately in its proper turn, but would here point out that the placing of the book in the paw of the lion, making him the "leone di San Marco," is the only visible sign, at least among the cabmen, of the thin veneer of Christianity, commonly overlaid upon Neapolitan paganism. In Rome these articles are not seen on horses' backs, though wolf skins, pheasants' tails, horns and crescents are plentiful enough. There, however, differing from Naples, are to be seen large quantities of silver rings, for human fingers, with a little pendent horn attached, like the one in Fig. 81. These are strung on rods, fifty or sixty in a row, and marked plainly in the shop windows, " Annelli contra la jettatura." That here shown was bought in the Piazza di Spagna.[340]

We are told [341] that petrified sharks' teeth owing to their tongue or horn shape were used as amulets against fascination in ancient times; probably they were fastened together, as boars' tusks are to-day, to form crescents.

Another singular form of horn amulet, is that of the combination of the two heads and fore legs of horned animals into a nondescript, as shown in Figs. 31-37. It will be seen later, from the illustrations of *Cavalli Marini* and other impossible animals, that charms made of a double-headed creature were rather favourites.

Horns were used as handles in various shapes for lamps of various kinds. Sometimes, as in Fig. 85, they have the crescent plainly marked with the name of the Ephesian Artemis, and in others, the plain crescent without knobs; plenty of these latter are to be seen at the Naples and other museums. Others again had handles of branching cows' horns, still pointing to the same deity in her cow-faced form (Fig. 86). Many of these lamps bore more than the single amulet of the handle: sometimes one, but often a number of objects are found upon them. That here shown has a scorpion upon it; a very

[340] I fear that in Rome articles of this kind have begun to find a place among the spurious curios called *roba Americana*, and expect soon to find the demand producing a like supply in Naples.

[341] Dodwell, *Class. Tour*, vol. ii. p. 34.

common central ornament was a Medusa's head, perhaps found more frequently than any other on this kind of lamp, belonging to pagan times. These

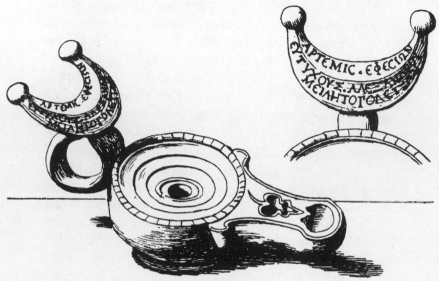

FIG. 85.—From *Symbolica Dianæ Ephesiæ Statua.*

lamps are generally of bronze, though often of terra cotta. Subsequently, in the Christian period, the central ornament in lamps of this kind changed to a cock or a cross, but most commonly of all, to what is miscalled the *labarum* — the Greek monogram ☧, the initials of χριστός.[342] These are the lamps commonly found in the Roman Catacombs. A number of lamps from Pompeii is to be seen at Naples of this general shape—most of them have on the flat centre a Medusa, a Tragic mask, a hand, and for a handle a crescent, the head of an ox, horse, dog, swan, or a serpent. These latter are

[342] This monogram was called χρῆσμα by S. Ambrose ; the staff of Osiris, to which it bears some resemblance, was called χρηστήριον (Higgins, *Ana-calypsis*, vol. ii. p. 204).

of course all identical as amulets with the same objects worn to-day by Neapolitan cab-horses. Who can doubt that the intention of these things upon the ancient lamps, was precisely the same as of those now on the horses, against the evil eye? [343]

We have noticed the cows' horns affixed to the model house from Senegal. The Bataks of Sumatra also place horns of oxen on the gables of their houses by way of finials. [344] Those who know Naples will not have failed to remark that many of the

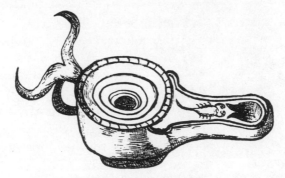

FIG. 86.—From Naples Museum.

houses near the Porta Nolana have cows' horns, often painted blue, fixed against the wall, especially upon an angle, at about the height of the first floor, at just the height of the famous *diavolo* of Florence, p. 231, Appendix II.

One of the entrances to Seville Cathedral, that which belonged to the original mosque, still retaining its horseshoe Moorish arch, leads from the famous Patio de los Naránjos (Court of the Orange-trees) into the Cathedral, and is a true relic of the

[343] The subject of terra-cotta lamps is referred to again in Chap. X.
[344] Report of M. Jules Chaine. See *Illustrated London News*, Sept. 12, 1891, p. 335.

noble Moslems who built the splendid tower of
Seville.   Over this door (Fig. 87) is hung by a chain
the tusk of an elephant, and
further out, but still commanding the same door-
way, swings from the roof
by another chain a large
crocodile, sent as a present,
no doubt as amulets of
special power, to Alonso el
Sabio in 1260, by the then
Sultan of Egypt, with a
request for the hand of the
Wise Alonso's daughter.
These two great amulets
have been hanging there
ever since, and lend a
strangely weird appear-
ance to the doorway of a
Christian church.   (See
Appendix II.)

FIG. 87.—At Seville.

Many of our readers will
probably have remarked
that on the framework of that remarkable structure
to be seen upon the Roman wine carts, which, rough
as it is, forms a folding hood to shelter the *contadino*,
there is almost always a small cow's horn.   It is
usually fixed to the side of the first piece of bent wood
at the front of the hood, but in such a way,
and in such a position, that it can be of no use
except as amulet or ornament.   Very often another
cow's horn is seen hanging upon the axle, underneath the cart, along with the usual lantern.

How shall we account for almost identical objects

to the crescents and horns we have been describing,
when we find them in use among the negro savages
of Ashantee ? Fig. 88 shows three iron standards of
native make, now to be seen in
the Museum at Taunton. They
are from 20 to 23 inches in length,
and by no means badly forged.
They were brought from the west
coast of Africa, where they are
used to stick into the ground "to
protect the crop sown from evil
spirits," or, in other words, from
the witchcraft of possessors of
the evil eye.

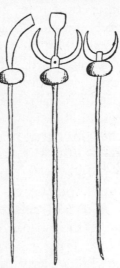

FIG. 88.

In these objects the crescent
surmounts the disc instead of enclosing it, just as it does in many
examples of the insignia of Roman
legions; and we cannot fail to
be struck with the remarkable coincidence. One of
the crescents has a prolongation of the stem ending
in a flat surface, which we suggest may represent
the head of the moon-goddess; and allowing for
difference of treatment, and the separation of unknown ages in time,[345] very remarkably preserves
the same old notion, typified by the neck and head
starting out of the crescent, of the terra-cotta figures
from Mycenæ, now in the Athens Museum (see
Fig. 68).

[345] Schliemann says (*Mycenæ*, p. 69) : "There is also a human head painted
on a fragment of pottery; it has a very large eye, and a head-dress in the form
of a Phrygian cap." Also (p. 71) : "I have been able to gather here more than
200 terra-cotta idols of Hera, more or less broken." "The head of those
idols is of a very compressed shape . . . the lower part is in the form of a
gradually widening tube." To this may be added that one of those sketched
by the writer is widened out so as to form a distinct stand, and perhaps to indicate female drapery.

The third of these iron objects, used for the same purpose as the others, is more difficult to explain. It is submitted, as at least possible, and even plausible, taken in connection with its more evident companions, that this may be intended for a horn, point downwards, as in Neapolitan harness. Although we profess to be dealing with facts, yet again we submit that when such facts as we here produce can be marshalled together, it is but reasonable to deduce an intimate connection, and therefore that they are the products of one and the same idea in Naples and in Ashantee.

No doubt among savage and half-civilised races, plenty of other examples can be found of the use of crescents and horns, in positions analogous to those already mentioned: indeed a cow's horn hung up over the doorway of a stable or cowhouse may be seen anywhere in Italy, and the writer is of opinion it may often be found even here in England. Certainly there is no need to go to stables here, to find handsomely-polished pairs of horns hung up in halls; and stags' "heads" cannot be called uncommon, even in houses where the owners never saw a deer except in a park, or in the Zoo.[346] Of course the enlightened owners would be indignant at any suggestion that these horns were put up as amulets, or for anything but ornament; yet, we ask, what first gave rise to the notion that these objects were suitable for ornament, or if there is any decorative propriety in them, say in the case of a suburban villa?

There is one custom, however, common amongst us enlightened English, as it is among Jews, Turks,

[346] See Jorio's remarks upon this, *post*, pp. 263, 264.

infidels, and heretics all the world over, that of fixing old horseshoes[346a] over, under, upon, or behind our doors. The English horseshoe is now somewhat of a conventional article—it is in itself an example of evolution ; but an Oriental one can scarcely be called anything but the crescent, whether as represented on the Turkish ensign, on the gems of ancient Rome, or on the iron amulets of Ashantee. We may without discussion assume that the horseshoe wherever used is the handy conventional representative of the crescent. The Buddhist crescent emblem is a horseshoe, with the toe pointed like a Gothic arch.[347] " The arch or bend of the mystical instrument borne by Isis—the sistrum—represented the lunar orbit." [348] May we not then safely say the same of the horseshoe? At the Ashmolean Museum is a small sistrum in blue enamel, from Thebes, evidently an amulet.

Here in Somerset horseshoes are nailed on stable doors, hung up to the ceilings above the horses, or fastened to the walls of the cowhouse, "to keep off the pixies," those malicious sprites who are said to come and ride the horses at night, so that "very often in the mornin', there they be, all a-brokt out into a sweat, the very same's 'off they'd a-bin hard to work." This does not occur where the stable is properly protected by the powerful crescent horseshoe.[349] Dwelling-houses are equally

---

[346a] See Jorio's remarks upon this, *post*, p. 260.

[347] Inman, *Ancient Faiths*, vol. ii. p. 262.

[348] Payne Knight, *Symbolical Language*, p. 101.

[349] The same thing is done by hanging up scythes or sharp instruments to the stable rafters, by which the pixies will be cut if they ride the horses.

> Hang up hooks and sheers to scare
> Hence the hag, that rides the mare,
> Till they be all over wet
> With the mire and the sweat.

guarded against the entrance of a witch who can
"overlook," by the shoe being nailed against the
"dreckstool" [350] or behind the door, especially if it
be a "half-hatch." [351]

Sometimes the shoe is found in combination with
other amulets. At this moment, within half a mile
of the spot where this is written, is a house with a
horseshoe nailed behind the door, and above it what
appears to be a book wrapped in black cloth. The
present occupier cannot say what the book is, but
nothing would induce him to have it disturbed or
examined. He believes devoutly in its power to
keep off "they there witches."

The editor of Brand (iii. p. 17) says that in 1813
he counted no less than seventeen horseshoes in
Monmouth Street, London, nailed against the steps
of doors. "Five or six are all that now remain in
1841." "That the horseshoe may never be pulled
from your threshold!" was one of the good wishes or
"sentiments" of the last century, and throws some
light upon the unwillingness of my neighbour in
Wellington to permit any disturbance of the protectors behind his door.

The late Duchess of St. Albans and her husband,
Mr. Coutts, had two rusty, old, broken horseshoes
fastened on the highest marble step, by which the
house at Holly Lodge was entered from the lawn.
The horseshoe has been also used for a talisman as
well as an amulet; for in 1687 it was believed in
Amsterdam that a stolen horseshoe placed on the

This observed, the manes shall be
Of your horses all knot-free.
                 Herrick, *Hesperides*, ed. Hazlitt, 1869, p. 305.
[350] Threshold ; low half-door. See *West Somerset Word-Book*.
[351] A horseshoe may be seen to-day nailed on the outside of a stable
door opening on to the principal thoroughfare of the town of Wellington.

chimney-hearth would bring good luck to the house.[352]

In the tombs of the kings at Thebes (that of Rameses IX. No. 6) the king is represented as receiving the *ankh*, or symbol of life, from different goddesses, each of whom, in several scenes, holds him hand in hand. In one case, however, Hathor is presenting him with a double phallus, which is curiously, but evidently with intention, made to take the form of a horseshoe! In Tunis, Cairo, Constantinople, Spain, Italy, and Sicily, plenty of horseshoes may be seen in the streets fixed to the houses, as the writer can testify. At the Paris Exhibition of 1889 was a reproduction of a street in Old Cairo. Over several of the doors was hung a crocodile, a powerful amulet; on one house, however, was not only the crocodile, but on his snout, and also on his tail, were perched horseshoes, the crescent symbol of the pagan Diana, used as an amulet by the Mahomedan iconoclast!

FIG. 89.

The lamp shown in Fig. 85 has the crescent handle almost in horseshoe shape. The curious amulet, too (Fig. 89), from the Etruscan Museum at Bologna, can hardly represent anything but a horseshoe, while the round knobs at the heels are matched by those on the lamp; the same knobs are often seen upon crescents. There is a necklace in the

---

[352] Brand, *Pop. Ant.* vol. iii. p. 18, ed. Bohn. In Cumberland this practice is very common; the writer has seen many upon various parts of the premises at Duddon Hall. One old one is nailed to the wall at the back of an ornamental temple in the garden—a building which is quite empty. The only explanation to be extracted from the natives is that the shoes are nailed up for luck. If more close and intimate relations could be established, we have no doubt of finding the way to other reasons.

Louvre consisting entirely of half-moons with these balls on the ends. What they mean must be left to others to explain. It will be seen by Fig. 81, which exhibits no single article, except the three mystic eyes, which is not sold in the shops of Italy as distinctly *contra la jettatura*, that the horseshoe is one of the common charms worn on the watch-chain. This is always in addition to, never in place of, the inevitable horn of coral or metal.

Among certain people there is an aversion, an antipathy, to iron, as bringing evil to those who touch it. Possibly this may partly account for the strange though powerful amulet (*phallus*) adopted by the blacksmiths of ancient Rome and Pompeii to counteract the effect which the constant handling of iron might be expected to bring upon them.

The negroes of the Gold Coast remove all metal from their persons when they consult their fetish— a practice with which Freemasons will not fail to perceive reasons for lively sympathy. So the men who made the needfire in Scotland had to divest themselves of all metal.[353] Another Scotch custom was that in making the *clavie* (a kind of Yuletide fire-wheel) at Burghead, no hammer might be used, the hammering must be done with a stone.[354]

Nearer home we know that one of the sights of Exeter Cathedral is the wooden Bishop's throne, with its canopy 60 feet high, constructed entirely without nails or iron of any kind ; this fact is always specially dwelt upon by the verger. We are told (Ex. xx. 25) as to building an altar : " If thou lift

---

[353] Logan, *The Scottish Gael*, vol. ii. p. 68.
[354] C. F. Gordon Cumming, *In the Hebrides*, p. 226 ; E. J. Guthrie, *Old Scottish Customs*, p. 223, quoted by Frazer, *Golden Bough*, vol. i. p. 173.

up thy tool (iron) upon it, thou hast polluted it."
So of the temple (1 Kings vi. 7) : " There was neither
hammer, nor axe, nor any tool of iron, heard in the
house while it was in building."

"At Cyzicus is the βουλευτήριον (senate house),
a vast edifice, constructed without a nail of iron ;[355]
the raftering being so contrived as to admit of the
beams being removed and replaced without the
use of stays. A similar thing, too, is the case with
the Sublician Bridge at Rome." This was a sacred
bridge, and it had to be kept in repair without the
use of either iron or other metal.[356]

Raja Vijyanagram, one of the most enlightened
of Hindoo princes, would not allow iron to be used
in the construction of buildings within his territory,
believing that its use would inevitably be followed
by smallpox and other epidemics.[357]

On the other hand, the very fact that iron is
deemed obnoxious to spirits, furnishes men with a
weapon which may be turned against them when
occasion serves. The dislike of spirits for iron is
so great that they will not approach persons and
things protected by the obnoxious metal. " Iron
therefore may obviously be employed as a charm
for banning ghosts and other dangerous spirits,"[358]
to which we may add—witches.[359] This feeling will

[355] Pliny, *Nat. Hist.* xxxvi. 24 (Ed. Bohn, vi. p. 345).

[356] It was the earliest constructed across the Tiber, by Ancus Martius, 114
A.U.C. It was called *Sublician*, because it was constructed entirely of wood.
No iron was used in its construction, on the strength of religious tradition,
nor was any ever used in repair even in Christian times down to the fall of
the Empire. The fact is noted by Dionysius, v. 24 ; Varro, v. 83 ; Ovid, *Fasti*,
v. 622. Pliny's account, assigning the rejection of iron to the difficulties of
Horatius Cocles in cutting it through, is absurd (Lanciani, *op. cit.* p. 40).

[357] *Indian Antiquary*, vol. x. 1881, p. 364.

[358] Frazer, *Golden Bough*, vol. i. p. 175.

[359] Let the superstitious wife
  Neer the child's heart lay a knife :

possibly account for the iron crescents of Ashantee, and perhaps for the adoption of the horseshoe as a potent form of the crescent, especially obnoxious to witches and pixies. In Morocco iron is considered a great protection against demons. In Scotland when a fisherman at sea uses blasphemous language, the first man who hears him calls out "Cauld airn," at which every man grasps the nearest bit of iron, and holds it fast for awhile.[360] The old binding contract among schoolboys on making a "swop," [361] "Tick, tack, never change back, touch cold iron!" is well known as a binding form of contract in several parts of England, and may well be a vestige of the same old belief as that of the Scotch fisherman, which seems to imply a seeking of the protection of the iron against the temptations of evil demons. In Wales it was believed [362] that touching with iron caused fairy wives to vanish. Professor Rhys tells a story of a young man at last winning a fairy maid, but she told him if he ever struck her with iron she would go away never to return. This of course recalls myths like Melusine and Undine.

According to authorities quoted by Frazer the same idea as to iron is very prevalent in India; especially is cold iron used by the performer of certain funereal rites, apparently to guard himself against the evil spirits which he may have set free from the dead man. So in North Scotland, immediately

Point be up, and haft be downe,
While she gossips in the towne,
This 'mongst other mystic charms
Keeps the sleeping child from harms.

Herrick, *Hesperides*, ed. Hazlitt, 1869, p. 305.

[360] E. J. Guthrie, *Old Scottish Customs*, p. 149; C. Rogers, *Social Life in Scotland*, 1886, vol. iii. p. 218.

[361] *Notes and Queries*, 8th ser. v. 160, 235, 354.

[362] Rhys, *Welsh Fairies*, art. in *Nineteenth Century*, Oct. 1891, p. 565.

after a death, a piece of iron, such as a nail or knitting needle, used to be stuck into all the meal, butter, cheese, flesh, and whisky in the house, "to prevent death from entering them." This custom is evidently the same in idea as that of the Hindoo, and is intended to keep off the ghost of the deceased. Various people ranging from Burmah to Roumania are careful not to use sharp instruments so long as the ghost of a deceased friend is thought to be near, lest they should wound it. In Transylvania they will carefully see that no knife is left lying with the sharp edge upwards so long as the corpse remains in the house, or else the soul will be forced to ride on the blade.[363]

Similar customs are recorded of the Chinese, the Esquimos of Alaska, the people of Celebes, Prussians, Lithuanians and Germans generally.

Professor Rhys believes aversion to iron to be a survival of the feeling implanted in man's early life, when all metals were new, and hence to be avoided. The like explanation is given respecting the dislike of first seeing the new moon through glass. Polish farmers having experienced a succession of bad harvests, set down this to the recent introduction of iron ploughshares; consequently, they gave up using them and took to the old wooden ones. Probably the same feeling, respecting the baneful effect of iron, gave rise to the many customs we read of, about not cutting the hair, especially when undertaking any important expedition. Such a custom was observed occasionally by the Romans, while the very name Lombards (*Langobardi*) implies that for

---

[363] Bastian, *Die Völker des östlichen Asien*, i. 136; E. Gerard, *The Land beyond the Forest*, i. 312; Schmidt, *Das Jahr und seine Tage in Meinung und Brauch*, etc., p. 40; Frazer, i. 176.

some reason the men allowed no cutting instrument to touch their beards. Six thousand Saxons once swore they would not cut their hair nor shave until they had taken vengeance of their enemies. The Nazarite of Scripture, too, was set apart by " no razor shall come on his head." [363a] No doubt this aversion to cutting the hair implied not only that the man should not be defiled by iron, but probably also, especially on the war path, that nothing belonging to the warrior should by any chance fall into the hands of his enemy—whose possession of so special a part of him as a lock of his hair, would enable him to work untold evil. The same dread of iron has doubtless given rise to the custom throughout Europe regarding children's nails. Everywhere, including England, it is the practice to bite off the infant's nails if too long, and not to cut them, at least for the first year, or until the child, who is peculiarly open to the attacks of all malignant influences, has grown strong. It is presumed that to postpone cutting will enable the child to get power to withstand at least one of the evils awaiting him, that which may be in the iron. English mothers in this respect hold to the same fashion, belief, custom or whatever may be the motive for the practice, as Hindoos. The latter cut the nails of the firstborn at six months, while other children, presumed to be weaker, are left for two years.[364] The Slav, Hare, and Dogrib Indians of North America do not cut their female (the weaker) children's nails till they are four years of age.

The same anxiety exists everywhere with respect to nails as to hair, teeth, or any other part of the

[363a] Judges xiii. 5.
[364] *Punjaub Notes and Queries*, ii. No. 1092.

body, lest it should fall into the hands of an enemy ;
hence here in England the nails bitten off by nurses
must be spit into the fire, and the cuttings taken off
by knife or scissors must likewise be burnt.   The
same with respect to teeth—a child's milk-teeth
must be thrown into the fire.   The writer well
remembers in his childhood being told to be very
careful when " shelling" his teeth not to lose one,
but to be sure to throw it into the fire, because "a
dog would be safe to pick it up, and then you would
have a dog's tooth."   This very thing has been said
with all seriousness in the writer's own house within
the past few days (July 1894).   A story is told [365] of
an Australian girl who fell ill of a fever, and persisted
that some months before a young man had come
behind her and cut off a lock of her hair : she was
sure that he had buried it, and that it was rotting
somewhere.   She persisted that this was the cause
of her sickness, and that as her hair rotted so her
flesh was wasting away, and when her hair was quite
rotten, she would die.

Out of all the evidence we have produced as to
the aversion to iron on the one hand, and as to its
potency in keeping off evil spirits on the other, we
may gain some clue to the notion underlying the
common use of the horseshoe : first, it is a handy
representation of the powerful amulet the crescent ;
and next, its power is greatly reinforced by its
material—the witch-hated cold iron.

[365] B. Smith, *Aborigines of Victoria*, vol. i. p. 467.

APPENDIX I

A VERY short excursion in the field of comparative religions will show how one idea seems to have come from the far East in the early days of mankind, and to have taken root in the minds of all races who came westward. We have already referred to the faith which led the Magi to follow the star to Bethlehem. Throughout the East it was the primæval instinct that a child was to be born of a celestial mother, who should destroy the spirit of evil and be the saviour of mankind. Not only so, but the mother was to conceive and to bring him forth from her own inherent power.[366] With the triune male deity we find a single female associated. " Her names are innumerable, ' Mother of all the Gods,' The Lady, The Queen, Mulita, Bilta, Ishtar, or the bright, pure being. She is also Ri, Alitta, Elissa, Beltis, Ashtoreth, Astarte, Saraha or Sara, Nana, Asurah, Tanith. All these and more are Babylonish, but elsewhere she is Athor, Dea, Syria, Artemis, Aphrodite, Rhea, Demeter, Ceres, Diana, Minerva, Juno, Venus, Isis, Cybele, Ge, Hera. As Anaitis she is ' The Mother of the Child '; reproduced again as Isis and Horus, Devaki and Christna, Aurora and Memnon. Even in ancient Mexico the mother and child were worshipped. In modern times she survives as the Virgin Mary and her Son. There were Ishtar of Nineveh and Ishtar of Arbela, just as there are now Maria di Loretto and Marie de la Garde."

Indranee (and her child), consort of Indur from the cave of Indur Subha, are again one and the same person. Fig. 74[367] really represents Mary, whose name is synonymous with maternity, but not with ordinary maternity occurring on earth, inasmuch as throughout the ancient mytho-

---

[366] Inman, *Ancient Faiths*, vol. i. p. 98 *et seq.*

[367] From *Asiatic Researches*, vol. vi. p. 393. I am quite aware that Lieutenant Wilford is said to have been imposed upon by stories invented for him. Into that controversy I need not enter, and merely give his statements for what they are worth. Prof. Max Müller refers to this in an article in *Nineteenth Century*, October 1894.

logies the celestial mother was represented as a virgin[368]
—the same " woman who has replaced in Christendom the
celestial virgin of Paganism."

The same author[369] records that in India, Christna,
Chrishna, or Vishnu, is usually called " the saviour " or
"preserver." "He, being a god, became incarnate in the
flesh. As soon as he was born he was saluted by a chorus
of angels or avators." " One of his names is ' the Good
Shepherd.' Christna cured a leper, a woman poured on
his head a box of ointment, and he cured her of disease.
He washed the feet of Brahmins. Christna had a dreadful
fight with the serpent Caluga. He astonished his tutor
by his learning. He was crucified, went into hell, and
afterwards into heaven. Christna and his mother are
always represented as black. His statue in the temple
at Mathura is black, and the temple is built in the form
of a cross. As Vishnu he is painted with a Parthian
coronet, when crucified. As Wittoba he has sometimes
the stigmata in his hands, and sometimes in his feet, and
one picture represents him with a round hole in his side :
to his collar hangs a heart."[370]

This account is so remarkable in its correspondence
with our Gospel narrative that it seems almost incredible
for it to be other than a paraphrase therefrom. Nevertheless, our author says : " There is every reason to believe
the legend to be more ancient than the Christian era."
The various illustrations in other books fully support the
foregoing. Chrishna is represented in Moor's *Hindu
Pantheon* (p. 67) with a nimbus as shown in Fig. 72, while
winged cherubs from above are sending down upon him
rays of light, just as we are accustomed to see in pictures
of the baptism of our Lord. He is also shown as crucified
in precisely the same way, and with a crown of thorns and
nimbus, just as we are accustomed to see in pictures of the
Crucifixion.[371]

[368] Inman, *op. cit.* vol. i. p. 253.   [369] *Ib.* vol. i. p. 400.
[370] *Ib.* vol. i. pp. 400-403.
[371] Much information on this subject may be found in Hislop's *Two
Babylons*, pp. 30-90. It is needless to say that we have no sympathy with

Isis and Horus were distinctly associated with a fish, for we find her represented as bearing a fish on her head

instead of the usual disc and horns (Fig. 90).[372] Another author says: "The most obvious and ancient symbol of the reproductive power of water was a fish.[373] Derceto, goddess of the Phœnicians, had the body of a woman ending in a fish. We have already remarked that Diana was sovereign of humidity, and was symbolised in the aspect of the goddess of the fertilising power of water by a crab. We venture to suggest that these considerations offer another solution of the origin of the fish as a Christian symbol of Christ. The acrostic or rebus explanation of the Greek word for fish has always seemed speculative and far-fetched, when viewed by the light obtained from other well-understood objects, such as the cross,

FIG. 90.

which have certainly been adopted from so-called heathenism. All these startling facts, so far from unsettling our weak minds upon the cardinal facts of our Christian belief, should but prove to us that they are founded upon an instinct planted in the breast of man as mysterious as his life, and just as inexplicable by his limited faculties. They do but point out the futility of what we in our pride call "knowledge," and suggest to us that the best motto modern savants could adopt would still be *Quod scis nescis.*[374]

Further, we suggest that the celestial mother and child were not only objects of faith and worship, but representa-

the purpose of this book nor with the spirit in which it is written. Moreover, judging from some of those we have endeavoured to verify, the references cannot be wholly relied on.

[372] Inman, *Ancient Faiths*, vol. i. Frontispiece; also p. 520.

[373] Payne Knight, *Symbolical Language*, p. 111.

[374] Upon this subject see Mr. Gladstone's remarks in a paper on "Heresy" in the *Nineteenth Century*, August 1894, p. 174.

tions of them were certainly used as amulets.   In support
of this we point to Fig. 91, a bronze
arm from a larger figure, holding out
a woman and child, in a manner which
candour must admit to be conclusive.
The bronze, of evident antiquity, was
obtained by the writer from a native on
the Nile.   It is scarcely a likely object
to have been forged.   Another piece
of convincing evidence is found in
the woman and child in both representations of the Mano Pantea (Figs.
148, 156).

FIG. 91.
From Author's Col-
lection.

APPENDIX II

THE evident defence of a Christian church by the horn
and crocodile amulets of Seville naturally leads to
the consideration of those very common though remarkable appendages to other Christian churches with which
most people are familiar.   It would be an interesting
study to ascertain when the grotesque and hideous things,
those nightmares in stone which we call gurgoyles, were
first adopted.   Where was the germ first planted ?   From
what kind of eggs were these fanciful birds, beasts,
fishes, and reptiles, first hatched ?   Without waiting, however, for an answer to these questions, we may venture
to assert that the idea from which they sprang must have
been the same as that we have been considering.   The
evil glance of a wicked eye might as well be personified as the great variety of other vices, such as avarice, lust,
and drunkenness, to say nothing of the virtues, graces, and
higher attributes, all of which have found their representations in personal shapes.   Precisely then as justice, mercy,
truth, find their expression in human female beauty, so
would their opposites, the ideals of evil, find theirs in the
fanciful and distorted shapes commonly understood by the
term fiendish.   The old conceptions of Gnostic days would

supply, from their *grylli* and other strange devices,[374a] a link
from the earlier days of Babylonian and Græco-Egyptian
times, when their gods were represented with human bodies,
but with heads of birds and beasts, more or less representing
the special qualities attributed to those deities. We have
seen, and have further to show, how strange objects have
been erected both in pagan and Christian times in many
public situations, with the object of protecting place and
people from the wicked and malignant influence of evil
spirits, emanating from the eyes of those by whom they
were possessed. These evil spirits all became actual
demons to those who believed in them ; and inasmuch as
they were all active agents of mischief and of evil, so it
was but natural to suppose their attacks would be especially directed against those buildings and persons, whose
purpose was to cultivate and to strengthen the opposite
principles of goodness and of virtue. Therefore amongst
those who firmly believed in these evil demons, and at the
same time placed much reliance upon antidotes or protective
amulets against their power, we should expect to find
visible and lasting precautions taken, particularly in the
case of buildings so liable to devilish attack as churches.
This is precisely what we do find. The Middle Ages, when
churches were rising in all directions, when the highest art
and the choicest gifts of the people were lavished upon their
religious buildings, were precisely the epoch when the dread
of the evil eye was the most real, when perhaps of all other
times the personality of spirits, good and bad, had become
most firmly imbedded in the belief of the people.

Therefore it was that the same idea which to-day leads
to the mounting of a piece of wolf or badger skin upon a
horse's bridle to scare the evil glance of the *versipelle*, induced our forefathers to carve in stone, and so to perpetuate
their fantastic conceptions of the wicked spirits they wished
to scare away from their sacred buildings. We all know
that our church bells have that as their original purpose,

[374a] For these see *Abraxas seu Apistopistus* Johannis Macarii, Antwerpiæ,
MDCLVII. Also King, *Gnostics*, and *Handbook of Gems*.

and, *a fortiori*, why should not the stone demons which adorn the angles and conspicuous parts of our Gothic churches?

It is said, too, that the same idea of frightening away the evil spirits residing in them, is that which has led to the custom of our gamekeepers, to gibbet the "varmint" in some conspicuous place, so that the devils inhabiting the bodies of cats, stoats, jays, and magpies may be warned of what awaits them if they do not keep a respectful distance from preserves of respectable birds and animals.

It has been well remarked quite recently to the writer : "We never see a real gurgoyle now on a modern church ; there are hideous things enough, but they have no life in them." The reason for this is not far to seek. The feeling and keen imagination which created the devils of our mediæval churches came of a lively faith in their reality. Nowadays such things are mere decorations, servile copies of the oddities invented by our forefathers, but without either knowledge or belief as to their meaning or intention. The consequence is, the inevitable lifeless failure of the modern stone-cutter. The monks of old saw the goblins they carved through the eye of undoubting belief.

Of course as time went on these grotesque demons and goblins, having been adopted as regular items of church decoration, lent themselves to the treatment of artistic and cultivated taste ; but there can be little question as to their original intention. No better example of what we are maintaining can be found than that of the famous Florentine *diavolo*, of which a rough sketch by the writer is annexed (Fig. 92).

In the first place, it was designed by one of the greatest sculptors of the Italian Renaissance, John of Bologna, or as he is called Giambologna, the same who created that most elegant of Mercuries standing tiptoe on a breath of air. Originally there were two of these little bronze figures attached to the angle of a Florentine palace near the once picturesque Mercato Vecchio, but one was stolen many years ago, and that here shown has, since the writer's last

visit two or three years ago, been removed into a place of
safety as a precious work of art.   In this case the figure
is of bronze, and was specially designed to be fixed to the
wall of the house, just as horns
are still fixed in Naples. Tradition says that from this spot
Peter Martyr preached, and
that he exorcised the devil,
who galloped past in the shape
of a black horse.[375]

It will be seen by this figure
that horns were not considered
specially the badge of honour
or of sanctity, as in the statue
of Moses. On the contrary,
our own popular notion of the
devil is more expressed in this
figure : horns and cloven feet
with a barbed tail being our
ideal.   Here he has the hairy
thighs of a goat or satyr, and
short horns ; but the feet are
not cloven hoofs.   We may
however take this figure as a
typical one, fully representing

FIG. 92.

the idea, in art and in fact, of just what we see petrified
upon the towers and angles of our churches.

There is a very extraordinary collection of grotesque
figures on the towers of Notre Dame in Paris.   They are
" like an actual body of fiendish visitors caught and turned
into stone as they grinned over the city." [376]   This idea of
" turning into stone " brings back to mind the old fancy
lying in the story of Perseus and the Gorgon.

[375] Horner, *Walks in Florence*, 1873, vol. i. p. 156.
[376] Pennell, *The Devils of Notre Dame*, 1894.   Many of our readers will
recall the grotesque *bracciali* upon the palaces at Sienna.

CHAPTER VII

TOUCH, HANDS, GESTURES

ONE of the ways by which the influence included in the general term Evil Eye is communicated, is by touch. Mere bodily contact, as in the case of contagious diseases, has always been held to be of much importance as a means of conveying injury, and both by practice and precept has always been carefully guarded against. "Eat thou not the bread of him that hath an evil eye" (Prov. xxiii. 6) means, avoid his presence lest you come into contact with him; he may be blind, but his touch is malignant. Great as may be the power of mere personal presence, such as the rubbing shoulders with one possessed with the terrible faculty, the effect is tenfold greater when there is the actual and intentional touching by the baneful person. In the mesmeric performances with which we are all familiar, the influence of the operator is vastly increased when he makes passes with his hands, and still more so when he actually touches his patient. Then it is that he seems to convey to his subject the invisible influence of his own will, whether that will be in the direction of good or of evil. These evidences of the effect of personal contact, which our senses compel us to acknowledge, have been existent in all time, and the consequence has been from the earliest days, that men have regarded with intense interest the instrument by which touch is commonly, and, when intentionally, always conveyed—the hand.   Not only is it the bodily member which specially differentiates man from all lower animals, but it is that by which in every way he makes his power known and felt.   True that man's relatives the Apes have four hands to our two, yet his are but prehensile instruments, incapable from the partial development of the thumb, apart from the brain-power of direction, of performing those thousands of intricate acts of construction, of musical touch, of significant gesture, which the human hand performs, and which mark it out as the faithful servant, as well as the natural symbol, of a higher power, that of a perfected intelligence.

If in past ages the hand has been looked upon as an instrument of evil when used by the malignant, much more has it been regarded as an instrument of good—the powerful protector against that special form of evil which was supposed to be flashed from one person to another, whether through the eye or the touch of malice.

It has ever been recognised that the differences of shape, texture, and general appearance of the hands of individuals are quite as great as in faces. Moreover, it has been noticed by long experience that certain kinds of hand are found to belong to the possessors of certain types of faces; and just as the life and character of the individual are to be seen in his face, so is his hand also the index of the mind.   Further, it is found that just as the features of a person's face distinguish his individuality and remain permanent, to be recognised by all who know him, so do the features—the shape, size, texture and markings on his hands—continue permanent, subject only to such changes as affect the features of his countenance.   This fact is so well established by scientific research and record, that its results are being now applied to the identification of criminals, whose hands are carefully photographed or in other ways portrayed, as well as their faces.   It is even proposed to apply the same method to the foot, which is also found to be different in every individual from that of every other.   Just as no two faces are alike, so are no two people's hands or feet.

The study of the hand as a quasi-science has of late become almost a mania, and the books on palmistry, or chiromancy, in all languages have become legion.   Upon the hand, however, as an index of the life and character, we have no wish to enlarge, but refer the curious reader to such works as *Shall I tell you your Fortune, my pretty Maid?* by Mrs. John White, which the writer bought at a railway bookstall for sixpence, and which is marked "Twelfth Thousand"; to *Chiromanzia, Fisiologia sulla Mano*, Giulio Adrieu, Milano, 1884; *Lira Una;* or to the costly and elaborate compilations on the subject, which have appeared at recent dates. Indeed, so much has the fad of palmistry run riot, that one of the "up to date" enterprising soap-boilers has recently made use of it in a really clever puff upon a great hand, as an advertisement in some of the illustrated papers.

Our business, however, lies rather with the sister - science Chironomy than with this.   The

latter is defined [377] as "the art or science of gesticulation, or of moving the hands according to rule
in oratory, pantomime," etc. To this definition we
venture to add, "the art of representing such gesticulation," etc., and this will be found later a needful
qualification. As a science we are told [378] that
chironomy is of great antiquity. " Numa Pompilius,
the successor of Romulus, publicly made use of the
art of chironomy, or of gesture with the hands, as
a means of counting" (or reckoning, *per conteggiare*).
" Not only Pliny the historian, but also Macrobius
assures us, that Numa, in establishing a religion for
the fierce Romans, caused a statue of Janus to be
made with two heads, or with two faces, but with
the fingers bent (*piegate*) in such a manner as to
represent, according to Pliny,[379] the number 350,
and according to Macrobius [380] the number 365."

In considering this evidence, we speak of making by the
hand a certain gesture, a certain sign, which may convey (*signi-
ficasse*) to all the Roman populace that which is meant by the
words three hundred and fifty. Here then we have the conventional sign. If Numa had used a manual gesture, unknown to
all, or if he had ordered the statue of Janus to be made with the
fingers folded in a way which had not been in accordance with
the previous habit or convention of the people, he would have
been considered the most foolish of mankind. And therefore
we are compelled to conclude the Romans to have then understood (*intendessero*) that part of *chironomy* as belonging to the
gesture of counting.[381]

---

[377] *New English Dictionary*, s.v. " Chironomy. "
[378] *Scoperta della Chironomia ossia dell' arte di gestire con le mani*, Dell'
Abate Vincenzo Requeno, Parma, 1797, p. 13.
[379] "Janus geminus a Numa rege dicatus, qui pacis, bellique argumento
colitur, digitis ita figuratis, ut trecentorum quinquaginta dierum nota per
significationem anni, temporis, et ævi se Deum indicaret."—Pliny, xxxiv. 7.
[380] " Simulacrum ejus plerumque fingitur manu dextera 300 et sinistra
sexaginta quinque numerum tenens, ad demonstrandam anni dimensionem."
—Macrobius, *Saturn.* i.
[381] Abate Requeno, *op. cit.* p. 14.

The Abate says that the Romans obtained their gestures from the Greeks; that the Greek word

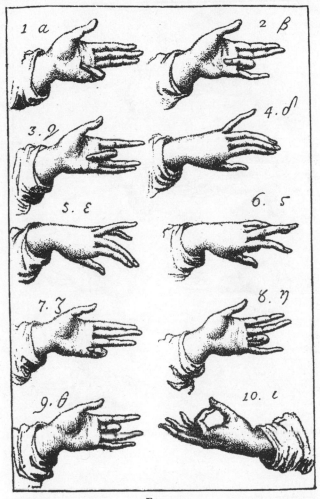

FIG. 93.

chironomia had been adopted (into Latin) to denote the art of gesture. He asserts that the invention of gestures for manual numeration was from the heroic

ages of Greece, and so of surprising antiquity ;
but he gives no hint as to the source whence the

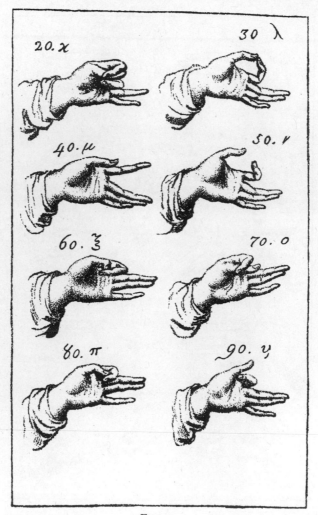

FIG. 94.

Greeks obtained it.   He traces the use of this
ancient method, and gives details of each position
of the fingers of the left hand, so as to indicate any

number up to 90 (Figs. 93, 94). For instance he says :—

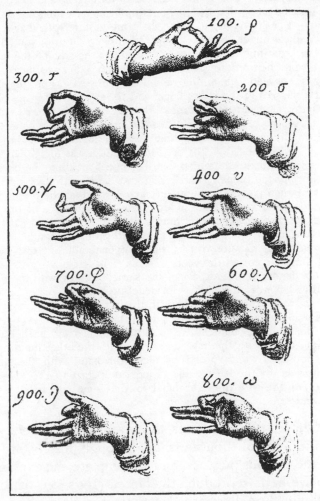

FIG. 95.

To indicate (*pronunziare*) the number 1, you have to bend the little finger (of the left hand) closely upon the palm of the hand. For 2, the ring finger is to be bent in the same manner. For 3, you do the same with the middle finger. For 4, you raise the little finger alone above the others. For 5, you raise the ring finger. For 6, you raise the middle and bend down the ring finger upon the palm. For 7, you raise the other fingers, and bend only the little finger so that the nail rests upon its own root, not on the palm. For 8, you are to make the same gesture with that called the medical finger, the next to the little finger. For 9, you do the like with the middle finger. For 10, place the nail of the index finger on the middle joint of the thumb. For 20, place the thumb between the middle and index fingers. For 30, unite gently the nail of the index finger and the thumb. For 40, place the index alongside the thumb. For 50, bend the index towards the palm like g, or Greek Γ. For 60, make the same bend with the thumb and at the same time press the bent thumb with the index surrounding it. For 70, bend the index as for 50, and fill the space with the thumb so that the thumb nail may be beyond the joint of the index. For 80, do the same with the index as for 70 ; then place the thumb in such a way that the thumb-nail may touch the joint of the index. For 90, make the nail of the index touch the root of the thumb.

No signs for the hundreds are made by the left hand. " One sees an exemplification of this, when Juvenal, alluding to Nestor, said that he counted the years with his right hand."[382]

To denote hundreds, make the same gestures with the right hand as have been described for denoting the tens with the left. Hence to indicate 100, make with the right hand the same sign as is made with the left for 10 (Fig. 95).

Consequently you denote 200 with the right hand in the same manner as 20 with the left ; and so on with the other hundreds.

Thousands are denoted by the right hand with the same gestures as by the left for the prime numbers 1 to 10. Hence 1000 is made with the right hand in the same way as 1 by the left, and so on.

Our author describes the way to denote tens up to hundreds of thousands, but enough has been extracted for our purpose, and to complete the explanation we here reproduce the plates (Figs. 93, 94, 95) with which he illustrates his subject, and which make it quite clear, so far as we have dealt with it.[383]

[382] Abate Requeno, *op. cit.* p. 40.

[383] Before venturing to reproduce this interesting system for which the Abate claims such antiquity, great pains were taken to ascertain if it is known and practised in our English systems of teaching the deaf and dumb. The

The second part of the treatise deals with the gestures used by ancient actors and pantomimists; but inasmuch as he gives no pictorial illustrations, we despair of interpreting with sufficient plainness to be of interest to the reader.

The ancients having contrived so complete a system of manual numeration, it needs little imagination to understand how the hand, the emblem and instrument of power, naturally became in itself one of the earliest of protective amulets, probably coeval with the phallic emblems, at which we have but hinted in a previous chapter.

The earliest examples we have of the hand as an amulet against fascination—and we must take it almost as an axiom that all amulets had originally that object—are found, as we should expect them to be, singly or used separately ; not combined with another object.   The very rude representations of the hand shown in Figs. 96-101, from sketches by the writer,

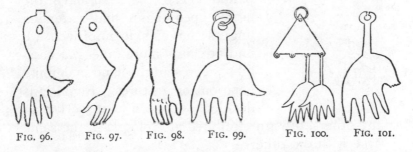

FIG. 96.   FIG. 97.   FIG. 98.   FIG. 99.   FIG. 100.   FIG. 101.

are from early Etruscan tombs ; all these are to be seen, with many more, in the Museums of the

constant reply of experts, as to whether this or any similar system of manual numeration was taught, has been : " I know of no ancient system " !   Only by a negative process has it been found that this system is not used by modern teachers.   It is therefore here recorded as bearing much on what has to be said upon gestures of the hand, so intimately connected with the belief in the evil eye.

Collegio Romano, of Cortona, of Bologna, and probably elsewhere. They are described as belonging " to the first age of iron," a period of extreme antiquity. The eyelets for suspension show that these objects were intended to be worn. They are mere pieces of bronze plate cut into the shapes, and about the sizes here drawn—perhaps a little larger. It is not easy to measure an article in a glass case. Fig. 100 has two hands remaining out of four which originally hung upon the same triangle. Whether or not the triangle represented anything more than a convenient shape for the suspender we cannot now decide — probably it did ; but the fact of finding four hands combined shows that already in those days, 500 to 1000 B.C., there was a tendency to pile up amulets by way of adding to their power.

Among all these very early hand amulets, in only one is any particular gesture depicted. All the rest have the mere open palm and extended fingers ; but as skill improved, we find attempts more or less successful to represent the hand in definite positions or gestures. Fig. 102 is decidedly of much later work than the others, though exhibited at Bologna in the same case with the others.

FIG. 102.

In the Ashmolean Museum are many examples of the open hand, in blue pottery, showing piercings or handle attachments for suspension as amulets.[384]

---

[384] Jahn, *Aberglauben,* etc., frequently uses this argument as a proof that the objects he is speaking of were used as amulets, *e.g.* p. 47, of a female figure with the hand on the mouth he says : " Die sich zum Theil durch den Henkel als Amulete ausweisen."

Several of these latter are Phœnician and may therefore be the same as Etruscan.

Besides the small ones intended to be worn on
the person, representations of the open hand are
very widely scattered, and in such a manner portrayed
both in sculpture and painting that we cannot but
accept them as examples of that kind of amulet
which was fixed in a conspicuous place for public
protection, such as the grillo of Pisistratus, the horns
on houses, and the gurgoyles on our churches.

Perhaps the most striking example of the use of
the hand as a symbol of power as well as of protection, is to be seen sculptured on the tombs, ex-
cavated by that monotheistic Pharaoh, Khuenaten
("the beloved of the Sun's disc"), at Tel-el-Amarna.
There he and his court are adoring the sun, whose
rays are stretching out towards them; but in every
case, and there are several such scenes in the tombs,
each ray terminates in an open hand.   The accompanying illustration (Fig. 103) is from *Wilkinson*,
vol. iii. p. 52, the only drawing available, but it is
unsatisfactory, and the writer regrets he made no
sketch on the spot.[385]   The date of these tombs is
given as 1500 B.C.,[386] and as their history is well
known, this is probably one of the most exact in
Egyptian chronology.   The use of the hand as a sign
of the divine presence and power is thus fixed at least
as early as the sojourn of Israel in Egypt, and some
time before the birth of Moses; it has continued to
be so used throughout the ages down to the present
day—alike by pagans, Mahomedans, and Christians.

Next probably in antiquity come the Etruscan

---

[385] Another plate, with the sun's rays terminating in a hand, is in
Wilkinson, i. 40.   [386] E. Wallis Budge, *The Nile*, p. 13.

and Greek hands, made evidently for use as household
amulets. Of these, two are to be seen in the Ashmolean. They are of bronze : one about six inches

FIG. 103.

high, and fixed upright upon a flat plinth ; another
of the same kind, but larger, is late Greek, found at
Taranto, in the temple of Dionysos. These are both
exactly like Fig. 104, which has lost its stand,
though retaining the pin by which it was fixed ; the
Oxford ones are both right hands. In the Naples
Museum two are alike, Nos. 5507, 5508, a right hand

and a left, probably of much later date than the
Etruscan, though of the same type of open hand
without special gesture.   The writer
believes that there are Greek examples
of the like kind at the Museums of
Girgenti and Syracuse; at Cortona
there certainly are more than one, and
also in the Museo Kircheriano at
Rome; but whether these latter are
Roman or Etruscan he has omitted
to note.[387]

FIG. 104.
From Naples.

Fig. 105 is an Etruscan statuette
from the Collegio Romano at Rome.

Here it looks rather more finished
and in better proportion than the
original, which is very long drawn
out.   The figure, about eight
inches high, is one of two; unlike
in other respects, both hold up
the right hand as shown, with
palm and fingers extended.   The
attitude is so marked in both
figures that they can only be
taken to be designed for the exhibition of this manual gesture.
They are placed with other
ancient bronzes found in Sardinia,
and are evidently of great antiquity, probably Phœnician.
Ancient statues of this kind, of

FIG. 105.

[387] In the Ashmolean Museum are three small
Egyptian amulets evidently for suspension.   They
are open hands of the usual blue pottery, but
small, and almost identical in type with many a coral hand to be seen to-day
in the Naples shops.   No doubt the open hand has been worn as a protection throughout the thirty centuries since these little charms were made.

unknown age, as well as modern Indian ones,[388] show that the pose and gesture of the hands are full of

FIG. 106.

meaning, and that many ancient statues, now regarded simply as works of art, were intended to exhibit actions that conveyed in their day very distinct ideas.[389]

Belonging to later times, over the great gate of the Alhambra (Fig. 106) called "*La Torre de Justicia*," where the King or his Kaid dispensed judgment in Oriental fashion,[390] is a large upright hand on the keystone of the outer Moorish arch, in defiance of the strict objection of the Moslem to images. It is sculptured in low relief, the palm outwards, with the fingers and thumb in natural position. On this hand Ford [391] remarks that some consider it

an emblem of hospitality and generosity, the redeeming qualities of the Oriental. Others think it a type of the five principal

---

[388] See Fig. 115, p. 267, which, though modern, probably represents by Oriental unchangeableness equal antiquity.

[389] This is fully supported by the account given by the Abate Requeno of the statue set up by Numa Pompilius, in which the pose of the hands was specially ordered.

[390] Deut. xvi. 18; Dan. ii. 49; 1 Kings vii. 7.

[391] Murray's *Handbook for Spain*, 1855, vol. i. p. 301.

commandments of the creed of Islam: "To keep the fast of Ramadan, pilgrimage to Mecca, almsgiving, ablution, and war against the infidel." Others refer to the Hebrew *jadh*, the hand of God, the Oriental symbol of power and providence. But the true meaning of it is a talisman over the portal against the much-dreaded "Evil Eye," at which Orientals have always and do still tremble. The Morisco women wore small *hands* of gold and silver round their necks, like the Neapolitans, and a substitute for the classical phallic symbol of defiance. In the *Sala de los Embajadores* is an inscription to the same purport: "The best praise be given to God! I will remove all the effects of an evil eye upon our master Yusuf," etc.

Fully agreeing with Ford as to its real meaning, it may be noted as a coincidence that the act of taking a judicial oath is performed by Jews and other Orientals by holding up the right hand as thus depicted, also that a hand in this position upon the shield is the modern heraldic sign of baronetcy.[392]

In the mosaics at Ravenna, seven centuries older than the Alhambra (Fig. 107), our Lord and two angels are all in the act of holding up the right hand in the attitude of benediction. One has the hand open and extended, another angel in the same group, not here shown, has the hand in the like position; at the same time more angels have the hand conspicuously making the other gesture here drawn, which we shall explain later.

In the Church of San Apollinare in Classe at Ravenna the saint is in the main tribune standing beneath a great cross, with the Apostles on either

[392] The arms of Ulster are simply a large hand in this position, filling up the entire "field." Perhaps the most apt and the best-known illustration of the holding up of the hand as a powerful gesture is the account in Exodus xvii. 11: "And it came to pass, when Moses held up his hand, that Israel prevailed; and when he let down his hand, Amalek prevailed." Then because he could not hold it up continually it was held up by Aaron and Hur. The Scriptures are full of examples showing the great importance of manual gestures.

side of him, represented by twelve sheep. He himself has both hands held up open, with palms outward, evidently in the act of benediction. Above the cross is an open hand coming out of a cloud,

FIG. 107.—From San Apollinare Nuova, Ravenna.   Mosaic of sixth cent.
From a Photograph.

while on either side is a figure kneeling apparently on a cloud, but each of these latter is plainly making a conspicuous gesture with the hand—one with palm open and exposed, the other showing only the thumb and two first fingers. Above the arch of the tribune is a large medallion showing our Lord in the act of blessing the holy chalice; this He holds in His left hand, while the right is raised, showing only the two first fingers and the thumb. On either side of the medallion are the typical symbol-figures representing the four Evangelists, each of whom seems to be presenting a book to the central figure.

St. Mark, the companion figure to St. Luke (Fig. 114), is shown with his right hand raised high, palm open and thumb extended. It is not of course suggested here that all these persons are making gestures against the evil eye, but they are singular pieces of evidence as to the importance of the hand itself, and of the position in which it is held both in acts of devotion and of benediction.[393]

Considering the open hand as a distinctly used amulet of both ancient and modern times, we would call attention to its frequency at Tunis, where it may be seen displayed in a variety of ways over doors, or drawn upon walls in connection with the remarkable works of pictorial art by which the Haji announces his right to wear the green turban. These paintings upon the walls of the houses of returned pilgrims, although meant to portray animals and trees, are of such an exceedingly crude and rough sort that they can hardly be held to transgress the law that no Moslem shall make any object in the likeness of anything in heaven above or the earth beneath. In Tunis also may be seen many shallow drums, mere hoops of about two inches broad, having parchment

---

[393] The frequent reference in Scripture to the lifting up of the hands fully confirms the importance of this attitude of prayer : "Lift up your hands in the sanctuary" (Psalm cxxxiv. 2). "The lifting up of my hands as the evening sacrifice" (Psalm cxli. 2). "I stretch forth my hands unto thee" (Psalm cxliii. 6). "He lifted up his hands, and blessed them" (St. Luke xxiv. 50). See also Psalm xxviii. 2, lxiii. 4, cxix. 48, and many other passages.

stretched on both sides, just as if an ordinary tam-
bourine had two diaphragms instead of one.   Each
of these drums has a hand upon it like Fig. 104
upon one side, and on the other a double triangle.

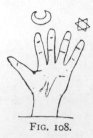

Some of these have, besides the hand,
a crescent and a double triangle, as in
Fig. 108 : in every case the crescent
is placed above the index and middle
finger, while the double triangle, which
we believe to represent the sun, is
always over the third and fourth finger.

FIG. 108.

The drawing is so rude that it is
difficult to tell whether the hand is right or left.

On inquiry about the meaning of these things,
they say the hand is that of the Prophet.   Seeing,
however, that these drums are all ornamented round
the rings with cowrie shells, fixed as they always
are with the opening in the shells outwards, one
could but form a further opinion : cowries have always
been distinct amulets against the evil eye,[393a] and it
is but reasonable to assign the same purpose to the
entire decorations.   Tunisian Moslems are like other
people, and pile up their defences by a combination
frequently alluded to.   The open hand is a very
common amulet upon Neapolitan cab-horses (Fig.
83) ; indeed it may be accepted as a well-understood
and completely-recognised protective amulet among
all nations, whether represented by painting, by
sculpture, or by gesture.   We give two more convincing examples from far-distant quarters.   On one
of the great marble columns in the church-mosque
of St. Sophia at Constantinople is a very remarkable

[393a] See Fig. 13.   Jahn also explains what these shells typify.   Phallic
students will readily understand them.

freak of nature.   There is a white mark in the dark
purple marble exactly like a spread-out hand; in
fact it is so good a representation that one naturally
fancies at first that it is artificial; but on close inspec-
tion it is found to be the natural marking of the marble.
It is about the size of the human hand, and is really
a conspicuous object when the visitor is conducted
to the front of it, as he is sure to be, by the guides.
The hand is near the *Mihrab* on the south side, about
seven feet from the floor, and is held in the very
highest reverence by the people as the hand of the
Prophet.   It is believed to protect all who go to
pray near it from the evil eye.   If this fine column
had, as some declare, a previous existence in an
ancient temple, who shall say to how many genera-
tions of men this strange piece of nature's art may
have been an object of veneration? [394]

In Fig. 77, from far-off North America upon the
Mandan chief's robe, is the representation of the
hand in the same position, placed there intentionally
to ward off the evil eye of his enemy and to protect the wearer.   How instinctively we throw up
our open hand with palm outwards as a gesture
prompted by surprise at any strange appearance,
or to ward off any threat not amounting to actual
violence!   It is also thus used involuntarily to stop
the undesired approach of any person or thing.   In
modern Neapolitan gesture-language "the raising
of the hands naturally with the palms opposed to
the object" signifies a negative to a question or

---

[394] This hand shows precisely the same gesture as those over the arch at the
Alhambra, and upon the drums of Tunis.   "The open hand was represented
on the coins of some of our Saxon kings in the tenth century; on one it is
accompanied by Alpha and Omega" (Twining, *Symbols and Emblems of
Early Christian Art*, p. 6).

demand.   It also signifies surprise, as with ourselves, and disapproval; [395] but to add effect to the
gesture when vehemence is intended, in addition
to the expression on his face, the actor violently
spreads out his fingers, "le dita saranno violente-

FIG. 109.

mente allargate l'uno dall' altro," precisely as drawn
upon the robe of Mah-to-wo-pa (p. 200).

Judging, however, from Canon Jorio's description of his plates, in four of which (Nos. 5, 6, 17, 18)
the attitude is shown, with descriptions in the text,
it would seem to be more like our own, an involuntary act of astonishment than of well-understood and
significant gesture. [396]   As a sacerdotal act it is of
course recognised everywhere, though he does not

[395] *Mimica degli Antichi*, Andrea de Jorio, *Napoli*, 1832, p. 227.

[396] Fig. 109, No. 17 of Jorio, is from a Greek vase published by Millin—
vas. ec. V. 1 tav. 66, by Inchirami, *Galleria Omerica*, ec. tav. 76.   He
says that of this picture Minerva is the *protagonista*, the central object towards
whom the eyes of all the other figures are directed.   The scene appears to
represent a council of armed heroes, amongst whom Minerva brandishes her
lance.   A careful study of the gestures leads to the conclusion that there is a
difference of opinion between those on her right and those on her left, for
reasons which he points out.

allude to it in that aspect, nor does he indeed to any
priestly action.

Precisely the attitude we are describing is to be

FIG. 110.

seen in a very characteristic painting by Perugino on
the soffit of one of the famous stanze in the Vatican,

Minerva turns her face to the right, while she raises her left arm with the
hand open; she seems to be in the act of stepping forward to the left, and is
pointing her left hand while brandishing her lance in the same direction. The
old man sitting on her right is holding his right hand spread out and reversed, as if to signify "Go gently," or "Don't excite yourself." The woman
standing raises her left hand with palm extended as if saying to the goddess,
"Listen! Keep quiet!" These two figures then being in tranquil attitudes
seem to say, "Wait; go carefully; the business is doubtful." The sitting
warrior has his left hand open, palm upward, a little raised—a position when
the hand is flat denoting a question asked, while the raising it upward denotes much disapproval of the words of his opponents. The standing figure
behind him has his right hand raised so as to show vivacity in his whole
body, and indicates his entire and active disapproval of the counsel of the others.
The whole picture represents Minerva proposing some great operation, which
those on her right discountenance, and advise prudent waiting, while those on
the left support and urge it with heat and animosity.

The whole picture is one of manual gesture telling a plain story.

Fig. 110, No. 18 of Jorio, is from a vase in the collection of Sir John
Coghill, and is fully described by Millingen. Jorio says the principal figure

that of the "Incendio di Borgo." In it our Lord is represented as ascending into heaven, but both hands are raised with open palms as though to wave off St. John and the other saints pressing around. In the four compartments of this vaulted ceiling our Lord holds one or both hands in special attitudes : in three making the sign with two fingers and thumb, the priestly benediction, and the fourth as above described, with both hands open wide, with palms outwards.

Among the Romans the hand was a specially favourite ornament, and was constantly placed upon household articles. In the Naples Museum are seen, from Pompeii and elsewhere, handles of stoves, braziers, and of many other utensils, flattened out into broad open hands where riveted to the body of the article. Door-knockers from Pompeii, of a pattern still commonly seen in Italy, have a hand grasping a ball, with the hinge at the wrist. We cannot look upon these hands as simply decorative, but suggest that they were used intentionally as well-known protective amulets, powerful indeed when simply open, but doubly so when bent into certain well-defined and recognised attitudes.

is Bacchus, closely watching the conversation of the other persons, who are at the same time making gestures as ancient as they are modern, relating to a special quarrel between the two women. The one on the left, fixing her eyes on her companion, and thrusting out her right forefinger to accentuate her look, says with emphasis, 'Thou !' That this 'thou' is intended as a reproach may be argued from her look ; but more certainly from the attitudes of herself as well as of her companion. Indeed she also stares back at her, lifts up both her arms in angry surprise and denial at the same time. Further, with the like significance, she throws back the upper part of her body, so as to enable her to steady herself on her feet. The other person, perceiving the anger of her opponent, raises her left hand and with thumb and forefinger makes the sign of love or friendship (see 5, Fig. 119). Jorio points out how cleverly the artist has told the story, and how plain all these things are to a Neapolitan : how that jealousy is shown in the left-hand woman, while the satyr goes on playing his pipes in apparent unconcern, while Bacchus also is taking the liveliest interest, etc.

In the Ashmolean Museum among the Egyptian amulets is a clenched hand pierced for suspension ; it is of rude modelling in blue porcelain, but it is evident from its general contour that it is meant for the same position as that shown in the Etruscan hand from Bologna (Fig. 102).

There is another of these in the Ashmolean which is also a small amulet to be worn, from Umrît, said to be Phœnician. The position of these hands is one which has evidently had a special meaning from very early times, and is still common everywhere, even here in England : in Italy it is so common that it has a technical name of its own, the *mano fica*. This has ever been a gesture of defiance and of insult among all nations. It denoted *per-summa ignominia* to the Romans,[397] and among all the Latin races it was connected with the fig,[398] and so conveyed a *hässlich* idea. In French *faire la figue*, Italian *far la fica*, Spanish *hacér el higo*, all denote this particular gesture of the thumb between the first and second fingers. Our English idiom of " Don't care a fig," which expresses the contemptuous idea, and implies the gesture, has its counterpart in the German *Fragen den Teufel*. The gesture is everywhere perfectly well understood, though the Teuton does not connect it with the fruit.[399] In classic times the hand in this position was well known as *manus obscœna*.[400] Everybody is familiar

---

[397] John Prætorius, *De Pollice*, Lipsiæ, 1677, p. 42. He refers to the Italian phrase " far le fiche."

[398] " The fig and the phallus were carried in processions in honour of Bacchus. Hence in Italy arose the term *far la fica*."—Payne Knight, *Symb. Lang.* p. 30.

[399] " To fig " (a person) is, " Einen durch Trotz oder Verachtung andeutende Verwegungen mit den Fingern beleidigen " (Hilpert).

[400] This is described by Ovid (*Fast.* v. 433) : " Signaque dat digitis medio cum pollice junctis."

" Favebant ii, qui manum in obscænum modum formabant."—*De Pollice*, 43.

with this gesture, which, if it has somewhat changed its meaning, has in all these ages by no means lost its force. The two following quotations seem to give it a northern habitat, but here in Somerset it is too common even to be noted.

Dean Ramsay remembered how in Yorkshire he and his school-fellows, from 1800 to 1810, "used to put our thumb between the first and second finger, pointing it downwards as the infallible protection against the evil influences of one particularly malevolent and powerful witch." [401]

They placed in the hand of the Midsummer Witch a vessel of the same kind with a long, narrow neck.

"It is filled with water," continued Judith, "drawn by herself from the sea on this very evening. Now, child, double thumb and come along."

Everybody knows that to double your thumb in your right hand averts danger. [402]

We have already fully described (p. 150) the amulet known as *turpicula res*, of which this *mano fica* formed one branch. Jorio, [403] who always calls this gesture *mano in fica*, says that there are many meanings conveyed by this sign (Fig. 111).

The most used amongst us is as an amulet against the evil eye; and the Neapolitans utter the expression, "*Te faccio na fica*," as if they would say to a friend: "May the evil eye do you no harm!"

This meaning is identical with that of making horns in the amulet sense; in fact when making this gesture they often pronounce the same sentence as they use in making horns against fascination.

FIG. 111.

[401] Atkinson, *Forty Years in a Moorland Parish*, quoted in *Athenæum*, May 23, 1891, p. 662.

[402] Walter Besant, *Dorothy Forster*, 1885, p. 7. Scene laid in Northumberland.

[403] *Mimica degli Antichi*, p. 155.

" *Mal-uocchie non ce pozzano !* " ([may] evil eyes not overwhelm you, literally, "throw down a well "). The only difference is that the *mano in fica* has a little more force than the horns in the idea of those who have faith in it.

Among Italians this gesture has the same meaning as among us and other people far and near— that of intense contempt or defiant insult. In this sense it is referred to by Dante,[404] and twice by Frezzi.[405] Trissino [406] also uses it, almost copying Dante.

Jorio describes this as a most insulting gesture, equivalent to our "A fig for you! Go to Bath!" except that the Neapolitan equivalent *fuori ₂ ·otta,* as a low, "outside-the-barrier" sort of place, carries infinitely more scorn than "to Bath." [407]

Another meaning of the sign, beyond the limits of our present purpose, is discussed under the heading : "*Invito turpe.*"

In offering or presenting any object to another

[404] " Al fine delle sue parole il ladro
Le mani alzò con ambeduo le fiche,
Gridando : Togli, Dio, chè a te le squadro."
Inferno, Canto xxv. 1-4.
[405] " E fe le fiche a Dio 'l superbo vermo."
Il Quadrir, ii. 19.
" E fe le fiche a Dio il mostro rio,
Stringendo i denti ed alzando le braccia."
Ib. iii. 10.
[406] " Poi facea con le man le fiche al cielo
Dicendo : Togli, Iddio ; che puoi più farmi ? "
L'Italia Liberata, Canto xii.
The latter authors are quoted by Cary.
[407] " Se poi viene un susurrone
E lodando vi scompone,
Presto il pollice volgete
Sotto l'indice, 'l tenete
A lui ritto ritto in faccia
Sin che parti, over si taccia."
Marugi, *Capricci sulla Jettatura,* p. 134.
The author says in a note : " This is the most efficacious of all the expedients up to this time practised. Make trial of it, and you will be grateful to me."

person in order to avert any evil which may accompany it from the giver, when the article is of such a nature as to need support of the closed hand (*pugno*), it ought, in such case, to be held in the position of *mano in fica*. If the object be such, *per esempio*, as a plate held by thumb above and finger under, then the other fingers are to be placed *a mano cornuta*, of which we have now to speak.

This position of the hand is shown five times in Fig. 112 by the hand alone, also grasping a key and a flower, as amulets in silver and other materials; also on the Indian goddess (Fig. 115) grasping rings.

The Neapolitans have but one *gesto* to imitate horns, but so great and so many are the qualities and diversities of its signification, that these (latter) apply not only to this gesture, but also to natural horns, to their resemblances, and even to their simple name.

Thus Jorio [408] begins his dissertation of over thirty pages upon *Corna, far le corna*, and after referring to the multitude of writings on the subject, says he shall consider it under the following heads :—

1. What kind of horns do the Neapolitans use? 2. The ideas they associate with horns, of whatsoever kind they may be, including the gesture and the word *horns*. 3. Finally, if the ancients had in whole or in part the same ideas and the same customs, or at least the same gestures, as the moderns relating to the horn. The words *horn* or *horns* are used indifferently, and apply alike to the horn alone or to the two which adorn the heads of *animali corniferi*.

He says of natural horns, that those of bullocks, the most used, are to be seen in gardens, on the top of palings, on the houses even of the nobility ; that in these latter, the horns of Sicilian oxen are most in request. Those of rams and goats, of which wine-

[408] *Mimica degli Antichi*, Napoli, 1837, p. 89.

sellers and the lower classes make most use, are
suspended in the inside of the houses, or at the
door, and sometimes in the window. Less common
are those of the stag, which may be seen dangling

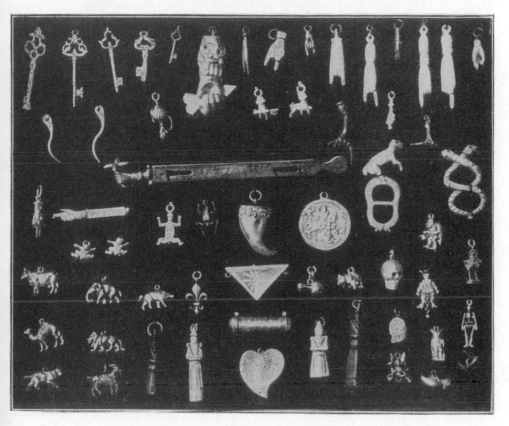

FIG. 112.—From the Author's Collection.

at the doors of chemists' and grocers' shops, who, if
they are able, obtain the horns of the elk, known as
the *Gran bestia*. Of buffaloes' horns scarcely any
are to be seen ; when seen they are suspended in dark
or ignoble places. These distinctions, not *di rigore*,

are often modified according to the ease with which any kind of horn can be procured.

Artificial horns are made chiefly for the convenience of carriage on the person. Hence they are fashioned in small sizes and with much elegance. The most frequent material is coral, but plenty are to be had in gold, silver, mother of pearl, amber, or lava. One of the vendors not long since exposed for sale some exceedingly minute *mani cornute*, in gold, silver, coral, etc., and the business done proved that the artist knew the wants of his countrymen.

Whether through lack of horns, real or artificial, or whether it be that among us (Neapolitans) the idea of the horn is so widespread and deeply rooted that few will be without one, the fact is, that they have at length got to consider as a real horn any object whatever that resembles it. The following objects are therefore most particularly used. The claw of crab or lobster, cocks' spurs, claws or teeth of animals, as those of tigers and wild boars, horseshoes, half-moons, etc.

The word horn. When the Neapolitan has need of a horn for any purpose, and has not either a real or artificial, nor anything resembling one, he makes use of the name, uttering the word *horn* or *horns* once or oftener according to the force he intends to give.[409]

As a gesture. The index and little finger extended, the middle and ring finger clasped by the thumb, as shown in many illustrations.

The hand thus posed and raised vertically gives a very good imitation of the head of a horned animal, and therefore we give to this gesture the name of the horned hand (*mano cornuta*). Just as this unique sign imitating horns has very many different meanings, so we attach to it all the diverse ideas which belong to the word *horn*.

---

[409] *Mimica degli Antichi*, Napoli, 1837, p. 92.

As a potent gesture protecting against the evil eye, the *mano cornuta* is constant and persistent. A Neapolitan's right hand is almost constantly in that position, pointing downwards, just as the hand charms are made to hang downwards, and in this position they take the place of an amulet worn habitually against unknown and unsuspected attacks. Of all the ideas connected with the *mano cornuta*, that of fascination holds by very far the largest place.

When, however, it is desired to use the sign specially against a particular individual, the hand so posed is thrust out towards him, and if there is no fear of his person, towards his very eyes, from which so much is dreaded. That is, of course, if he be present, but if absent, the sign is made in the direction of his supposed whereabouts.

Jorio [410] tells a story of a sprightly Napoletana who was over-credulous of the effects of fascination.

Observing that another lady whom she believed to be a *jettatrice* was highly praising the beauty of her husband, and especially of his well-formed thighs and legs, she wished to have recourse to the horn. Not having at hand the grand preservative, nor being able to supply it (openly) by a gesture, and what is more, not believing the repetition by her lips of the word *corno, corno, corno*, to be sufficient, she pretended to have need of a handkerchief. She therefore put her hand into her husband's pocket, and there made the *mano cornuta*. Then, with the points of her index and little fingers well extended, began to stab the thigh bone of her husband with such force, as if she wanted to pierce through it (*bucarlo*) : indeed, if she did not pierce it, it was only because she could not. Nor did she leave off her preventive operation until the believed *jettatrice* turned her talk in another direction. Neapolitan ladies wear little horned hands of various materials suspended at the end of a necklace, which is ordinarily hidden in the breast; but whenever a person appears who is suspected of being a jettatore, the hand quickly goes to the necklace, and the amulet is brought out, dangling in the direction considered necessary. As etiquette does not permit this to be

[410] *Mimica*, p. 100.

done openly in society, they pretend to be adjusting the kerchief, but the fact remains, that they seek to make sure of, and to touch if possible, the *gran preservativo del fascino.*

Over and above its use as a preventive gesture, the *mano cornuta* when raised vertically towards the person's own forehead denotes what some consider an ornament, the exalted horn ; but on the other hand, when pointed towards the chin, it implies conjugal infidelity to the husband. This idea is not by any means confined to Italy. In Brand, under the heading "Cornutes," is a long chapter upon this subject, and we gather that at least in Brand's time the gesture made with the little and fore fingers had the same meaning here in England that it has still in Italy—where at the present day the gesture made, as last described, is looked upon as an unpardonable insult which blood alone can wipe out. Amongst ourselves the gesture seems to have quite died out and become forgotten, the result, we hope, of improved morals ; but during the seventeenth century the perpetual allusion to cuckolds and horns is a distinct blot upon the literature of the period. Shakespeare has many allusions to the subject, though less in proportion than many of the coarser dramatists.[411]

Addison complains[412] that "cuckledom is the basis of most of our modern plays," showing that it was still common talk. We know it was a frequent topic in the last century, yet now the words seem quite to have dropped out of literature. No quotation

---

[411] "It shall hang like a meteor o'er the cuckold's horns" (*Merry Wives of Windsor*, Act ii. Sc. 2). "An old cuckold with horns on his head" (*Much Ado about Nothing*, Act ii. Sc. 1). Marston in his *Malcontent*, Act iv. Scene 5, calls Agamemnon, Prince Arthur, and Hercules, cornutes. So also Ben Jonson in *Every Man in his Humour*, Act iii. Scenes 3 and 6, also in Act v. Scene 5, alludes to both horns and cuckolds.

[412] *Spectator*, No. 446.

of the word could be found for the *New English Dictionary* later than 1728 without going to Ford's *Spain*, where the word is referred back to the sixteenth century.

Both the gesture and its implication are still well known in all European countries. "Faire les cornes à quelqu'un !" "Porter les cornes"; "Far le corna a uno"; "Portar le corna"; "Llevár los cuérnos"; "Einem Hörner aufsetzen" ("to cuckold any one"); "Hörner tragen," are all identically the same in meaning.

How the notion first arose and where, are points of great difficulty. Brand discusses the question at great length, gives many recorded opinions, but leaves it unsolved. He places its origin according to the earliest data he produces at the time of the Crusades; but Jorio declares the ancient Greeks to have used the horns, and also the gesture, in the same signification as at present: further, he dwells on the extreme antiquity of the use of the fingers as representing them. He considers the cornucopia of Amalthea the she-goat, the symbol of abundance, to have been an amulet.[412a] Also he places the Rhyton of Dionysus in the same category, as well as the musical horn; and he winds up by declaring that their signification " è particolarmente di amuleto contro del fascino." He describes the various amulet horns, their shapes, their being deprived of all ornament except at the point, their mode of attachment or suspension, their representation in (ancient) pictures and bronzes accompanied by the phallus, especially at Herculaneum, where they appear also upon the household utensils (*arnese*). He also refers

[412a] See *Mano Pantea*, post, p. 318.

to the horns found among the fruits depicted on
the walls of Pompeii, and says that "our Neapolitan
fruiterers," who display their goods so openly outside
their shops, "never fail to place among them a fine
pair of horns, for the purpose of keeping off other
folk's envy, evil eyes, fascination." [413]

He refers to the only two isolated horns of metal
discovered, one of bronze, the other of iron; both
are solid, and so could never have been cups, and consequently they could have been of no use except for
suspension.   He also describes the heads of two
oxen, from the mouths of which proceeds the phallus.
The latter are referred to and depicted by Jahn, Taf.
V.   Another bronze from Herculaneum, no longer
to be seen in the Royal Museum, is an ox's head, intended for suspension, on which are grouped three
half-moons and three phalli.

Jorio describes at length, in much detail, a plaster
(*intonaco*) from Herculaneum in which one of the male
figures is making the *mano cornuta* with the left
hand.   He gives his full reasons why the figure is
not intending insult, or for any of the other purposes
(than the protective) to which the gesture is applied,
and concludes the long discussion by declaring that
"at such an action, one of our Neapolitans would
not have hesitated a moment to exclaim : *Benedica !
mal-uocchie non ce pozanno !*"   He says the Museum
has abundant examples of this gesture as an amulet
contro al fascino, and concludes with : "In the vast
field of amulets, every one was known to the
ancients, and the moderns have not added thereto
one single *Corno*." [414]

---

[413] *Mimica degli Antichi*, p. 109.
[414] *Mimica*, p. 120.   It has already been remarked that every species of

Again, the sixth century mosaics[415] of Ravenna give us further illustrations. In Fig. 113 the remarkable hand appearing from the clouds, representing the Almighty, is very plainly in the position we have been considering, and looking at the scene in which

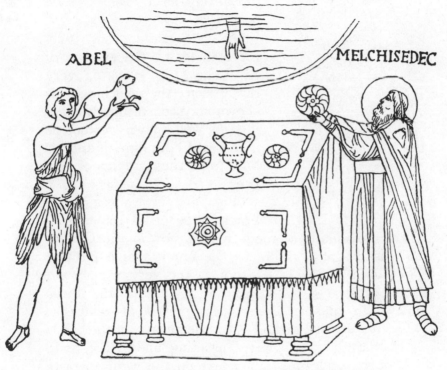

ABEL   MELCHISEDEC

FIG. 113.—From San Vitale, Ravenna. Mosaic of the sixth century.

it occurs we cannot but regard it as a feature of great importance. In the same church and in others at Ravenna the hand is seen coming out of the clouds,

charm of whatever kind soever against the evil eye is called in the vernacular *un corno ;* hence the above. Later on we shall see that he is mistaken, or at least some have been invented since his day.

[415] The illustrations from the Ravenna mosaics are all from photographs in the writer's possession, obtained on the spot.

especially in the scenes of Abraham's sacrifice of
Isaac (Fig. 116), and of Moses putting off his shoes
before the burning bush (Fig. 117); but in no other
case known to the writer does
the *Dextera Dei* appear so unmistakably as a *mano cornuta*
as in Fig. 113.

A bull standing and fully
represented, as the symbol of
St. Luke (Fig. 114), is very
rarely seen ; the saint himself is
shown very conspicuously making the well-known gesture as
if to guard both himself and his
bull from the assaults of evil
eyes.

FIG. 114.

Fig. 115 is from a small
brass statue of an Indian god-
dess, evidently of modern date, now in the County
Museum at Taunton. The unmistakable position
of both hands is a proof of the very widespread
importance attached to the gesture of the *mano
cornuta*, and is a convincing proof of what has
been before remarked—that the gesture of the hands
in ancient statues has a meaning, and is not, as in
modern sculpture, dependent on the whim or taste
of the artist. It is to be noted here also that this
Indian statuette has one of the horned hands pointed
down in true *more Neapolitano*.

When we see the same thing in the early Christian
art of the sixth century at Ravenna, and in the present
day pagan art of India, we are compelled to admit
that symbolism is independent of religious faith, and
that there is something in special positions of

the hands, which both pagan and Christian alike
recognise.

The several gestures in the Ravenna mosaics are
both interesting and remarkable ;
perhaps the more so from the fact
that none of them (except the *mano
cornuta*) are referred to as sacerdotal gestures in any of the books
on modern gesture language in
Italy, exhaustively dealt with by
Canon Jorio. Nor does he once
refer to any of those manual positions which must have been perfectly familiar to him as a priest.
Three positions of the right hand
raised are recognised as pertaining
to the act of sacerdotal benediction.
Of these, the two most usual are the
open hand for deacons and inferior
clergy shown by one angel, and that
of our Lord and the second angel in
Fig. 107 ; the latter is that of the
Roman *mano pantea*. This position
is that which is still the proper
one for bishops of the Western
Churches, but in the early Church,
and down to the eighth century, a

FIG. 115.

third position was used : instead of the thumb the
little finger was raised ; and this is still the attitude
of benediction in the Orthodox Greek Church. In the
early mosaics at Ravenna, dating before the great
schism, we find all three positions. The Almighty
hand from the clouds in both the scenes here produced
(Abraham and Moses, Figs. 116, 117) has the first,

second, and fourth fingers extended, with the third or *anularius* closed upon the palm. The same position is depicted on the angel next but one on the right of our Lord enthroned, in the famous series at San Apollinare Nuova.[416] Again, in

FIG. 116.—From San Vitale, Ravenna.

the scene of the three men entertained by Abraham (Fig. 116), supposed to represent the three Persons of the Holy Trinity, they are severally making all three of the gestures described. Two are raising the right hand in the act of blessing, of whom the central figure makes the orthodox Greek

[416] This angel is not shown in Fig. 107, but in the great mosaic it appears next the angel with the open hand.

sign, while the personage on his left makes the
Western sign, and the third shows the open hand.
The position of the thumb
and two first fingers raised
seems to be the only one
in which "Il Redentore" is
portrayed, when in the act of lifting
the right hand in benediction. The
third figure in this scene, not being
treated as sacerdotal in character, has
his right hand laid naturally upon the
table; the two others have the left.

Fig. 117.

It is certain that these gestures
are intentionally depicted, and also
that they denote sacerdotal rank; for
later, by many centuries, we find the
same thing in the Giotto frescoes
at Assisi. There Saint Francis is
painted with his hands displayed so as to exhibit
the stigmata, but, inasmuch as he was never
a priest, his hands are simply crossed upon his
breast; while a mitred bishop, in the next panel, has
his right hand lifted in the benedictory gesture,
which by that time had become the only one used
in the Western Church.[417]

Among the simple amulets there are two other
positions of the hand, as shown in Fig. 112. The
forefinger alone extended is referred to by Jorio
very frequently as a gesture, but not described by
him as one used against the evil eye, yet the writer

[417] The importance attached to manual gesture in the rites of the Roman
Church is proved by the minute directions as to the position in which the
celebrant is ordered to make the sign of the cross at Mass. He is to turn the
little finger of the right hand towards the object which he is to bless, keeping
the right hand straight with the fingers extended and joined together with
the thumb (from *Pontificale Romanum*, Venetiis, 1836).

knows well that it is undoubtedly made and sold
thus, as an amulet for that purpose. Those shown
were purchased at a shop in the native quarter of
Naples, and the writer believes he has seen the
single forefinger, pointed up, fixed upon a horse's
back, but could not find one in the shops which
supply the saddlers. This gesture is, however, very
clearly marked in Fig. 74, where the Indian goddess
Indranee is shown as the celestial mother with her
child. The hand having the points of thumb and
forefinger touching, as shown in No. 3 on Fig. 118,
though also extremely common, with a great variety
of uses in the gesture language, is not, as a mere gesture, an amulet according to Jorio.[418] Jorio quotes the
Abate Requeno's system of numeration, and points
out that the sign so made means thirty (Fig. 94),
and that in number-lore thirty signifies *le nozze*
(marriage), while sixty represents widowhood. We
cannot follow these authors into all their ramifications, which are outside the evil eye, but the hand
in this position is, we repeat, commonly made and
sold as an amulet against it, although the gesture
itself is not one. It will be noted from Fig. 118,
No. 3, and Fig. 119, No. 5, that it is made with
both right and left hands, whereas the left only
signifies thirty, while the right in this position denotes three hundred. As a horse amulet this position of the hand is rather a favourite ; and we may
consider it to be adopted by those cabmen who
desire the custom of ladies—it being well understood
by all what the gesture indicates (*le nozze*). As a
gesture, however, it may be one of the most insult-

---

[418] The hand in this position is, however, made and sold as an amulet.
One of these is on Fig. 83 as a horse amulet, and a small one in coral is on
Fig. 112, among the charms for personal wear.

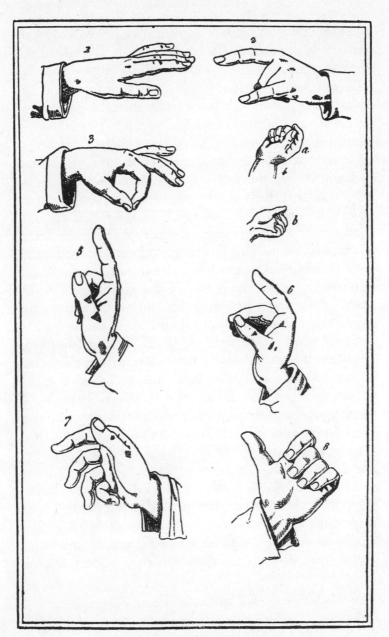

FIG. 118. See Description, p. 274.

ing, though its chief significance, according to Jorio,[419] is *inimicizia* (enmity); but by slightly altering the shape so as to form a circle it has a totally different signification, *disprezzo* (contempt). In both these meanings there is a distinct flavour of defiance, and perhaps on that account it may have been adopted as an amulet in the concrete form.[420]

Examination of any varied collection of charms will show that the hand is a common amulet in itself, also that it is used in combination with other objects: sometimes merely grasping them, and sometimes, while grasping the actual charm, making at the same time the important protective gesture.[421]

The silver hand grasping the dart is a prominent one on Fig. 112, and is one of the commonest to be seen. Another in coral holding a short sword appears on the same plate just above the serpents. In the Woburn Marble (Fig. 24) the gladiator is grasping a short sword; and again in the Cimaruta (Chap. X.) one of the branches ends in a hand grasping a sword. Moreover this arm grasping a dart, spear, or sword in various positions is one of the commonest of heraldic crests of the present day. One of the charms (on Fig. 112) is a key, and another the lotus; both are in *mano cornuta*. Two others are the *mano in fica*, one combined with a shell and the other with a flower-bud of some sort. The important one, however, is that at the end of the spada or sword. This is a hand grasping the lotus, and is no doubt considered a very potent charm.

---

[419] *Mimica*, pp. 46, 126.

[420] This gesture is called the Phallic hand (Forlong, *Rivers of Life*, p. 461).

[421] This is seen again in the Indian goddess, Fig. 115, who is grasping two large rings while making the *mano cornuta* with both hands.

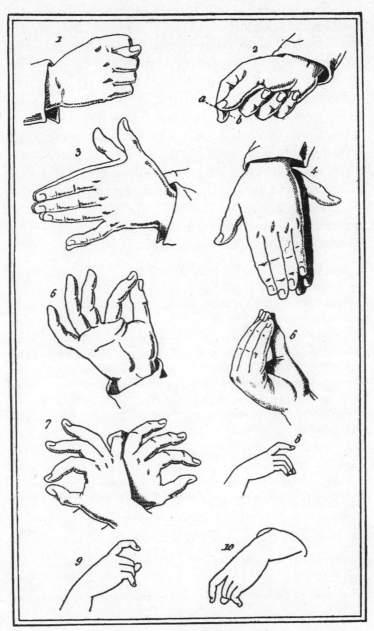

FIG. 119.   See Description, p. 276.

The spada is of silver, about six inches long, and is worn in the back hair by any girls rich enough to procure one. The specimen here shown has been much worn, and is a decidedly bright and effective ornament. Another coral arm is grasping a fish ; a hand grasping a fish, perhaps a dolphin, is also to be seen on the Cimaruta. The fish is an undoubted amulet, as may be seen on the gems, Figs. 16, 18.

None of these things are alluded to by Jorio, and we may accept it therefore as an axiom that the only two gestures, apart from the concrete, which of themselves constitute protective amulets, are the *mano cornuta* and the *mano in fica*.

We have reproduced here, as not out of place, the three pages of illustrations given by Jorio of the principal gestures in common use among Neapolitans of to-day. Concerning these, he has given full explanations and descriptions in the text. They are not, of course, strictly connected with our subject, yet so much has been said respecting manual gesture, and so many amulets exist in which the position of the hand is an important factor, that we cannot think these numbered attitudes, with a translation of their corresponding interpretations, will prove uninteresting.

FIG. 118.

1. Adagio. Minaccia. Mediocramente.
2. Mano cornuta pei suoi diversi significati.
3. Giustizia. Perfetto. Minaccia.
4. Poco.
5. Additare (*v.* l'Indice III). Indice solo disteso.
6. Schioppetto pei diversi suoi significati.
7. Ladro.
8. Bere. Additare.

1. Gently, soberly. Threat, menace. Indifferently, middling, so so.
2. Mano cornuta in its various significations.
3. Justice. Perfection, all right. Threat.
4. Little (in quantity).
5. To point with the forefinger. (He gives no less than twenty different meanings for this gesture.)
6. A gun, a musket, in its various significations.
7. Thief.
8. Drink. To point.

FIG. 120. See Description, p. 276.

Of course, where two or more significations may be given by the same position of the hand, the meaning is supplemented by facial and other expression. Jorio gives 32 pages to the explanation of No. 2, Fig. 118.

FIG. 119.

1. Mano in fica.	1. (Sufficiently explained.)
2. Danaro.	2. Money, coin.
3 and 4. Stupido.	3 and 4. Stupid, blockhead.
5. Amore.	5. Love, liking, attachment.
6. Chiedere.	6. To ask, to beg, to request.
7. Condotta versipelle.	7. Cunning, malicious conduct or behaviour.
8. Schioppetto.	8. Gun, musket.
9 and 10. Disprezzo.	9 and 10. Contempt, disdain.

FIG. 120.

1. Silenzio.	1. Silence, hold your tongue.
2. Negativa.	2. Denial, no.
3. Bellezza.	3. Beauty.
4. Fame.	4. Hunger, I want food.
5. Besseggiare.	5. To make a long nose, to mock, etc.
6. Fatica.	6. Labour, fatigue.
7. Stupido.	7. Stupid, blockhead, donkey, asses' ears. See p. 416.
8. Guercio.	8. Squint-eyed.
9. Ingannare.	9. To cheat, to deceive.
10. Astuto.	10. Crafty, cunning.

Only a study of the curious book itself can afford full information upon all these gestures.

CHAPTER VIII

THE CROSS

AMONG modern amulets, used specially and avowedly against the evil eye, the cross finds no place; for the simple reason that it has taken its position as the great Christian symbol, whereby its connection with times preceding Christianity has been severed, and its meaning modified to its later purpose.

Of all simple signs it is the easiest to make and the most common, whether ancient or modern. In these latter days it is often but a mere mark, like the chalk cross made by an artisan upon his work, or the sign-manual of our parish marriage register, yet in many of its forms and uses it has a very distinct and special meaning.

Among the ancient Egyptians the cross was very common. Standing on a heart (as in Fig. 121) it was the symbol of goodness [422]; the same form in hieroglyphic writing is the ideograph *nefer* or the phonetic *n*.[423] It is shown thus on a tablet depicted by Maspero [424] together with a Calvary cross. These tablets (*dalles*), found in considerable numbers, were slabs of stone, whereon were sculptured models, to teach the apprentices their trade;

[422] Wilkinson, vol. iii. p. 352.   [423] Budge, *Nile*, pp. 55, 65.
[424] *Arch. Egypt.* pp. 190, 191.

and they show examples of stone carving in all
stages from the mere outline to the finished work.

At the Ashmolean Museum are undoubted amulets
from ancient Egypt, such as Figs. 121, 122. Quite
as ancient as any of these is a small ornamental cross

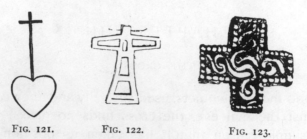

FIG. 121.   FIG. 122.   FIG. 123.

amulet of gold, found by Schliemann in the third
sepulchre at Mycenæ, now in the Athens Museum
(Fig. 123) [425] rather suggesting serpents in combination. Several other cross ornaments were found
in the same tomb, but they are not of this distinct
character. We are told that the Spanish conquerors
of Mexico were astonished at finding the cross
in common use by men whom they knew to be
heathens, and that they managed to ingratiate themselves with the natives by displaying the cross upon
their standards. Many crosses appear also on the
ancient Peruvian hieroglyphs (Fig. 126).

What the true symbolical meaning of the cross
may be, is a vexed question. On the one hand,
many hold it to be distinctly phallic; in India it
is always so considered, while others say the
"theory is monstrous and devoid of evidence." [426]
All authorities, however, agree that the T or tau

---

[425] He (Schliemann, *Mycenæ and Tiryns*, p. 66) says : "The cross with
the marks of four nails may often be seen " upon vases and other pottery.
[426] Baring-Gould, *Myths of the Middle Ages*, p. 358.

cross is the symbol of life [427] in both its forms, *i.e.* either the simple T, or with the loop handle attached. The latter is the *crux ansata* or *ankh*, seen in the hand of most of the Egyptian gods of the later period. In one or other of these forms it is traditionally held to have been the mark set upon Cain; also upon the houses of the Israelites in Egypt, to preserve them from the destroying angel.

The rod Moses stretched over the Red Sea and with which he struck the rock is supposed to have been topped with a cross; on the Tau the brazen serpent was upraised. Mediæval writers thought the two sticks gathered by the widow of Sarepta a type of the cross; but in Ezekiel ix. 4 the mark to be set on " the foreheads of the men that cry," etc., was certainly the T; for the Vulgate has : "Et signa Thau super frontes virorum gementium." Many authorities accept this rendering : St. Jerome "refers again and again to this passage"; SS. Cyprian, Augustine, Origen, and Isidore allude to it ; also Bishops Lowth and Münter ; " but there need be little doubt as to the passage." [428]

In the roll of the Roman soldiery after a battle it was customary to place T against those who were alive, and Θ against the killed.

In the Roman Catacombs is found the T or St. Anthony's cross ; in those very early days of the Church it symbolised the belief in the eternity of that life upon which the departed soul had entered. This was probably the transition period, when the cross had not yet been fully recognised as the special symbol of the Christian faith.

[427] Budge ; Wilkinson ; Baring-Gould ; Smith, *Dict. Bib.* etc., wherein many ancient authorities are quoted, forming the basis of modern research.

[428] Baring-Gould, *op. cit.* p. 377.

The ancient Britons worshipped the ⊤ or Tau as a god, and among Northmen of old the same figure was "the hammer of Thor," the Scandinavian Jove; reversed thus ⊥, it is the *yoni-lingam* symbol of the Hindoos.[429]

The *crux ansata* form is exceedingly wide-

FIG. 124.—Ancient.   FIG. 125.—Modern.

[429] Much discussion has taken place from time to time as to what was the real shape of the cross on which our Lord was crucified. The famous graffito found on the Palatine, now in the Kircherian Museum in Rome, seems to settle the question. Whether it is an actual blasphemous caricature, as most people believe, or whether it was, as King (*Gnostics*, p. 90) says, "the work of some pious Gnostic, of his jackal-headed god," is the question. A close examination of the photographs or of the original shows that the man who scratched it used two strokes to form ⊤, and that he afterwards added a short one over, to carry the superscription; for the line is perfectly distinct from the main upright line of the cross. Had he not been accustomed to the *tau* cross and none other, as the one with which he associated crucifixion, he would not so carefully have made his down stroke exactly meet the horizontal one, but would, as we should, have begun at the top, some way above the line of the arms. A comparison between King's plate, p. 90, and a photograph from the original, will show very clearly what we mean. In King's, the upright line is continuous from the superscription to the feet. In Lanciani, *Ancient Rome*, p. 122, is a photogravure which completely confirms the writer's own close observation, and enables him entirely to dispute Mr. King's explanation. In the photographs from the original, there is nothing to suggest the head of a jackal; it is even in his own drawing distinctly equine. Moreover, being in Rome a very short time after the find, the writer saw, and knows well, the spot whence the whole piece of plaster had been removed to the Museum, and there close by on the same wall was another graffito, possibly by the same hand, of a donkey turning a conical mill-stone with a plain inscription,

spread.[430] Not only is it found in the sculptures
from Khorsabad, from Nineveh, and in the Palmyra
sculptures now in the Louvre, but further east
in Persia and India. More remarkable still is it
to find the same sign in far-distant Peru, where
it appears as an actual shape cut through great
blocks of granite (Figs. 124, 125), both ancient
and modern at Cuzco, and also in the remarkable
hieroglyphics of the Incas reproduced in Fig. 126.[431]
The ancient Cuzco block at the time of the Conquest was used for the execution of criminals. The
head was inserted face down in the round aperture,
and a piece of wood jammed into the slot so as to
hold the neck tight ; the body was then seized,
violently lifted, and the neck dislocated.[432] There
are no means of ascertaining what the Incas intended by this *crux ansata*, but the fact remains that
it existed, and is found repeatedly in ancient Peru.
The cross was known in South America in several
other forms besides the *ankh*, as appears from the
hieroglyphics of Peru.

which read, *Labora asine*, etc. This has also been removed. Inasmuch as
the graffito is known to have been almost contemporary (A.D. 69) with the
event depicted, it forms a most convincing link in the chain of evidence that
our Lord suffered upon a *tau* cross. The spirit which would lead to such a
graffito as that here discussed is abundantly exhibited in Acts xxviii. 22.
Probably it was drawn while St. Paul was in Rome, when "this sect" was
spoken against.

[430] This subject is treated at great length by an anonymous writer in a
volume called *Phallism* (London, privately printed, 1889), but his facts are
different, and do not lead to the same conclusion as those here produced.

[431] A close examination of these inscriptions shows a strange general
resemblance to Egyptian characters. It will be noticed that the cross in
various shapes is very frequently used. The writing here reproduced is
reduced to one-fifth ; the original is now in the Museum of Cuzco. Wiener
says that although written about the end of the sixteenth century, the style
and characters are those used before the Conquest. The document was
found in the valley of Paucastambo, "dans le pays perdu de la Bolivie, à
Sicasica."

[432] Wiener, *Pérou et Bolivie*, p. 724.

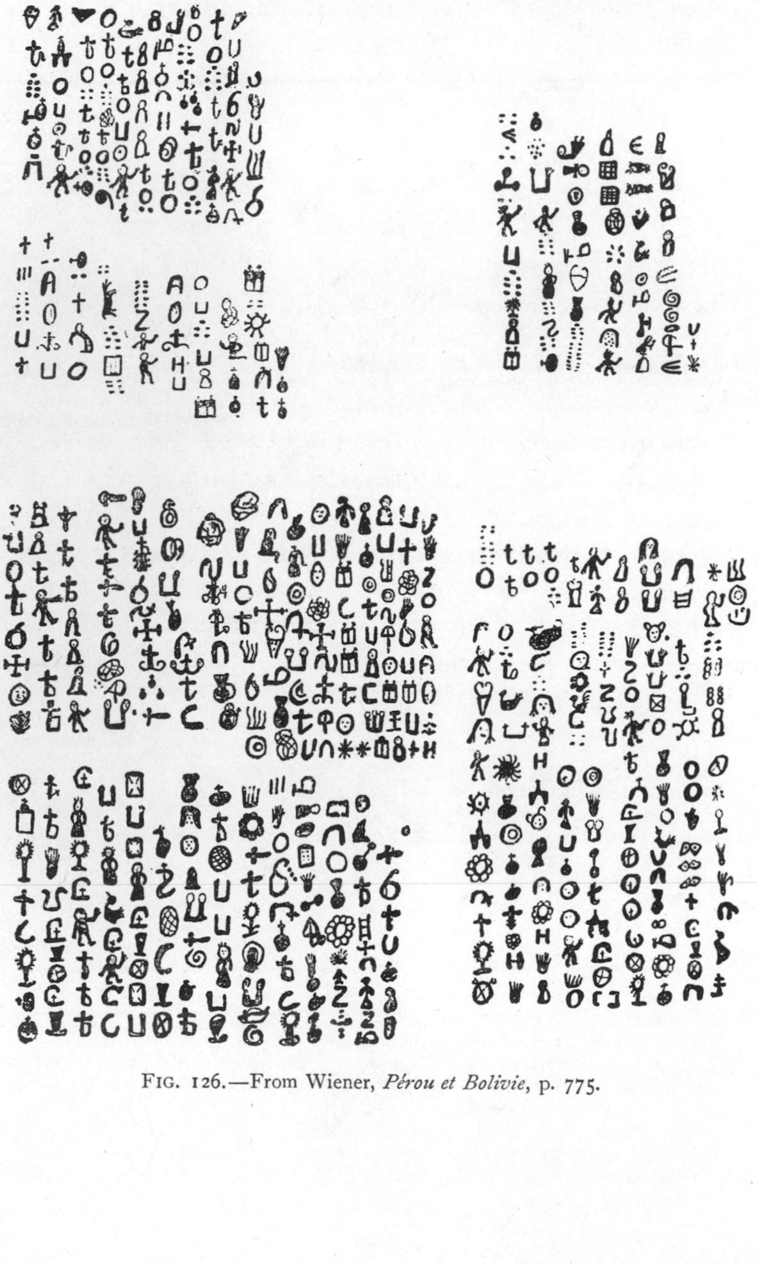

FIG. 126.—From Wiener, *Pérou et Bolivie*, p. 775.

A device almost exactly similar [433] is found on coins of Asia Minor, Cilicia, and Cyprus. It is placed on a Phœnician coin of Tarsus beneath the throne of Baal. Another is on a Sicilian medal of Camarina.

It is, however, in Egypt that this symbol, sometimes called the Cross of Serapis,[434] is most commonly to be seen in the hands of kings and gods alike. One scene [435] represents Amenophis II. having a double stream of these figures, alternated with the symbol of purity, poured out upon him by the gods Horus and Thoth. This same act is also a subject of sculpture at several places, and by the outpouring of life and purity denotes the king's purification, to fit him to stand before the god of the temple. In each case the king so purified also held the *ankh* in his right hand.[436]

Besides these, the same cross is in a way personified with arms and hands holding the symbol of purity. Especially were these noted by the writer at Medinet Habou and at Edfou (Figs. 127, 128). At both these temples the figures are repeated in rows, side by side, so as to form a decorative dado.

The meaning of the *crux ansata* wherever found is testified "in the most obvious manner," [437] denoting fecundity and abundance in the way universally understood by this symbol throughout India.[438] And

[433] Baring-Gould, *op. cit.* p. 362, who gives illustrations (Figs. 19, 20, p. 344) and quotes Raoul Rochette, *Mém. de l'Académie des Inscr.* tom. XVI.

[434] Payne Knight, *Symbol. Lang.* p. 238.

[435] Wilkinson, *Anc. Egypt.* iii. 362.

[436] In Fig. 103 it will be noticed that one of the Sun's hand-rays is holding the symbol of life to the lips of Khuenaten. In the other plate referred to (Wilkinson, i. 40) two of these same hand-rays are holding the *ankh* to his lips and to those of his wife.

[437] C. W. King, *Gnostics*, p. 72.

[438] Ardanari Iswara is represented (Forlong, *Rivers of Life*, vol. ii. p. 374, Pl. xiv.) as a female standing on a water-lily with the *crux ansata* as her only

we may remark that the use of this cross as the
symbol of fertilisation is perfectly consistent with the
sign being that of the kind of life therein typified.[439]
All these examples are of ancient usage, but there

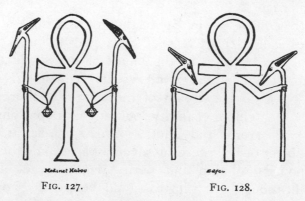

Medinat Habou   *Edfou*

FIG. 127.   FIG. 128.

will be little difficulty in showing that it has been used
throughout the Middle Ages, and that it is found to-
day in a form but slightly modified. At the present
day in Cyprus the women wear this cross as a talisman.[440] It is believed to keep off the evil eye and
to prevent or cure barrenness.

Fig. 129 is a coin of Ethelward :[441] besides a
smaller one in the inscription, there is a cross on
the centre of each side ; one of these is the *crux
ansata* in a form which is still more "obvious"
than that usually seen in the hands of Egyptian
gods or kings, or even upon the Indian Iswara.

ornament. Her right hand is raised in the position on which we have more to
say—that of the *mano pantea*.

 [439] "In solemn sacrifices all the Lapland idols were marked with the ♀ from
the blood of the victims. . . . It occurs on many Runic monuments in Sweden
and Denmark long anterior to Christianity."—Payne Knight, *Symbol. Lang.*
p. 30. One author (Forlong, *op. cit.* i. 317) asserts that this symbol was
adopted as the ancient pallium, which was shaped thus. He gives an illustration of it, as worn by a priest.

 [440] General di Cesnola, *Cyprus*, p. 371. [441] From *Archæologia*, vol. xix.

The object of a cross on each side of this coin
was the customary one, of placing protective amulets
against the evil eye upon coins, medals, and seals,
as well as upon buildings, public and private.
One of these amulet seals, having the sun and
moon upon it, was in actual use by the Dean
and Chapter of St. Andrew of Wells (Fig. 137),

Aethelweard.

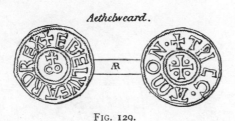

FIG. 129.

down to a comparatively late period—long since
the Reformation.   A careful consideration of the
coin of Ethelward will help us to understand its
later developments, especially if we look upon both
crux in corde (Fig. 121) and *ansata*, undoubted
amulets for suspension, as practically the same
things; for we cannot fail to see that all the
devices are but modified forms of one and the
same symbol.   On a cylinder from Babylon [442]
there is a figure holding a *crux ansata*, reversed
from its usual Egyptian position, and having the
cross upwards and the ring beneath.

Our next stage is shown in Fig. 130 where the
Third Person of the Holy Trinity, the "Lord and
Giver of Life," holds this same symbol, but slightly
changed, in His hand.   Again, in Fig. 131 the
Father Almighty holds the same symbol under His
left hand.   The only difference is that in both of

[442] Münter, *Religion der Babylonier*. Köpenhagen, 1827.

these examples the cross is upon the globe as well as above it.[443]

On a bas-relief from the Roman Catacombs is a representation of the Lamb, but instead of the usual flag He holds a staff, with a ball and cross on the

FIG. 130.—French MS. of fourteenth cent. FIG. 131.

top, precisely like the conventional orb and cross in the hand of kings and queens.[444] The historic gradation of the use, from remote ages to the present day, of this symbol of life in perpetuity as the badge of sovereignty, makes it clear, however unwilling

[443] Wilkinson, vol. ii. p. 344, gives a number of necklaces made up of amulets such as we have dealt with. Among these is a large scarab with the T cross upon it, just as is seen upon the orb in the hand of the First and Third Persons of the Holy Trinity, Figs. 130, 131. See also Fig. 141.

[444] These figures are from *Symbols of Early and Mediæval Christian Art*, by Miss Louisa Twining, to whom I am indebted for kind permission to reproduce.

devout worshippers of royalty may be to assent, that the object we know so well as the orb and cross, is nothing else but a powerful amulet against the evil eye.

Those who remain sceptical as to our chain of facts will perhaps be convinced by the following. In days when brewing used to be done at home, the writer, as a boy, has often watched and helped the operations. When the malt was steeped in the "mashing vat" our old man used to cover it up with cloths "to let it steevy"; but before doing this he never failed "to zet the kieve." This was to make upon the surface of the mash "two hearts and a criss-cross," as in Fig. 132. Inquiry always brought the same answer: " Nif didn zet the kieve, they there pixies wi'd safe to spwoil the drink." The figure of a heart is made with the utmost ease by placing the two forefingers together at the indentation, and then moving each simultaneously so as to meet at the bottom, and make the two sides. Precisely the same sign used constantly to be made on the fine soil of a bed after sowing any special seeds, such as cabbage, onions, etc., so that it may not be over-looked.[445] Here then we have a distinctly modern

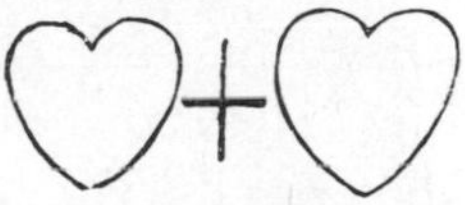

FIG. 132.

---

[445] The same thing was done all round the countryside when people used to bake at home. The barm put into the dough is called "setting the sponge." The batch is then lightly covered and left all night "to rise." It is at this time that the "two hearts and the criss-cross" were and are made upon it, precisely similar in kind, and for the same purpose, as upon the mash in brewing, or on the seed-bed. It is of course to this old custom that Herrick refers in his *Hesperides*:

This I'll tell ye by the way,
Maidens, when ye leavens lay,
Crosse your dow, and your dispatch
Will be better for your batch.

amulet of the same identical elements as that on the coin of Ethelward ; for by merely bringing the two hearts together, and slightly rounding them, with the cross placed on the top, we have the "obvious" figure itself.

Whatever may have been the notion of the designers of St. Peter's in Rome and St. Paul's in London, the fact remains that each of these great Christian churches bears on its highest point the orb and cross of royalty, no other than the *crux ansata* (a symbol of the perpetuation of life in one aspect, and a potent amulet in another), raised high above the people, like the famous cricket of Pisistratus at Athens, the crocodile at Venice, the devils on Notre Dame, and the *diavolo* at Florence, protecting them from the wicked glance of the evil spirits expected to lurk around when the bells are silent. Of course all this will be set down as pure speculation ; but of such cavillers we would ask, first for a better explanation of the ball and cross, and next for any explanation whatever of the maintenance of bells other than that they represent an ancient custom, founded, like the orb and cross, on an ancient belief.[446]

That the cross was actually worn as an amulet in ancient times is clearly proved by the fact that two

> In the morning when ye rise,
> Wash your hands and cleanse your eyes.
> Next be sure ye have a care
> To disperse the water farre ;
> For as farre as that doth light,
> So farre keeps the evil spright.

[446] This belief is not merely a superstition of the early or mediæval Church, but of much more ancient times. Bells were adopted from heathendom by Christians, though they have been rejected by Mahomedans.

> " Temesæaque concrepat æra
> Et rogat ut tectis exeat umbra suis."
>
> Ovid, *Fast.* v. 441-2.

men called Kharu (Syrians) appear on Egyptian sculptures actually wearing it suspended to the neck.[447]

At the British Museum may be seen a large cross amulet suspended from the neck of Tiglath Pileser in the great tablet from Nimroud.   At this day necklaces made of a string of crosses are worn by the Indians of Peru,[448] but these latter may be from Christian sources, though that is by no means even probable.

There are other kinds of cross among the variety used in heraldry or ornament, which certainly have a mystery about them, and some of which are amulets.[448a]   Foremost among these is the *svastika* of the Hindoos, the fylfot - cross or *gammadion*, called also by some the "catch L," ⊐⊏.

Among the Hindoos this was the mark or sign of Vishnu,[449] the beneficent preserver of life.   It is proved now to be a sun symbol, by Mr. Percy Gardner, who has found a coin of the ancient city of Mesembria in Thrace, on which is the fylfot with a sun on its centre.   The name of the place means the city of " Mid-day," and this name is also figured on some of its coins by the legend ΜΕΣ ⊐⊏,[450] which clearly and decisively proves its meaning.   This form of cross was early adopted among Christian symbols, for it is found in the Roman Catacombs of

---

[447] Wilkinson, *Anc. Egypt.* i. 246.   [448] Wiener, *Pérou et Bolivie*, p. 667.
[448a] Those especially known as *fleurie*, and *fleurettée*, have each limb tipped with the *fleur-de-lis*, while the cross *botonée* is tipped with the fig-leaf. Both of these fantastic ornamentations have distinctly phallic meanings which add power to the cross as an amulet.   See Inman, *Anc. Faiths*, pp. 150-165.   [449] C. W. King, *Gnostics*, p. 229.
[450] Goblet d'Alviella, *Migr. des Symb.   Athenæum*, No. 3381, p. 217. See Letter from Prof. Max Müller, *Athenæum*, No. 3382.   Also R. P. Greg, *On the Meaning and Origin of the Fylfot and Svastika.*   1884.

the fourth century.[451] As a mystic sign it is said to have travelled further than any other symbol of antiquity.[452] It was known in Iceland in the ninth

FIG. 133.

century; it is known all over Asia, including Japan;

[451] Brownlow, *Roma Sotterranea*, vol. ii. p. 177.

[452] It occurs on an old stone cross in company with Ogham inscriptions at Aglish (J. Romilly Allen, *Christian Symbolism*, p. 97) in Kerry. On these the arms are reversed so as to make it appear to turn against the sun. In King's *Gnostics* the *svastika* is shown both ways.

all over Europe from Iceland to Greece, Sicily, and
Malta.   It is found on the oldest Greek coins, on
Etruscan vases, and on the Newton Stone, an ancient
Celtic monument at Aberdeen.[453]   Comte Goblet
traces it to the Troad as its birthplace, some
thirteen hundred years before Christ.   Schliemann
found at Mycenæ a terra-cotta dish, on one side of
which "are engraved a number of ⊐⊔s, the sign
which occurs so frequently in the ruins of Troy."[454]
He says the same sign was often found on vases and
pottery.[455]

From its appearance on coins and from its being
a sun sign we may accept the conclusion that the

FIG. 134.

fylfot was an amulet against the evil eye "of
wonderful diffusion."   We are told that the *triskelion* or *triquetra* is a modification of the fylfot,
and that it was adopted as the badge of Sicily by
Agathocles about 317 B.C. and later by the Isle

[453] King, *Gnostics*, p. 176.
[454] *Mycenæ and Tiryns*, p. 77.   This would put the date indefinitely
further back than Comte Goblet does.   [455] *Ib*. p. 66.

of Man.[456] We are told [457] that the arms of Sicily and the Isle of Man consist of three human legs of identical pattern, except that the latter are spurred. With all deference to high authority we would point to the illustration Fig. 133, which is from a photograph of an ancient relief at Palermo, with the Gorgon's head in the centre, whereas the Manx arms are plain and have no head. The same device with the head was found on a Greek altar in Malta (Fig. 134) [458] and on a gem (Fig. 135).[459] The Manx arms are borne by several old English families, and are said to have been brought to England by Crusaders returning *viâ* Sicily. All this does but support and confirm what we have remarked as to the real meaning and basis of modern heraldry.

FIG. 135.

[456] On an ancient Etruscan vase found at Volci, now in the Museum of Rouen, is a scene representing a fight between Athena and Enceladus. On the shield of the fallen giant is the triskelion : the legs are naked, meeting in the centre, without the Gorgoneion (Daremberg et Saglio, p. 102).

[457] Goblet d'Alviella, *op. cit. Athen.* No. 3381, p. 217.

[458] From *History of Malta*, Boisgelin, 1805, p. 18.

[459] King, *Handbook of Gems*, p. 361.

CHAPTER IX

THE MANO PANTEA

THE hand in the attitude of sacerdotal benediction, having the two first fingers and thumb extended, was an amulet against the evil eye long before the Christian era. Fig. 136 is from the Naples Museum (about eight inches high), No. $\frac{5595}{1737}$, from Pompeii. Being mounted on a stand, its purpose is evidently the same as the plain open hand (Fig. 104).

FIG. 136.

Jorio [460] has nothing whatever to say about this position, henceforward called that of the *Mano Pantea*. As a gesture by the common people it is not used at all, but is evidently left for the priests alone,[461] being specially the attitude of our Lord in the act of benediction, as shown by the Ravenna mosaic (Fig. 107, p. 248).

Of the three men entertained by Abraham, the one who may be supposed to represent the Second

---

[460] Possibly Canon Jorio was a Freemason as well as a priest. In either capacity he would be quite familiar with the gesture.

[461] In a scene (*Canon. Misc. MS.* 378, Bodleian; before referred to in connection with Roman insignia, Chapter V.) representing a dispute between Epictetus and Hadrian, both are represented as making this sign. This mediæval design is, of course, only historical, as relating to the period in which it was produced, but it is nevertheless a valuable testimony to the then universal practice of significant manual gesture.

Person of the Trinity, as already described, holds
the right hand thus, while the central figure, the
First Person, is making the Eastern sign of benediction, also explained, with the first, second,
and fourth fingers.   Again, in the great twelfth
century mosaic of our Lord on the tribune of the

FIG. 137.   FIG. 138.

Cathedral of Monreale in Sicily the attitude is the
same as in Fig. 107 though six centuries later,
and twelve centuries later than Fig. 136.   Although
this position of the hand is that usually assigned to
Him, it is by no means restricted to the Second
Person, for there are several instances where the
Almighty Father is shown in this attitude, and, further,
the Holy Spirit is portrayed in human form with the
right hand raised in this gesture [462] (Figs. 130, 131).

[462] In Fig. 131 all the Persons of the Holy Trinity have the right hand in
the same attitude.   The seal of the Dean and Chapter of Wells (from an autotype
in Canon Church's *Early History of the Church*, from the "Wells Manuscripts,"
1894), here reproduced (Fig. 137), which was in constant use down to the

There are very interesting examples of this
special attitude, attributed not only to all the
Persons of the Holy Trinity separately, but in two
cases Miss Twining [463] (in Plates xxxiv. xxxv.) represents the Trinity by one single, seated figure, who,

FIG. 139.

in both plates, is lifting the right hand in the position
we are now discussing.   There are many other examples of this attitude attributed to the Almighty
Father, where the hand alone, or *Dextera Dei*, in
this position is shown coming down from the clouds.
Fig. 139, from the Norman tympanum at Hover-
ingham, Notts,[464] shows this Almighty hand reaching down to St. Michael fighting with the dragon.[465]

last century, has the *Dextera Dei* in the attitude we are describing.   Moreover, it contains the Gnostic pagan symbols of the sun and moon, and on
that account we can but consider them as placed on the seal as a protective
amulet, like those so frequently seen on other seals and coins.

[463] *Symbols of Early and Mediæval Christian Art*, 1852.   Fig. 138 "is
from Plate xxxiv., the Benedictional of St. Ethelwold, a Saxon MS. of the
tenth century."   The Trinity in Unity is the idea set forth in both examples
referred to.

[464] J. Romilly Allen, *Christian Symbolism*, 1887, p. 163.

[465] In Miss Twining's book are many representations of the First Person
by the hand alone in several positions, especially on Plate ii., where it appears in the usage of the Eastern Church, from a Greek MS. of the tenth
century.   On the same plate are seven examples of the hand posed as in

As a modern amulet to be worn, the writer has
never seen a simple hand thus posed,
but always with other attributes
placed upon it. Thus combined it is
one of the most remarkable of all the
composite charms known against the
evil eye, whether of ancient or modern
times. The original from which Figs.
147, 148 are taken is now in Berlin,
but there are in the Kircherian Museum in Rome

FIG. 140.

FIC. 141.

FIG. 142.

two or three others similar in type, but widely differ-

Fig. 140. This hand is from the portal of the Cathedral of Ferrara, of the
twelfth century. This was the form of the ancient " Main de Justice," sur-
mounting the staff which was used in France at coronations, and was preserved in the treasury of St. Denis. This hand appears on the seal of Hugh
Capet, and was continued till the time of the Renaissance (Twining, op. cit.
p. 6).

Plate xxxii. shows two examples of the Almighty and of the Holy Spirit in
human form, each of whom has the right hand thus raised.

Plate xxxviii. shows the Holy Trinity (Fig. 141) as two persons seated,
both holding up the right hand as before, with the dove descending between
them (from a MS. in the British Museum, of the fourteenth century). Both
Persons are holding the orb with the left hand, on which is the sacred T
of life. A second Fig. on this, and another on Plate xxxix. show all three
Persons in human form, and all with the right hand thus raised, from a
French MS. of the fourteenth century in the Bibliotheque Nationale. Again,

ing in detail.   They are all from 6 to 8 inches high.

FIG. 143.

All are in the same attitude that we have been

FIG. 144.

FIG. 145.

describing, but each one has a varying combination

the orb and T are shown in the left hand of the Father.   These are all from
Miss Twining's book.

Fig. 142·represents Christ in Glory on the tympanum of a doorway in Ely
Cathedral.   Fig. 143 is the same subject, also on a tympanum of a doorway
at Essendine, Rutlandshire.   Fig. 144 is another Christ in Glory, from a
MS. of the Gospels at S. Gall in Switzerland.   Fig. 145 is a very early

of symbols upon it. One of these hands is in the British Museum (Figs. 156, 157), two are at Cortona,

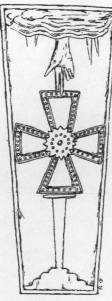

FIG. 146.

well known to the writer, in addition to those in Rome, mentioned above. Besides all these, Jahn gives particulars (p. 101) of fourteen other examples known to him, of which he says some are about the natural size, and some a little smaller; but he seems quite ignorant of the fact that they are made in Rome to-day and worn as amulets. Of these so-called "votive hands" Jahn says (p. 102) that two have inscriptions upon them; of these, one in the Barberini collection in Rome has

CECROPIVS · V · C · VOTUM · *Solvit,*

and the other in London, in the possession of Lord Londesborough, has :—

ΖΟΥΠΟΡΑϹ ΕΥΞΑ
ΜΕΝΟϹ ΑΝΕΘΗ
ΚΕΝΟΑΒΑΖΙ
ΕΑϹϘΙΤΚΟϢϢ

He says the first lines are clear, *i.e.* Ζούπορας εὐξάμενος

treatment of the same subject from a sculptured slab on the Saxon church of Daglingworth in Gloucestershire.

In all these illustrations the right hand of Christ is raised in the same attitude, and examples might be multiplied to any extent, but enough have been produced to show distinctly that it was not represented by accident, but that it was the recognised gesture throughout the Middle Ages, especially onward from the time of the separation of the Eastern and Western Churches.

I am indebted to Mr. J. Romilly Allen for his kind permission to copy these cuts from his *Early Christian Symbolism,* 1887.

Fig. 146 is from a coffin-lid, at Lullington in Somerset, of the thirteenth

ἀνέθηκεν Σαβαζίῳ.   Not so the last.   In a note he says: "Keil" (*Arch. Anz.* 1854, p. 517) "recognised the word ἐπηκόῳ, which is common in votive inscriptions, without explaining the rest."   Jahn

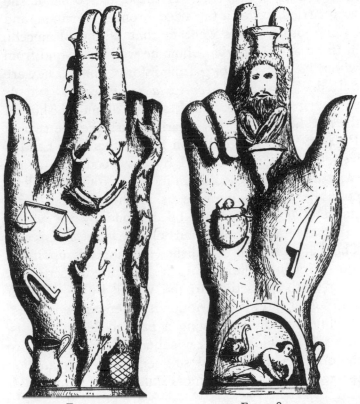

FIG. 147.   FIG. 148.

himself offers no explanation. The position of the hand, he says, is still the one used in taking the oath,[466] and a sign used by priests.

century, and is the only example of the use of the *Dextera Dei* known to the writer on a tomb or coffin; but of course there may be others.

[466] In either the *Graphic* or the *Illustrated News* of December 17, 1893, is a large picture of German troops swearing fidelity to the Kaiser; every man has his right hand raised in this position.

On Fig. 112 will be seen two specimens of this hand as a modern amulet, bought at two different shops in Rome. One is a charm to be suspended from the watch-chain, and the other is mounted as a brooch. As these are so small, the writer tried to get a full-sized bronze specimen, and among other shops went to that of Sig. Finocchi, in the Piazza Minerva, whom he well knew, and from whom he was sure of getting information. They are only made as charms *contra la jettatura*, in gold or silver, he said, and while talking about it, showed the one he was himself wearing, just like the two on Fig. 112, but of gold. In Rome this little hand is well known, and is called by everybody the *Mano Pantea*. The same charm in silver, quite complete, possibly of Roman make, is in the shops at Constantinople, but has not been found by the writer either at Smyrna, at Athens or elsewhere in Greece. The name is well established; it appears upon the brooch itself, and further upon the printed description, given with the article to the writer, by the jeweller who sold it. This description is given below in full.[467]

The reason for giving a printed description is, that this article is of very superior workmanship to the ordinary charm, and so needs some explanation to account for its costliness; also to explain that it

---

[467] MANO PANTEA. Contro il Fascino. (Giojello per Ciondolo.) "Questa mano è esattamente imitata in piccola proporzione da quella di Bronzo al naturale che già era nel Museo di Gian Pietro Bellori in Roma, e se ne ha il disegno nell '*Opera del Grevio*, vol. xii. p. 763, donde fu ricavata.

"L'alto delle dita e i simboli che la ricoprono, cioè il Busto di Serapide, divinità propizia agli uomini, il coltello, il serpe, il ramarro, il rospo, la bilancia, la tartaruga, due vasi, la figura della donna col bambino e un altro oggetto ignoto, formano un gruppo di Simboli che uniti insieme si credevano essere potenti a respingere gli effetti del fascino; e queste mani grande le tenevano in casa per proteggerla contro ogni cattivo influsso della magia o del mal occhio, quelle piccole le portavano indosso per esserne difesi."

is an exact copy of the antique, and therefore
superior in every way to the ordinary goods sold,
etc. The term *Pantheus* is dealt with by Mr. King,
Gnostics, pp. 80, 81. It signifies a combination of
many attributes, expressing the amalgamation of
several ideas into one and the same form.[468]

Comparison with the illustration here printed
shows that it differs from that given by Jahn (Taf.
IV.), although the symbols are nearly the same.
Jahn's represents the top of the index and middle
finger broken off, has no scarab, nor the nondescript
article called *oggetto ignoto* by the Roman jewellers,
but which it is here suggested is the whip of Osiris or
courbash of modern Egypt, of which two separate ones
are plainly shown on the British Museum hand (Figs.
156, 157). The whip is the symbol of rule [469] and
government ; in Egyptian sculptures always in the
right hand of Osiris.[470] This explanation of a doubtful object is rather confirmed by its being placed
immediately over the Vase or *Cantharus*, one of the
recognised symbols of Osiris. Apuleius says that
water in an urn represented Osiris. It was consecrated to him as the life-giving water-god—the Nile.
This two-handled vessel was sacred to Bacchus
in Roman times, and that it was a veritable amulet
is proved by the fact of its being the sole device

---

[468] In Daremberg et Saglio, p. 256, are remarks upon the various attributes collected upon single amulets called " Panthées " (*Pantea signa*), *e.g.*
of Harpocrates, Fortuna, Venus, Cupid, Minerva, etc. Montfaucon says of
a representation he is describing : " Panthea or Polythea, that is adorned with
the symbols of many divinities " (Montfaucon, *Antiquity*, etc., Trs. by D.
Humphreys, vol. i. p. 10).

[469] E. A. Wallis Budge, *The Nile*, p. 80.

[470] The *flagellum* in the hands of Osiris had another meaning as a restorer
of virile power, which, in the light of Egyptian sculptures, seems very probably to be the idea, leading to its adoption upon the *Mano Pantea*. Upon
this subject see Hargrave Jennings' *Phallicism*, p. 273. Apuleius says the
flagrum is the proper sign for a *seminator* (see *De Pollice*, p. 211).

upon the shield of one of the Amazons, painted on a famous vase at Arezzo (see Dennis, *Etruria*, vol. ii. p. 387).[471] Moreover, when we consider that the whole of the symbols here combined, beginning with the bust of Serapis, are essentially Egyptian, it is but reasonable to interpret the unknown from the well known.[472]

Serapis, or Jupiter Serapis, the Egyptian divinity whose bust is placed upon the *mons Jovis* of the hand, was chiefly worshipped at Alexandria. His cult was introduced into Greece in the time of the Ptolemies, and afterwards, against much opposition,[473] into Rome. One ruined temple at least still exists in Italy called a *Serapeon*, and others called *Iseons*, in which latter, Isis as well as Serapis was worshipped. The best known of the former is at Pozzuoli, and of the latter at Pompeii. That at Pozzuoli specially recalls the connection of that port with Alexandria. In a ship of Alexandria trading with Italy St. Paul sailed, and so landed at Pozzuoli (Puteoli, Acts xxviii. 13). The Egyptian divinity was Osiris, called Osiris-Apis or Serapis,[474] who in Egyptian sculpture often has the head of the bull Apis, crowned with the disc and horns like Isis. He was essentially a sun-god; so also is Jupiter Serapis, an attribute symbolised by the flower-basket or *calathus* upon his head, to express the height of the sun above us.[475] Innumerable are the statues,

---

[471] There are plenty of Egyptian vase amulets, pierced for suspension, in the Ashmolean Museum. Their shape and general type show their object conclusively. At the same place is an Etruscan necklace of gold canthari.

[472] Pretorius has learnedly explained that a brazen jar typified the brightness of the Great Goddess (*De Pollice*, p. 210).

[473] Smith's *Classical Dict*. s.v. " Isis."

[474] Wilkinson, *Anc. Egypt.* vol. iii. p. 87.

[475] King, *Gnostics*, pp. 65, 66.

bas-reliefs, and gems connected with the worship
of Serapis, who, though lord of the sun, cannot
be separated from Isis and other moon goddesses.[476]

On gem talismans the bust of Serapis is very
common, having the legend, either in full, EIC ΘEOC
CAPAΠIC, or abbreviated, E.Θ.C. "There is but one
God and he is Serapis."   EIC ZΩN ΘEOC.   "The
one living God." Who can fail to note here the
prototype of the Mahomedan "Allah il Allah"?

Often the intention of the amulet is fully expressed, as NIKA O CAPAΠIC TON ΦΘONON, "Baffle
the evil eye, O Serapis!"[477] In the later Roman
fashion, the Almighty Jove most usually wears the
castle - like crown,[478] something like that of the
Ephesian Diana, again showing the direct link
between *Osiris-Isis* and *Jupiter-Diana.* It is remarkable that on the dome of the so-called Arian

---

The god is reputed to have answered a question of Nicocreon, King of
Cyprus—

> A god I am such as I show to thee :
> The starry Heavens my head, my trunk the Sea,
> Earth forms my feet, mine ears the Air supplies,
> The Sun's far-darting, brilliant rays, mine eyes.

"Hence it is apparent that the nature of Serapis and the Sun is one and in-
divisible. Isis, so universally worshipped, is either the Earth, or Nature, as
subjected to the Sun." This is the true idea expressed plainly on the statues,
as well as in the word *multimammia*, before referred to as one of the names
of Diana, who was Isis herself.

[476] Even here in England the worship of Serapis existed in Roman times.
In the Museum at York is a dedicatory tablet, found in ruins of Roman brick-
work, which clearly proves that a temple stood there. The inscription is
|DEO SANCTO | SERAPI | TEMPLUM A SO|LO FECIT | C. L. HERONY|MIANUS
LEG. | LEG. VI. VICT.|. Perhaps the most curious fact about this monument
is one which nobody seems to have noted. On each side of the inscription is
repeated a sort of compound amulet, of which two *caducei* and a sun are plain
enough ; but there is another object, called in the guide-books a "moon-
shaped shield," but which close examination shows to be nothing more nor
less than the double phallic *fascinum*, the common amulet in Rome at the
time of the Serapis cult.

[477] King, *Gnostics*, p. 70.

[478] This was called the *calathus*, which really means a work-basket (see
King, *Gnostics*, p. 64). This head ornament is probably the second vase,
referred to by the Roman jeweller ; otherwise there are not *due vasi*.

Baptistery at Ravenna, of the sixth century, where there is a representation of our Lord's baptism, the dove is descending in visible form, but the First Person in the Trinity is represented sitting on a rock, as an old man with white beard, and on his head a sort of crown identical in shape with that upon Jupiter Serapis (Fig. 148).[479]

Most, if not all, of the other symbols upon the *Mano Pantea*, like those upon the every-day-of-the-week amulet (Fig. 19), also belong to one or other of the last-named deities of the sun and moon.

At the bottom of the palm is a kind of semi-circular frame, found in all these hands known to the writer, besides six of those named by Jahn, containing a woman suckling a child, in this one with a bird keeping guard over them. Who can doubt these to be the same persons as those shown in Chapter VI. and Appendix I.—Devaki and Crishna, Isis and Horus, or the universal celestial mother and child? The bird is perhaps the cock, found on so many other amulets, gems, and medals. He represents the dawn, which in all ages he has proclaimed, and so typifies Diana, explained later; or he may mean Phœbus, another name for Osiris, the Sun,

---

[479] The same kind of crown is shown on the three heads of Diana Triformis on Fig. 149 from King's *Gnostics*, p. 205, No. 5. The obverse of this medal shows Abraxas having the head of a cock, and ending in two serpents, with a pair of pincers gripping the tail of each; beneath lies a thunderbolt. The god is holding an elliptic-shaped shield over his left arm, while he brandishes a mace with his right. The threefold figure is said to represent Bhavani, whom we have shown to be the same person as Isis or Diana. On p. 202 is a gem having Serapis with this *calathus* crown; three others are given in King's *Handbook of Gems*, pp. 72, 367. All of these latter have the curled ram's horn, often seen upon and marking them as Jupiter heads.

FIG. 149.

watching over his consort the Moon (Isis), who is
nursing their son Horus.[480] It may be, however,
that this bird represents the eagle, another symbol
of Jupiter, and often seen with him on gems and
statues.   A very remarkable comment upon this
bird (in Jahn's plate it is quite nondescript, and
looks like a goose with eagle's beak), and upon the
attitude here displayed, is in Dr. Phene's description of some Hittite monuments in Asia Minor.
He says:[481] " The symbols are a crouching bird on
a level with the face of Sesostris, and close to it a
sceptre. . . . The bird usually found in Hittite
inscriptions . . . is the eagle, and the position is
one of majesty, which he considered implied kingly
power, and hence the crouching and humbled bird
was a king bereft of his power."   The bird on the
Mano Pantea cannot be said to be crouching, neither
was it in the illustration which Dr. Phene gave, nor
is either of the birds represented on the Woburn
marble (Fig. 24).[482]

Upon the figure of the woman and child, Jahn
remarks (p. 104): " It has been rightly considered
that these hands are *ex votos* for a safe delivery, and
that the others, on which are other objects, are *ex
votos* for other good fortunes."   To this opinion we
take objection, upon the ground that all these hands
are constructed to stand upright, upon a flat surface,
whereas ancient as well as modern *ex votos*, such as
phalli, hands, legs, etc., were prepared for suspen-

---

[480] The cock also typifies Mercury (see Montfaucon, i. p. 79), and is also
the attribute of Abraxas, the Gnostic Sun God, the later form of Osiris and
Jupiter.

[481] *Brit. Assoc. Report*, 1892, Cardiff, p. 814.

[482] It may be that this bird is the crow, which appears on the Woburn
marble, and is figured on several Gnostic gems (*Abraxas* Joh. Macarii,
Antwerpiæ, 1657, Tab. V.) in the same attitude.

sion. Moreover, *ex votos*, when intended simply as such, were in old times generally mutilated or broken, and the writer has never seen or heard of a bronze one.[483] These hands were therefore intended to be placed somewhere in the house, and not in the temple. Further, all have a number of objects upon them, each in itself a well-known amulet, specially used against the evil eye, and fashioned in a very lasting material. All these devices would be useless and meaningless upon a mere *ex voto*, which in old days, as now, we know to have been some single object—an arm, a leg, a breast, or an ear—representing in itself more or less accurately the benefit received or the member healed. Moreover, we have the complete analogy of compounded and complicated amulets in the many gems and medals among the ancients, while among the moderns we have the striking example of the *Cimaruta* in its manifold forms. Of this latter, Jahn never seems to have

---

[483] We have seen how Chinese kill their money, and other people the arms offered to the dead. The following shows a continuance of the custom among Europeans :—

At Isernia in the Terra di Lavoro, during 1780, at the church of SS. Cosmo and Damian especially, but also " Nella fiera ed in Città vi sono molti divoti, che vendono membri virili di cera di diverse forme, e di tutte grandezze fino un palmo.

" Sopra delle tavole in ogn' una vi è un bacile che serve per raccogliere li membri di cera. Questa divozione è tutta quasi delle Donne, e pochissima quelli, o quelle che presentano gambe e braccia, mentre tutta la gran festa s'aggira a profitto di membri della generazione. Io ho inteso dire una donna ' Santo Cosimo benedetto, così lo voglio,' etc.

These offerings of wax were received by a priest, who said in response to each gift : " Per intercessionem beati Cosmi, liberet te ab omni malo " (Payne Knight, *Worship of Priapus*, 1865, p. 10). The strange part of this business was that all these wax figures thus offered to SS. Cosmo and Damian were broken before being placed in the basket. The actual breaking of the gift was part of the devotional offering.

It is said (Murray's *Handbook to Southern Italy*, 1868, p. 52) that the sale of the objectionable *membri* was prohibited by the Government in 1780, but ten years later than that Sir R. Colt Hoare was able to procure these specimens of the forbidden emblems. Similar ones, though of the classic period seventeen centuries earlier, are to be seen at the Naples Museum.

heard, though he mentions the *mano fica* and one or
two other modern charms. With all deference to
learning, it is stoutly maintained that all these hands
were not votive, but prophylactic, pure and simple.
Thus the whole amulet would be specially potent
for the protection against fascination of mothers and
new-born infants, as well as for adults in general.
Our deliberate opinion is, that these hands, having
such pantheistic symbols upon them, were for the
same purpose as the Teraphim of Scripture, or the
Lares and Penates of classic days. They were
probably held in much the same estimation as a
crucifix is to-day by a devout Christian.

It is suggested that what Jahn calls a bracket
supporting the bust, may be meant for a cornucopia,
and if so, its meaning would be at once evident.[484]

The next of the amulets, the scarab, is of all
others, perhaps not even excluding the mystic eye, the
most commonly seen and found in Egyptian tombs.

Its frequent occurrence in sculpture, no less than
the authority of numerous ancient writers, shows the
great importance attached by the Egyptians to this
insect. "It was the emblem of the sun, to which
deity it was particularly sacred."[485] In the scarab
we have another symbol of Osiris, the Sun-God, and
consequently of his successor Serapis, the supreme
divinity of our complex amulet.

Pliny[486] says: "The insect in its operations pictures
the revolution of the sun." These "operations" are

---

[484] This opinion is strengthened by the undoubted cornucopia upon the
similar hand (Fig. 157). Later, the cornucopia will be noted upon two of the
statues of Diana (Figs. 175, 177), and also on the *grillo* (Fig. 28). Cornu-
copias are often seen on gem amulets, and are said to have the same potency
as the horn on which we have already said so much.

[485] Wilkinson, *Anc. Egypt.* vol. iii. p. 345.

[486] *Nat. Hist.* xxx. 30 (vol. v. p. 454, Bohn).

the habit it has of making pellets of clay, and rolling them along. The scarab was also a symbol of the world, and as a hieroglyph, under its name Ptah-Xeper, it signified the Creative Power.[487]

From the belief that there were no females, and that all of the species were males, it was considered the symbol of virility and manly force, hence it was engraved upon the signets of Egyptian soldiers.[488]

The scarab may be considered [489] as : "(1) An emblem of the sun ; (2) of Ptah, the Creative Power, and of Ptah-Xeper ; (3) of Ptah-Socharis Osiris ; (4) of the world ; (5) connected with astronomical subjects ; [490] and (6) with funereal rites."

Upon the *Mano Pantea* we may safely consider it under either, or all of the four first meanings ; and hence as it was in Egypt a powerful amulet to guard both living and dead, so we may well believe it was adopted as such by the Romans along with the Serapis cult. It will be noticed that our jeweller's description passes over the scarab, which is nevertheless very distinct on the original bronze.

On the back of the hand we have the frog, which our friend calls a toad (*rospo*).[491] This is a common

---

[487] Wilkinson, *Ib.* iii. 345, 346. E. W. Budge, *Nile*, pp. 55, 63. Wherever seen as a hieroglyph it is always drawn with wings folded, so as to exhibit plainly the T of life on its back.

[488] Plutarch, *De Iside*, 10, 73.

[489] Wilkinson, *Anc. Egypt.* vol. iii. p. 346.

[490] It occurs in some zodiacs in the place of Cancer. *Ib.* iii. 346.

[491] In this manifest error he is not alone ; indeed it is not at all uncommon here in England, for people living in towns not to know frogs from toads. In a *Catalogue Descriptif d'une Collection d'amulettes Italiennes envoyée à l'Exposition Universelle de Paris*, 1889, by Dr. Joseph Bellucci, Pérouse, 1889, frogs are all written *crapaud*. Signor Bellucci has published also a *Catalogo della collezione di amuleti*, Perugia, 1881, but I have not been able to compare the French with the Italian. There is, however, no manner of doubt that *rana* and not *rospo* is the creature intended. Bellucci's catalogue contains almost none of the charms and amulets we are dealing with. No doubt in his search for *curios*, he, like Jorio, Valletta, and others, overlooked the common things under his very nose. He appears to have collected upwards of four thousand

amulet against the evil eye.   In Naples the simple
frog amulet is called a *Sirena*, like the more
elaborate one of which a description follows later.
It is not only now worn (see Fig. 112) by Italians,
Greeks, and even Turks, but it appears on many
ancient gems and medals (see Fig. 17).   It is commonly of metal, but when cut out of amber or
coral is of greater power.   The frog also was among
Egyptians " a symbol of Ptah," because, as Horapollo says, " it was the representation of man in
embryo, that is, of the being who, like the world, was
the work of the Creative Power, and the noblest production of his hands." [492]

   " The importance attached to the frog in some
parts of Egypt is shown by its having been embalmed, and honoured with sculpture in the tombs
of Thebes.   The frog was the symbol of *hefnu*,
100,000, or an immense number.[493]   It sat on a ring
or seal, a sign occasionally used in lieu of the *Tau*
or 'life.'"   Again we are told, "la
grenouille rappelait l'idée de la renaissance." [494]   Fig. 150 is from Maspero's
Archéologie, p. 235.   Jahn gives a plate
(Taf. IV.) of a terra-cotta lamp, now
in the Berlin Museum, having an eye
for centre, round which are the frog, scorpion, phal-

Fig. 150.

---

objects, but they seem to be largely composed of stones, meteoric and other.
One only (No. 25, Tab. XI. p. 66), " Sirène *en os*, contre le mauvais œil et
la fascination," may be a frog.

   [492] Wilkinson, *Anc. Egypt.* vol. iii. pp. 15, 340.   Pignorius (*Mensæ
Isiacæ Expositio*, p. 23) says the frog and the cynocephalus are symbols of
Isis ; but the cynocephalus standing, with its hands raised towards heaven,
Horapollo considers to have been the symbol of the rising moon.

   [493] Wilkinson, iii. 353.   Budge, *Nile*, p. 57.

   [494] This idea arose from its being born without feet, and in an altogether
different form from that it grows into.   Moreover, it was said to typify the
decline of disease, and by the growth of its feet the gradual power of the

lus, snail, and two monkeys' heads (*cynocephalus*); the spout is formed of a horned mask. The frog is shown on the Kertch necklace (p. 135) as one of the special amulets. There is also an ancient bronze frog amulet,[495] prepared for suspension, in the Ashmolean Museum.

Pliny says :[496] " To this the Magi add some other particulars, which, if there is any truth in them, would lead us to believe that frogs ought to be considered much more useful to society than laws." He gives directions for a particular manipulation of the frog, by which a wife conceives an aversion to all paramours. One kind (*phrini*), known to the Greeks, have protuberances like horns. He also says, there is a small bone on each side of a frog. That on the right side has many wonderful properties ; one is, that if thrown into boiling water it will immediately cool, and that it will not boil again till the bone be removed. The little bone from the left side, on the other hand, has the property of making it boil. It will also assuage the fury of dogs, and if put into drink it will conciliate love and end discord or strife. It is also worn for a talisman as an aphrodisiac.[497]

FIG. 151.

patient in convalescence to walk about (Pretorius, *De Pollice*, Lipsiæ, 1677, p. 211).

[495] The frog was evidently an amulet among the Incas of Peru. Fig. 151 is a bracelet from Wiener's *Pérou et Bolivie*, p. 669.

[496] Pliny, *Nat. Hist.* xxxii. vol. vi. p. 22 (Bohn). All this is dwelt on by Delrio, *Disq. Mag.* iii. p. 32. He shows the connection of frogs with Diana.

[497] Looking at the frog from this point of view, it is indeed in strange

One of the two frog charms on Fig. 112 is that common in Rome, while the clumsier one is Neapolitan. The two shown immediately beneath the *Mano Pantea* on the same plate are from Constantinople, sold openly as charms in the bazaars. Evidently the frog as an amulet is widely used among various races, ancient and modern.[498]

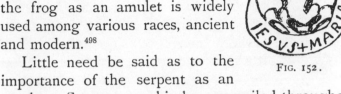

FIG. 152.

Little need be said as to the importance of the serpent as an amulet. Serpent worship has prevailed throughout the ages. It is the type of eternity, and with its tail in its mouth the symbol of perpetual union.

There is hardly a country of the ancient world where it cannot be traced, pervading every known system of mythology.[499] Babylon, Persia, India, Ceylon, China, Japan, Burmah, Java, Arabia, Syria, Asia Minor, Egypt, Ethiopia, Greece, Italy, Northern and Western Europe, Mexico, Peru, North America, all yield abundant testimony to the same effect respecting serpent

---

company when we find it combined, not with the crescent merely, but with that symbol, manifestly in its adoption as a Christian one. The book, under the paw of the lion of St. Mark, representing his Gospel, is the only combination of pagan and Christian with which we are acquainted, save and except the solitary example here produced in Fig. 152. This amulet, belonging to my friend Mr. Neville Rolfe, has every mark of having been much worn, and we cannot but suppose that the original possessor, while believing in the virtue of the pagan symbols, was also up to her light a devout Christian, and without reflecting upon the incongruity, desired, as so many others have done, to pile up appeals for protection just like Lucius Zethus of old, lest any on whom reliance was placed might feel themselves overlooked. The writer believes this particular modern frog amulet to be absolutely unique. Frogs made of gilt metal and cut in amber are worn as amulets by children in Burmah. Necklaces consisting entirely of strings of little frogs of these materials are to be seen in the Pitt Rivers Museum, Oxford, from Mandalay.

[498] From Figs. 151, 153, 154 it will be seen that the frog was used commonly as a decoration in ancient Peru. These are also from Wiener's *Pérou et Bolivie*. It would seem that in Peru frogs retain their tails, although, as is well known, in Europe the tail disappears as the legs grow, making it still more apt as a symbol of man in embryo, who has lost his tail by evolution.

[499] Kalisch, *History and Critical Comment.* on Gen. iii. 1.

worship, and point to the common origin of pagan systems wherever found.

The intimate connection of the serpent with the idea of the Medusa adds to the evidence that her myth came from the East; for there the  serpent has always been the symbol of an evil demon.[500]   On the other hand, the Phœnicians adored it as a beneficent *genius;*[501] and in Egypt, one of the earliest homes of serpent worship,[502] it was looked upon as a protector, *tutela loci*, the guardian of tombs.   Every tomb of the kings yet opened there has the serpent sculptured erect on each side of the doorway as the symbol of the watchful, protecting deity.

Fig. 153.

It was called Thermuthis, "and with it the statues of Isis were crowned as with a diadem."[503] It was the mark of royalty. Egyptian kings and queens have an asp on the front of their crowns as a sign of the invincible power of royalty.   There was another serpent called Aphôphis, the giant, which was looked upon as the

Fig. 154.

type of evil.   It was said to have been killed by Horus, and this myth is no doubt the same as that of Apollo and the Python in Greek mythology.   In Egypt the serpent was both worshipped and hated, probably at different times, and in accordance with

[500] Inman, *Ancient Faiths embodied in Ancient Names*, vol. ii. pp. 710, 712.   Also vol. i. pp. 497, 498.

[501] Smith's *Dict. of the Bible*, s.v. "Serpent."

[502] *Ophiolatreia*, privately printed, 1889, p. 1.   This book deals very fully with the subject, but gives no references.

[503] Wilkinson, *Anc. Egypt*. vol. iii. p. 334.

the origin of the several dynasties maintaining the cult. We find the same thing as regards the crocodile. At one place it was worshipped as a god, and at others, *e.g.* Edfou, it was hunted and slain as a venomous beast.

A very large live serpent was kept, according to Ælian, in the temple of Æsculapius at Alexandria, and according to Pausanias there was another in his temple at Epidaurus ; both were carefully tended as objects of worship. We all know that a serpent is the usual accompaniment of ancient statues of the god, and in this connection is said to typify health. It is also said [504] to denote the condition or duration of the disease, and hence it may be described as the symbol of diagnosis. Livy [505] and several authors relate that when a pestilence broke out in Rome, the Delphic oracle advised an embassy to Epidaurus, to fetch the god Æsculapius. While they were gazing at the statue of the god a " venerable, not horrible," serpent, which only appeared when some extraordinary benefit was intended, glided from his hiding-place and, passing through the city, went direct to the Roman ship, where he coiled himself in the berth of Ogulnius, the chief ambassador. On arrival in the Tiber the serpent leapt overboard and escaped on an island. Here a temple was erected to him in the shape of a ship, and the plague was immediately stayed. [506] Delphi was the

---

[504] *De Pollice*, Lipsiæ, 1677, p. 210.

[505] Livy, x. 32. Lanciani, p. 69, says this happened in A.U.C. 459, and that the Sibylline books were consulted. The answer was : " Æsculapium ab Epidauro Romæ arcessendum." There is confusion between the Sibylline books and the Delphic oracle.

[506] This temple of Æsculapius was on the island now called S. Bartolomeo, and became the greatest sanitary establishment in the metropolis. It is a striking proof of the vitality of tradition, that not only the island, but the very

stronghold of serpent worship in Greece, and a singular fact remains. The oldest known monument in Europe, an undoubted relic of ancient serpent worship, is now to be seen still standing in the Atmeidan or Hippodrome at Constantinople. It is the original column, brought from the temple of Apollo at Delphi, and was set up where it now stands by Constantine, about A.D. 324.

It consists of [507] "the bodies of three serpents twisted into one pillar of brass. Their triple heads had once supported the golden tripod which, after the defeat of Xerxes, was consecrated in the temple of Delphi by the victorious Greeks." It bears the only known inscription still extant, which is actually contemporary with the Persian wars. It was erected soon after the battle of Marathon.[508] The surface of the Atmeidan is now several feet higher than the base of this famous column, which stands in a sort of pit. Originally the serpents had three heads, now all have disappeared—one is said to have been knocked off by Mahomet himself, who exclaimed against it as an idol. No sooner had he done this than a great number of serpents began to be seen in the city.[509] The writer can testify to the great veneration with which this precious relic of the past is still regarded by the Turks, who look upon it as one of the great protectors of the city.[510]

spot on it where once stood this temple, always has been, and is now, the seat of a hospital, that of San Giovanni di Calabita (Lanciani, *Anc. Rome*, p. 70).

[507] Gibbon, *Dec. and Fall*. Milman, vol. ii. 1846, p. 13.

[508] Professor Mahaffy, *Nineteenth Century*, May 1894, p. 859.

[509] *Ophiolatreia* (privately printed), p. 87.

[510] Those who have seen this famous old-world monument, said to have the name of *Mycenæ* engraved upon it, cannot but be struck with its singular resemblance to many of the twisted columns at Venice and elsewhere in Italy. Who knows but the idea in them may have sprung from the Delphic pillar? Looking again at the serpent as the guardian of doorways : may not

In Greek and Roman mythology the serpent Agathodemon was the attribute of Ceres, Mercury, Æsculapius, and Hecate-Diana, with, of course, their Egyptian prototypes in their most beneficent qualities; while Python was a fearful monster, which only a god could overcome and destroy. The same fierce enmity, abject fear, submission and worship regarding the serpent, are found to-day among Hindoos and Mahomedans of India, as well as among savages of Africa and America. Without attempting to explain the story of the brazen serpent in the wilderness, it may be pointed out that to the Israelites, just come out of Egypt, the worship of Agathodemon was perfectly familiar, and that it was to them the symbol of life and health.

The temples in Cambodia, of which the French produced large models at more than one Paris Exposition, show that they were guarded by a great avenue of serpents, and the same objects are seen at the entrances to Chinese temples.

That our Celtic forefathers were Ophiolaters [511] is proved by the so-called Druidical remains at Abury and elsewhere. Just as serpents are carved on the rock to guard the tombs of the kings at Thebes, so, the writer observed in the early Celtic tomb of Gavr Innis at Locmariaker, in Brittany, are two serpents sculptured on the rock inside the entrance. [512]

---

the very usual twisted mouldings, following the sides and arches of doorways in Venice, be also descendants of the serpents of Delphi? In fact, may we not apply this to mouldings in general of that type which generally go by the name of *cable*? The armour of Agamemnon was ornamented with a three-headed serpent. Menelaus also had one on his shield. Spartans and Athenians said they were of serpent origin, and called themselves *Ophiogenæ*.

[511] See Sir R. C. Hoare's *Ancient and Modern Wiltshire*; Davies's *Mythology of the Druids*; Borlase's *Cornwall*; Stukeley, *Abury, a Temple of the British Druids*, 1793.

[512] Even in far-off Peru we see a serpent carved upon the pier at the

We are all familiar with the two serpents, called the *Caduceus*, in the hand of Mercury. This was a true amulet which he carried as the staff of a messenger to guard him against the malevolent glances of those who would impede his errand.

The two serpents in congress are the Rod of Life.[513] The *caduceus*, the special symbol of Mercury, was used sometimes alone as an amulet on engraved gems. Of one of these Mr. King gives a specimen (*Gnostics*, p. 70). Among modern amulets the two bone specimens, bought at Sienna, shown on Fig. 112, bear signs of much wear, and so prove that the same belief as of old still survives.[514]

In West Africa the serpent is still used as an amulet to protect the crops. Fig. 155 is an iron one from Ashantee, now in the Somerset County Museum along with the other objects shown on Fig. 88. Lastly, on Fig. 8 the serpent is shown in connection with

FIG. the crescent; and upon the Cimaruta (Fig. 155. 162) it forms the horns of the half-moon, thus doubly augmenting its power as a protection against the evil eye. The serpent plays so large a part in Egyptian worship,[515] that we may well consider it to

---

entrance of a bridge over the Pachachaca near Chavin (*Pérou et Bolivie*, p. 561).

[513] Forlong, *Rivers of Life*, p. 223.

[514] An object very similar to one of them, with an animal mounted upon it, is represented on a terra-cotta plaque (Fig. 181) from the collection of the late Sir W. Temple, found at Pozzuoli, and now in the British Museum. This is probably a goat, which in Egypt (Wilkinson, *Anc. Egypt.* vol. iii. p. 30) was a sacred animal, a favourite of Isis. In Greece, according to Herodotus, the goat was sacred to Pan, and in Roman times we well know that it was the symbol of Priapus. Hence its obvious meaning as a modern charm.

[515] Upon the subject of serpent worship see King, *Gnostics*, p. 26, who gives a chapter on Ophites, and again, at p. 73, another on Agathodemon

be closely connected with the worship of Serapis, as well as the moon - goddesses, and therefore we find it upon every *Mano Pantea* known to the writer. That it was an ancient Græco-Roman amulet, is proved by the several gems and medals (Figs. 14 - 19) which were avowedly against the evil eye. We see serpents also in the hands of the three-formed goddess shown on Figs. 149 and 163.

The annexed drawings (Figs. 156, 157) are from a bronze hand in the British Museum, belonging to the collection of the late Rev. Payne Knight, which does not appear to have ever been

Talismans or Serpent Amulets; but the best account is by Dr. Moritz Winternitz (*Der Sarpabali, ein altindischer Schlangencult*, Wien, 1888). He gives an immense array of authorities and many remarkable facts.

Traces of serpent worship may be seen, not only in the architectural features at Venice and elsewhere, but in the peculiar spiral and interlaced ornament found upon the early Greek tombstones at Mycenæ—represented in Schliemann's *Mycenæ and Tiryns*, pp. 81-96, especially those on p. 91, which are certainly intended to represent serpents. Strangely, we find here in Great Britain sculptured ornaments identical in idea and almost in fact. The writer was attracted to the Greek tombstones on the spot at Mycenæ, and in the museum at Athens; he has therefore rather had his eyes open since then for similar objects. There is, in one of the Dolmens of Brittany, near Locmariaker, a stela-shaped stone at the end of one of the tombs, on which the device rudely cut is manifestly serpentine.

Mr. J. Romilly Allen in his *Monumental History of the Early British Church* gives as a frontispiece two panels, which he calls *plaitwork*, from a cross at Llantwit Major; also on p. 211 there is a similar design from the cross of Gilsuith and Berhtsuith at Thornhill in Yorkshire; and at p. 212 is an interlaced design from the cross of Utr and Froka, at Kirk Braddan, all of which are serpent patterns, while the latter shows unmistakably two serpents' heads.

Again, in Dolton Church, North Devon, there is a very remarkable font of early date, having the same interlaced serpent pattern upon it. The like is on a stone in the pavement of Saxilby church in Lincolnshire, and on a slab at Northampton, and on the shaft of a cross at Rothley Temple in Leicestershire. On the Dolton example the Rev. G. F. Browne says: "The centre panel shows two serpents, head downwards, biting their own and each other's tails." Four photographs of these panels are published by Mr. Winslow Jones in an article in the *Transactions of the Devon Association*, vol. xxiii. p. 200. There are also sculptured stones of the same character in various parts of Italy, all seeming to show that at least the recollection of serpent worship has existed in Western Europe down to the early Middle Ages, and long since the adoption of Christianity.

published, and which is not one of those described by Jahn.

In this beautiful, nearly life-size hand, the serpent is by far the most conspicuous amulet upon it, for it

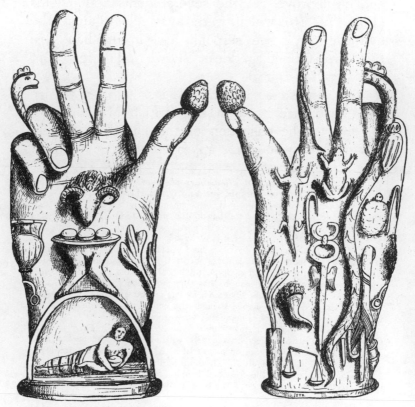

FIG. 156.

FIG. 157.

is evidently intended to be seen from whichever side the hand is looked at. In this case, moreover, there is not only the large serpent, but also a small one, so as to seemingly pile up the power of this protecting, watchful guardian. It is suggested that the smaller represents the Asp of Egyptian royalty. A comparison of the two (Figs. 147, 148, and 156, 157), which may be considered as typical of all the known hands, will not fail to show points of agreement in them, and prove that, whatever their purpose may have been, it was the same in all alike.

In five out of the six medals and gems (Figs. 14-19) there is a serpent; in both these hands he is in connection with the third or medical finger, as the representation of the healing god Æsculapius, and in both cases he is given the same position on the back of the hand.

The woman and child in the arched frame are on both hands alike, but in the Payne Knight hand there is no bird to watch over them.

The frog, it may be noted, in both cases seems to have its proper position, and that well known, aphrodisiac, was surely placed by design in close relation to the middle finger, the ancient *digitus infamis*. The ram's head occupying nearly the same position as the head of Jupiter, appropriately upon what is known to palmists as the *mons Jovis*, must be taken as the symbol of that divinity, who is constantly depicted with ram's horns upon his head.

The Cantharus, or two-handled vase, appears on both hands. The remarkable table with three flat cakes upon it, is much more difficult of explanation. It seems to be an offering of bread to the Almighty Jove, and one cannot but be struck by the coincidence of these three cakes with those shown on the table in Figs. 113, 116, on the altar of Melchisedec, and before the three strangers entertained by Abraham. We do not assert the connection, but the threefold aspect of Egyptian gods is dwelt upon elsewhere, and these cakes may well typify offerings to the greatest of the gods in his threefold character. All the known hands of this class appear to be Roman, and of the period of the empire before Constantine.

The crocodile, also on both the hands, was an Egyptian amulet : it was worshipped as a god, called Sebek in Lower Egypt, and there was a city called *Crocodilopolis* by the Greeks, from the cult there practised ;[516] hence it here finds an appropriate place.[517] As the type of the generation of divine wisdom, we understand the crocodile upon Minerva's breast, in those gems and statues where she is not wearing the ægis, but which represent her as the goddess of wisdom and learning.

As an amulet to be worn on the person, the crocodile does not appear to be very commonly used ; but as a protector against the evil eye it has been adopted by many people. Among the amulets on the necklace shown on Fig. 21 is the head of a crocodile. Its present use in Cairo and Tunis does but perpetuate the belief which displayed itself in the gift of the crocodile, now hanging over the door of Seville Cathedral (Fig. 158). This was an un- doubted amulet in 1260, and all must remember also the crocodile upon the column on the Piazzetta at Venice, on which stands St. Theodore. Now this column, with its companion bearing the lion of St.

[516] E. W. Budge, *The Nile*, p. 162.

[517] Like the serpent, the crocodile as a dreaded monster was hated as well as adored. At Edfou we see Horus spearing the crocodile, and of course recognise him as the antitype of Michael and the Dragon. Indeed by some it is held that the Leviathan and Dragon of the A.V. of Scripture referred to the crocodile (Smith, *Dict. of Bib.* s.v. "Dragon "). As Sebek (Wilkinson, iii. 189 ; E. W. Budge, *Nile*, p. 94) he was a sun-god, and worshipped as the life-giver ; thus he fitly became a Gnostic symbol. Pignorius (*Vetustissimæ Tabulæ*, p. 23) says the lizard or crocodile (*Lacertus*), like the lion, dragon, and eagle, was sacred to the sun.

Mark, was erected in 1329, only seventy years after
the famous *Lagarto* was set up in Seville ; and we
maintain that as Pisistratus set up a column bearing
a cricket, in the Agora at Athens, to
guard the people from the evil eye,
so did the Venetians set up their
columns for the like purpose.   We are
told[518] that these columns so completely
formed a part of the *idea* of Venice,
that they were repeated in "most of the
cities subject to its dominion."   What
could be the *idea* other than that here
suggested ?   We see how in Naples
to-day the lion of St. Mark is placed on
the horses' backs, avowedly as an amulet,

Fig. 158.

contra la jettatura ; is there not then every reason
for believing that the dread of that influence was
quite as great, and that the means taken to counteract it were as many, if not even more numerous, in
the Middle Ages than at present ?   It cannot therefore be unreasonable to assign the same meaning to
the mediæval crocodile and lion at Venice as to the
modern lion at Naples, and the modern crocodile at
Tunis and Cairo.

In Portugal a favourite object in pottery is a
lizard or crocodile, so made as to hang flat against
the wall.   The writer has one such, which he bought
in Lisbon certainly as an amulet, and always regards
as such.

In Figs. 14-17 the crocodile appears in every one
of the five combinations, while even the serpent is
wanting in one — clearly proving the importance
attached to it as an amulet for wear in Roman times.

[518] Murray's *Handbook to Northern Italy*, 1860, p. 343.

The crocodile was believed to conceive by the
ear and to bring forth by the mouth—a strange notion
indeed, yet it has been perpetuated as a Christian
one in the hymn [519] of S. Bonaventura, the Seraphic
Doctor,[520] who (born 1221 in Tuscany) lived at the
precise epoch when the cult of the B.V.M. had
begun to occupy such a disproportionate place in
the Services of the Church,[521] just at the time when
the legend of ancient Egypt respecting Isis, itself
derived from still older sources, had been adapted to
her successor.   An ancient gem, belonging to the
late Rev. C. W. King, shows Serapis seated : before
him stands Isis, holding in one hand the sistrum,
in the other a wheat-sheaf, with the legend H KYPIA
ICIC AΓNH, "Immaculate is our lady Isis."   "The
very terms applied afterwards to that personage who
succeeded to her form, titles, symbols, rites and
ceremonies." [522]   "Her proper title, Domina, the
exact translation of the Sanscrit *Isi*, survives, with
slight change, in the modern Madonna" (*Mater
Domina*).

The scales, so prominent upon most of these

[519] "Gaude, Virgo, Mater Christi,
　　　Quæ per aurem concepisti
　　　Gabriele nuncio.
　　　Gaude quia Deo plena
　　　Peperisti sine pena
　　　Cum pudoris lilio."

The whole idea of the conception by the crocodile is but another example of
the strong belief in the power of the senses to convey actual tangible effects
to the body.   Hence the Crocodile or Lizard "is the type of the generation
of the Word, *i.e.* of the Logos, or Divine Wisdom."   Here is a satisfactory
explanation of the crocodile placed upon Minerva's breast, as seen on some
gems.   The crocodile denotes both the accession of wisdom and the silence
of the wise.   Of old it was considered to have no tongue, and hence it was
the symbol of silence.   Pliny says it is the only land animal which lacks the
use of its tongue (Pliny, *Nat. Hist.* viii. 25 ; vol. ii. p. 287, Bohn).   The
lizard and the crocodile seem to have been regarded as the same species.

[520] Jameson, *Legends of the Monastic Orders*, p. 288.
[521] "Savaric," by Canon Church, in *Archæologia*, vol. li. p. 24.
[522] King, *Gnostics*, pp. 71, 72.

hands, are passed over by Jahn, but they serve at least to confirm the Egyptian character of all these amulets.   At the time when these hands were made in Italy, the weighing apparatus was always, as it is to a large extent to-day, of the steelyard type.   Of all the scales in the Naples and Pompeian Museums every one is a steelyard; whereas in the innumerable representations of weighing, found on Egyptian paintings and sculptures, whether of souls by the recording Thoth, or of merchandise by various persons, the machine is nearly always an equipoised beam and two scales.[523]   In judging then of the true meaning of the scales upon the *Mano Pantea*, we must take into account the fact that, as a representation, they were conventional, of an object not unknown, but at least such as the Roman users of these hands were unaccustomed to.[524]   Although the Egyptians had another kind of balance it is rarely seen.

As a separate amulet the scales are not used so far as the present writer is aware, nor can he pretend

[523] Wilkinson, ii. p. 247.   The steelyard is found in Egypt, but of distinctly Roman type, and of a late age when Egypt was much under Roman influence.   By his admirable illustrations of the *Distribution of Mythical Beliefs* at the British Association at Oxford, 1894, Dr. Tylor showed not only the widespread similarity of the idea of the actual weighing of souls in the next world, but also that the method of representation was equally diffused; in fact it would appear that the belief itself, and the form of the scales in which the weighing is represented, have gone together as part and parcel of the whole conception.   Early Egyptian, Japanese, and Christian English, each in his own peculiar fashion, depicted the same equipoised balance, with the soul in a suspended scale on one side, and the goddess Mut (Truth), or some other counterweight in the other.   Moreover the demon, depicted according to the several popular beliefs, was in each case awaiting the result, and if possible to claim his victim.

[524] The scales are said to represent September, the autumnal equinox, and thereby the seventh month of the disease, and so of convalescence, for certainly by the seventh month the patient has regained his health.   The three fingers upraised of the hand described "denote 200, that is six months and twenty days—the time between the two equinoxes" (Pretorius, *De Pollice*, Lipsiæ, 1677, p. 213).   Here we have another system of numeration, this sign differing from that given on p. 239.   It is, however, very interesting, as proving the importance attached to manual attitude.

to explain their meaning in these combinations. Jahn, too, says (p. 106) that he cannot explain them. In Egyptian art the scales appear whenever Osiris sits in judgment upon a human soul, and they are accompanied by Thoth the scribe. The same idea has descended through the ages into Christian art. In pictures of the Last Judgment, the Archangel Michael is often represented as holding the scales of Justice, in which the soul shall be weighed. That the scales on both our hands do represent an amulet, we must maintain, for they form one of the signs of the Zodiac, and nearly all the other objects are known to be amulets.[525]

The tortoise appears on both the hands here shown, as well as on the Florentine gem (Fig. 17). Moreover, Jahn says that "there are little ones made of bronze, of precious stones, and of amber, sometimes with other amulets hanging on a necklace, so that the meaning of the tortoise as an amulet cannot be doubted."[526] Of the hands catalogued by Jahn, no less than twelve have the tortoise upon them.

Pliny says:[527] "The flesh of the land tortoise . . . is highly salutary for repelling the malpractices of magic and for neutralising poisons." He gives many diseases for which, when eaten, the flesh is a cure; also "the blood of the land tortoise improves the eyesight and removes cataract." In one way which he details, the shavings of the shell are an antaphrodisiac, and in another strongly the opposite.

[525] Libra was an aphrodisiac talisman. Proserpine was the holder of the balance in old Zodiacs, and the Romans called her Libera (Forlong, *Rivers of Life*, vol. i. pp. 171, 172). This somewhat helps our argument as to the meaning of the Sirens in Chap. X.

[526] Jahn, *Aberglauben*, etc., p. 99. v

[527] Pliny, *Nat. Hist.* xxxii. 14 (vol. vi. p. 15, Bohn).

The urine, according to adepts in magic, has marvellous properties ; the eggs also are a remedy for scrofula and other evils. The catalogue of remedies given by Pliny, for which the tortoise can be used, is no less than sixty-six.[528]

A tortoise - headed god occurs as one of the genii in the tombs ; but it does not appear that the tortoise held a rank among the sacred animals of Egypt.[529]

The tortoise is very often depicted with and as an emblem of Mercury, like the *Caduceus.*[530] Jahn gives particulars of the various symbols on the hands known to him, and thus proves that all were similar in type though differing in detail.

On the British Museum hand (Figs. 156, 157), which Jahn had never seen, is a remarkable feature, not uncommon, though the writer has seen one only. Jahn says the pine-cone appears upon no less than nine of the hands known to him. It is also among the amulets strung upon the Kertch necklace (Fig. 21). The position given to it upon the tip of the thumb marks it out as an object of considerable importance, and its frequent use shows it to have been considered as a powerful amulet. The pine-tree was sacred to Zeus, and an attribute of Serapis ; it was beloved of virgins. Ovid calls the pine *pura arbor.*[531] The cone had however a phallic meaning, and Layard says the pine-cone was most used in the cult of Venus.[532]

The fig - tree on the hand had also a phallic

---

[528] The tortoise was sacred to Cybele (*De Pollice*, p. 212). The tortoise was a phallic amulet, and being considered an androgynous animal, was an apt symbol of the double power (Payne Knight, *Symb. Lang.* p. 29).

[529] Wilkinson, *Anc. Egypt.* vol. iii. p. 329.

[530] Montfaucon, vol. i. p. 79.

[531] Ovid, *Fast.* ii. 25-8.

[532] Forlong, *op. cit.* i. 59.   I cannot find it in Layard's books.

meaning. It was borne in the processions of Dionysos at the Eleusinian mysteries.

The bee was a symbol of Diana (see Fig. 17).

Three objects near the tail of the serpent are probably intended for a knife, a strigil, and a distaff.

The horseshoe figure with two rings at the ends is difficult to explain. There is an object almost exactly like it upon the breast of a Greek statuette in the Ashmolean; and also it is very like the small amulet (Fig. 89) from Bologna. The hand from the British Museum shows a greater number of amulets upon it than any other with which either Jahn or the writer is acquainted.

In six of those catalogued by Jahn is found the frame with the woman and child at the breast. One especially, he says, possesses images of the gods Cybele and Mercury. Two others have Mercury, and two have a bearded figure in a Phrygian cap. This latter seems in a way to connect them with the famous Woburn marble (Fig. 24). Moreover, one of the heads of Diana Triformis is represented as wearing a Phrygian cap.[533] Another has a full-length figure sitting on the palm of the hand in Phrygian tunic and hose, and having both hands uplifted, pointing with the forefinger extended as in the Phrygian worship of Cybele, Bacchus, and Mercury.

Only three known hands have the Serapis head. On four an eagle sits on the two upraised fingers, grasping a thunderbolt in its claws. The oak-branch of Jove is found on two; on another is the lyre of Apollo. The *Caduceus* is on three; the pincers of Vulcan are on two. One has the egg-

[533] Montfaucon, vol. i. p. 94.

shaped helmet worn by the Dioscuri (Castor and Pollux) ; two others have the Thyrsus ; one a vine-branch ; and no less than nine of those known to Jahn have the two-handled Cantharus. One has the moon, which Jahn says is perhaps the badge of Mars (*der Harnisch dem Ares*). Besides all these there are the symbols of the Phrygian orgies— the tympanum on one, bells on one, crotala (kind of cymbal) on two ; cymbals on three ; the Phrygian flute on four ; knife on two ; and the whip on four. The ox head is on two, and the ram's head on five. Egyptian cultus is again represented by the sistrum upon two of these hands. What seems like a round offering cake, divided by cross lines into four parts, appears upon two hands. They are precisely like the round, flat cakes found at Pompeii, now in the Naples Museum, and at Oxford, except that the terra cottas in the Ashmolean are not only imitation loaves, but smaller than real ones, thus doubly cheating the dead.[534]

The scales are found on no less than nine, and Jahn gives besides a list of animals depicted on these hands—a bird, unknown, on two ; a frog on ten ; a tortoise on twelve ; a lizard or crocodile on nine ; but he does not say on how many he has noted the serpent. He remarks that it is certainly not by chance that we meet again and again with the same animals, which play so significant a part among protectives against the evil eye ; all the less so (*i.e.* by chance), as amongst the other symbols met with, come out the well-known signs of the phallus on one, and the vulva also on another.

[534] We would refer again to the cakes upon the tables in Figs. 156, and 113, 116 from Ravenna. In any case the coincidence is remarkable.

If we would now finally settle the proper meaning of these animals, the fact is distinctly proved that in all those allied religious representations which display the richest arsenal of superstitions and witchcraft, a signification is given to those animals, which makes them serve forthwith as amulets.[535]

He winds up his treatise with a description of six different magic nails. One of these, now in the Collegio Romano, is here reproduced (Fig. 159).[536] Jahn remarks that nails have much to do with human superstitions; that the well-known ancient Etruscan custom of *clavum figere* was not merely intended to mark the date, but, as Livy relates, it is said over and over again by tradition of the

FIG. 159.

[535] Jahn, *Aberglauben*, etc., p. 106.

[536] "It has on one side the inscription ΙΑΩCΑΒΑΩΘ (*Jao-Sabaoth*), together with two signs, obscure to me, and three stars." One of the doubtful objects is, we suggest, the pincers seen upon many Gnostic amulets, and especially in the three plaques (Figs. 181, 182, 183). "The other three sides are inscribed with cursorily drawn animals— amongst these are (*a*) two serpents, two birds, a bee, a frog, then an unknown creature; (*b*) a long serpent, then a θ; (*c*) a stag, a lizard, a scorpion, and a hare, with another unknown, doubtful animal—besides these there are placed on either side three stars and a little indistinct sign." The object next to the stag, "unknown," is certainly like one upon the tablet of Isis (Fig. 185), whatever it may be intended to represent.

On this large nail are the same objects and animals with which we have been dealing already. The only new one is the hare. Even this we see on the insignia of the Constantia Legion (Fig. 64), jumping over the sun's disc. Moreover, we know that hares were held in much esteem among the ancient Britons as magic-working animals. Cæsar says that they made use of hares for the purpose of divination. They were never killed by them for food. Queen Boadicea is said to have had a hare concealed in her bosom, and after haranguing her soldiers to raise their courage, she let go the hare so that her augurs might divine whether the omens were good or evil from the turnings and windings made by the frightened animal. The omen was favourable, and

ancients, that pestilence was stayed when a nail was
driven by the dictator.[537]

It is also shown by Pliny how disease could be
cured in this way ; [538] and by the Romans the mere
utterance of the word *defigere* implied a nail driven,
and thereby an act by which fascination or witchcraft was countervailed.[539] In Greek tombs nails
have been found amongst other amulets used for the
dead as well as for the living. In the present day it
is sought by human wisdom to strengthen the power
of these nails ; hence a nail by which some one has
been slain on the cross, or a nail from a shipwrecked
vessel, has quite a special power ; the first against
intermittent fever and epilepsy, and the latter against
epilepsy.

Many of these nails had inscriptions and symbols
of magic power engraved upon them, and once more
we repeat that each added symbol was supposed to
increase the collective power of the whole. Most of
the separate symbols found on these nails have
been already described as protectives against the
evil eye—*a fortiori*, the nails were potent amulets.
Moreover when we perceive in these latter days
that all these same animals and objects, together
with cabalistic writings, appear in constant use as

the multitude set up a shout of joy, upon which the Queen seized the
opportunity, led them to the battle, and gained the victory (Borlase, *Antiq.
of Cornwall*, p. 135). No doubt it is this old belief in the hare as an ominous
animal that has survived in our steadfastly held modern one that it is an ill
omen to see a hare cross the path.

[537] " Repetitum ex seniorum memoria dicitur pestilentiam quondam clavo
ab dictatore fixo sedatam" (Livy, vii. 3 ; viii. 18, 12 ; ix. 28, 6). *Cf.* the use
of the words *præfiscini* and *favere* explained elsewhere. They were the
colloquialisms, the *slang* of the Roman populace.

[538] xxviii. 6, 17, as quoted by Jahn, p. 107. I cannot find this passage.

[539] How remarkably this custom of ancient Rome is perpetuated, according to Jorio, in modern Naples, where the mere utterance of the word *corno*
is a defence against the *jettatura* !

avowed protectors against fascination, we are not
only confirmed in our judgment of their meaning
in the ancient form, but we are taught how strong,
how lasting, and how universal, is the belief.

In the light gained from ancient amulets we
easily see the meaning of most of the other objects
on Fig. 112, every one of which is openly sold to-
day as *contra la jettatura*.

The large tiger's tooth in the centre is by no
means uncommon. Real tigers' teeth set as a brooch,
forming a crescent, are plentiful enough here in
England, though their owners hardly look on them as
amulets.   Much value is placed on every part of a
tiger as a protective charm in India.

Pliny says : [540] " The canine tooth of the wolf, on
the right side, is held in high esteem as an amulet."
Also : [541] " A wolf's tooth attached to the body prevents infants from being startled, and acts as a preservative against the maladies of dentition ; an effect
equally produced by making use of a wolf's skin,
attached to a horse's neck (it) will render him proof
against all weariness, it is said."   If wolves' teeth
were so precious in olden times, while they were
tolerably plentiful, of how much greater value would
be that of one of a *gran bestia*, like a tiger ! We
see the analogy of setting greater value upon the
scarcer article, in Jorio's remarks on Neapolitan
shop and house keepers (p. 259 sq.). Again, in
Pliny's day, the wolf skin was an amulet ; we see
and know the use made of it to-day.

The medal with St. George and the Dragon is
with some a favourite, but of course we can only now

[540] *Nat. Hist.* xi. 63 (vol. iii. p. 59, Bohn).
[541] *Ibid.* xxviii. 78 (vol. v. p. 364, Bohn).

consider it as an adaptation of the story of Perseus and Andromeda to the exigencies of mediæval saint-lore. San Georgio is a favourite saint both in Italy and in Greece; we have seen that Mascagni always carried him.

The Gobbo or hunchback is much more common, and is an undoubted survival from ancient days. The Egyptian god Bes is represented as deformed,[542] and he is frequently seen in connection with Horus, when the latter typified death. The number of statuettes of Bes still in existence shows that he was looked upon with veneration, and his cultus may well have descended to the modern Gobbo, an undoubtedly favourite charm. Among the Egyptian amulets in the Museo Kircheriano are many veritable Gobbi, almost exactly like those represented on Fig. 112, though of course without their modern dress. The Gobbo is sold as a charm in silver at Constantinople.[543] There are also one or two small Phœnician figures in the Ashmolean, which are undoubted hunchback amulets. Monte Carlo gamblers did not invent their lucky Gobbo.

FIG. 160.
From Peru.

The bull and the cow are of course the symbols of Osiris-Serapis, and of Isis-Hathor respectively.

[542] Wilkinson, vol. iii. p. 148 *et seq.*

[543] Fig. 160, judged by its eyelets for suspension, is an undoubted amulet. It is from a "figurine en bronze trouvée pres de Cotahuacho," in Peru (Wiener, *Pérou et Bolivie*, p. 715). Comparison will show how strikingly like this figure is, in general type, to two others upon the Kertch necklace (Fig. 21). Upon the same page from which this was taken are seven others which we can only consider of the same sort. One of these is wonderfully like Bes, and bears witness again to the world-wide idea, that grotesque, gurgoyle, devil-like images, were protective against the spirits they were supposed to represent. In these illustrations Peru and the Crimea are brought side by side!

Capo di bove is a very favourite ornament of Etruscan and Roman times, seen alike on the famous Cortona lamp, on the mausoleum of Cecilia Metella so well known to all tourists, but more than all upon the Ephesian Diana (see Fig. 69).

The elephant appears as an amulet on ancient gems (see Figs. 15, 16), and has more said about him by Pliny than perhaps any other animal. In Egyptian sculptures he appears among "the presents brought by an Asiatic nation to an Egyptian king,"[544] but from the representations of ivory, brought from Ethiopia, he would not seem to have come first into Africa from Asia. He may therefore be taken to represent a present of a different or superior breed, just as an Arab barb may be sent now as a present to England. He was not a sacred animal, though the hippopotamus was.

Mercury is frequently depicted[545] riding on an elephant, and from his exceeding intelligence he was a symbol of Mercury. The elephant is said by Pliny to be very fond of women ; and the old seventeenth century Jesuit, Nicholas Caussinus, says that " Ad adspectum virginis mitescit."[546] The evidence is abundant that from the earliest times he has been looked upon as something more than a mere beast, and has had a higher intelligence accorded to him

---

[544] Wilkinson, *Ancient Egypt.* vol. iii. p. 295.

[545] Montfaucon, vol. i. p. 80.

[546] *De symbolica Ægyptorum sapientia.* Coloniæ Agrippinæ, 1623, p. 320. He says that his fury is instantly tamed by the arrival of a beautiful woman, quoting Ælian for his statement. Also that he is the type of the incarnation, and of conjugal fidelity.

" Pudicitia flos morum, honor corporum, decor sexuum, integritas sanguinis, fundamentum sanctitatis, præjudicium omnis bonæ mentis."—Tertullian, *De pudicitia.*

The elephant is said to be duplex in heart and in disposition, and that it is well known he may be both incensed with anger or pacified and made docile by the speech of black men (*De symbolica*, p. 322).

than to any other animal. Our experience in India confirms the opinions expressed by both Tertullian and Caussinus.

Of the pig and wild boar, both of which appear on Fig. 112 as modern amulets, we have somewhat more direct evidence. In Egypt both were held in abhorrence as unclean animals unfit for food. It was unlawful, says Herodotus,[547] to sacrifice the pig to any gods but to the moon and Bacchus, and then only at the full moon. Except on this occasion the people were forbidden to eat its flesh. Even then they did not eat the pig, which was sacrificed before their door, but gave it back to the person from whom it was purchased. Plutarch considered the pig to be connected with the worship of Osiris, and it also appears in the legend of Horus. There were "many small porcelain figures of sows . . . found, of a later period," and probably we may with reason consider them as amulets. The boar is represented in a tomb at Thebes, and he was "an emblem of Evil." In the Judgment scenes, when on weighing the soul it is found wanting, it is condemned by Osiris "to return to earth under the form of a pig, or some other unclean animal."[548]

In Greek mythology the pig as an amulet becomes clearer, and helps us further in the explanation of another important modern charm of which we have yet to speak.[549]

The pig was sacred to Demeter,[550] and of course

[547] Herodotus, ii. 47. Wilkinson, iii. 167, 297 *et seq.*

[548] For illustration of such a scene see Wilkinson, iii. 466.

[549] The pig was sacrificed to Artemis, as may be seen by a relief on a sarcophagus at Constantinople (Daremberg et Saglio, p. 168).

[550] Frazer, *Golden Bough*, ii. 44-60. The whole subject of the pig is carefully and elaborately worked out ; *inter alia*, the times and mode of eating of its flesh are produced (p. 47) as evidence of a sacramental partaking of the body of a slain god. See also Lobeck, *Aglaophamus*, p. 831.

also to her "daughter and double," Proserpine, whom we have proved to be *unam eandemque*. It came at length to be "an embodiment of the corn-goddess herself"; and at the Thesmophoria, a festival confined to women, representing the descent of Proserpine into the lower world, it was customary for the women to eat swine's flesh, to throw pigs, cakes of dough, and pine-branches into the *megara*, or chasms of Demeter and Proserpine. These appear to have been sacred caverns or vaults. We are not told where these caverns were, but we assume that they were either at or near Eleusis, the centre of the Demeter cult. The limestone rocks at the back of the temple of Eleusis might well have many caves in them. In Crete, also an ancient seat of Demeter worship, the pig was esteemed very sacred and was not eaten.

The Greeks could not decide whether the Jews worshipped swine or abominated them, "for they might neither eat nor kill them," so that if eating was forbidden on account of uncleanness, the unlawfulness of killing them tells still more strongly for their sanctity. Frazer believes that swine were rather sacred than unclean to the Jews, and that, in general, so-called unclean animals were originally sacred, and that they were not eaten because they were divine.[551]

Wilkinson [552] gives a full account of the Eleusinian

---

[551] *Golden Bough*, ii. 51. In England, where pork was the only meat in general use, it came as a surprise when the Crusaders told their countrymen of other people besides the Jews who held swine in abomination. The wild stories current were believed and recorded even by so famous a historian as Matthew Paris, who says that the Mahomedans despise pork because the Prophet, having gorged himself till he was so insensible as to fall asleep on a dunghill, was attacked there by a litter of pigs, and so suffocated. For this story, and more of the same kind, see Buckle, *Hist. of Civil.* i. p. 314 *et seq.*

[552] *Ancient Egyptians*, vol. iii. p. 387 *et seq.*

mysteries, the most noted solemnity of any in Greece ; instituted in honour of Ceres, by which name he always speaks of Demeter. (Frazer also uses the Roman name Proserpine when referring to the Greek Demeter.) There were gradations in these as in some more modern mysteries, to which the initiated appear to have been advanced according to merit. "About a year after having sacrificed a sow to Ceres, they were raised to the greater mysteries, the secret rites of which . . . were frankly revealed to them." The "manner of initiation" is described at some length, also the different names of the various parts, properties, and several persons concerned. A perusal of this very accessible description is recommended to students of modern Freemasonry.

Wilkinson says the mysteries were derived from Egypt. Another great authority [553] says : "The tale of Demeter and Persephone, with all the adornments of Greek fancy, is thoroughly Sikel in its essence, the natural growth of a creed in which the power of the nether-world held the first place." We are told previously that the Sikels were one of the early races of settlers in Sicily, from whom the island took the name of *Sikelia*. Whence these people came we are not told, but their primitive worship seems to have been overlaid by the "gorgeous trappings of Greek fancy." "The Sikel deities and their worship were merged in the Greek deities and their worship."

The Greek conquerors of Sicily adopted the pre-existing sacred spot of the Sikels, nearly in the centre of the island, the ancient Enna, now Castro-giovanni, a hill-fortress well suited for a religious

[553] Freeman, *History of Sicily*, vol. i. p. 169.

centre.   To this famous spot the fancy of the
Greeks transferred their legend of Demeter and
Persephone, and it is [554] very pertinently asked
whether the Latin Ceres, Libera, and Dis were ap-
proximations in sound to the names of the original
deities of the hill of Enna (as it is called by Italians,
not of Henna, as the exact Professor persistently
writes it).

Although no mention of swine occurs in the account of the Demeter cult of Enna, yet we may
reasonably conclude that their traces are to be seen
in the very remarkable terra-cotta vases, shaped
like a pig, with only a small aperture in the back, to
be found in the Museum of Girgenti.   The writer
made two sketches of these, and believes there are
others at Syracuse, but has no note of the fact; he
has, however, never seen any of the sort elsewhere.

It should not be forgotten that in Roman lustrations also, the sow was one of the regular animals
sacrificed to the Olympic gods.   It stands first in the
compound word for these—*suovetaurilia;* and the
sow is a prominent object on two of the monuments
still existing on the Roman Forum.   At the Ashmolean, among the Egyptian amulets, are seven sows
in porcelain, all pierced, and of the size intended to
be worn, or to be attached to the dead.   These
were, of course, sacred to Isis.   There are also
several pig amulets, marked late Greek, among the
so-called *ex votos*.   The pig or boar appears as the
badge of more than one Roman legion in Pancirollo;
and a boar's head is common in modern heraldry;
but evidence enough has been adduced to show that

[554] Freeman, *History of Sicily*, vol. i. p. 177.

the modern Italian charm sold in the Roman shops is a true survival of a very ancient cult.

Immediately under the pigs in Fig. 112 are placed four remarkable figures : of all the modern charms here depicted these have most the appearance of a savage fetish, or a South-Sea idol, and yet strangely, they alone pretend to be Christian. They represent St. Anthony of Padua, and were purchased on a great Fair day at the door of the mosque-like cathedral there. There were two mat-baskets full, each containing a number far too large to be even guessed at, but in quantity much over a bushel in each ! It will be seen that each is furnished with a ring, for suspension, and the immense number on sale proves the greatness of the demand by the *contadini* coming to the Fair. The prompt answer of the woman who sold them—*contro malocchio*—to the question what they were worn for, is sufficient proof of their being used as amulets against the ever-present evil eye. We have said that Christian saints *per se* are not amulets, and, excepting these curious objects, the medal of St. George, and perhaps the saints on Neapolitan harness, none have been seen during the many years the writer has been on the look-out for these things. Nor does the saint in either of the two former cases form more than a convenient peg on which to hang a long antecedent belief.

Frazer [555] asks : " May not the pig which was so closely associated with Demeter be nothing but the goddess herself in animal form ? " and then he says : " But after an animal has been conceived as a god, or a god as an animal, it sometimes happens

[555] *Golden Bough*, vol. ii. p. 44.

that the god sloughs off his animal form and becomes anthropomorphic." Precisely so, and by merely carrying the argument to the next stage, and applying it to the case in point, we see that the pig, a well-known and potent amulet, would be improved upon and strengthened by the Padovani through the adoption of their patron saint, not as such, but as the personal embodiment of his own saintly attribute, the pig. Thus we are brought to a modern development of this very ancient idea, and in St. Anthony, as a charm against the evil eye, we see him first as the embodiment of his favourite animal, and through it of Demeter, and so also of Isis.

It will at once be objected that the pig never was the attribute of the Franciscan Saint Anthony of Padua; but no difficulty whatever arises from any such contention. At Padua their patron is Il Santo, they recognise no other, and just as the individualities of the heathen gods and goddesses have been transferred, combined, and assimilated, so all the legends and miracles of the earlier and more famous hermit Saint Anthony are appropriated and ascribed to the mediæval monk who adopted his name. It is but the old story repeated: "Argos destroyed Mykênê and took its glories to itself."[556]

The real Saint Anthony, the founder of the Cenobites, or, in other words, of Monasticism, was a native of Alexandria, and was canonised in A.D. 357.

The ancient custom of placing in all his effigies a black pig at his feet, or under his feet, gave rise to the superstition that this unclean animal was especially dedicated to him and under his protection. The monks of the Order of St. Anthony kept herds

[556] Freeman, *Studies of Travel—Greece*, p. 112.

of consecrated pigs, which were allowed to feed at the public charge, and which it was a profanation to steal or kill : hence the proverb about the fatness of a " Tantony pig." [557]

The facts here given show that the effigy of St. Anthony as an amulet is a development of mediæval and later times ; but its power in the particular locality of Padua is none the less, probably all the greater, on that account. The facts are interesting, moreover, as demonstrating how charms grow up and take root.

The story of the sow and her thirty pigs in connection with Alba Longa seems to have no bearing on the case of the pig as an amulet.

It will be evident that many of the remaining charms in the writer's collection, a few of which are shown on Fig. 112, belong to the same category as St. Anthony, but not having so clear a history, are far more difficult of explanation.

The *fleur-de-lis* as an amulet is, of course, in its present shape, quite modern, or at least a recent development. It is said to represent the phallus,[558] which is also typified by the trefoil and the fig-tree. Again it is said [559] that the lily, of which the *fleur-de-lis* is the conventional sign, is the same as the lotus. This latter we know was a symbol of Isis, and was indeed the sacred flower of the ancients, typifying the combination of the principles of the earth's fecundation,[560] and therefore of fertility. It is this attribute of Isis which the lotus specially symbolised.

By a singular permutation, the flower borne by each (Isis and Madonna), the lotus, ancient emblem of the sun and fecundity,

---

[557] Mrs. Jameson, *Sacred and Legendary Art*, 2nd edition, 1850, p. 436. On " Tantony Pig," see also Hone, *E.D.B.* i. 1826, p. 119.

[558] Inman, *Ancient Faiths*, vol. i. p. 522.   [559] King, *Gnostics*, p. 72.

[560] Inman, *op. cit.* vol. ii. p. 396.

now renamed the lily, is interpreted as significant of the opposite quality,[561] *i.e.* of chastity, virginity.

This is no more strange than the fact that their connecting link, Diana, should by some be taken as the type of virgin chastity, and by others, in her Ephesian form, as that of prolific maternity. Later we shall see the lotus-lily playing an important part ; and accepting the fact that the *fleur-de-lis* is a modern representation, we are fully supplied with a reason for its adoption as a modern charm *contra la jettatura*.

As to the fungus or toadstool, it is another phallic symbol, and has connection with the worship of Priapus ; but, not desiring to pursue that branch of the subject, the writer omitted to note the reference, and cannot now recover it. He must therefore frankly place the fungus among his *oggetti ignoti*, merely stating that it is commonly worn with the same object as all the rest.

The skulls must be considered as portions of the skeleton, which seems [562] from early times to have been considered as a protective amulet. In our day these objects are rather looked on as representing Time or *Chronos* in his aspect of Death, and so as a *memento mori ;* but of their use as charms throughout Italy there is no question. The harlequin too, which is really quite an ingenious little toy, throwing out his legs and arms when the chain is pulled, must be accounted for as an amulet, from being rather like a skeleton ; if not, it also can only be explained by the fact that it is something strange, and likely to attract the eye.

The owl is, of course, the symbol of Athena-

[561] King, *Gnostics*, p. 72.   [562] *Ibid.* p. 213.

Minerva, and appears upon an Athenian coin, now
in the British Museum, representing the patron
goddess.[563] "The owl on the reverse proves it to
be Minerva." [564] To the same goddess were also
sacred the serpent, the cock, and the olive-tree.
Montfaucon gives many representations of the owl
in company with Minerva.

Two others appear among our small charms,
these are the monkey and scissors, and the sabot,
about which nothing can be said further than that
they are strange, and likely to attract the attention
of a beholder, thereby baffling his evil eye.

It is remarkable that the camel, though known
to have been in Egypt at least as early as the time
of Abraham, has never yet been found on any paintings or hieroglyphics ; [565] nor does it appear to have
been sacred to any deity. The only reason the
writer can suggest for its being among modern
charms is, from its being held nowadays by Arabs
and all camel-owning people to be, with the
horse, the most subject of all domestic animals to
injury from the evil eye. Certainly a camel never
journeys without his amulet. The commonest protection is a string of coarse blue-glass beads hung
on his neck, and a little bag containing words
from the Koran ; these are used also for the
horse. It may be that, the animal itself being
so highly sensitive to the effects of fascination,
its effigy is considered attractive to the malignant
glance, and so may absorb its influence to the
protection of the wearer. This notion probably
contributes to the frequency with which repre-

563 Smith, *Dict. of Antiquities*, s.v. "Drachma."
564 Montfaucon, *Antiq.* vol. i. p. 86.
565 Wilkinson, vol. ii. p. 101 ; vol. iii. p. 301.

sentations of all domestic animals are used as protectors.

The lion, the dog, and the goat are sacred to Jove, to Mars (or, as Mr. King says, to Mercury), and to Pan or Priapus. They have been already dealt with.

P.S.—The little figures of St. Anthony, each with a ring for suspension, are referred to in connection with the fair at Padua, by Miss Symonds in *Days spent on a Doge's Farm.*   1894.

CHAPTER X

THE CIMARUTA, SIRENE, TABLETS

AMONG those who have written upon Neapolitan superstitions, one only is known to the writer who has even alluded to the most curious of all the many charms worn there against the evil eye. Mr. Neville Rolfe, in *Naples in 1888*, gives a description of this remarkable amulet, to the infants of Naples just as common to-day as the "coral and bells" were until recently among ourselves. Like many other every-day facts, such as local names for common objects, they are so familiar that nobody notices them, or perceives that they are at all strange ; otherwise we cannot suppose that residents, like Valletta, Marugi, or Jorio, would have failed at least to make some reference to what must have been as familiar to them as their own garments.[566] The number of specimens in the writer's collection[566a] show how common they are ; and moreover that every single one is different from every other. Of these any number of duplicates might have been obtained, and further search will no doubt bring to light many fresh examples. A careful study of these curious objects,

---

[566] These remarks apply equally to the *Mano Pantea*, respecting which there is a hiatus of eighteen or twenty centuries between the hands herein described and the present day. [566a] See Fig. 81, p. 203.

which neither Story nor the writers of guide-books ever seem to have heard of, shows a likeness in the general plan, maintained even in its most simple and elementary forms, that amply justifies the name by which it is universally known.   The *cima di ruta*, or, in Neapolitan, the *cimaruta*, "sprig of rue," tells its own tale.

Although so complicated, and in some cases compounded of so very many different individual amulets, yet all are traceable to one and the same root.

We cannot find any notice of this charm through-out the Roman or mediæval periods, nor indeed is

FIG. 161.

there any amulet like it, known to the writer, in any of the museums where one would ex-pect to find such things,[566b] except one.   In the Bologna Museum among the very earliest Etruscan amulets is a small bronze object of which Fig. 161 is a careful drawing, and about the actual size.   Comparing this, and its clearly ostensible purpose as an amulet for suspension, with the elaborate modern charm, every candid observer must admit the remarkable similarity of general form and evident design in both.   It is much to be regretted that no other ancient example of this kind can be produced ; but even so, and while living in hopes of further finds, it is not unreasonable nor speculative to conclude that we have here the germ,

[566b] The Cimaruta, being always of silver, has probably when worn out been treated as bullion, and if so its absence is accounted for.

and that the "sprig of rue" is one of the very oldest
of existing amulets. We may safely give it an
Etruscan or early Phœnician origin; for we must
always remember that
the objects among
which it appears are
labelled by experts, as
found in tombs, "della
prima età di ferro."

Looking, too, at
the almost oriental un-
changeableness of the
Neapolitan character,
it is no less reasonable
to look upon the name
itself of the amulet as
a tradition of remote
antiquity; and it is
easy to see, even with-
out evidence to prove
it, how upon the simple
sprig new symbols
have been grafted, so
that each of its tips

FIG. 162.

From the Collection of Mr. Neville Rolfe.

has been made to carry a charm in itself, until at
last we have the multiplied aggregation comprised
in the modern amulet (Fig. 162).

Worn upon the breasts of infants in Naples and
the neighbourhood, it is considered their special
protector against the ever-dreaded *jettatura*.

Mr. Neville Rolfe [567] gives a list of eight different
symbols, but in addition to these we have to point out
several other features which may be recognised in it.

[567] *Naples in 1888*, p. 116.

To begin with the title-role : No plant had more virtues ascribed to it in ancient times than rue, and the belief in these has continued down to the present day.

Pliny [568] says the ancients held rue in peculiar esteem ; that the plant has a great liking for the fig-tree and for that tree only, and that it thrives better under it than anywhere else.   He says it is one of the most active of all medicinal plants, and one of the principal ingredients used in antidotes. " Every species of rue, employed by itself, has the effect of an antidote if the leaves are bruised and taken in wine." It is good for the stings of ser-pents — " so much so, in fact, that weasels when about to attack them, take the precaution first of protecting themselves by eating rue." It is good too for " stings by scorpions, spiders, bees, hornets and wasps, the noxious effects produced by can-tharides and salamanders, and the bites of mad dogs." He quotes Pythagoras, Harpocrates, and Diocles, as to the value of rue in a great number of diseases, and in his last paragraph says that " of all the plants that are grown, rue is the one most employed for the maladies of cattle " ; altogether he cites it as being a remedy for eighty-four diseases or ailments. [569]

---

[568] Pliny, *Nat. Hist.* xix. 45 (Bohn, vol. iv. pp. 192, 252, 256).

[569] Molto men, che l' erba ruta
O l' ortic' acut' acuta
Facci' a voi venir le carte
Con guadagno d' ogni parte ;
L' o' provat' e sono stato
Tutto quanto sbaragliato.
Marugi, *Capricci sulla Jettatura*, Napoli, 1815, p. 107.

On this the Editor remarks in a note : " This is the common belief about rue, but I have found no good in it.   I have read in the *Trino Magico* that he who keeps the ortica along with the millefoil is secure against incantation. I know nothing of it."

Gerard speaks much of the virtues of rue, but all herbalists call it " herb of grace." [570]

Culpepper says : " It is an herb of the Sun, and under Leo."

It is suggested that inasmuch as rue was hung about the neck as an amulet in primæval times [571] against fascination, and we know of no other herb that was so used, it may on that account have acquired its name in the Middle Ages. It was, moreover, believed to be of all herbs the most potent restorative medicine, and as a beneficent remedy this was, *par excellence*, the plant bestowing grace or favour upon such as used it.

No doubt our amulet from Bologna was one of those hung about the neck over three thousand years ago ; and it may fairly be contended that it represented the same herb whose reputation has lasted through the ages ; which in these latter days has by some means acquired for itself alone among plants the name " herb of grace." With rue as the

---

[570] There are various opinions as to the reason for calling it the " herb of grace." One is apparently formed upon Shakespeare's use of the word in *Hamlet* (Act iv. Sc. 5) : " We may call it herb-grace o' Sundays " ; that " it was used on Sundays by the Romanists in their exorcisms " (Brand, vol. iii. p. 315) ; but there is no evidence of this, and Shakespeare uses the term several times without any reference to Sundays.

> . . . Here in this place
> I'll set a bank of rue, sour herb of grace :
> Rue, even for ruth, here shortly shall be seen,
> In the remembrance of a weeping queen,
> (*Richard II.* Act iii. Sc. 4)

has hardly a Sunday flavour. The notion that rue was the " bitter herb " with which the Passover was to be eaten as a sign of repentance seems but little better.

The quotation from Bishop Taylor, in Webster, as to " trying the devil with holy water," or in Johnson, from Miller, " An herb of grace, because holy water was sprinkled with it," are equally unsatisfactory ; and until something better is found by Dr. Murray for the *N.E.D.* we must leave the question amongst our *insoluta*.

[571] " Rutam fascini amuletum esse tradit Aristoteles." — Wierus, *De Præstigiis Dæmonum*, lib. v. cap. xxi. col. 584.

basis of our amulet, we have to account for the conventional shape which the spray assumed even in
Etruscan days.

In all the complete specimens here produced
(Figs. 81, 162), it will be seen that the Cimaruta
has three main branches; and considering the
material of which these charms are always made,
in connection with the other symbols on this
complex object, we can come to no other conclusion than that the three branches are typical of
Diana Triformis[572] or of her prototypes. Epithets
are given to her denoting that she is the giver of
light and life, benefits also attributed to Proserpine,
and these " make it seem that she (Proserpine) was
also thought to be concerned for women in labour,
which cannot appear strange if we consider her as
the same goddess with Diana, who being in three
different capacities, as conversant in heaven, earth,
and hell, has three distinct names : in heaven she is
Σελήνη, the *Moon ;* upon the earth Ἄρτεμις, *Diana ;*
in hell Περσεφόνη, *Proserpine ;* whence are those
epithets whereby the poets denote her threefold
character as τρίμορφος, *triformis, tergemina,* with
several others." [573]

---

[572] " Montium custos nemorumque, virgo,
    Quæ laborantes utero puellas
    Ter vocata audis, adimisque letho,
    Diva triformis."
              Horace, *Ode* III. xxii. (*not* Ode xxiii. as
                        quoted by Potter).

[573] Potter, ii. 317. Fig. 163 of Diana Triformis is from Jahn, p. 87. Apart
from its illustrating the same idea that we see so constantly carried out in Indian
statues—several heads and arms upon one body—it shows a quaint custom of
ancient Rome, where, as the inscriptions show, they used to set up figures of
the gods in places not to be desecrated or polluted : in fact to answer the same
purpose as the modern police notices in London or Paris. Besides the inscription on the base of the panel here shown, Juvenal records another : " Ad
cujus effigiem non tantum meiere fas est." The Romans appealed to religion
to enforce sanitation.

Considering her in another threefold character, she is Hecate, Diana, Proserpine.[574]

Montfaucon pictures a statue of this goddess, whom he calls Hecate, in three positions, so as to bring each form alternately to the front.

FIG. 163.

1. On her head is a crescent; above that a flower (the lotus), "the usual mark of Isis." She holds two torches in her hands, and thus represents *Diana Lucifera*.

2. She wears a Phrygian cap with rays of light proceeding from it, and holds a sword in one hand with a serpent in the other. "Servius says she

[574] Montfaucon, vol. i. p. 92.

(Diana) presides over health, of which the serpent is the symbol." [575]

3. She is crowned with laurel, holding a key in her right hand, and ropes in her left. "The key belongs properly to Hecate; she was guardian of Hell, where she reigned with Pluto. The ropes referred to her office of guardian of Hell for reasons evident to all the world."

One of the attributes of Diana was the especial protection of women in childbirth, and by Cicero she was maintained to be one and the same as *Ilithyia* or *Lucina*. Horace also invokes her :—

> "Sive tu Lucina probas vocari
> Seu Genitalis." [576]

In this attribute we have Diana Lucina as the direct forerunner and counterpart, in Neapolitan belief, of Madonna del Parto.[577]

This charm must always be of silver, and each one has to bear the hall-mark; without this the poorest will not have it.

Silver was Diana's own metal—in Greece, in Ephesus, and in Rome alike. Demetrius who made the *shrines* (*housis*, according to Wiclif) was a silversmith.[578]

[575] Montfaucon, vol. i. p. 94.

[576] Horace, *Carmen Sæculare*, l. 15.

[577] In the confusion of the various deities, many of the most opposite qualities have been ascribed to one and the same personality, until all individuality may be said to have been completely lost. We read (*Symbolica Dianæ Ephesiæ*, p. 19) : "Isidis, Cereris, Dianæ, et Cybeles attributa Lunæ etiam adscribi." And again : "Hecate porro Diana, Luna, et Proserpina a Festo et Diodoro Siculo pro uno eodemque numine accipiuntur. Exinde Diana triformis fingebatur." Virgil (*Æn.* iv. 5, 11) also writes :—

> "Tergeminamque Hecaten, tria virginis ora Dianæ."

"Diana had also the name of Trivia, by reason of the power she had over all ways" (Montfaucon, vol. i. p. 16). This view would give another explanation to the three diverging branches of the Cimaruta.

[578] Acts xix. 24. We may note *en passant* that the passage translated

We turn our silver in our pockets when we first see the new moon or Diana ; and in fact the silver moon is something more than a mere figure of speech.[579]

In all complete specimens two of the attributes are never wanting. These are the crescent and the hand, with which the tip of every spray is made to finish, reminding one of the sun's rays on the sculpture in the tomb of Khuenaten (Fig. 103), except that here the hand, when alone, is bent

FIG. 164.

into the gesture already described as a potent amulet[580] in itself—the *mano fica,* and in the other cases is made to grasp some other object. The half-moon on Fig. 162 in itself combines two other symbols, namely horns, already dealt with, and a serpent enclosing the crescent.[581]

(ver. 35) "image which fell down from Jupiter," is in Wiclif's and the Rheims versions "child of Jupiter."

[579] Upon Diana in her Moon character, see Lobeck, *Aglaophamus,* pp. 72, 1062.

[580] The amulet (Fig. 164) here produced is a late example of the classic *fascinum.* It is from Pignorius (*Vetustissimæ Tabulæ Æneæ,* Venetiis, 1605, p. 16 *in dorso*).

"Hinc Neurospasta apud Lucianum, et remedium, præbiave in collo pueris res turpicula, Fascinus videlicet, quem infantium custodem appellas Plinius, hujus amuleti speciem ex ære, lapide lazuli, corallo, et chrystallo ; hic damus in gratiam eruditi lectoris."

[581] Besides being associated with Diana, the serpent was an attribute of another goddess. Minerva or Athena is represented as accompanied by a serpent. "The Tower of Athens, which was guarded by a serpent . . . this serpent which guarded the house stood by the door" (Montfaucon, vol. i. p. 85). This completely accords with what we have remarked as to the serpent being placed at the entrances of tombs and temples ; but on the Cimaruta as an infant's amulet the serpent has more probably to do with health than with the guardianship of doors, although, as we shall see immediately, even in that respect it typified Diana. Hygeia, the goddess of health, is represented as sitting on a rock with a serpent coiled in her lap,

The key, which like the crescent takes a prominent position, appears in every perfect specimen. We may therefore conclude that it is an important amulet; this key also is compounded. On the Cimaruta the bow of the key is always shaped like a heart as on Fig. 162. In Fig. 112 the key appears singly, *i.e.* without the heart, in many shapes more or less ornamental, clearly proving the position it holds in Neapolitan estimation as a simple charm to be worn by adults, as well as in its compounded form by infants. As an amulet it has a distinct phallic significance.[582]

There can be little doubt that the key is another of the symbols of Diana, and relates to her in the form of Luna, or in her proper name of Diana, the wife of Dianus; for *Janus* and *Jana* are but alternative forms of one and the same word. As keeper of the gates of heaven, Jana was entrusted with her husband's key to open the portals for the exit of Aurora and the life and light giving Phœbus, as well as to close the gates of night. The key might possibly be also regarded as an attribute of Hecate-Proserpine, who as mistress of the lower world might open the gates and free the imprisoned spirits.[583] A medal represents her with a key in one hand and a serpent in the other.[584] It is a remarkable fact, and not to be overlooked in connection with Diana and the Cimaruta, that the Neapolitan

opening its mouth to seize a pot of ointment in her left hand (Montfaucon, vol. i. p. 181).

[582] Payne Knight, *Symb. Lang.* p. 30.

[583] Montfaucon, vol. i. p. 94.

[584] Diana, in her alternative name Jana, presided over the doors and thresholds of all houses. "Nigidius assures us that Apollo is Janus, and Diana, Jana; and that the key is their proper attribute" (Montfaucon, vol. i. p. 16). In one of her three forms she holds a key in her hand.

vernacular for a witch is not, as in ordinary Italian, *strega*, but *Janara;* evidently conserving the ancient belief.   In the Bologna Etruscan Museum are several finger-rings, having little keys attached to them, precisely like the horns attached to the modern rings in Rome (Fig. 81).   They are far too small for use, and can only have been worn as amulets, thus proving the antiquity of the key as such.

The heart has already been shown as an ancient symbol in connection with the cross, and it is suggested that in the key with the heart-handle may be a conventionalised representation of the *crux ansata.*   We may safely accept the heart as implying an allusion to the maiden goddess "whose affections were regulated by the key of prudence." [585]

One of the writer's specimens (Fig. 81) contains two birds, and assuming that they are not meant for the same bird, we consider one to be the cock and the other the eagle.

The cock on several gems, like Fig. 14, is either alone or combined with Apollo in a *grillo*, as in Fig. 165.[585a]   He is regarded as a "solar animal," [586] and thus sacred to the sun-gods, Osiris, Serapis, Jupiter, Apollo.   The cock is also the symbol of Mercury, denoting vigilance.   He is sometimes represented as holding an ear of corn in his bill, meaning that "only vigilance can produce plenty." [587]   As a watch-

FIG. 165.

[585] Rolfe, *Naples in 1888*, p. 118.   [585a] *Handbook of Gems*, p. 95.
[586] Wilkinson, *Anc. Egypt.* vol. iii. p. 320.
[587] It is the general opinion that the Sun, Serapis, Mithras, Dis, Typhon,

ful guardian, who will drive away the fiercest beast, even a lion, the cock is a singularly appropriate symbol for the protection of an infant, and hence possibly he is placed on both sides of the Cimaruta, and also upon the *Mano Pantea* to guard the woman and child. His crow is said to be the praise offered to the sun-god, when Chanticleer proclaims the approach of day. It is said that even the lion is afraid of a cock, and that his eye is all-powerful as an amulet (see Fig. 13); also that all demons with lions' heads vanish instantly when the cock (or his image) is presented to them. May not this be the reason why a weathercock is placed high on our church towers? See remarks on Gurgoyles in Appendix II. Pliny [588] says "the lion is terrified—still more on seeing the crest, or hearing the crowing of the cock." The eagle is well known as Jove's own bird. It is shown alongside him on the gem (Fig. 18) as an amulet. In Montfaucon most of the prints of Jupiter have an eagle accompanying him.

The sword or dagger grasped in the hand appears not only as a separate charm on Fig. 112, but is in the hand of the gladiator on the Woburn marble (Fig. 24) and in several of the hands of Diana Triformis (Fig. 163). This may represent the knife shown on the *Mano Pantea* (Fig. 148), or it may be the dart of Diana Venatrix as on Fig. 112.

The fish grasped by the hand is among the separate coral charms shown also on Fig. 112. The fish appears also on the Cortona lamp (Fig. 50) and on various gems and medals (Figs. 14-18). In

Attis, Ammon, and Adonis were one and the same god (Montfaucon, vol. i. p. 10). To these we must certainly add the Gnostic god Abraxas, and hence the cock may symbolise any one of them.

[588] *Nat. Hist.* viii. 20 (vol. ii. p. 269, Bohn). See also *Ib.* p. 496.

some it appears as a dolphin.   The dolphin was the special attribute of Neptune, but Diana-Proserpine was a sea goddess, and it may as an amulet refer to her, inasmuch as it is on her statue (Fig. 175).

Lastly, the flower must be intended for the lotus, the symbol of Isis, *i.e.* of Diana.[589]

To sum up: we have in this highly composite and therefore powerful amulet, no less than thirteen separate and distinct symbols, any one of which by itself may be taken as prophylactic against the dreaded evil eye.   These are: 1, Rue; 2, Diana Triformis; 3, Silver; 4, Hand; 5, horned Crescent; 6, Serpent; 7, Key; 8, Heart; 9, Cock; 10, Eagle; 11, Sword or Dart; 12, Fish; 13, Lotus. [589a]

Of all the many charms combined in the Cimaruta we find on close study that there is scarcely one which may not directly or indirectly be considered as connected with Diana, the goddess of infants, worshipped to-day by Neapolitans as zealously as ever she was in old times by the men of Ephesus and Rome; the only change is in her name.   Many a Demetrius, who still makes her silver shrines, flourishes near the Piazza Margherita, though nowadays he knows her only as La Madonna; she is, however, his goddess, his "regina del Cielo, della terra, del parto, ed anche del Inferno."

[589] In addition to Isis and her descendants, the lotus is sacred to Lateshmi, who, as the partner of Vishnu, is the goddess of prosperity, or the Indian Abundantia.   The flower in Egyptian mythology was also sacred to Horus, who is very commonly represented seated on a lotus.   In King's *Gems* this is quite a favourite subject, also in *Abraxas*, etc.

The lotus was also the symbol of the Roman Ceres, the corn goddess, the type of plenty.   Lotus-seeds were mixed along with wheat-ears in the cornucopia of Amalthea, the she-goat, the very emblem of abundance.

[589a] Probably there are other charms to be found in specimens not seen by the writer.   It is, however, curious that those recognised should be precisely thirteen in number—an undesigned coincidence, but naturally connecting itself with the number, on which we remark in Chap. XI.

Figs. 166-169 are all modern amulets in daily use, and all alike avowedly *contra la jettatura*. These are all for suspension, and are mostly pro-

FIG. 166.—From the Author's Collection.

vided with chains by which to hang. Like all Diana charms, they are of silver. Unlike the Cimaruta, these are always made both sides alike, for the reason that they are worn by women outside the dress, or hung up in the house, speci-

ally in the window. Although all pass under
the general term *Corno*, which is Neapolitan for
amulet, these particular objects are known as
Sirene, or *Cavalli Marini* respectively. In all the
former the female figure is crowned. In one she
is seated on a double sea - horse, though usually
the horses are represented by their two tails rather
than two heads. There are, though very scarce,

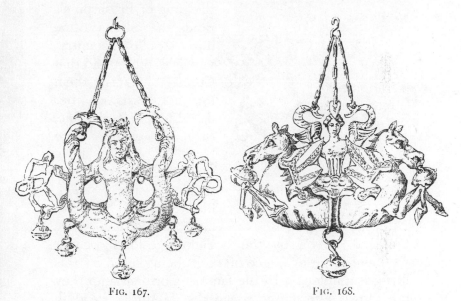

FIG. 167.   FIG. 168.

From the Collection of Mr. E. Neville Rolfe.

specimens of the figure on a single sea - horse.
Readers who are familiar with Abraxas gems will
notice the Gnostic influence so plainly visible in
these double-tailed mermaids.

By far the most difficult problem connected with
this subject has been to account for these strange
objects as amulets at all; and next, for their being
known in Neapolitan as *sirene*.

First, then, we are in the very home of the
Sirens : their islands are close at hand ; the pro-
montory of Ulysses is, next to Capri, the most
visible object from
Naples.   Parthenope,
one of the Sirens, is a
name of the city itself.
" Hyginus writes that at
the time of Proserpine's
rape, the Sirens came
into Apollo's country,
which is Sicily, and that
Ceres, to punish them
for not assisting her
daughter   Proserpine,
turned   them   into
birds." [590]   We have
plenty of representa-
tions of the *Sirens*,
birds with women's
faces, as they were
believed to be by the ancients ; and moreover
we have some evidence of their being used in this
form as amulets.   In the famous Cortona lamp they
are shown alternating round the Medusa's head in
company with the *capo di bove*, fish and Priapus, all
well-recognised amulets (see Fig. 50).

FIG. 169.—From the Collection of
Mr. E. Neville Rolfe.

The arms of the Neapolitan family of Petronia
are a siren, Parthenope, playing a flute.[591]   On a

[590] Montfaucon, vol. i. p. 245.

[591] *Les Sirènes, ou Discours sur leurs forme et figure*, Paris, 1691, p. 65.
"Anciennes médailles, qui sont les monuments les plus sûrs et les moins
suspects" (*Ib.* p. 60).   "On y remarque, outre les aîles, les pieds et les
jambes d'un Cocq attribuez aux Sirènes par la plûpart des anciens auteurs,
quoique d'autres disent que les Sirènes avoient la partie inférieure de Pas-
sereaux" (*Ib.* p. 66).

medal belonging to them she is represented as a
female standing, having wings of the angel kind,
but with a bird's tail and legs. There is thus everything about the locality of Naples to connect it with
the Sirens, and we know their conventional shape,
but whence did the notion come, and how are we to
connect them with Proserpine? [592]

The Etruscan lamp once more directs us to
Egypt. There we find that Isis was represented

FIG. 170.—From Wilkinson, vol. iii. p. 107.   FIG. 171.

with wings (Fig. 170) as a flying goddess. This is a
step forward; but Wilkinson, vol. iii. p. 115, shows us
precisely what we are looking for (Fig. 171). This
is the goddess *Hathor*, holding precisely the same
relation to Isis as the Ephesian Artemis held to the
chaste Roman Diana; or rather we may say that
Hathor was to Isis what Proserpine was to Diana.[593]

[592] As to the mere word Siren, the meaning is not of much consequence,
for women's long, trailing skirts were formerly called *Sirens*. A horrible, discordant instrument giving a warning hoot from a lightship is called a Siren.
The frog amulet in Naples is called a Siren : " Nos toiles de soie . . . si fines
et si diaphanes, q'à peine les voyoit-on sur le nud, sont appellées Syrènes par
Hesychius" (*Les Sirènes*, Paris, 1691, p. 48).

[593] In *Tabula Bembina sive Mensa Isiaca*, by Dr. W. Wynn Westcott,

On Egyptian paintings and sculptures we have Hathor represented as a bird-woman; that is Isis, that is Proserpine, that is Diana. How do we know that the crowned figure sitting on sea-horses, called a Siren, is Proserpine, and therefore Hecate, and therefore Diana the protectress of women in child-birth, and therefore a suitable amulet for the use of

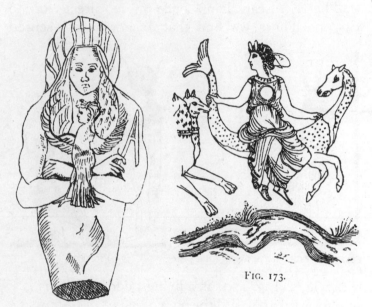

FIG. 172. — From Pignorius.

FIG. 173.

women as a guardian against the evil eye? No candid reader will refuse to admit that in the bird-woman Parthenope, on the Cortona lamp, we have the same person as the bird-woman Hathor in Fig. 171. Further, if any doubt remained, we have a representation of Isis herself (Fig. 172) holding her own siren attribute, just as we shall see the same

1887, is the same bird with woman's face as the attribute of Isis herself—not of Hathor as in Fig. 171.

goddess represented by the statues of the Ephesian
Diana bearing the distinguishing symbols belonging
to her under that title.

Fig. 173 is from a photograph purchased in
Naples. It is part of the very large Greek vase of
Pluto and Proserpine, No. 2959 in the Museum.
The figure on the sea-horse is undoubtedly Proserpine. It is a colossal vase of the transition
period, about the third century B.C., with twenty-
two figures, nearly all named. This one has been
of great service in identifying figures found upon
other vases.

FIG. 174.

The three-headed Cerberus sufficiently marks
the locality. We invite attention next to Fig. 174,
half-size of a drawing by the writer from another
late Greek vase of about the same date, found at
Capua about 1888, now belonging to Mr. Neville
Rolfe. The latter has no other ornament than this
solid block upon a gray ground. The vase is of
course a small one, but there is no doubt as to its
genuineness. It will hardly be disputed that these
two Greek paintings represent the same idea and
the same person. From these the reader is asked
to turn to the five statues of Diana (Figs. 69, 175-
178) taken from Bellori. Upon these seem to

be crowded the various symbols of Diana, every one of which in some place or other is to be found as a separate amulet. Upon four of these statues, perhaps four or five centuries later in date than the

FIG. 175.   FIG. 176.

Greek vases, is to be seen, nearly in the same position, the female on the sea-horse.

Will any person venture to deny that the several representations here brought together are anything else than the prototypes, the direct parents of the modern Neapolitan amulet shown on Fig. 168, and of all those shown on Figs. 166, 167? Inasmuch, too, as we know the ancient ones to represent Proserpine-Diana, so it is maintained that the modern amulet called a siren also represents the same deity.

FIG. 177.   FIG. 178.

There are in Montfaucon, and in other books of classic art, plenty of female figures sitting on sea-horses, but these are called Nereids. No one will venture to call those here produced by that name, and possibly some of the so-called Nereids may in reality be Proserpines.

Such a chain of evidence, connecting in the most obvious manner the beliefs of to-day with the mythology of perhaps thirty centuries ago, is not often to be found ; and again, judging from the known to the unknown, it is reasonable to maintain that most of the habits and customs now persistently upheld by the people would, if they could be thus traced, be found to have their beginnings in the same dim ages of obscure antiquity. Conversely, there is hardly a custom or occult practice of the ancients which may not be traced somewhere or somehow amongst their modern descendants. The statuette (Fig. 175), well known to the writer, is now in the Museum of the Collegio Romano. The others are in private collections. It is strange that not one of these four seems to have been known to Montfaucon, or to his authorities. He has, however, the more typical statue of the Ephesian goddess (Fig. 69), in which she appears as the patroness of maternity. Those which have the attribute of Proserpine so prominent, appeal more to the Roman ideal, although they are matronly in appearance.

It is difficult satisfactorily to interpret the various attributes upon the four statues from Bellori. In general type they are strikingly alike, though each one is different in detail. Every one has the *corona turrita*, by which the author of *Symbolica* says *vertex insignitur*. This is usually the attribute of the Phrygian Cybele as well as of Diana. The two Farnesian statues have wreaths or floral crowns ; in the centre of each is no doubt her own flower—but which ? The rose, chrysanthemum, heliochrysum, lotus, were all sacred to Diana. One has the sun upon her crown, while every one wears a half-moon on her breast with the horns downward, just as these amulets are now always worn by horses.

The object above the crescent on three statues is said to represent a crab, but the whole looks more like a scorpion, with the crescent to represent his claws. We are distinctly told [594] that the crab was suspended to the neck of Diana of Ephesus because it was sacred to her. Hence we find the crab on the breast in Fig. 69, and also engraved on gem amulets (see Fig. 17).

All four statues have two busts upon them, which the present writer does not pretend to explain; a single bust, something like one of these, appears as an amulet on the Kertch necklace (Fig. 21).

Another feature common to three of the statuettes is that they have in each case, both above and below the sea-horses, a group of three nude Graces; and the upper group in each shows the outer figure holding a cornucopia. The lower groups have wings, and in one they are holding the wreaths in their hands, probably the same wreath that two of the other statues have on their heads. Moreover, it will be noted that on the breast of Fig. 69 are two draped females holding up a wreath, and also on this latter are shown two of the nude females in line with the three stags' heads.

The fourth statue (Fig. 178) has but one row of Graces, without anything in their hands. It is difficult to determine the meaning of these nude figures. They may possibly represent Diana Triformis. [595]

[594] *Symbolica Dianæ Ephesiæ.* Romæ: Typis Mascardi, 1657, p. 25. Kindly lent by a friend.

[595] One would like to know if the little groups of similar figures in blue enamel in the British Museum from Sardinia, or the like in the Ashmolean, and elsewhere, from Egypt, can be in any way connected with those on the Diana statues.

Every one of these five statues has both hands posed in distinct gesture-like attitudes, and every hand is open.

The *cavalli marini* (Figs. 166-169) of course represent the same sea-horses as those upon the Diana statues. The sea-horse is an amulet apart, worn equally by the cab horses and upon the breasts of Neapolitan women. On the statues these creatures seem to have heads more like goats than horses. The same may be said of the silver charms. Nevertheless they are all known as *cavalli*.

Each of the statues wears a veil, reaching to the ground upon four, but curtailed to a mere head-dress on the fifth (Fig. 69). These are like the veils often worn by brides, not to hide but to set off the face. Upon Diana the veil represents night—" Velo Dianæ nox indicatur." Moreover, it is the symbol of modesty and chastity.[596]

In the British Museum is an ancient terra-cotta flat bottle, having on both sides the same figure, brandishing in the right hand a sword and in the left a scabbard. All that is known of it is that it was purchased at the Durand sale, described in the " Cabinet Durand," by De Witte, Paris 1836, No. 1550. It is called a Scylla, but on what grounds we are not told. Fig. 179 is from a rough sketch by the writer, but it is sufficient to suggest the general resemblance of this figure to the Proserpines upon the Diana statues and upon the Neapolitan amulets. The two dogs are true Diana symbols, but there is no sign of a crown. One striking feature is in common : the dolphins on the water-bottle are matched by the dolphin alongside the

[596] *Symbolica Dianæ*, pp. 20, 21.

Proserpine on Fig. 175. In any case the coincidence is strange, and does not appear to have been noticed before.[597]

The same conception of the double sea-horse, combined with fish tails, is apparent in the Durand

FIG. 179.

bottle, though the twist is not in the same direction as that invariably seen in the Abraxas and in the Sirens (Figs. 166, 167).

Considering how much these charms vary, and the singular individuality there is in all of them, notwithstanding the very rough work of Neapolitan silversmiths, it is yet remarkable that they should all be so true to their respective types. It cannot therefore be surprising that after all these centuries the modern charm should not have de-

[597] A similar female figure, ending in two fishes' tails, and with the forequarters of two dogs of precisely the same character as those on Fig. 179, is in *Bull. Arch. Nap.* An. VII. Tav. II.

veloped a far greater divergence, and that it still .
keeps so near to its prototypes on the Greek vases
of two thousand years ago. Such divergences as
there are, doubtless arise from their having had to
pass through the mill of the Gnostic influence,
whereby they adopted new forms without, however,
departing from their own types. The bells upon
these various objects are all much alike, and of one
conventional kind. So indeed are the bells upon
our children's corals, and strangely ours are always
of the same special pattern and size as these Neapolitan ones; but stranger still, on the walls of
Medinet Habou are these same little bells upon the
personified *crux ansata*, Fig. 127. Are these mere
coincidences? Is it also a coincidence that the coral
we use was also an ancient protective amulet for
children, and that we have it always mounted with
silver? Is it also mere coincidence that two of the
sirens shown on Fig. 166 end in whistles like our
baby's toy? [598]

We cannot explain the exact likeness in the little
bells between those on our baby's amulet and on
that of the ancient Egyptians or modern Neapolitans;
still the peculiar shape remains the same from the
time of Ptolemy X. and during all the eighteen
centuries since Pliny wrote. The little bells of
brass seen upon horses are different: in shape
they are mostly globular. " Le son de l'airain " was

[598] The god Fascinus "was identical with Mutinus or Tutinus, and was
worshipped under the form of a phallus. . . . As the guardian of infants, his
peculiar form is still unconsciously represented in the shape of the coral
bauble with which infants are aided in cutting their teeth " (Bostock, note to
Pliny, *Nat. Hist.* v. 290, Bohn).

Pliny says: "Branches of coral hung at the necks of infants are thought
to act as a preservative against danger" (*Nat. Hist.* xxxii. 11. vol. vi. p.
12, Bohn).

thought to have a prophylactic virtue. Little bells
of this metal were employed in certain rites, but
also worn as amulets. They are often suspended to
the phallus.[599]

We omitted to refer to one of the amulets upon
the Naples cab horses on Fig. 83, the man in a
boat. This is said to be Osiris, the Nile, or water,
by which the sun fertilises and nourishes the earth.
The old confusion between the several deities here
appears again ; for Horus is also depicted as sitting
on a lotus (his usual representation), and also in a
boat. He also is a sun-god,
and as much confounded with
his father Osiris as is Demeter
with her daughter Persephone.
Fig. 180 represents Horus [600] on
a lotus, holding the whip of
sovereignty in his left hand,
with his right as usual raised

FIG. 180.

towards his lips in token of silence. Above are the
regular Gnostic symbols, (the Turkish) sun and
moon. His boat is the sacred *baris*, terminating
at the prow in the head of an eagle or vulture,
and at the stern in that of a bull—both symbols of
the sun.

All these latter accessories do not appear on the
Neapolitan horse charm, but the idea is the same.
Of course the *capo di bove* is the old favourite,
repeated all round the tomb of Cecilia Metella,
the Cortona lamp, and in two rows of three each
on the statue of Diana (Fig. 69), where they are
flanked by dragons and griffins, which were sacred to

[599] Daremberg et Saglio, p. 258.
[600] From King's *Gnostics*, p. 205. Many similar figures are given in
Abraxas.

her.[601] Even these latter are compounded creatures, and so represent double attributes, all pointing to the sun : the dragon or flying serpent with a lion's head, and the griffin or lion with vulture's head and claws. The serpent is here supposed to represent the inner senses and the quickened understanding.[602] The bee is specially sacred to Diana and Ceres. It is the symbol of virginity, as testified by many ancient authorities.[603] Our custom of beating kettles, ringing bells, and making other noises to cause swarming bees to settle, is not a modern one. Varro (*De re rust.* iii.) says : "Who does not know that dispersed and wandering bees may be got to one place by cymbals and rattles (*plausibus*) ? "[604]

Among symbolic amulets are some very remarkable objects which have hitherto met with rather limited attention.

One of these Jahn (p. 52) calls a wonderful monument and, moreover, a distinct amulet. It is a terra-cotta plaque, circular in shape, with a sort of handle projection on one side. It is like a very shallow bowl with a flat rim round the edge, within which are huddled together a number of very remarkable objects. This one is now to be seen in the British Museum (Fig. 181). The drawing reduced from Jahn's book is by no means satisfactory, yet it is for our purpose much clearer than a photograph. The plaque came to the

[601] *Symbolica Dianæ*, pp. 38, 39.
[602] King, *Gnostics*, p. 35.   [603] *Symb. Dian.* pp. 44, 45.
[604] Claudianus also sang (*Symb. Dian.* p. 47)—
          "qualis Cybeleia quassans
          Hyblæus procul æra senex, revocare fugaces
          Tinnitu conatur Apes."
The bee will be seen upon the Mano Pantea (Fig. 157), and upon the gems, Figs. 17, 28, as well as on Diana, Fig. 69.

Museum by the bequest of Sir W. Temple, who
described it as found at Pozzuoli. Jahn says his
illustration is one-third of the original size, but the
plate itself does not exceed six inches in diameter.
The purpose of this terra cotta, besides serving for a
very compound amulet, is not referred to by Jahn,
although tablets of this character cannot have been

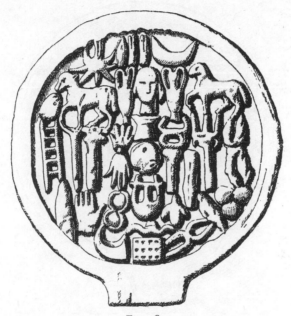

FIG. 181.

uncommon in classic times ; for we read of another
found in Amyklai, described by Aberdeen in *Wal-
pole's Memoirs*, p. 452. Moreover, there is in the
Ashmolean Museum a complete specimen with a
portion of another, brought by Mr. A. Evans from
Taranto.

All these seem to have a projection by way
of handle. Fig. 182 represents the Oxford disc.

Fig. 183 is in the Naples Museum, and there is another in Berlin. Comparison of these illustrations will convince the reader that, whatever their purpose may have been, they generally convey the same idea, and are as much alike as any of the examples of the ancient *Mano Pantea* or of the modern *Cimaruta*. The material is the same, and

FIG. 182.—From Photogravure in Mr. A. Evans's *Tarentine Terra Cottas*.

the size, about 5 inches in diameter, is nearly alike in all : the various objects represented upon them all are not raised but rather deeply sunk.

A glance is sufficient to show that many of the objects represented are the same in each, though their position upon the respective plaques varies. In the London and Naples tablets they seem to be arranged in lines vertically, and more or less horizontally ; in the

Oxford one they seem to be divided into four segments, with a number of the articles ranged round
the circumference, the rest being roughly radiated
from the centre. Moreover, the latter tablet has a
hole, apparently for suspension, which the British
Museum one has not.

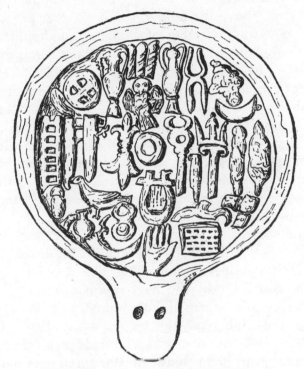

FIG. 183.—From *Bull. Archeol. Napolet.* No. 120, 1857.

On the top of Figs. 181 and 183 we see our old
friends the sun and the moon very distinctly. In
the other, both are also represented, but in different
positions. The three upright objects between the
sun and moon in Fig. 181 appear likewise in all the
tablets. Jahn says he does not know what they are.

Mr. Evans says they are distaffs, and that a fourth, a larger one, is also there.[604a] We presume he means the horizontal object alongside — these distaffs, he says, are wound round with wool.   There is a large upright object beneath the ladder in the British Museum tablet which Jahn does not refer to, but which Minervini says is an acorn.   In the middle of the next row, above the ladder, is a head over an object like an *ambos*.   Neither of these can be identified on the Oxford tablet, although Mr. Evans seems to see in it the "head of a nymph."   In each tablet is seen a pair of Amphoræ, or Canthari; and again we are reminded of the Cantharus upon both our examples of the Mano Pantea.   These represent, we are told, the Dioscuri (Castor and Pollux).   On either side of these is a sheep, but there is nothing to match them in the Oxford or Naples tablets.   This animal, however, closely resembles that upon the modern bone amulet from Sienna (see Fig. 112).   In front of one sheep at the top of the ladder is, according to Jahn, an oval thing which may be a mussel.   On the Oxford tablet is something like it on the right of the distaffs.   In the next row is a round object in the centre, which Jahn cannot explain.   Then come the club and the trident—the latter very plain on all the plates.   The ladder is plain on all, and Jahn says between the torch and ladder is a two-pronged fork (*Zweizack*), and that this is an attribute of Hades.   The lyre and bow appear on all, and next the lyre (on the left) what he thinks is meant for a pair of cymbals.   The open hand is plain on all ; the right hand in two, and left

[604a] *Recent Discoveries of Tarentine Terra Cottas,* p. 45 (from *Journ. of Hellenic Studies,* 1886).

in the other. To the right of the lyre is a leaf, the meaning of which, Jahn says, is not clear, but it is surely the phallic fig-leaf. The pincers are distinct on all, as they are upon the nail, Fig. 159. One other object, common to all the tablets, which neither Jahn nor Mr. Evans attempts to explain, is the oblong slab with twelve square holes in regular lines. Three flat discs, on all the plates, Mr. Evans thinks may be coins, but three similar discs are upon the table on the hand, Fig. 156, apparently as an offering to Serapis. There are, besides these, several objects upon the Oxford tablet not to be found upon those of the British Museum or Naples. First, the upright column above the crescent, which Mr. Evans calls the club of Herakles, we submit is much too important an object upon this combination of attributes to be the symbol of either of the lesser gods. It is suggested that this may be one of the pillars of Hermes on which that god engraved all knowledge.[605] The objection to this is that the caduceus has already typified him. Still there may be two symbols like the sun and thunderbolt for the same god. Again, there is a bird, but hardly a dove;[605a] it would rather be intended for a cock or an eagle. The object near the bird, called a lover's knot by Mr. Evans, is, we suggest, much more probably a scorpion. The "curved object" is manifestly the same as Jahn calls a *Füllhorn*, but it rather represents a scythe or sickle; which of them is the tunny or the grapes which Mr. Evans sees we cannot explain.

Jahn finishes his description of Fig. 181 with the

[605] King, *Gnostics*, p. 208.
[605a] A. J. Evans, *op. cit.* p. 46.

remark that "surely are distinguishable over and above the stars, the symbols of Zeus, Poseidon, Hermes, Herakles, Apollo, Artemis, Hephaistos, perhaps of Pluto and of Demeter: the cymbals may typify Dionysos or other orgiastic deities; the cornucopia Tyche (Fortuna)." The well-known symbols of various deities here brought together make it pretty evident that the rest, which we cannot identify, all belong to the same category, and are grouped here for a like purpose. Upon the general aspect of these tablets Mr. Evans points out that their wheel-like character renders it highly probable that they were used for stamping cakes in use on various religious occasions. The segmental division certainly recalls the cakes still to be seen in the Pompeian room at Naples, and the same thing appears on the cakes set before the "three men" by Abraham (Fig. 116), from the early Ravenna mosaics. Loaves or cakes so marked are still sold in the streets and markets of Naples, while our own hot-cross buns perpetuate the same form, though now under a Christian guise.

It is much to be desired that the British Museum authorities would have a cast made from the plaque in their possession (Fig. 181), for it, like all the other similar tablets, is an unmistakable mould. Examination of the convex casts placed alongside the mould (Fig. 182) in the Ashmolean, and of a fragment of another in the same case with it, shows much more distinctly what the objects are intended to represent, than can be determined when one only looks at the concave mould. Another matter of interest is, that the fragment at Oxford is an exact duplicate of the plaque in the British Museum

(Fig. 181), and is broken in a line from about the centre of the ladder, passing through the lyre to the centre of the three discs, and preserves the objects above that line. The cast makes clear several objects which Jahn evidently did not understand in the perfect plaque of Sir W. Temple. It is remarkable that duplicate moulds, identical in pattern and in shape, should have been found at Pozzuoli and Taranto. The Naples example is both clearer and sharper, as well as in much better preservation than the others. The engraving published in the *Bullettino Archeologico Napoletano*, No. 120, 1857, from which we take Fig. 183, has been badly copied in Daremberg (p. 256), but without acknowledgment.

We also give here a copy (Fig. 184) of a terra-cotta lamp from the collection of Signor Barone, also published in the *Bullettino Archeologico Napoletano*, vol. iii. p. 182, Tav. VII. Another plaque of the same kind is at Berlin, too indistinct and wanting in definiteness to be worth reproduction, yet a large number of the objects can be readily made out, and are common to all the others here shown. In the arrangement of objects it matches Fig. 182, particularly in the division into four segments ; but in this Berlin plaque is one very noticeable and remarkable point— it has a border almost identical in pattern, if not actually the same, as that shown on the lamp, Fig. 184. Attention is particularly invited to this, inasmuch as we hope by these drawings to prove what was the object of these terra cottas. A mere glance at the three cuts, really representing five distinct moulds, is sufficient to prove that the purpose is the same in all, and that the majority of the objects represented upon them are identical, and therefore must

all symbolise the same ideas or persons. Besides
these, there is another plate of the like kind in
the Louvre, which however the writer has not seen.
The greater plainness of the objects upon Fig. 184,

FIG. 184.

together with their proper convex forms in the casts
at Oxford, and a general comparison of all together,
enable us to correct Jahn, and to determine what
certain obscure objects are in each of the moulds.
Minervini (Editor of the *Bullettino*) writing on Fig.
183, remarks upon the great similarity between
this and Jahn's plaque (Fig. 181). He insists that

the whole is an amulet symbolising many divinities ; that a horizontal line through the centre of each of these plates passes through a series of identical objects.

Minervini says that the open hand has not been sufficiently considered by Jahn ; that it seems to point upward to the numerous symbols depicted above it ; that he considers these hands to be of the same meaning as those Jahn calls votive hands, here dealt with in the chapter on the Mano Pantea.

Beginning on the left, he compares the two *seriatim*. The ladder, he remarks, is doubtful in its meaning to Jahn, but we see in both plaques the symbols of the twelve great gods. Ceres however is wanting, whereas on Barone's lamp she is represented by the ear of corn ; and he maintains that what seems to be a ladder is *arnese di tessere*, i.e. a loom, and that it represents Ceres in all cases. In every one of the moulds seen by the writer there is the ladder unmistakable.

The next symbol, he says, is a lighted torch with the flame turned to the left. This, Jahn says, is a two-pronged fork ; but he is surely wrong, for that would mean nothing.

On Fig. 181 is a nondescript object above the ladder, corresponding in position to what Minervini calls a flame. Now, as in the Ashmolean plaque there is an undoubted torch, we think that in both moulds a torch with flame turned to the left comes next the ladder, and that it represents Vesta; so asserts Minervini. On the lamp we see the torch most distinctly. Next comes a scabbard, which Jahn took for the torch. It is very plain, and shows the ring by which it is attached to the belt (*balteo*) on Fig. 183. This is for Mars. The scabbard is shown on the lamp, and is probably intended by one of the objects upon the Mano Pantea which we could not explain. Minervini in one of his articles calls this a quiver (*turcasso*), but corrects himself afterwards. The thunderbolt appears in all the plaques, and needs no explanation. On the lamp it is superseded by the eagle.

Next, according to Minervini, is the patera in the centre, representing Juno. In the cast of the fragment at Oxford this centre is marked distinctly with a cross, which seems to point to its being an offering cake.

Next comes the caduceus of Mercury, plain on all the plaques, and also on the Barone lamp. The trident of Neptune is on all the moulds, but on the lamp he is represented by a dolphin.

Next is the club of Hercules, followed by an object which is not easily explained. On Figs. 181, 183, between the caduceus and trident, there is in each what Minervini says unhesitatingly is a knife in the latter; and if this be so, it is doubtless a knife in the other. In the B.M. tablet (Fig. 181) is a large double object next the trident. We believe this to represent the two separated objects in Fig. 183, which are the club and possibly, as suggested by Minervini, a distaff simply, or a distaff filled with wool (*conocchia o pennecchio*). Against this, however, his own argument respecting another of the objects tells with some force. Speaking of the cymbals, he refutes Jahn's opinion, and says it is impossible to suppose two symbols of the same deity upon one monument. Now, as Mr. Evans says that the three upright objects found on all three

of our plaques represent three distaffs, and also that
another object on his (Fig. 182), near the ladder, is
a large distaff, it is very difficult to reconcile authorities.[605b]   The three objects referred to have every
appearance in Mr. Evans's cast of being rather
three spools or bobbins, for the winding of the
thread is distinct upon them, and therefore I should
say they represent the three Fates.   But I can offer
no opinion as to the larger object, also said to be a
distaff.

In all three moulds, and also on the lamp, are
found the tongs or pincers of Pluto or rather
Vulcan.   Minervini says that he believes these to
represent the shears of the Fates rather than the
tongs of Pluto ; but here again he is inconsistent
with his own dictum.   He says he cannot attempt
to explain the obscure article near (*i.e.* below) the
telajo (loom) of Ceres.   Whatever this may be,
there is the same nondescript at the foot of the
ladder in all three plaques.   Jahn calls this a shell,
but in his mould (Fig. 181) it appears more like
an acorn.   I would suggest rather that in each case
this object is meant for a pine-cone ; the same
symbol is found upon the lamp and on the hand,
Figs. 156, 157.   Minervini believes the object called
a fig-leaf by Jahn, close to the lyre (Fig. 181), to
be the same as that on Fig. 183, between the tongs
and the moon.   This he thinks to be a bunch of
grapes for Dionysos—a bunch of grapes certainly

[605b] Minervini's opinion is not supported by evidence.   We see on the
Mano Pantea and on the Cimaruta the same deity typified by two different
symbols.   Moreover, on the gem, Fig. 17, the same symbol, the bee, is
repeated twice over.   Again, on the week-day gem (Fig. 19) every one of
the symbols may be construed to represent one or other of two deities only.
See also the sacred *baris* (Fig. 180), and Diana (Fig. 69).

appears on the lamp.   He wildly asserts that the
three objects between the vases, which are certainly
more like reels of yarn, are three masses of incense,
and that they recall the well-known verse of Ovid:—

"Et digitis Tria Tura tribus sub limine ponit."

He says this is proved by the adoption in some rites
of three lumps (*grani*) of incense.   This, to the
present writer, seems far fetched.

The three discs near the trident are very evident
in Figs. 181-183; and in Mr Evans's cast from Fig.
182, the object at the top of the caduceus is very unmistakably intended also for them though obscure on
the mould.   They represent the three sacrificial
loaves, doubtless the same as are on the hand, Fig.
156.   It is a coincidence to be noted that upon
the table spread by Abraham (Fig. 116) we see the
same number of round cakes, each, too, marked
with a cross.   Near the lyre on Fig. 183 is a bird,
which Minervini says is certainly the Iynx, or dove
of Venus.   A bird also appears plainly on the Oxford
cast, and also on the lamp.

The undoubted owl upon the Naples plaque of
course means Minerva.   Upon this Minervini says
that the same position in Jahn's drawing is occupied
by a head over an anvil, but that this is a modern
restoration!   It is certainly very indistinct, and the
head may be a creation of Jahn's draughtsman; but
on the other hand there is a head upon the lamp,
and also we find a head upon the Isiac tablet from
Pignorius (Fig. 185).   It has been suggested that
one of the obscure objects on the Ashmolean mould
may represent a head.   Minervini believes that the
head in Fig. 181 is really an owl, and the anvil its tail.

Near the hand beneath the bird, is the strigil
accompanied by the vase of oil, " or rather the
xistrolecito, a well-known symbol of bath and
palestra." These are called *strigil and guttus* in
Smith's *Dictionary of Antiquities.* The square
tablet in all the plaques is, according to Minervini, a
tabella representing athletic laws of the gymnasium
and palestra. I prefer to follow the example of
Jahn and Evans, by saying I do not know what it
is. On comparing them together no candid reader

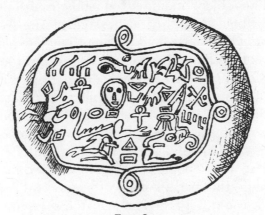

FIG. 185.

will deny that all these moulds were certainly intended for the same purpose, particularly as duplicates were found so far apart as Pozzuoli and
Taranto.

Although very different in the general arrangement of the objects represented upon it, yet the
lamp shows so much resemblance, and it has so
many symbols belonging to the other combinations,
that it is but reasonable to consider them upon
the lamp as representing the same ideas or cult
as upon the plaques. In the centre is a winged

female seated, whom we may take to be a divinity, surrounded by so many symbols that she seems to be intended for Fortuna Pantea, who is called upon a Roman monument FORTVN : OMNIVM· GENT·ET·DEOR. In her left hand she holds a cornucopia, from which appear flowers and grapes. In her right she holds a patera, which she is presenting to a serpent twined round an altar of offerings. At the top is a beardless head, enclosed in an ornament like a crescent. Beneath the crescent is a wheel-like object mounted on something unknown, but the whole strikingly suggestive of the Ashantee crescents (Fig. 88); and we may fairly explain the whole as the sun and moon. We see also the eagle; the Dolphin ; [606] the scabbard, or, as Minervini calls it, the quiver ; the club ; the sistrum of Isis ; the lyre ; the tongs (these are no shears) ; the caduceus; the thyrsus of Bacchus, having the pine-cone at the top ; the cymbals of Cybele, Bacchus, and Juno, suspended to the "pomegranates of Proserpine," and near them the ear of corn of Ceres. There is a second serpent, Agathodemon, often seen in connection with Fortuna, [607] which is climbing up behind and looking over her shoulder, much in the same position as that on the hand (Fig. 157), whereon again two serpents are represented.

Presuming that the illustrations, here brought together for the first time, have been duly examined and compared, we must now try to ascertain the true object of the moulds represented by three of them.

---

[606] On the dolphin as a symbol of Neptune see Müller, *Handbuch*, § 398, p. 645, Ed. Welcher.

[607] On this see Gerhard, *Agathodæmon und Bona Dea*, p. 18 sq.

Heydemann, writing in the *Gazette Archéologique*, 1883, p. 7, quotes Lenormant as of opinion that they are intended for the making of mirrors in bronze. M. Albert Dumont and M. Robert de Lasteyrie support this opinion, while M. Henzey says they have served to mark the religious impression upon sacrificial cakes.   Mr. Arthur Evans assumes this to be an unquestioned fact, as he simply calls them "moulds for sacred cakes."   He says later (p. 49) that it seems "highly probable" that this was their purpose.   Heydemann disagrees with both these opinions, and supports Jahn in the contention that they belong to the class ἀποτρόπαια, that is of prophylactic amulets ; and he goes on to compare the various specimens of moulds known to him, but not including those now at Oxford, and gives to some of the objects an explanation differing from any yet noted : for instance, he finds a thimble, a rosette, a key, a wing, a lizard, etc., but admits that the objects are often very indistinct.   After disputing several contentions of Minervini, he points out that in every case there is an umbilicus, round which the symbols are placed.   In this last belief the writer fully agrees with him ; at the same time it is evident Heydemann is not a careful observer, for he asserts that the plaque of Sir W. Temple (Fig. 181) and that of Mongelli at Naples (Fig. 183) are certainly from the same model.   It has been stated that the Berlin terra cotta (published in the *Gazette Archéologique*) in general arrangement resembles that at Oxford (Fig. 182), but in addition there is a border with a pattern like that on the Barone lamp.   Moreover, this lamp is of almost the exact size of all the known terra-cotta moulds of this sort, while of course the figures

upon the Barone and all other lamps are raised by
having been shaped in a concave mould.   Looking
then at the great demand there must have been for
lamps of all kinds, and at the peculiar and exactly
similar shapes of these moulds found in various
places to that of the lamp, Fig. 184; looking also
to the fact that lamps so frequently bore objects
upon them which were obviously intended as
amulets; we have little hesitation in setting aside
all the other theories advanced, and maintaining
that these were the moulds with which the potter
shaped the top of the peculiar flat-shaped lamp
shown on Fig. 184.   In the specimen we have,
there is a round hole just below Fortuna's arm, to
pour in the oil.   In forming a lamp from the other
moulds, the maker would cut a round hole in the
soft clay just in the centre, at the spot where in each
mould there is left a suitable umbilicus.   There is
no evidence whatever that the sacrificial cakes bore
any such devices as are upon these plaques.   More-
ever, the symbols are so small that in a material
like dough they would have simply appeared as
shapeless, meaningless excrescences, whereas the
plaster cast at Oxford shows that in a fine material
like terra cotta each symbol comes out in convex
form, distinct and fairly sharp, merely requiring the
ordinary hand trimming to make it as clear and
distinct as the representations upon the many lamps
in our museums, and especially on that of Barone at
Naples.   The border pattern upon the Berlin mould
completely destroys the sacred cake theory.   The
plain border round our Oxford, Naples, and British
Museum specimens, would be pared off by the work-
man in fitting the soft top on to the body of the lamp.

It is of course possible that bronze also may have
been cast in these moulds, for the many specimens
of the Mano Pantea are all cast in a mould of some
sort, and the symbols upon them have been dressed
and trimmed afterwards, just as the statuettes of
bronze or of terra cotta have been finished up after
being cast.   These things could no more have been
used for sacred cakes than the other moulds exhibited
alongside them at Oxford—from which ornamental
plaques, statuettes, and other artistic objects have
been made.

The lamps they were intended to shape were of
the commonest form, and lent themselves con-
veniently to the collocation of a number of symbols
such as are found on these moulds, as well as upon
many lamps.   We submit they were intended, in
the same way as the more costly bronze hands, to
display constantly an assemblage of amulets in a
cheap material analogous to the wax *ex votos* now
seen in churches, as compared with the very same
objects often alongside them in more costly silver.

Somewhat allied to the remarkable terra-cotta
plates we have been discussing is the curious tablet
illustrated in Pignorius,[608] of which Fig. 185 is a
copy.   Many of the objects drawn upon it are
very obscure, yet amongst them are some we
recognise as old acquaintances ; and there can be
little doubt of the whole being a protective amulet
against the evil eye, and that it is a veritable Mensa
Isiaca.   The head probably represents a skull, or
possibly it may be the same person as the bust in
Fig. 181.   Over it is the mystic eye.   The triangle,
whether with base or apex downward, is a well-

[608] See also Inman, *Anc. Faiths*, vol. i. p. 108.

known phallic symbol. Both occur upon this plate. The typical hoe or plough shown upon Egyptian *ushebtiu* (Figs. 1, 2) and in the hands of Isis, Fig. 172, with more than one *crux ansata*, and two arms with hands palm up, are all very plain.

CHAPTER XI

CABALISTIC WRITING—MAGICAL FORMULÆ

FROM the protective amulets, specially intended to attract and baffle the evil eye by being worn on the person, or otherwise conspicuously displayed, we pass to another class of protectives, depending for their potency not upon symbolism so much as upon direct invocation of those powers or deities, typified by the various symbols, we have been considering. Of this class there are two distinct kinds : first, the written formulæ of many sorts ; and next, the spoken words or actions, all tending to the same end. Both kinds, moreover, may be either concealed from view and hearing, or openly displayed.

Of the former, of course, the well-known Jewish phylacteries are the most obvious examples. Their virtue was supposed to rest in the written words shut up in the little leather case ; their Hebrew name was *tephillim*, but the name by which we know them in the New Testament sufficiently proves that they were amulets.[609]

On Turkish horses and Arab camels at this day are hung little bags wherein are passages from the Koran ; on Neapolitan horses, too, besides all the

---

[609] The *tephillah* of the arm and of the forehead have been already explained (p. 124), and the Scripture texts recited.

hands, horns, and wolf skin, is very frequently a little canvas bag, containing a prayer to the Madonna, or a verse of Scripture, but always with the same end in view—the *jettatore* must be countercharmed, in case the ostensible amulets should fail.

Through the kindness of Mrs. Charles Elton we are able to present a facsimile of a true phylactery from Abyssinia, where such things are common at the present day. The language of this charm, though Amharic, "is not the vernacular, but wholly that of the sacred books, called by the people Geez." At the present time no Ethiopic scholar in Europe reads it, and I am fortunate in having at last found a translator. The full transcription and glossed translation here given are the work of the Rev. R. Weakley of Alexandria, in whose service is a native Ethiopic "debterah" or scribe. This man read it easily, and dictated to Mr. Weakley, who has thus rendered it into English. It appears that these charms are quite common, and there is a class of disreputable men in Abyssinia who get their living by concocting and writing them for their ignorant countrymen.

Mr. Weakley has added some very valuable notes, which render the whole much more intelligible, and the present writer desires fully to admit the obligation, and to express his thanks for this unique rendering into English of a most curious document —a document proving up to the hilt all the statements put forward as to the world-wide prevalence, even in these latter days, of the firm belief in the power of the evil eye.[610] The eyes themselves

[610] In Mr. Theodore Bent's *Sacred City of the Ethiopians*, pp. 165, 166, are facsimiles of charms of just this character, and also drawings of several

appear in two places, peeping out at the beginning
and at the middle of the writing.

TRANSLATION

1. Bè asmă āve, wa weld, wa mănfars kĕdoos,
   In the name of the Father and the Son and the Holy
   Ghost,
2. Ahadĕ Amlack. Salot.
   One God. Prayer.
3. Bénter hamamer băryā wa āyēnet.
   For (against) the sickness of the slave (epilepsy) and the
   (evil) eye.
4. Awlo-mela-el: Metowé-mela-el: Corooking.[611]
5. Bè illoo asmat
   By these names
6. Adi hinna imhemamer barya wa āyēnet,
   Deliver her from the sickness of the slave (epilepsy) and
   the (evil) eye,
7. Āyēné sella wa āyēné Zār,
   The shadow of the eye and the eye of the Zār,[612]

---

leather cases like the one here produced (Fig. 186). There is also a learned
chapter on "Inscriptions," by Dr. David Heinrich Müller of Vienna, but none
of the charms are described or translated. In fact it is confidently believed
that at present there is no European now in Europe who can read them, or
the one here lithographed.

[611] Mr. Weakley's Notes. Secret names of God.

[612] Zār. The following paragraph is copied from Isenberg's *Amharic
Dictionary*, C.M.S. London, 1841—a very scarce book—under the word
"Zār," p. 156: "Name of a sort of demons or genii, to whose influence the
people of Shoa and the Gallas ascribe many changes in man's bodily constitution and general welfare; such as health and disease, pregnancy, birth, death,
change of weather, success or disappointment in several undertakings, etc.
They believe that these invisible beings are eighty-eight in number, and
divided into two equal parties; forty-four of them being united under one
chief, called Warrai, and the other forty-four under another chief whose
name is Māma. In Shoa these Zārs are worshipped, we were told, by those
who are in the habit of smoking tobacco, except foreigners; and we persuaded ourselves that that very custom is, by those Shoa people who followed
it, observed in honour of those imaginary beings. After having witnessed an
extraordinary instance of Zārolatry in our own house, where we saw an
otherwise intelligent and respectable woman alternately smoking and praying to the Zārs with great vehemence until she was mad, and then killing a
hen whose brain she ate and became quiet again; after this, I say, we
inquired into several instances where we met with smokers, and found that
they all were worshippers of the Zārs. In the state of phrensy, into which
they work themselves by vehemently smoking, praying, and shaking of the
head, their language alters so as to call everything by names which are
known only to the Zār worshippers."

8. Ayēné sāve wa ganen,
  The eye of men and demons,
9. Coorsăt wa feltăt,
  Colic and headache,
10. Wegăt wa serksecăt was shentemăt.
  Rending, and sharp pain, and painful micturition.
11. Ikerba lamatka welata Tekla Haimanoot.[613]
  Keep thy servant, the daughter of Tekla Haimanoot.

12. Avē isăt, weld isăt, wa manfar kĕdoos isăt,
  The Father is fire, the Son is fire, and the Holy Ghost
  is fire,
13. Maisaromoo lè aganàt.
  The chain of the demons.
14. Betaranyou : Bejune : Cashoon : wa Veaifa-satavias :
15. Mashfatanersh : Keeyakee : Borons : Carïtyanos.[614]
16. Bè illoo asmat iseromoo lè aganant.
  By these names chain the demons (viz. the following),
17. Baria wa Legewon, Dabas wa Jinn, Salawogi wa Fagen,
      and   and   and
  Zār wa Nagergar : Didk wa chunafār :
      and   : plague and sudden sickness ;
18. Mitch wa Mitat ; Nahavi wa goosimt :
  Sharp pain and stroke ; the hunter and the toucher ; [615]
19. Tavive wa Booda : [616] Googooha wa tigrida :
  The clever-wicked and sorcerers ; choking and wild
  paroxysm ;

---

[613] Tecla Haïmanoot, "one of the most celebrated Abyssinian saints, a native of Shoa, who flourished in the thirteenth century " (Isenberg's *Amharic Dictionary*).

[614] Secret names of God.

[615] *i.e.* the demon who hunts to death, and the demon who touches gently to death.

[616] *Cf.* "Taviv wa Booda." The latter word in Isenberg's *Dictionary* is explained "as an adjective : '*Mad*,' Esp. '*sorcerer*,' generally '*sorceress*.' The Abyssinian's belief in witchcraft goes so far as to ascribe to its influence not only every kind and degree of mania, epilepsy, *Chorus S^{ti}. Viti*, but also several other nervous and febrile complaints, such as hysteria and delirium, as well as every obstinate disease for which they know no remedy. Their idea in those cases is, that either some demon or a Booda must have taken possession of the patient. The Falashas of Semên and the neighbourhood of Gondar, skilful artisans in general, and a number of other people possessed with more than common skill or genius, are looked upon as Boodas. The hyæna is generally believed to be a transformation of a Booda."

These people have been so called ever since the days of Herodotus, see *ante*, Chap. I. p. 28.

LEATHER CASE,

Showing marks of much wear.

BACK OF SCROLL.

❧ Ethiopian Charm, and Case, ❧
CIRCA 1840.   *(HALF SIZE.)*

20. Fira wa nedad : Magua wa mansho :
    Fever and ague ; fever and periodic illness.
21. Cama iyikravoo imlaila amatea Welata Tekla Hai-
    manoot.[617]
    Lest they approach her, (and fall) on thy servant, the
    daughter of Tekla Haimanoot.
22. Sloter d'ngaze megraray aganent.
    The prayer of fear to Him who rules the demons.

23. Coltekolcol, Coltekolcol, Coltekolcol, Colte- (Repetition
    kolcol, Coltekolcol, Coltekolcol, Coltekolcol.   in Sevens.)
24. Hajirji, Hajirji, Hajirji, Hajirji, Hajirji, Hajirji, Hajirji.
25. Gohajir, Gohajir, Gohajir, Gohajir, Gohajir, Gohajir,
    Gohajir.
26. Gorgovajir, Gorgovajir, Gorgovajir, Gorgovajir, Gorgovajir,
    Gorgovajir, Gorgovajir.[618]

27. Bè illoo asmat, Ikaba imdingaza aganant,
    By these names keep her from the terror of the demons,
28. Baraya wa magaña, Zār wa kuraña, Algoom wa
    [Koomaña.[619]
        still birth,   evil possession, dumbness
    [and standing sickness.
29. Adihinna, lamatika, Welata Tekla Haimanoot.[620]
    Deliver her, thy servant, daughter of Tekla Haimanoot.

30. Wa gāzoo zalizoom lé zilmat, firha wa dangaza Diāvolos
    (fikat)
    Then he whose face is covered with darkness, feared and
    trembled ; the archdevil.
31. Rigo bihooterlidat besiga Amlacka bè seaol.
    When he saw the mighty one who was born in the flesh
    (even) God, in hell.
32. El ; M'el ; Jan'el ; Ililfarsangana-el ; M'el ; Telk-el ;
    Walil-el ; Z'el ; B'el ; M'el.[621]
33. Fatare samayat wa midir, Adihinnani lamatika Eon Kalloo
    deerè taviv wa booda goorgooha wa tigrida, Welata
    Tekla Haimanoot.

---

[617] See note 613, p. 392.   [618] Secret names.
[619] Koomaña, "standing sickness." A disease which works impercept-
ibly and fatally while the person affected is "on his feet," *i.e.* going about
as if in health.
[620] See note 613, p. 392.   [621] Names of God.

The creator of heaven and earth, deliver me, thy servant, from every ill by the evil, wicked, and sorcerer choking and paroxysm daughter of Tekla Haimanoot.

Back of Scroll

Continuation : there being not sufficient space below the last line on the face.

34. Isma alvo negar Zèyesano lè Egziàwehair.
Nothing is impossible with God

The figures and letters after the above form a talisman, signifying in words: "Bind him! Bind him! Bind him!"

Coming back from Abyssinia to England, we subjoin to the above the following genuine recipes. They are taken from a book which belonged to the "Conjurer" referred to in note 80, Chap. II. p. 55 :—

A Receipt for Ill Wishing

Take a handful of white salt in your right hand and strewe it over the Backs of all your cattle : begin at the head of the near side and go to the Tail, and from the Tail to the head up the off side, and as you let it out of your hand say these words: " As Thy servant Elisha healed the waters of Jericho by casting salt therein, so I hope to heal this my Beast: in the Name of God the Father, God the Son, and God the Holy Ghost. Amen."

If any Cattle is bad, do thus

Cut a bit of hair from between the Ears, a bit from behind each Shoulder, and a bit from the Stump of the Tail, a little Blood, a Teaspoonful of Gunpowder, and put the whole into a small Bladder, and tie the top of it ; then get some Green Ashen wood, and make a fire, and set it on the brand *irons*, and take the Bladder into your right hand, and say those words: " I confine all Evil, and all Enemies of mine and my cattle into the fire for ever, never to hurt me or mine any more for ever: in the Name of God the Father, God the Son, and God the Holy Ghost. Amen." Then drop it into the Fire, and let it burn out. Read the first thirteen verses of the 28th chapter of Duteronomy (*sic*) and no more every morning before you go to see your Cattle.[621a]

The Ethiopic and the Somerset charms are exactly contemporary. The man who used the latter was well known to the writer.

The manufacture of mystical writings is a very ancient art ; so also is the teaching how to ascertain propitious days. *Dies fasti* and *nefasti* were household words in ancient Rome. Much light is thrown on this art by a very remarkable papyrus in the British Museum (No. XLVI. Greek) of about the second century A.D. It came from Egypt, and was discovered in one of the later tombs. The magic arts practised in the early years of the Christian era, which Irenæus, Origen, Epiphanius, and other Fathers lay to the charge of the heretics of their day, are herein laid bare.[622]

Several spells are given in this document for various purposes, amongst which is one for producing an immediate vision of the god evoked by the operator. Besides the words of incantation, we are told (p. 5) "in a brazen cup with oil, anoint your right eye with water taken from a boat that has been wrecked, and the left [mixing some] Coptic *stibium* with the water. And if you cannot find water from a boat that has been wrecked, take some from a wicker wherry that has been submerged."

Various charms are given for discovering a thief; for driving away evil spirits ; for compelling a thief

---

[621a] These recipes are inserted here by way of comparison of language with the Abyssinian ; naturally their place would be in the next chapter.

[622] The part preserved is apparently imperfect ; but an account of it with a translation alongside the text is given by Mr. Charles Wycliffe Goodwin for the Cambridge Antiquarian Society, 1852, in a paper called *Fragment of a Græco-Egyptian Work upon Magic*.

to confess ; but the chief interest of the papyrus lies in the following translation :—

Take a sheet of hieratic paper, or a leaden plate, and an iron ring, and place the ring upon the paper, and mark both inside and out with a pen the form of a ring. Then having described the circular outline of the ring, write upon the said outline, inscribing upon the paper the name, and the characters on the outside, and inside the thing which you wish not to happen, or that such a man's mind may be bound so as not to do such and such a thing. Then placing the ring upon its outline which you have made, and taking up the parts outside the outline, sew up the ring with thread, so as to completely conceal it, piercing through the characters with the pen, and when you wish to bind, say : " I bind such an one not to speak to such an one ; let him not resist, let him not contradict, let him not be able to look me in the face, or to answer me, but let him be subject to me as long as this ring is buried. And again I bind his mind, and his senses, his desires, his actions, that he may be sluggish towards all men . . . and let not such a woman marry such a man. Common words."

Then taking it to the grave of one untimely dead, dig four fingers deep and put it in and say : " O ! departed spirit whosoever thou art . . . I deliver to thee such an one, that he may not do such a thing." Then having covered it up depart.—And you will do it best in the waning of the moon.—The words written within the circle are these (several lines of Greek) : let such a thing not be done, as long as this ring is buried. Bind it with knots, making strings for that purpose, and thus deposit it. The ring may also be cast into a disused well, or into the grave of one untimely dead. And after the characters write also these words below the ring as a base (five lines of Greek) and the . . . spell which you also place within.

We give a facsimile (Fig. 187) of the figure to which the above refers, taken from Mr. Goodwin's paper ; to this for further particulars the reader is referred. So valuable a relic of the doings of past ages ought to be well known.[623]

Written charms of this kind, intended to cast a spell as well as to be protectives, have been found

[623] See also R. Stuart Poole in Smith's *Dict. Bible*, s.v. " Magic," p. 197.

of late in several places. They were first discovered
at Athens in 1811 by M. Fauvel. These latter are
on leaden tablets, and are called κατάδεσμα or *diræ*.
They professed to bind persons by name precisely

FIG. 187.

in the same manner as is done in that just described,
and in the Ethiopic charm. The whole household
of the man named are placed under the same spell.[624]

Among the gems at the British Museum is a very
beautiful little golden scroll, which was found rolled
up in a gold case of precisely the same shape as the
Ethiopian charm. It is of course very minute, being

[624] Miss L. Macdonald, *Proc. Soc. Bib. Archæol.* Feb. 1891, p. 162 sq.
In the article quoted from, much information is given about tablets and
injurious inscriptions. The author refers to the papyrus we have mentioned
known as the "Goodwin Cambridge Fragment." There is also a similar
"binding" Latin inscription quoted by Jahn, *Aberglauben*, p. 55.

no thicker than an ordinary lead pencil, and about two inches long.[625] It is marked Petilia·S·Italy [C·I· 5772 M·].

There does not appear to be anything which may be termed Magical in the words, but neither is there in passages from Scripture or the Koran worn at the present day. It is very difficult in most cases to perceive any connection between the actual words or figures used, and the purpose for which they are inscribed. This one is based on the ancient Orphic mysticism.[626] The shape of the case and general conditions, however, prove it incontestably to have been a charm for the protection of the wearer.

Frommannd's book is a perfect mine of written magic spells against fascination, which in many cases

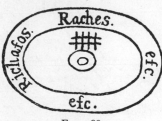

FIG. 188.

have to be prepared with such accompaniments as white of egg mixed with oak charcoal, to be wrapped in paper having Fig. 188 upon it. A prayer is to be uttered in German gibberish, of which he says: "Sed modus hic est absurdus, impius, magicus et Diabolicus." In the same chapter he discusses the meaning of *cauculator*, whence German *Gauckler*. He inquires whence Okos Bokos? He says: "Agyrtæ vocant *Okos Bokos*, vocabulis a vero vel ficto nomine Itali cujusdam."[627] He gives several

[625] The case is described in *Bullettino dell' Istit. di Corr. Archeol.* 1836, p. 149.

[626] On this see Lobeck, *Aglaophamus*, p. 643. A facsimile of the original inscription with a translation into literary Greek by Mr. Cecil Smith will be found in an article by G. Comparetti, in *Journal of Hellenic Studies*, vol. iii. p. 112.

[627] Here is a new etymology of *hocus pocus* for Dr. Murray! For this he

versions of the well-known *Abracadabra*, which was *amuletum insigne* not only against hemitritæum, but also against fevers and other maladies. This famous cabalistic form is of very ancient date, for even in the third century it was a traditional pre- scription, set out at length by Qu. Serenus Am- moniacus,[628] physician to Gordian Junior.[629] He directs it to be written in the form of an inverted cone, *i.e.* each line of repetition drops the final letter until A alone remains as the apex. Frommannd (p. 309) says that this is like the amulet of the Talmudists, worn on their necks against blindness.[630]

Very closely allied to these writings for the pro- tection of the living, is the remarkable custom still surviving in Russia, of placing in the hands of the dead a sort of passport to the nether-world almost precisely analogous to the "Book of the Dead" of ancient Egypt, see *ante*, pp. 50, 51.

At the burial of the late Czar we read :— [630a]

A prayer was chanted, described as the Prayer of Absolution. It begins with the words : "Our Lord Jesus Christ, by virtue of His divine grace, gift, and power given to His holy Disciples and Apostles to bind and loose the sins of men," and, going on to cite the text in question, prays Christ to forgive all the sins, including excommunication and others of the gravest categories, by His love for man and by the prayers of the Virgin Mary, Mother of God, of the holy Apostles, and of all saints. This prayer is not merely read, it is likewise printed on a scroll of

---

quotes Voetius, lib. iii. *Dispp.* p. 542. Ady (*Candle in the Dark*) says that in King James's time a juggler went about who called himself "the King's Majesty's most excellent *Hocus Pocus*" (Hone, *Year-Book*, 1832, p. 1477). This seems to match Frommannd.

[628] Frommannd, pp. 45, 307.

[629] King, *Gnostics*, p. 105, gives a translation of the Abracadabra prescription.

[630] He gives the Hebrew formula, and several others written in the same cone shape.

[630a] *Daily Telegraph*, Nov. 20, 1894 ; also *Spectator*, Nov. 24, 1894, p. 733.

paper, which the officiating priest places in the hands of the corpse as a document enabling him, when wandering about in the spirit world during the first few days after death, to pass on his solitary way unmolested by evil spirits.

There is abundant evidence in all lands of the value attached to certain words, usually written, though they may be merely uttered, to keep off evil from, or to bring good to, the user. The well-worn "blessed word Mesopotamia" proves that the idea survives, though allied to crass ignorance. The many Scriptural or other inscriptions upon old houses here in England, and perhaps more commonly upon the Continent, or the passages from the Koran upon the houses of Mahomedans, are much less in reality the expressions of piety than protective charms against the origin of every misfortune—the evil eye.

The first words of the Gospel of St. John in any of the Aryan languages have always been held of great virtue when carried on the person. These should be written upon virgin parchment, enclosed in a goose quill, an hour before sunrise on the first Sunday in the year.[631]

Brand (iii. 319) gives a number of similar inscriptions, which were called *Characts*, but the real collector of them must go to Frommannd or Delrio. The former quotes Voetius, who says that the beginning of the fourth Gospel was worn as an amulet from the times of the Apostles themselves.

For the bite of a mad dog the following words are to be written upon the crust of a loaf, which, *transfixo pollice*, is to be applied three several

---

[631] Thiers, *Traité des Superstitions*, i. 414. Freemasons again will recognise something here.

times. The performer is to repeat the Lord's Prayer five times for the five wounds of Christ, etc.[632]

S	A	T	O	R
A	R	E	P	O
T	E	N	E	T
O	P	E	R	A
R	O	T	A	S

For the mad dog's bite, also: " Hæc verba pani azymo inscripta, Affra, Gaffra, Gaffritan, etc., prodesse dicuntur."

A curious formula against the plague is—

†. Z. †. D. I. A. †.

These are the initials of a number of prayers and recitations. † = " Crux Christi salva me." Z = " Zelus domus libera me." † = " Crux Christi vincit et regnat," etc. D = " Deus! expelle pestem de loco isto," etc. I = " In manus tuas Domine commendo animam meam," etc. A = " Ante cœlum et terram Deus erat," etc. † = " Crux Christi potens est ad expellendam pestem a loco isto."

Another charm against wounds by sword, cut and thrust (*für Hieb und Stich*), is the following, written also on virgin parchment ; to be worn on the person :—

† A 3 6 ma 9 † † † etc.
Diese Figur sey in Gott gesegnet, etc.

The following is to be used as an amulet engraved upon a sword : " Hoc qui dextre velit uti amuleto."

Ich beschwere dich Degen gut,
Dass du nicht von mir sollst bringen Blut.
Diss zehl ich dir Schwerd schneid zür Buss
In den Namen der 3, Gestern, Gafalon, Samalecti, etc. etc.

---

[632] Frommannd, p. 46. We are told (J. Lewes André, in *Reliquary*, October 1893, p. 195) that this is a Roman charm found at Cirencester on a piece of plaster ; it evidently was well known elsewhere ; also that it was written upon the binding cloth of a woman in the Middle Ages. The Cirencester charm had the same words differently arranged.

Other amulets to be worn against fascination [633] are the following, engraved upon silver plates.

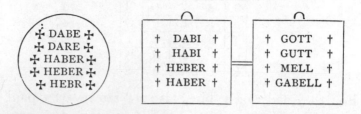

Besides seventeenth-century metal objects of this kind to be worn as charms, there are a great many written formulæ in Latin and German, or rather in gibberish, intended both to be worn as amulets in suitable cases like the three on Fig. 112, and to be uttered in mumbo-jumbo incantation.

Combinations of figures, too, have long had high reputation as efficient protectors, particularly those called magic squares—in which certain numbers are arranged in rows, so that their sum, in whatsoever direction it may be taken, always produces the same result.

The following common example is perhaps the simplest :—

4	3	8
9	5	1
2	7	6

It will be seen that addition of any three figures in line will produce 15. Another square taken in the same way makes 72 in each line. This latter is

<hr />

[633] *Tract. de Fasc.* p. 306. Many other cabalistic formulæ will be found.

28	35	2	7
6	3	32	31
34	29	8	1
4	5	30	33

said to be a veritable amulet, and if your enemy's name be written underneath it, and you wear this as a charm, his envy will be baffled and his eye will be powerless against you.[634]

Not only do we find great store set upon the many combinations such as these, but very wonderful things are done with figures outside the sphere of magic, so that the ignorant may well have become impressed by the power of numbers whether expressed in writing or not. The curious results certain people delight in producing from numbers found in the Revelation and other sacred books are but proofs of the still surviving idea that mystery lies in the very numbers themselves. What wonderful prophecies have been obtained by manipulation of the figures recited in the Book of Daniel, whereby the end of the world has been so often foretold, and the "number of the beast" deciphered!

In an article called "In Calabria-Passeggiate," by Caterina Pignorini-Beri,[635] is a description of what was seen in a peasant's house :—

In an angle just over the doorway was affixed a horseshoe; above this were two horns painted, and beneath were placed the two magic numbers (*numeri fatali*) 8 and 9 to avert the *jettatura*. "Why is this?" I asked. The old woman replied: "Against

---

[634] *Chambers's Cyclopædia*, s.v. "Magic."
[635] *Nuova Antologia*, Roma, Luglio, 1883, p. 71.

the evil eye, Miss" (" *Pel fora fascino, signorina* "). "And what is the evil eye?" "Ah!" said the old woman, pointing the fore and little fingers towards the ground :—

"Ah! eight nine, eight nine!"[636]

"But why eight nine?"

"*Eccellenza*, the witches (*streghe*) say *six* and *seven*."

No other explanation was obtainable—perhaps it is the only one that can be given, owing to the terror of witchcraft which inspires all southerners, gentle and simple alike. It was indeed a new thing to break the *seven*, the famous cabalistic *seven*, which has pursued humanity for six thousand years, by (the use of) the next number. In fact the poor woman had given me something more than others—she had given me a valid reason for the *fora fascino*, and I could not grumble.

The authoress does not further explain the numbers, but she calls at another ground-floor tenement (*botteguccia*), and remarks that the usual bed was not in the room, nor were the numbers 8 and 9, nor the horseshoe, nor the painted horns to be seen. The owner was a corporal of *bersaglieri*, and therefore arrived at a state of new civilisation which took no note of such things. She concludes her remarks with the regretful "Ahime! Non tutti sono più calabresi in Calabria!"

In Calabria the words which we should translate by "amulet against the evil eye" are *fora fascino*. The authoress in another place (p. 66) speaks of the utterance of the numbers 8 and 9 as a charm *per allontanare la malia*. So far as the present writer knows, of all Italians the lottery-loving Calabresi alone furnish an example of the belief that the mere utterance of particular numbers is a protective charm.

We all know of the common belief in "the luck in odd numbers." We shall see it later in the many

---

[636] It is to be noted as a curious coincidence that the magic square sums up in each line the same product as these two potent factors—$8 \times 9 = 72$.

repetitions of "three times" as to spitting. The
old saying "Third time lucky" is familiar to everybody.

Three has always been looked upon by both
Jews and Gentiles as a specially complete and
mystic number. In Scripture, three is given as an
exact measure, while other numbers were used indefinitely, merely to convey the notion of several, or
of a great many, precisely as we now speak of dozens,
scores, or thousands, when we do not even imply
any definite number. There were three great
feasts; there were three cities of refuge, and the
number three is several times repeated in connection
with them; three alternatives were offered to David,
and two of these had each the special element of
three in it. So we have the three Christian virtues;
three great witnesses; and endless other examples of
the use of three as something more than a mere
numeral. The three-sided triangle is said to be
symbolic of deity, pagan as much as Christian. The
Egyptians had triads of divinities, specially worshipped in particular cities, while the Romans had
their Diana Triformis. In the Hebrides the accounts given in Chap. II. on sun-worship show that
each act was performed three times. We are told[637]
that in Ireland a cure for whooping-cough, called
there *chin-cough*, is to pass the child three times over
and under a donkey, certain prayers being said
during the operation. So spitting as a preventive
act had to be done three times, and in the many
recited acts to be performed it will be noted how
often "three times" occurs.

It is not merely as an odd number that three

[637] Le Fanu, *Seventy Years of Irish Life*, 1894, p. 113.

of all others was held so specially sacred; yet
the preference generally for odd numbers is not
only old but still abiding. As a matter of course
an odd number of eggs are put under a hen.
Indeed this is so thoroughly recognised, that one
sees constant advertisements of choice eggs for sale
at so much "per sitting." A sitting of eggs is a
number just as well known as a baker's dozen—
thirteen. The notion is that a brood is certain to
be odd in number, and that therefore to set an even
number of eggs is certain waste. The fact, however, remains that as often as not an even number
of chicks are hatched; still the custom is to set
thirteen, and no luck is expected from an even
number. Again, military salutes are always odd in
number. A Royal salute is twenty-one guns. The
valiant "Thirteen Club" is in itself an evidence of
the belief that if odd numbers generally are lucky,
thirteen sitting down together at a meal is held to
be unlucky—indeed fatal to one of the party. This
notion is said by some to be based upon the
experience of past mortality: that out of thirteen
adults, the chances are strong that one will die during
the next year. Moreover, under the well-worn para-
dox that exceptions prove the rule, thirteen is a specially unlucky number, except for the setting of eggs.

Perhaps in these latter days, however, the magic
number seven is the one most used. It is that of
the *strega* in Calabria, and of the white-witch in
England. A seventh son of a seventh son is a born
doctor—he has miraculous powers of healing by
touch.[638] "The doctor" is the recognised name here in

---

[638] Lupton, *Notable Things*, 1660, bk. ii. p. 25. See also Thiers, *Traité
des Superstitions*, 1679, p. 436.

Somerset of a seventh son; and it is very commonly held that he should be trained for one, as a matter of course. Seven has always been a mystical number. Balaam had seven altars built by the sun-worshipper Balak, three distinct times. Elisha ordered Naaman to wash in Jordan seven times. Elijah sent seven times to the top of Carmel. The days of Creation were seven; seven weeks divided the great feasts. There were seven Churches in Asia; the great dragon of the Revelation had seven heads; there were seven angels with seven vials; besides a host of sevens, where perhaps only an indefinite number was implied.[639] Curiously, too, the common name for the dormouse is the " seven-sleeper," no doubt from the Seven Sleepers of Ephesus.[640] We west-country folks talk of a person who sleeps soundly as a " proper zeb'm-slaiper." [640a] Again, there is a very common belief that in seven years a man changes every atom in his body, and that each seventh year of his life is a climacteric in which he has to pass through dangers physical and moral. The sixty-third year, that is the ninth septennial period, is the " grand climacteric "—the year specially perilous to old men. The very common term of leases for seven, fourteen, or twenty-one years, is believed to originate in the idea that it is desirable to reconsider conditions and to renew agree-

[639] In the *Nineteenth Century* for October 1894 is an article on " The Seven Lord Roseberys," discussed, however, in twelve divisions!

[640] For an account of the Seven Sleepers see Baring-Gould, *Curious Myths of the Middle Ages*, p. 93. At Ephesus the story is devoutly believed. The writer has been shown into the cave in which they slept.

[640a] " For no sooner did Abraham pay the eighteenpence than he slept as sound as a sebem-sleeper, and began to get the good of his victuals."—W. Raymond, " Love and Quiet Life," *Somerset Idylls*, 1894, p. 206. See *West Somerset Word-Book*.

ments in accordance with the recognised stages of human life.

The numbers of certain days and months are considered fortunate or otherwise according to certain modes of reckoning, wherein the rationale or the logic is by no means obvious.

A curious little black-letter book called *A Concordancie of Yeares*, by Arthur Hopton, 1612, gives a chapter headed " Of the infortunate and fatall dayes of the yeare," etc., which throws some light upon the methods of " wise men." It sets out the infortunate days, beginning—

> January the 1, 2, 4, 5, 10,[641] 15, 17, 19.
> February the 8, 10, and the 17.
> March the 15, 16, and the 19.
> Aprill the 16 and 21. Not so euill the 7, 8, 10, 20;

and so on through the year. He says that " astrologers will have in every moone 2 infortunate daies, wherein they recount it most unhappy to begin or undertake any kind of worldly affaires." These he specifies, and says " it is therefore very ill to have a child borne in them, for feare of an euill death." The most unfortunate days of all the year are " January the 3 day, July the 1, October the 7, Aprill the 30, August the 1 and the 31." Those in the former table were only " infortunate," while these latter appear to be fatal.

There were also two days in every month called *Ægri, mali and Ægyptiaci*. On *Ægri* " if any fell sick they should hardly or never escape." On *mali* " evill affections of the Constellations " would frustrate any kind of work, and *Ægyptiaci* were un-

---

[641] The present writer has no practical reason to complain of this day, during the many "happy returns of it" for which he has given thanks.

lucky because they were so thought by the Egyptians, and because "they do also note unto us the
10 plagues of Egypt in these verses" :—

> Sanguis, rana, culex, muscæ parvæ, pecus, ulcus,
> Grando, locustæ, nox, mors, prius orta necant.

We are told how to discover lucky or unlucky
days, and that "these infortunate days were noted
alwaies in the Romane Kalender, notwithstanding yᵉ
inhibition of Augustine, saying : 'Calendas mensium,
et dies Ægyptiacos, non observetis.'   But yet to
satisfie all, take them in the ensuing verses" :—

> Armis Gunfe, Dei Kalatos, Adamare dabatur.
> Lixa memor, Constans gelidos, Infancia quosdam.
> Omne limen, Aaron bagis, Concordia laudat.
> Chije linkat, Ei Coequata, Gearcha Lisardus.

Of the words in these four lines of gibberish he
says that

every two serve for one moneth, the first standing for
January.   If therefore you desire to know the first of the two
former fatall daies in any moneth, count so many daies from the
beginning of the moneth, descending, as the first letter in the
first word is distant from A inclusively, according to the
Alphabet, and where that number ends, there is a fatall day : as
in Aprill, L (beginning Lixa) is the 10 letter in the Alphabet,
therefore the 10 day is fatall, and according to the number of the
first letter (in order of yᵉ Alphabet) of the secōd sillable, yᵉ said
houre of yᵉ said day is vehemently to be suspected.

In similar fashion, but "ascending," he shows
how to reckon the second fatal day ; but we are not
told how or by whom the magic verses were composed, whereby such discoveries can be made.

CHAPTER XII

SPITTING, INCANTATION, AND OTHER PROTECTIVE ACTS. PIXIES

In the story told by Jorio of the Neapolitan woman (p. 261), another side of the question, so far only hinted at, is opened out. It is the effect believed to exist in certain actions, performed openly, secretly, or in the way of incantation. When, in talking with a stranger, a Neapolitan keeps his hands behind his back in the position described as *mano cornuta*, he does precisely what is meant: he performs an act unknown to the person against whom it is intended, but which the actor believes will shield him from the possible harm coming to him from the other party. Acts of this kind are performed with a twofold object: in the one case to keep off injury; in the other to bring about what is desired, such as secretly touching a hunchback at Monte Carlo. Among the latter are all such acts as are done or said "for luck." How common it is at cards when a player has had a run of ill fortune, to get up and turn his chair three times "to change the luck." On Christmas Eve 1889 the moon was two days old. Two keepers and two beaters were just about to go home after a day's shooting. "There's the new moon," said one. "Ees, and

over the right shoulder, too," said another.   "Turn
your money vor luck," said number three.   "I han't
a-got nort but a penny," replied number one.   "Oh!
thick idn no good, must be zilver," said number three.
This kind of dialogue is to be heard every day; and
is only given here because it is specific, and was
spoken in the writer's own hearing.   Almost the
same thing comes from South Africa.

Mr. G. S. Foot writes to the *Spectator* of
October 29, 1892, respecting the doings of some
native boys.

> On looking out, I saw them one after another take lighted
> brands from the fire, and throw them towards some object in the
> sky.   They then stood in a praying attitude, and loudly shouted,
> "Give plenty money!"   They replied to inquiries: that all boys
> thus greeted the new moon; and it was found to be a universal
> custom among the Mashonas.

The marriage of the Czar Nicholas II. furnishes
a curious fact in this connection, and like the rite of
the passport for the dead (see p. 399) shows that in
Russia practices are solemnised which in more
western countries would be classed as magic.

> By orthodox theologians the symbolical meaning of the golden
> and silver rings is explained thus: The gold ring bestowed on the
> man signifies that he is to be as the sun to his future wife, irradiat-
> ing her with his light.   She is given the silver ring, inasmuch as,
> like the moon, she receives her brilliancy from her husband.   The
> changing of rings, which ends by leaving to both their own, sym-
> bolises union and concord of husband and wife.[641a]

Very nearly allied to this is the custom at fairs
or markets for the seller, on being paid for cattle, to
give back a silver coin "for luck."   So much is this
a recognised custom, that in close bargains a very
frequent stipulation is made for so much "to
luck."   Luck money, too, should always be silver.

[641a] *Daily Telegraph*, Nov. 24, 1894.

Further, it is common among the regular market-dealers, when the "luck money" is handed back to the buyer, for the receiver to spit on it "for luck." The same habit of spitting on a coin is very common also by the receiver when won in a bet, or when it is the first money received for the day.[642]

This custom of spitting opens up quite a wide subject, for not only is it practised in the hope of obtaining good fortune, but in all ages, and almost among all peoples, it has ever been considered as an act to safeguard the spitter, whether against fascination or other evils. Among the ancient Greeks and Romans "the most common remedy against an invidious look was spitting; it was hence called *despuere malum*." [643] According to Theocritus "it is necessary to spit three times into the breast of the person who fears fascination."

Old women were accustomed to avert the evil eye from children by spitting into their bosoms: this was done three times—three being a sacred number. "Hence Damœtas . . . having praised himself, adds that by the advice of old Cotyttaris he had spit thrice into his bosom to prevent fascination." [644]

[642] Jahn (p. 84, n. 234) says : "I have often as a boy seen the fishwives of Ellerbeck, when they had got handsel (first money, *Handgeld*) from my mother, how they spat upon it. They say that brings them specially good luck (*besonderes Glück*). They will not tell the reason ; certainly it is done to keep off witchcraft." Here in the west a very common way of begging a cup of cider is : "Maister, I be that dry, I could'n spat a zixpence." This surely means that the speaker is so dry that if a sixpence were given him he could not spit on it for luck, as well as the other and more obvious one as to the amount of his possible expectoration.

[643] Dodwell, vol. ii. p. 32, gives the following authors, who all mention the same thing. Theocritus, *Idyl.* vi. 39; Tibullus, *Eleg.* i. 2, 54; Petronius, *Sat.* 131; Persius, *Sat.* ii. 32; Pliny, *Nat. Hist.* xxviii. 3, 4; Seneca, *Consol. ad Marc.* 9; Plautus, *Captivi*, III. iv. 23.

[644] Potter, *Archæol. Græc.*, vol. i. p. 417. Potter also quotes the same authors as Dodwell.

It was usual to reprove arrogant persons by bidding them spit into their bosoms.[645] Among the ancient Greeks it was customary to spit three times into their bosoms at the sight of a madman, or one troubled with epilepsy.[646] This was done in defiance of the omen, spitting being a sign of contempt and aversion.[647]

Another method of averting fascination from infants was this : they tied a thread of divers colours about the neck of the infant (compare the coloured ribbons on horses, and the coloured worsted on the *fattura della morte*), then spat on the ground, and taking up the spittle mixed with dirt upon their finger, put it upon the infant's forehead and lips. Moreover, this had to be done with the *digitus infamis*. As to the latter, there is no doubt as to which is the finger of disgrace.[648]

> And lest enchantment should my limbs infest,
> I three times dropt my spittle on my breast ;
> This charm I learnt from an old sorceress' tongue,
> Who harvest-home at Hypocoon's sung.

[645] Spitting was in the Middle Ages not only a protective, but also an injurious act, for we read :—

> I can worke wyles in battell,
> If I but ones do spattle
> I can make corne and cattle
> That they shall never thryve.
>
>   Bale's *Interlude—Idolatry*, 1562, sig. C. 2.

[646] Theocritus, *Idyl.* xx. 11.   [647] *Ibid.* v. 66.

[648] In an old treatise on the hand we read that the names of the fingers are derived from their use, their position, and their size. The ancients had another name for the index, which they called *salutaris* "quod eo salutarent deos suos inter adorandum quippe non Romani solum, sed et aliæ gentes solebant dextræ manus priore digito in erectum pollicem residente." The obvious pun in this well accords with the spirit of the older writers. The salutation of the god with the forefinger was followed by the kiss, hence we readily perceive how our word salute includes to kiss. Those who are familiar with St. Peter's statue in Rome will readily understand this, and thereby will not fail to perceive another practice of Christian times handed down from pagan ancestors. Prætorius writes : "Even nowadays we teach our boys that the right index is to be kissed (as a salutation) to persons worthy of honour, and to offer the index of honour and reverence " (Prætorius, *De Pollice*, Lipsiæ, 1677, p. 14).

In the Greek Church kissing is still more practised than even in the

Pagan lustration was performed with the middle finger.

> Th' obscure old grandam, or the next of kin,
> The new-born infant from the cradle takes,
> And first of spittle a lustration makes :
> Then in the spawl her middle finger dips,
> Anoints the temples, forehead, and the lips.

Thus Dryden translates that part of the second satire of Persius in which occurs the line—

> "Infami digito, et lustralibus ante salivis."

The improper and indecorous placing of the hand and fingers is also to be classed among derisive grimaces. Formerly the middle finger expressed the utmost contempt and ignominy when thrust out, with the other fingers closed. On that account it is called *infamis* and *impudicus*.[649] Isidorus Hispalensis says : "When any one wished formerly to mock contumeliously, or to signify the utmost derision, he used to thrust out the middle finger." It is said[650] that when certain visitors came to Demosthenes, who did not salute him with the

Roman. There were several names for the middle finger, such as *medius*, *longus*, *remus* (oar), *medius navis ;* also it was called *impudicus*, *infamis*, and *medicus*. It is still known as the medical finger. "Why it is called *medicus* I am unable to learn, unless it is because we are thereby most strongly bound to the wrist and vital arteries." (*Ib.* p. 15).

It is also called *magnus* from its size, as compared with *parvus*, denoting the two extremes in size. "The third finger is called *medio proximus* (next the middle) or *anularis* (ring finger) by the later Greeks."

On the thumb (*pollex*) we have another pun : "Nam pollex unus tantum pollet, quantum vix cæteri" ("For one thumb is worth all the rest"). With us moderns in the West, however, the thumb is the type of clumsiness : our vernacular for a person who is very awkward with his hands is, "He's all thumbs."

[649] *De Pollice*, p. 41. "Quo loco Cornutus, infami digito (*i.e.* of Persius *Sat.* ii.) ait, id est medio, qui obscœnitatis est et subjicit." Martial (ix. 70) also says :—

> "Impudicus etiam Priapi cantor eodem modo,
> Derides quoque fur, et impudicum
> Ostendis digitum mihi minanti."

[650] Laertius, *De vitis Philosophorum*, lib. vi.

index, he recognised them with his stretched - out middle finger.

There was much discussion among old writers upon this gesture. Suetonius calls it "the hand formed in an obscene manner"; others declare it *impudicitiam ostendere*.

Besides this thrusting out of the middle finger, there was another sign of contemptuous mocking grimace, made by the interposition or insertion of the thumb between the index and middle finger, so that the thumb projects beyond, while the rest of the fingers are contracted into a fist. This is the greatest indignity of all mocking gestures, " dicitur ab Italis Far le fiche." [651]   In the theatres they had three ways of expressing disapproval or derision of the actors by the hands, besides the well-known hissing, shouting, thrusting out the tongue, and other facial contortions. These were : First, by making with the hands what was called a crane's bill, "Pinsente etiam rostro ciconiam manibus quandoque exprimebant"; secondly, by imitating asses' ears, "Et imitabantur aliquando asini auriculas"; thirdly, by the thumb gesture (*mano in fica*), "Tertium, cum manus in obscœnum modum formata." The latter was evidently the most forcible : indeed it seems to have become so common as to be signified by the mere word *fauere, i.e.* properly to applaud, but practically to recognise the actor in either way, by applauding or disapproval. This was precisely analogous to other cases where it was customary to say *præfiscini* or *defigere*. In fact these were slang words of the Empire. It was evidently considered an extremely vulgar sort of disap-

---

[651] *De Pollice*, p. 42 ; already sufficiently dealt with.

probation, for we read, "Turpissime contra aliquem favere," *i.e.* "It is most disgraceful to express disapproval of any one by thrusting out the *mano fica*."

What was the nature of the crane's-bill gesture is not very clear. Persius says (*Sat.* i.) :—

> " O Iane, a tergo quem nulla ciconia pinsit."

We are told that jokers make the stork (crane) by joining all the fingers ; they then place them to the lower part in the likeness of a crane's bill.[652] There is much discussion of this performance, but in the absence of any drawing it is difficult to explain ; the *a tergo* will perhaps suggest something. So also we are told with much detail how the asses' ears were imitated. The two hands were applied to the temples and the fingers moved backwards and forwards. This attitude survives in No. 7 (Stupido) of the Neapolitan gestures on Fig. 120.

Passing from manual gestures, already dealt with, we find *spitting* upon many occasions to be a widespread practice, nor need we turn to ancient times for plenty of examples of belief in its efficacy as a protective act, besides those performed for luck.

To spit on cut hair before throwing it away is thought in some parts of Europe sufficient to prevent its being used by witches.[653] This is of course analogous to the various precautions taken to prevent hostile persons getting possession of any part of or belonging to another.[654]

[652] *De Pollice*, p. 43.
[653] Zingerle, ⸜*Sitten, Braüche und Meinungen des Tiroler Volkes*, Nos. 176, 580 ; *Melusine*, 1878, c. 79. Frazer, *Golden Bough*, vol. i. p. 204.
[654] Spitting on the hair is of course regularly practised in Naples.

> " Nell' uscir dal vostro tetto
> La mattina su del petto
> Ben tre volte vi sputate ;

It is quite commonly said here in Somerset :
" Nif you do meet wi' anybody wi' a north eye, spat
dree times."[655]   Why always three times ? why three
times by the nurses of old days, except that there is
some virtue added by the number three ?

Those afflicted with obliquity of vision have
ever been accounted as dangerous by hard-headed
as well as superstitious people.   Even in London
the enlightened, these beliefs are not extinct.   The
Morning Herald of August 16, 1839, records that
two women were fellow-lodgers, but unfortunately
one of them squinted, and the other, to avert the
supposed consequences from the defect in the first,
considered she could only protect herself by spitting
in her face three times a day.[656]

In many parts of England, certainly here in the
west, it is a common saying: " Always spat dree times
'nif ee do zee a piebald 'oss."   Piebald horses are
thought uncanny nearly everywhere.

Country people generally have well - known
occasions when to spit ; indeed the act is almost as
naturally performed as to breathe.

Not long ago, in shooting, the writer with others
came upon a dead dog which was most offensive.
One keeper said: "Here's a pretty breath"; the other
said : " Mus' bring a showl an' bury un " ; but both
accompanied their words with deliberately spitting

Quando poi vi pettinate
I capei, che son condutti
Li sputate tutti tutti."—Marugi, *Capricci*, p. 103.

The Editor remarks in a note to the above that Thiers says one spits
three times on the hair pulled out by the comb before throwing it away ; and
further he says, Tibullus enjoins spitting on the breast, giving his precise
words : " Despuit in molles et sibi quisque sinus."   He adds : "I do not fail
to do this always, and I have found the benefit of it."

[655] The same thing is recorded in Hone's *Year-Book*, 1831, p. 253.

[656] Brand, vol. iii. p. 50.

on the ground. This is almost invariable, and has
been noted by the writer hundreds of times. Whenever an offensive smell is perceived there is often a
coarse joke ; but if ten or a dozen are working together all spit, though probably few of them have
actually smelt it. Moreover, it has been noticed that
the action is not the violent ejection of saliva, but the
deliberate voidance of all the moisture in the mouth,
often accompanied by the usual "hawking" to clear
the windpipe. All this is done with evident uncon-
sciousness ; it seems an involuntary action, the result
of pure animal instinct. No one is ever told to spit
in such cases, but it is the most sanitary act which
can be performed under the circumstances. Germs
of disease present in fœtid matter can only pass
into the body through the breathed air, and hence
to void the saliva which may have been impregnated
by the foul odour is as natural an act, and as involuntary, as the closing of an eye at a threatened
blow. This is surely one of Nature's own lessons.
Those who are too polite to expectorate, will find
upon careful scrutiny that a bad smell causes a flow
of saliva to the mouth. Who knows whether "good
manners" may not have had some bad effect, and that
many a case of diphtheria might have been avoided
if it had never been considered vulgar to spit ?

Great virtue is and was always believed to
belong to fasting spittle, both as curative and protective.[657] To lick a wart first thing in the morning
is one of the well-recognised cures ; the same is held

---

[657] Their beads of nits, bels, books and wax,
      Candles, forsooth, and other knacks :
      Their holy oyle, their fasting spittle ;
      Their sacred salt here, not a little,
      Dry chips, old shooes, rags, grease, and bones.
                    Herrick, *Hesperides*, "The Temple."

respecting disorders of the eyes, a slight wound, or
any irritation of the skin. Pliny says[658] fasting spittle
is a sovereign preservative against the poison of serpents, and that " we are in the habit of spitting as
a preservative against epilepsy, or, in other words,
we repel contagion thereby ; in a similar manner we
repel fascinations, and the evil presages attendant
upon meeting a person who is lame in the right
leg." He also refers to spitting three times on the
breast, and says it is the practice in all cases where
medicine is employed to spit three times on the
ground ; also to mark a boil, when it first appears,
three times with fasting spittle. His remark that
pugilists and other persons, before making an effort,
spit in the hand in order to make the blow more
heavy, shows that familiar modern practices of the
like kind are not quite of yesterday.

Pliny shows how lichens and leprous spots may
be removed by constant application of fasting spittle ;
that crick in the neck may be cured by carrying
fasting spittle to the right knee with the right hand,
and to the left knee with the left.

As charms against the evil eye, he mentions
spitting into the urine the moment it is voided, of
spitting into the right shoe before putting it on,[659] and
of spitting while passing any place where danger has
been incurred. Pliny continues : " When a person

[658] Pliny, *Nat. Hist.* xxviii. 7 ; vol. v. p. 288, Bohn.
[659] This is still practised in Italy.

> D' una cosa traggo al gioco
> Io vantaggio poco poco,
> Ed è questa, l' appaleso ;
> Di sputar quand 'ò del peso
> Sulla scarpa del piè dritto,
> E poi starmi zitto zitto.—Marugi, *Capricci*, p. 108.

The Editor remarks on this, that he has practised it with *qualche sorta di profitto*.

looks upon an infant asleep [660] it is usual for the nurse to spit three times upon the ground ; and this, although infants are under the especial guardianship of the god Fascinus, the protector not of infants only but of generals as well, and a divinity whose worship is entrusted to the Vestal Virgins. The image of this god is attached beneath the triumphal car, to protect the victorious general against the effects of envy. Hence the expression *præfiscini.*" [661]

Quite recently a friend of the writer was travelling in Greece in the neighbourhood of Sparta. A country woman had a baby on her back, carried in the usual skin employed for that purpose. The traveller being a lady naturally wished to look at the baby, and was in the act of uncovering its face, when the mother turned round in the greatest anger, and of course snatched away the child. The dragoman explained that the mother dreaded the evil eye, and that if the lady wished to see the child, she must first spit on it three times. This she did, and was at once permitted to look on the baby's face, having provided the recognised antidote against the stranger's glance. [662]

The act of restoring sight to a blind man with fasting spittle is attributed to Vespasian by two authors. [663] The man is said to have besought him "ut genas et orbes oculorum dignaretur respergere oris excremento." A singular and very remarkable com-

---

[660] Bring the holy crust of bread,
  Lay it underneath the head ;
  'Tis a certain charm to keep
  Hags away, while children sleep.
      Herrick, *Hesperides*, ed. Hazlitt, 1869, p. 304.

[661] Ellis, Note to Pliny, *Nat. Hist.* v. p. 290, Bohn.

[662] Alexander Alexandrinus also wrote : " Fascinationes saliva jejuna repelli, veteri superstitioni creditum est " (Ellis, Note to Brand, vol. iii. p. 260).

[663] Suetonius, *Vespas.* 7 ; Tacitus, *Hist.* iv. 8.

ment upon the means which our Lord Himself took
to open the eyes of the man born blind, is seen in
the fact that He did not despise as " mere superstition " the acts which in His day were held to be
effectual, but that " He spat on the ground, and
made clay of the spittle, and He anointed the eyes
of the blind man with the clay." He knew the
medicinal value which was set upon saliva by the
people, but instead of spurning such means, He
thought right to make them the conductors of His
miraculous power.[664] We find the same course
followed in the case of the deaf and dumb man
(St. Mark vii. 33).

A modern traveller[665] relates that in Corfu he
unwittingly expressed his admiration for two children
of his host. The grandmother on his repeating the
praise became agonized, and nothing would suffice
to appease the parents and others present but that
he should spit in their faces. This he did, and the
children submitted as if well accustomed to have
their beauty first lauded and then protected. This,
however, was not enough : the mother then made a
paste of dust and oil from the lamp burning before
the Virgin and anointed their foreheads. We are
not told which finger the Corfiote woman used to
apply her paste, but it was probably the middle
finger—the same as was undoubtedly used for the
purpose at the time of our Lord's miracles ; for
Petronius, who was an actual contemporary (died
A.D. 66), mentions the putting of dust combined with
saliva upon the forehead with the middle finger.[666]

[664] See Trench, *Notes on the Miracles*, p. 294.
[665] Dodwell, vol. ii. p. 36.
[666] " Mox turbatum sputo pulverem medio sustulit digito frontem repug-

Mungo Park relates that among the Mandingoes the ceremony of naming a child takes place at eight years old. First his head is shaved, then the priest utters a prayer, while all the company whisper in the child's ear, and spit three times in his face, after which they name the child, etc.

This is but the gross performance of a ritual which is still practised in civilised countries. In ordinary Roman baptism, before the water used " In nomine Patris et Filii et Spiritus Sancti," the priest exorcises with spittle the ears and nostrils of the infant,[667] besides anointing with the chrism or holy oil.[668]

Dr. Gregory, in his lecture to the British Association at Oxford, 1894, said that after a quarrel with the chief of the Masai in East Africa, the renewal of friendship was signified thus—"we spat upon each other," the Masai equivalent for shaking hands.

The application of the lustrant spittle with the middle or *infamis digitus* may be the reason why the more important rite of anointing with the chrism or holy oil should be so specially and distinctly

nantis signat . . . hoc peracto carmine ter me jussit expuere, terque lapillos conjicere in sinum."—Petronius, *Sat.* 131.
This, too, confirms Persius (*Sat.* ii. 32) :—

> " Frontemque atque uda labella
> Infami digito, et lustralibus ante salivis
> Expiat."

And the two quotations prove clearly not only which finger was to be used, but that the middle was the *digitus infamis*.

> Sacred spittle bring ye hither ;
> Meale and it now mix together,
> And a little oil with either.—Herrick, *Hesperides*.

[667] F. Chance, *Notes and Queries*, 8th ser. v. 137.

[668] It has even been discussed as to whether, in the absence of water, spittle might be used for the baptism itself, but this latter is denied (G. Angus, *Notes and Queries*, 8th ser. v. 192). With further regard to spitting, we must not forget that salt is put into the child's mouth during the baptismal rite in order to make him *despuere malum*, or as it is called vernacularly " spit out the devil."

ordered in the several Rubrics [669] to be performed with the thumb, the symbol of power. Such is however the fact, and the custom is retained in our own Church of using the thumb in that part of the baptismal service where the priest says "(We) do sign him with the sign of the cross."

Of all the arts practised by magicians, ancient and modern, but especially the latter, in cases of witchcraft, "ruling the planets" is one of the commonest. Astrology has ever held a leading place in all the occult sciences, and it will not be possible to overlook the evident connection between many of the objects which are well-known amulets and the names by which all men have agreed to call very many of the heavenly bodies. We have seen how the sun and moon are represented by many gods and goddesses in every mythology. The phases of the moon regulate the times for many operations, while each of the planets bears a name denoting to the most civilised people in the world one of the days of the week, and also a pagan divinity. Moreover, our Saxon-English Tuesday, Wednesday, Thursday, and Friday, very strikingly illustrate that which has been so often dwelt on—the assimilation of ideas by which the personification of any idea by one race migrates and takes up its place in another with similar attributes or symbolic signs, but with names expressing the modified notions of the imbibing race.

[669] *Rituale Romanum*, Romæ, MDCCL. (Baptism of Infants). "Deinde intingit pollicem in sacro chrismate, et ungit infantem in summitate capitis in modum crucis, dicens Deus Omnipotens, etc. . . . Postea pollice faciat signum crucis in fronte et in pectore infantis," etc. . . .

The same direction as to the use of the thumb is given in the Rubrics for Extreme Unction, Confirmation, Ordination of Priests, Coronation, Consecration of an Altar, etc. . . .

It is strange that animals should have become
so connected in thought with the various constellations and Zodiacal signs; but so it is, and the connection is evidently of the utmost antiquity, because
since history began, civilised races have all adopted
the same ideas, and in their several languages denote
the same animals.[670] We are told [671] that the star
stories of Greeks and Egyptians (which we inherit)
are in direct correspondence with the like legends
among modern savages, yet many of them call stars
and constellations by names representing animals
different from those we call them. Nearly all savage

---

[670] The Greeks had two names for the great northern constellation, which
remain to this day—the Great Bear and the Wain. Our modern name of
" King Charles's Wain " is but a very ancient one, revived with a prefix commemorating some modern event. No amount of imagination can see any
real resemblance between the grouping of the points of light we call stars,
and the animals or things whose names have been given to them, yet the
idea took such root in primæval minds that it has survived unchanged to
this day ; like the belief in the evil eye, it is quite unaccountable, and only to
be set down among the facts that are. See Appendix III.

Very many are the beliefs here in England and all over the world relating
to falling stars. The most widespread is probably that which connects them
with death or birth. Among the shepherds of the Apennines, a falling star
is a death portent ("Ecco un altro avviso di morte; chi sa mai a chi toccherà?"
(Bellucci, *Le Stelle Cadente e le loro leggende*, Perugia, 1893, p. 10.) This
author recounts various other fantastic fancies. The same is held in the
Val Anzasca concerning events to happen to some one living in the house
on which it appears to fall. In Russia a falling star signifies an actual death
—in Lapland that of an infant. If so common a sight in some places
presages death, we naturally should expect to find the complementary notion
in others. In Somerset every falling star denotes a birth, while in Norfolk
it proclaims a child begotten.

In New Zealand a falling star is a kick which one god gives to another
weaker than himself. The universal belief in the living, animal character of
heavenly bodies is shown in the belief of the people of Guiana, who say that
falling stars are *l' orina* of the other stars, while the Loochoo Indians say that
they are *excrementi delle stelle* (Bellucci, *op. cit.* p. 29).

After having written so much upon the existing belief in animal portents,
it is amusing to read in the *Spectator* of Nov. 24, 1894, p. 725, that " the
belief in animal portents . . . no longer survives in our century" (!) Two
days after this (Nov. 26) a Somerset friend writes : " Does not the death of
a lion still give anxiety to many a woman expecting childbirth ? " This latter
is a curious and unsought confirmation of the remarks on p. 76 *ante*.

[671] A. Lang, *Myth and Custom*, p. 124. See also Goguet, *L'Origine des
Lois*, on this subject.

nations, such as the Australian aborigines, even those without picture writing, call the stars by names of men and animals, and have all sorts of legends to match.

Reference has been made to the practices anciently employed at weddings: how songs of a lewd character called *Fescennina* were commonly a part of the performance; but even in the present day elaborate acts are common whose object is still the same—that of averting the evil eye from the newly married pair. At a marriage among the Jews of Tunis, after the religious ceremony, the bride is taken into an upper room, accompanied by all her friends, who remain with her. The bridegroom having retired with his friends, without taking the slightest notice of the bride or any one else, she is seated on a chair placed upon the usual divan. Her mother-in-law now comes forward, unveils her, and with a pair of scissors cuts off the tips of her hair. This last ceremony is supposed to be of great importance in driving away all evil influences that might do harm to or enter between the newly married pair.[672] We are not told what is done to the hair cut off, nor of any ceremony in the cutting to countervail the touch of iron. Both matters are doubtless carefully looked to, though unnoted by a stranger. The birth of a daughter is a cause of grief, etc., while a son is so greatly prized that they not unfrequently compass his death by the very means taken to secure his life. Their one great anxiety is to keep him from the influence of the evil eye, and with this object in view they keep him carefully concealed within thick curtains for some time after his birth, while a

[672] Mrs. Reichardt, *Good Words*, Jan. 1893, p. 47.

smoking light is kept burning within those curtains day and night ; in this way poisoning the air for the poor little victim. Not only this, but large squares of paper with flaming hands and outspread fingers, pieces of bone, and shells (of course cowries), are everywhere hung about and exposed both within and without to avert the evil eye.[673]

In Africa, and also in the Eastern Archipelago, where the belief is universal, it is thought to be most dangerous to be looked at while eating. Possibly this arises from the notion among savage and therefore hungry people, that to see another eat excites envy, the mainspring of the malignant glance. The kings of Kacongo (West Africa), of the Battas (Sumatra) or of Loango may not be seen eating. It is a capital offence to see the King of Dahomey at his meals. "No Warua allows others to witness their eating or drinking, being doubly particular with regard to members of the opposite sex ; and on *pombé* being offered, I have frequently seen them request that a cloth might be held up to hide them while drinking." [674] When the King of Tonga eats, all turn their backs. Any who saw Muato Jamwo, a great potentate of the Congo country, eating, would certainly be put to death. In these cases it is thought that if the king is looked at while eating, he will shortly die. This dislike to be seen eating is

[673] This making of smoke is aptly matched in the Apocryphal account following. "Then the angel said : ' Open the fish and take the heart and the liver and the gall and put them up safely.' So the young man did as the angel commanded him ; and when they had roasted the fish, they did eat it. Then the young man said to the angel : ' Brother Azarias, to what use is the heart and the liver and the gall of the fish ? ' And he said to him : ' Touching the heart and the liver, if a devil or evil spirit trouble any, we must make a smoke thereof before the man or woman, and the party shall be no more vexed. As for the gall, it is good to anoint a man that hath whiteness in his eyes, and he shall be healed ' " (*Tobit*, vi. 3-8).
[674] Cameron, *Across Africa*, vol. ii. p. 71.

by no means confined to savages. Turks of all classes object to be looked at while eating, and, stranger still, the Pope himself always takes his meals alone.

Hiding the face too, by way of protection, is a recognised mark of sovereignty in certain parts of Central Africa, where the king's face must be veiled. In Wadai the Sultan always speaks from behind a curtain; no one sees his face except his intimates and a few favoured persons.[675] Here we see of course the dread of a stranger's eye. Among the Touaregs of the Sahara all the men keep the lower part of the face, especially the mouth, veiled constantly. In West Timor a speaker holds his right hand before his mouth in speaking, lest a demon should enter his body, and lest the person with whom he is conversing should harm his soul by magic.[676]

A young New South Wales man must always cover his mouth with a rug in the presence of a woman, after his initiation into the mysteries of his tribe. So strongly is the danger felt, that many kings are not suffered to leave their houses, lest evil should befall them through being seen. The King of Loango is confined to his palace, and may not leave it after his coronation.[677] The King of Ibo also may not leave his house even to go into his town unless a human sacrifice is made to propitiate the gods. Consequently he never goes beyond his own premises.[678] In Mandalay a strong paling, six feet high,

[675] Mohammed Ibn-Omar el Tounsy, *Voyage au Darfour*, 1845, p. 203. *Travels of an Arab Merchant*, abridged by Bayle St. John, p. 91.
[676] Riedel, " Die Landschaft Dawan oder West-Timor," in *Deutsche Geog. Blat.* x. 230, quoted by Frazer.
[677] Bastian, *Die Loango-Küste*, i. 263.
[678] Crowther and Taylor, *Gospel on the Banks of the Niger*, p. 433.

lined every street through which the king was likely
at any time to pass, and the people had to remain
behind this fence when the king or any of the
queens went out. No one might attempt to look
through or over this blind,[679] of course from the fear
lest his eye should work mischief.

To this day the kings of Corea are shut up in
their palace; so also was the King of Tonquin, who
was allowed out two or three times a year, for the
performance of religious ceremonies. The day
before his coming forth, notice was given to the
inhabitants to keep out of the way the king had to
go, for the people were not allowed to look upon
him. The women were compelled to remain in their
houses, and durst not show themselves under pain
of death — a penalty which was carried out on
the spot, even if disobedience occurred through
ignorance. Thus the king was kept invisible to all
but a chosen few.[680]

Although in all these cases we are not told distinctly why these precautions were taken, yet, knowing what the belief was, there can be little hesitation
in assigning them to it, and to their dread of per-
mitting so precious a life as their king's to be subjected to the blighting influence.

Our own customs regarding children may be distinctly referred to the same primæval belief in the
liability of infants to the blighting effect of the
stranger's eye. It cannot be pretended that it is
necessary to its health that a baby's face should be
always carefully covered up whenever it is taken out
of the house, or even in the house, into the presence

[679] Shway Yoe, *The Burman*, i. 308.
[680] Richard, *History of Tonquin*, in Pinkerton, ix. p. 746.

of strangers. Moreover some nurses would not think of exhibiting baby without fastening " the coral and bells " upon its neck. Both mamma and nurse would indignantly repel any suggestion of superstition, nevertheless the coral is in the material itself a powerful amulet. Its shape keeps the remembrance of the old classic *fascinum*, the Priapic symbol, while the silver and the bells recognise the power of Diana, the type of all the motherly protectresses of infants, which have already been dealt with at such length.

The practice of veiling a woman's face throughout the East cannot be wholly referred to male jealousy : such may be the declared reason, but the women's own reluctance to show their faces to a stranger eloquently proclaims the real one.

Besides the various means taken by many people, and specially by Neapolitans of to-day, to keep out of the way of the *jettatore* known or unknown, there are very many precautions taken to baffle his maleficence besides those openly or secretly worn amulets, already sufficiently discussed. Even here among ourselves we have well-known rites, so to speak, which must be classed as preventive medicine. One such performance by a woman who believes herself to be overlooked is to take the shift off over her head, turn it three times withershins (*i.e.* from right to left—*wiederschein*—against the course of the sun), then hold it open, and drop a burning coal through it three times ; then put it on again.

We cannot fail to see that several old ideas are here preserved. The going against the way of the sun is a sort of defiance, like repeating "the Lord's Prayer backwards." It is in the same category as the defiant act depicted in Fig. 24. The burning coal may be a relic of ancient fire-worship, and so on the other hand a propitiatory act of sun-worship; while the three times accords with the spitting three times, and with the value set upon the mystic three.

One of the most widespread customs connected with fire, certainly found in Yorkshire, in Devon, Somerset, and throughout East Anglia—and probably in every county between those limits—is that of standing up the poker against the bars of the grate to make the fire burn. Everybody knows it, everybody does it, and believes it to be effectual. Superior persons consider that it causes or divides the draught; but those who know, say that the making of a cross with the poker and the bars, drives the devil out of the chimney, and so enables the fire to burn—this at least is the firm belief in the west country. Further, it is held that the devil cannot endure that any fire shall be hotter than his own, and "so makes it his business to try and put others' out." Of course the iron with which the cross is formed adds power to the charm.

The importance of progressing in all matters from left to right, or in the path of the sun, is made evident by our having a word specially to denote the deviation from this course. Here in Somerset quite recently, and within the writer's own knowledge, a number of children were brought to be baptized, and of course were ranged in a group around the font. The officiating minister not being accustomed to such a number, or not knowing the custom, began with the child on his right hand, of course following on in order and going round to the child on his left. This action caused great indignation: some parents who had never before seen the importance of having their children baptized at all, were quite sure that now they had not been done properly, and must be taken to another church " to be done over again." Thus it was held of far greater moment that the parson should proceed from left to right, than it was that the children should be baptized or not. Some of these children were growing into adults. In the same direction is the belief that in Confirmation it is most unlucky to be on the left side of the bishop, and so to receive his left hand : people are constantly warned to be careful to avoid this when their children are about to be confirmed. This objection is now becoming obsolete, from the fact that Confirmation is performed less perfunctorily, and candidates are, at least in this diocese, confirmed singly and not in pairs.

Not long ago a farmer lost two cows, for whose illness he could only account by the certainty that they had been "overlooked." He rode a long way to consult a wise woman, who decided that he was right in his diagnosis. She told him to find a horse with three nails in the near hind shoe (three again) ; he was then to pull out the middle nail and scratch the witch with it, otherwise all the rest of his cows would die.

The witch was not scratched, because the farmer, after much search, was unable to find the right horse with the right nail, but for all that he does not appear to have lost any more cows. Perhaps his will to scratch the witch was as good as if the deed had been accomplished.

Through the kindness of the Editors of *Somerset and Dorset Notes and Queries* I am enabled to print the following interesting quotation from that Magazine previous to its publication in vol. iv. part xxviii. (December 1894).

WITCHCRAFT IN SOMERSET.—It is hardly credible, but there exists, even in our day, a belief in witchcraft in some parts of Somerset.

The following incidents happened during this year. A poor woman, the mother of a large family, had for a period of two years a series of misfortunes : her husband was ill, two children were injured accidentally, they were all laid up by a prevailing epidemic. The woman herself, no doubt tired and worn out, came to the conclusion that in this long and bitter trial, which she considered was undeserved, there must be an evil agency at work, and she pronounced herself " overlooked." Once the idea took possession of her, it seemed to spread through the family, her husband and children testifying that they saw strange - looking little black objects sitting on the boxes at night : these little things used to try to pull them by the feet out of bed.

She became so thoroughly convinced that she was bewitched that she went to interview a wise man who lives at Wells. He took the same view of the case, and said that he would have to pray for her, the point at interest being, who had bewitched her? She had to go through a list of names—names of women; after mentioning many, and not the right one amongst them, as she was turning away, remembering one more she mentioned her, and that one the wise man pronounced the woman who had bewitched her. He told her that he could break the charm and take away the power of the witch, but it would take a lot of prayer and work. He then gave certain directions which the woman and her husband were to follow, in order to break the spell. About the hour of midnight she and her husband were directed to sit in front of their fire and burn salt, and for the space of one hour no conversation had to pass between them, only they had to repeat the following words :—

> This is not the thing I wish to burn
> But Mrs. ——'s heart of —— Somerset to turn,
> Wishing thee neither to eat, drink, sleep nor rest
> Until thou dost come to me and do my request ;
> Or else the wrath of God may fall on thee
> And cause thee to be consumed in a moment. Amen.

This accomplished, they were to retire backwards to the foot of the stairs, climb the stairs still backwards, repeating at the same time the Lord's Prayer also backwards, and then not speak a word to one another till they were in bed; in this way they would break the spell.

The man and his wife tried this, with implicit faith that the enchantment would be broken, or the evil eye averted.

[Our correspondent wishes to remain anonymous, but I can vouch for the truth of the story; in fact, I know the locality and some of the characters quite well.   EDITOR FOR SOMERSET.] [681]

Nearly akin to being overlooked, people are often said to be Pixy-led, when in the dark they lose their way. The writer has heard of many cases of this kind, for which probably the· " Jack-o'-lantern " is responsible. In one case well remembered, an old farmer was coming home from market across a well-known common in West Somerset. By some means his poor old mare was made to leave the track; probably her rider would not have seen very straight if it had been light; but finding his steed getting into a "soft place," his full wits returned, and at the same time an owl began to hoot. He at once began to cry out : " Man a-lost! man a-lost! Here's half a crown and a leg o' mutton! Man a-lost." It appears that after all he was not far from help; but he firmly believed he had been pixy-led, and the story clung to him till his death. Many such cases might be recounted, but the safeguard against such is to "turn your coat in an' out," when the evil sprites are confounded. [682]

[681] To house the hag you must doe this :
Commix with meale a little pisse
Of him bewitcht ; then forthwith make
A little wafer or a cake ;
And this rawly baked will bring
The old hag in.   No surer thing.
          Herrick, *Hesperides*, ed. Hazlitt, 1869, p. 305.

[682] If ye feare to be affrighted
When ye are by chance benighted,

In 1890 some men were ripping bark in a wood near Torrington. One of them declared that on stooping down to pick up a tool a strange feeling came over him, and while totally unable to raise himself he heard peals of discordant laughter all around. It flashed upon him that he was *pixy-led*, but his presence of mind forsook him, and he was unable to turn his coat inside out, a sure talisman (*sic*) against the spells of pixies. As the man did not return at the usual time, his wife, hearing from the others that he left work when they did, at ten o'clock went to look for him. Arriving at the place where they had been working, she met her husband dripping wet. "Where have you been?" she said. "I've a-bin pixy-led," says he, and then he told her how the pixies had held him fast for five hours, and that at last he crawled away, not knowing where he was going, and tumbling head over heels into the stream. As soon as he could get up he knew where he was and made his way homewards. "You girt fule, why didden 'ee turn your pockets inside out?" was all the comfort he got from his better half; "then you would have been able to come away tu wance." The man firmly believes in pixies, because a tailor named Short was *pixy-led* in the same wood some years ago. It is known that he was sober. No intoxicants had been tasted for the day by either of the party (abridged from *Western Daily Mercury*, June 6, 1890).

May Eve seems the time when these sprites—

In your pocket for a trust
Carrie nothing but a crust.
For that holy piece of bread
Charmes the danger and the dread.
Herrick, *Hesperides*, ed. Hazlitt, 1869, p. 346.

called by way of propitiation the "Good People"—
are most to be feared.   This name is, of course, a
reflection of the same notion conveyed in the old
saying about taking off your hat to the devil, *i.e.* be
polite and deferential to your greatest enemy.   It
is on May Eve the pixies are supposed to be most
inclined for mischief.   In Ireland it is thought that
then the evil eye has more than its usual vigilance
and malignity.   "The nurse who would then walk in
the open with a child in her arms would be repro-
bated as a monster." [683]   Youth and loveliness are
thought to be especially exposed to peril, therefore
not one woman in a thousand will then show herself
abroad.   Nor must it be supposed that conscious
ugliness is any protection ; on the contrary, neither
grizzled locks nor the brawny hand of the roughest
ploughman exempt from the blast.

The *blast* is a large round tumour which is
thought to rise suddenly on the part affected by the
baneful breath cast on it by one of the "good
people" at the time of their vindictive malice.   Here
in Somerset the belief in Pixies, Brownies, Little
Folks, "good people," is still very prevalent.

Many a quaint practice is silently performed
from mere habit, while the person so acting has no
sort of knowledge why he does so and so, nor would
he admit that he had any superstitious intention.

Many of the acts performed by country folk are
so common that they escape the notice of all but
close observers, and like many dialectal forms of
speech entirely escape record, because they have
not happened to come in the way of one looking out
for such things.   Any one who sits and gazes stead-

[683] Hone, *Everyday Book*, vol. i. p. 594.

fastly into the fire is usually suspected of the evil eye. The countercharm against such is called "Turning the Coal," and is worked by the suspecter's quietly taking the tongs and then turning the largest coal in the fire right upside down, saying at the same time, either aloud or softly, " The Lord be wi' us." This is believed to throw the evil gazer into confusion, so that his vision is dispelled, and for the time his evil intentions are thwarted. It is said that in the case of a true possessor of the evil eye, if the coal be turned upon him, he feels as if the fire were upon his heart; that he has often been seen to put his hand to his breast with "Oh !" and that he is unable to move so long as the live coal is held with the tongs. After this performance he is considered to have no more power over that house. Many curious stories are to be found in Scott's *Discovery of Witches*, and in Ady's *Candle in the Dark*, by which we see that " eye-biting witches," who caused disease among cattle, and other evils, were in former days commonly executed. Indeed executions for witchcraft or working evil with the eye are recorded so late as the last century.

In Ireland fire is believed to be a great protection against fairies and witches. " Whenever churning is going on, a small bit of burning turf is put under the churn to prevent the abstraction of butter by the 'good people.'" "Another custom is that any one coming into a house where churning is going on must take the churn-dash, and churn for a few seconds. His doing this prevents a person with the evil eye, should any such come in, charming away the butter, or otherwise spoiling the churning." [684]

[684] Le Fanu, *op. cit.* p. 104.

Diseases of all kinds being the direct result of fascination, charms of various sorts have been thought effective against them.   The carrying of the knuckle-bone of a sheep, called commonly a "cramp-bone," as a preventive against that ailment, is still a daily practice.   I have known persons, well to do, and by no means generally ignorant, who always had one about them.   It must never have touched the ground or its virtue is lost; consequently I have known it placed in a little bag and tied to the pocket or the dress, lest it should fall.   This has been done within my own knowledge by both a lady and a gentleman.

The carrying of a lump of camphor in the pocket may scarcely fall into this class, still it seems a little like the pills good against an earthquake. Crooked sixpences, especially with holes in them, are becoming somewhat obsolete, but well within the writer's memory they were much prized as protective amulets.

At Westleigh, in this neighbourhood, it was up to a recent time the custom carefully to preserve all teeth extracted; women used to hide them in their back hair.   This was done to prevent enemies or dogs getting hold of them, and betrays the same caution that is displayed in the more usual burning of teeth, lest injury to a part may affect the whole, dealt with in the chapter on Sympathetic Magic, p. 74, regarding other rejections of the body.   That which prevents injury may well be called protective. These persons were afraid both to burn their teeth and also to incur danger through their falling into malignant hands, so they hid them.

The personality of disease, or perhaps its direct

cause by personal evil influence, is shown by some Jewish customs.

A few days ago in the Polish town of Dzialoszice, the population of which has lately been decimated by cholera, the Jewish inhabitants, of the Chassidim sect, put on curiously-formed helmets and cuirasses made of pasteboard, and armed themselves with wooden javelins. Thus equipped, they formed a procession, and with clashing cymbals and the chanting of some kind of dissonant dirge, proceeded to a given rendezvous.[685]

Of course this was a defiant challenge to the demon of cholera.

The Chinese also exhibit much the same idea —that the spirit of the disease is the chief factor, and not the condition of their own bodies.

During a cholera outbreak two years ago in Chin Kung, on the Yangtsze-Kiang, placards were posted up, urging on the people the necessity of cleansing their hearts, saying nothing about cleansing their houses. The priests also sold charms against the disease, which, being put on board paper boats, were set adrift down the river, and were supposed to carry the disease away to sea.[686]

In all these cases where devils, or diseases, or misfortunes had to be dealt with, the underlying belief was ever present that all were emanations from an evil eye.

APPENDIX III

THE Australian aborigines, who seem to have considerable notions of astronomy, have a name for the Pleiades, which signifies a flock of cockatoos—an object most familiar to them. Their tradition is [687] that once upon a time they were a certain queen called *Gneeanggar*, and her six attendants, and that the star *crow* fell in love with the queen, but was so unsuccessful in gaining her affections that he determined to get possession of her by stratagem. He knew they

---

[685] *Daily News*, Sept. 18, 1894.   [686] *Public Health*, Aug. 1894, p. 376.
[687] James Dawson, *Australian Aborigines*, Melbourne, 1881, p. 100.

were very fond of white grubs, and finding out when they
were going in search of them, he determined to change
himself into a grub.   In this form he bored into the stem
of a tree, where he was sure to be observed by the queen
and her attendants.   He was soon discovered, and one of
the servants thrust in her bone-hook, which the women
use for extracting grubs.   Of this he broke the point, and
did the same to the hooks of all the other five attendants.
The queen then put her beautiful hook into the hole : he
knew that it was hers, and allowed himself to be drawn
out, when he immediately changed himself into a giant,
and ran off with her from her maids.   Ever since the loss
of the queen there have been only six stars in the Pleiades
representing her six servants.   This story is well known
in Western Australia, and with some variations in South
Australia also.

These people have their own names for most of the
heavenly bodies.

Like the German sun, theirs also is feminine and the
moon masculine.   The larger stars are sisters of the sun
and moon.   The Milky Way is the big river.   The dark
space of the Milky Way is *bunyip*,[688] an animal something
like a horse.   When the natives first saw a horse they
thought it was *bunyip*, and would not go near it.

Jupiter they call " Strike the Sun," a feminine name.
Venus is the " Mother of the Sun."

Canopus they call *crow*, Sirius *eagle*, Antares *big-
stomach*, and say the glow-worm took its light from this
star.

The three stars in Orion's belt are the sisters of the
eagle (Sirius), and always follow him.

These people believe in a good spirit as a gigantic
man living above the clouds.   " His voice, the thunder,[689]
is listened to with pleasure," as that of a friend.   The bad
spirit, who is evidently much more considered—for fear is
ever stronger than love in the savage breast—is called " the

688 Lumholtz, *Among Cannibals*, 1889, p. 202.
689 Dawson, *op. cit.* p. 49.

maker of bad-smelling smoke"; he is the author of every ill. "At times he assumes the form of a large, ugly man, and though not provided with wings like the white man's devil, he flits and darts from place to place with the rapidity of lightning, is very mischievous, and hungers for the flesh of children." He is believed to live deep underground, and commands a number of inferior spirits. No human being has ever returned from the place called *Ummekulleen*, where he, *Muuruup*, lives. There is nothing but fire there, and the souls of bad people get neither meat nor drink, and are terribly knocked about by the evil spirits. Every adult has a wraith, or likeness of himself, which is visible only to himself, and to him only before his own premature death. Good people go off to a beautiful country above the clouds, where life will be enjoyed for ever. Friends will meet and recognise each other, but there will be no marrying, as the bodies will be left upon earth. The shades of the wicked wander miserably about the earth for one year after death, frightening people, and then descend to *Ummekulleen*, never to return.[690]

These really very remarkable notions are so much like our own that one would have expected to find these savages had lived long in contact with Europeans; but we know that this cannot be so, and that their beliefs in a future state must be the relics of some unknown previous condition of civilisation, or they must be the innate ideas of primitive man. The *Wuulon* and the shadow referred to (p. 72) would seem to point to their descent from a higher Oriental stock—a contention further borne out by Dawson (p. 54), who describes a conveyance of land regularly signed and sealed. He says "the reader will be interested in these traces of civilisation among a people who have hitherto been considered the least civilised of all nations."

Closely connected with astrology is the poetical notion

[690] Dawson, *op. cit.* p. 51. See also on this subject Tylor, *Prim. Cult.* i. 274 *et seq.*

called the " Music of the Spheres," a term very often used
without the slightest knowledge of its true meaning.   It
was an ancient belief that each of the vowels of the
alphabet represented the sound uttered in its revolution
by one particular planet ; these all combined form one
eternal harmony to the glory of the great Creator of the
Universe.   This is the meaning of the lines in Addison's
well-known hymn :—

> For ever singing, as they shine,
> " The hand that made us is divine."

India, again, seems to have been the birthplace of this
beautiful idea, which even in Plato's day was quite
familiar, for he makes the seven notes proceed from a
siren seated upon the several spheres, set in motion by
the Fates.[691]

Another interpretation of the seven vowels is that they
represent the ineffable name of the Creator, the mystic
Jehovah, the great " I Am."   This explanation is supported
by the fact that " these combinations of the vowels often
appear purposely to include and veil from the profane
sense the sacred triliteral IAΩ."

The same author tells us [692] that " talisman is but the
corruption in the Arabian mouth of 'Αποτέλεσμα, the
influence of a planet upon the native ; hence astrology is
called ἡ 'Αποτελεσματική."

From astrology we are naturally led on to other
practices, by which men in all ages have sought to solve
the insoluble and to know the unknowable.

Magical arts, by which we mean all the various forms
of divination and enchantment practised by the ancients,
were said by the Greeks to have been invented in Persia,
or, as we have it, Chaldea.   The Μάγοι originally were
wise men, philosophers, given to the study of nature and
the contemplation of the stars and heavenly bodies.   From
these higher pursuits they gradually declined, and following
the bent of their natural humanity, which makes fear the

[691] King, *Gnostics*, p. 93.   [692] *Ibid.* p. 115.

strongest of motives, they began to propitiate the spirits of
the evils they dreaded, rather than to render thanks to the
good spirits from whom they at least admitted all good
things to proceed. Hence they took to the invocation of
demons, leading on to what we now call black arts.

These practices are said to have been introduced among
the Greeks by a certain Œthanes, who came over with the
invading army of Xerxes, and who propagated the rudi-
ments of magic. They were afterwards extended and
developed by Democritus, through contact with the Phœnicians. It is clear however that the seed fell into suitable
soil, which moreover had, long before Œthanes, been well
prepared by the primæval belief in the evil eye—a belief
which had become so confident, that we find, as already
related, the wise Pisistratus had caused a great amulet in
the shape of a grillo, a locust or cricket, to be set up on a
column in the Agora at Athens, as a protector against the
dread influence.

The greater arts practised by the ancient Greeks
were :—[693]

1. Necromancy (Νεκρομαντεία) the commonest of all
the magic arts, by which answers to matters relating to
this life were obtained from the dead. Closely allied,
and belonging to this, was Psychomancy (Ψυχομαντεία),
by which the dead were called up or made to appear in
airy forms like shades or ghosts. This was the art,
however it may have been practised, of the Witch of
Endor.

Among the old Greeks there were particular places set
apart as specially appropriate to this art, called Νεκυο-
μαντεία. Of these, two were the most remarkable : first
Threspotia, where Orpheus restored to life his wife
Eurydice, and where Periander, tyrant of Corinth, was
affrighted by the appearance of his wife Melissa, whom
he had murdered ; secondly, the next most noted spot

---

[693] Fuller accounts of all these, together with the details of a large number
of subsidiary enchantments, will be found in Potter's *Archæologia Græca*,
vol. i., and in Pliny's *Letters* and *Natural History*.

was at the famous cave of the Sibyl, on the Lacus
Avernus, between Pozzuoli and Baiæ in Campania, about
ten miles from Naples.   This latter is celebrated by Homer
and Virgil in their stories of Æneas and Ulysses.   The
writer can testify that it can still be entered and explored,
though somewhat flooded by water, consequent on recent
volcanic disturbance.

2. Hydromancy ('Ὑδρομαντεία), divination by the images
or other appearances caused to appear in water, as of a
fountain.   Often this was performed with a basin and then
called Λεκανομαντεία.

Frequently the same art with a like result was practised
with a mirror or looking-glass, and hence called Κατοπτρο-
μαντεία.   Sometimes it was performed in vessels of water,
the centre of which was called Γαστήρ, and hence this
divination was called Γαστρομαντεία.   The latter was
performed thus : Round vessels were filled with clear
water, about which were placed lighted torches ; they
then invoked the demon, in a low, murmuring voice, and
proposed the question to be solved.   A chaste boy or a
pregnant woman was appointed to observe with the
greatest care and exactness all the alterations in the
glasses, at the same time desiring, beseeching, and also
commanding an answer, which at length the demon used
to return by images in the glasses, which by reflection
from the water represented what should come to pass.[694]

There can be no doubt that Joseph had learnt this art
of divination from the Egyptians.   It was his divining
cup or bowl which was found in Benjamin's sack.   " Is not
this it (the bowl) in which my lord drinketh, and whereby
indeed he divineth ? " (Gen. xliv. 5).   Again, when brought
back, Joseph himself said to his brethren : " What deed is
this that ye have done ? wot ye not that such a man as I

---

[694] Potter, *Archæol. Græca*, i. 408.   Copied verbatim in Robinson's *Grecian
Antiquities*, p. 271, from whom Mr. Goodwin repeats it in *Fragment of a
Græco-Egyptian Work upon Magic*, Cambridge, 1852, p. 22.   The modern
Persians apply the word Jain, signifying a cup, mirror, or even globe, to
magical vessels of this kind.   See R. S. Poole in Smith's *Dict. of the Bible*,
s.v. "Magic," p. 197.

can certainly divine ? " (Gen. xliv. 15). He evidently took it for granted that his brethren would believe he could ascertain by magic who had stolen the money and the cup.

3. Crystalomancy (Κρυσταλλομαντεία) was performed with polished and enchanted crystals, wherein future events were discerned by certain marks and figures which were caused to appear.

4. Dactylomancy (Δακτυλομαντεία), or divination by enchanted rings.

5. Onychomancy ('Ονυχομαντεία) was performed by the finger-nails of an unpolluted boy. These were covered with soot and oil, and when turned to the sun they reflected the desired image.

6. Aeromancy ('Αερομαντεία), divination by appearances in the air.

7. Lithomancy (Λιθομαντεία), divination with a precious stone called *siderites*. By a stone of this kind, Helenus is reported to have foretold the destruction of Troy. Precious stones were not only used for the purpose of divination, but were in themselves held in the highest esteem as amulets or charms against the evil eye chiefly, but also against diseases.

Of all relics of the occult arts perhaps, the beliefs attaching to famous stones, from the Scone stone under the Coronation Chair, to the moonstones and toadstones of fable, are in these days as conspicuous as any. How many stories we find nowadays turning upon the safe keeping of some mystic stone, or precious gem, whose loss is fatal to its possessor or his family.

Another subsidiary divination was by the well-known crackling sound made by laurel leaves in burning. The word Daphne (δάφνη), the Greek for laurel, is said to be δα-φωνή (from the sound), *i.e.* the noise made by the leaves in burning.

8. Coscinomancy (Κοσκινομαντεία), divination by a sieve, which, according to Theocritus, was used by an old woman [695] in telling silly people their fortunes.

---

[695] Archbishop Potter makes Theocritus call the old woman a *gypsy* !

9. Axinomancy ('Αξινομαντεία) from 'Αξίνη an *axe* or *hatchet*, which was posted on a stake and was supposed to turn at the name of the guilty person. Perhaps here we have a clue to the origin of our vernacular "bury the hatchet," although Longfellow (*Hiawatha* xiii.) makes the custom North American.

10. Cephalonomancy (Κεφαλονομαντεία), divination by broiling an ass's head on coals. The jaws were said to move at the name of the guilty person.

11. Alectromancy ('Αλεκτρυομαντεία), by a cock. Twenty-four letters were laid on the ground with a grain of corn on each; the cock magically prepared was then let loose, and the letters from which he picked the corns in order were joined and produced the required name.

12. Sideromancy (Σιδηρομαντεία), conjuring with a hot iron, on which they laid an odd number of straws. The result required was obtained by observing the contortions made by the straws in burning.

13. Molybdomancy (Μολυβδομαντεία), by noting motions and figures in molten lead.

14. Tephromancy (Τεφρομαντεία), divination by ashes after exposure to the wind.

15. Botanomancy (Βοτανομαντεία), conjuring with herbs, especially 'Ελελίσφακος, or salvia.

Sometimes fig-leaves were used, and then it was called Sycomancy (Συκομαντεία). The diviners wrote names and questions on leaves, which were then exposed to the winds. Those remaining furnished the answers sought.

16. Ceromancy (Κηρομαντεία), divination by the forms assumed by melted wax dropped into water.

17. Pharmacy (Φαρμακεία). This was perhaps the most commonly practised as well as the most powerful of all the black arts, and has doubtless left its mark upon the poisoner's craft of later ages. It consisted in divination by means of medicated drugs, both vegetable and mineral, called Φάρμακα. Some of these were believed to be of great efficacy, and capable of imparting their venom

to persons at a considerable distance. So widespread was the belief in the potency of these poisons, that special charms or amulets, called Φάρμακα σωτήρια, were provided to counteract them. These were: *herb moly*, which preserved Ulysses from the enchantments of Circe, laurel (daphne), sallow-tree, rhamn or Christ thorn, fleabane, the jasper stone, and many others mentioned by the mediæval writer Albertus Magnus and by Orpheus in his book *De Lapillis*.

Certain rings also were used as countercharms, which were called by Aristophanes, in his *Plutus*, Δακτυλίους Φαρμακίτας.

Both Democritus and Pythagoras were reputed to be skilful in pharmacy. The Thessalians, particularly the women, were most celebrated among the Greeks as practisers of it. Besides all these, a great many other forms and modes of enchantment were devoutly used by the ancients. The more powerful incantations were firmly believed to be capable of even drawing the moon from her path.[696]

The *moon*, indeed, was thought to preside over the art of pharmacy, while *Hecate*, who, as we have seen, was but one of the persons or attributes of Artemis or Diana Triformis, was supposed to have been the inventor of it. Hence both these goddesses, really the same, were invoked by its adepts. Whenever the moon was eclipsed it was thought to be the effect of magicians ; and at such times it was usual to beat drums and kettles, to sound hautboys, trumpets, or any instruments making a great noise, to drown the voices of the sorcerers or evil workers, so that their charms might be impotent.

To this great art of pharmacy, on the other hand, belong all the charms, amulets, and enchantments against poison, venom of serpents, with all diseases ; and hence of course our modern use of the word.

---

[696] See Ovid, *Metamorph.* vii. 207 :—
        " Te quoque, Luna, traho" ;
    Virgil, *Eclog.* viii. 70 :—
        " Carmina vel cælo possunt deducere lunam."

The faith in the power of magic arts was simply unbounded, as is testified by nearly all the classic writers. Tibullus (*Eleg.* II. i. 43) says that a certain famous enchantress could not only draw down the stars from the sky, but could change the course of a river.   Further, she could make snow to fall in summer.

Horace, Lucan, Ovid, all bear similar witness : how that not only could they cause earthquakes and lightnings, but even could make the dead come out of their tombs. Hence we see that what was held to be a protector against the witch, or the witchcraft capable of producing such calamities, soon got to be considered a specific against the evil itself.   Thus our joke about pills good against an earthquake was once a serious fact devoutly believed.

We find that certain of these incantations had to be performed during the increase of the moon ; and similarly we read in the old herbals of Gerard, Turner, and Culpepper, how greatly the influence of the moon is to be considered in taking the remedies they prescribe.

Even Plato speaks of the Thessalian enchantresses as able to remove the moon from the sky, and he is followed by many other writers.   This account is moreover confirmed by both Tibullus and Virgil.   All stories are, however, capped by Pliny, who gravely states that an entire olive orchard, belonging to one Vectius Marcellus, was drawn by enchantment across the public road, while the land on which it was placed was made to go back and take the place previously occupied by the olive orchard.[697]

Ovid, too, gives some very strange stories of how, by incantation, the stars distilled blood and the moon became of a bloody purple.

> His mother was a witch, and one so strong
> That could control the moon, make flows and ebbs,
> And deal in her command without her power.
> *The Tempest*, Act v. Sc. 1.

Magicians were also believed to be able to raise the gods of the upper and lower world, and compel them to answer

[697] Pliny, *Nat. Hist.* xvii. 38 (vol. iii. p. 527, Bohn).

questions. Pliny, again, even gives the names of the herbs they used for this purpose. It appears, however, that the raising of the gods was not the same as the commoner necromancy, but must have belonged to the highest powers of the adepts in pharmacy, seeing that herbs were employed for the purpose.

It is, of course, futile to speculate as to the means, the extent to which these things were done, or, indeed, as to the truth of any of these wonderful stories. All we can say is, that in the Bible are abundant references to the wizards and magicians who "did so with their enchantments." We cannot believe them implicitly in the light of our present knowledge, neither can we explain them away, least of all can we venture to scoff at so many, so various, and in other respects so truthful witnesses.

A magical operation, almost precisely similar to the ancient Greek Γαστρομαντεία, is recorded as witnessed by himself in Mr. Lane's *Modern Egyptians* (vol. ii. ch. xii.), except that the mirror was of ink instead of clear water. This performance is now called *darb-el-mendel*. The chaste boy was the medium as of old; and the magician informed him that formerly those who alone could see the images, were the boy and a pregnant woman, to whom, however, modern experience seems to have added a virgin and a black female slave. The whole business is minutely described, and the form of invocation, written, as translated by Mr. Lane, was readily given to him. The main influence is said to be achieved by the first two words. We give the invocation, and refer the inquirer for full information to Mr. Lane's book.

Magic Invocation and Charm

Tarshun! Taryoashun! come down!
Come down! be present! Whither are gone
The prince and his troops? Where are El Ahmar
The prince and his troops? Be present,
Ye servants of these names!
And this is the removal, and we have removed from thee
Thy veil; and thy sight to-day
Is piercing! Correct: correct.

Besides this invocation there was the very common magic square with Arabic numerals making 15, as shown on p. 402. The only difference is in the position of the figures, which of course makes no change in the result so long as 5 is kept in the centre. The same applies to the squared words—*tenet* must be in the centre.

We are then told minutely what the boy said he saw ; but from "holding the boy's hand all the while" he was looking intently into the ink, it appears rather like a case of hypnotism, plus a good deal of apparatus in the way of a chafing dish, frankincense, and coriander seed, so that "the fumes became painful to the eyes." The boy, however, was evidently not an educated medium, as he was taken from a crowd, and was Mr. Lane's own selection. The description of the objects seen by the boy, as elicited by leading questions, shows that these questions are evidently ancient and traditional forms, while the general resemblance of the objects said to be seen in the ink, to the appearances mentioned in the papyrus, No. XLVI., described in Mr. Goodwin's paper (see p. 395), is quite obvious. We are thus brought to perceive that this art as now practised in Egypt has changed but little in two thousand years.

INDEX